THE HIDDEN COST OF ECONOMIC DEVELOPMENT

Modern Economic and Social History Series

General Editor: Derek H. Aldcroft

Titles in this series include:

Arms and the State
Sir William Armstrong and the Remaking of British Naval Power, 1854–1914
Marshall J. Bastable

Insuring the Industrial Revolution
Fire Insurance in Great Britain, 1700–1850
Robin Pearson

Lives of the Philadelphia Engineers
Capital, Class and Revolution, 1830–1890
Andrew Dawson

Studies in the Interwar European Economy
Derek H. Aldcroft

Whatever Happened to Monetarism?
Economic Policy Making and Social Learning in the United Kingdom Since 1979
Michael J. Oliver

Disillusionment or New Opportunites?
The Changing Nature of Work in Offices, Glasgow 1880–1914
R. Guerriero Wilson

Raleigh and the British Bicycle Industry
An Economic and Business History, 1870–1960
Roger Lloyd-Jones and M.J. Lewis

Battles for the Standard
Bimetallism and the Spread of the Gold Standard in the Nineteenth Century
Ted Wilson

The Hidden Cost of Economic Development

The Biological Standard of Living in Antebellum Pennsylvania

TIMOTHY CUFF
Westminster College,
New Wilmington, PA, USA

ASHGATE

Published by
Ashgate Publishing Limited
Gower House
Croft Road
Aldershot
Hampshire GU11 3HR
England

Ashgate Publishing Company
Suite 420
101 Cherry Street
Burlington, VT 05401-4405
USA

Ashgate website: http://www.ashgate.com

British Library Cataloguing in Publication Data
Cuff, Timothy
The hidden cost of economic development : the biological standard of living in antebellum Pennsylvania. – (Modern economic and social history)
1. Stature – Pennsylvania – History – 19th century
2. Nutrition – Pennsylvania – History – 19th century
3. Quality of life – Pennsylvania – History – 19th century
4. Pennsylvania – Social conditions – 19th century
5. Pennsylvania – Economic conditions – 19th century
I. Title
306.4'61'09748'09034

Library of Congress Cataloging-in-Publication Data
Cuff, Timothy.
The hidden cost of economic development : the biological standard of living in antebellum Pennsylvania / Timothy Cuff.
p. cm — (Modern economic and social history)
Includes bibliographical references and index.
ISBN 0-7546-4119-8 (alk. paper)
1. Cost and standard of living—Pennsylvania—History—19th century. 2. Stature—Pennsylvania—History—19th century. 3. Pennsylvania—Economic conditions—19th century. I. Title II. Series: Modern economic and social history series.

HD6993.P4C84 2004
339.4'2'0974809034—dc22

2004008256

ISBN 0 7546 4119 8

Printed and bound in Great Britain by MPG Books Ltd, Bodmin, Cornwall

This book is dedicated to my father and my brother,
neither of whom lived to see its publication,
and to my wife and daughters, Carolyn, Laura, and Margaret Rose,
who, although they had their doubts, did.

Contents

List of Figures

List of Tables

Modern Economic and Social History Series
General Editor's Preface

Economic and social history has been a flourishing subject of scholarly study during recent decades. Not only has the volume of literature increased enormously but the range of interest in time, space and subject matter has broadened considerably so that today there are many sub-branches of the subject which have developed considerable status in their own right.

One of the aims of this series is to encourage the publication of scholarly monographs on any aspect of modern economic and social history. The geographical coverage is world-wide and contributions on the non-British themes will be especially welcome. While emphasis will be placed on works embodying original research, it is also intended that the series should provide the opportunity to publish studies of a more general thematic nature which offer a reappraisal or critical analysis of major issues of debate.

Derek H. Aldcroft
University of Leicester

Preface

The American economy grew rapidly in advance of the Civil War. Between 1840 and 1870 per capita net national product increased significantly as did value added in the agricultural sector. Urban areas, old and new alike, grew quickly. Yet, outside of a small circle of specialists, it is hardly known that, amidst all this bustle, there were also signs of adversity associated with the structural changes accompanying the transition from an economy that was primarily agricultural to an industrial one – a development known as the onset of modern economic growth. In fact, there are indications that the health and biological well-being of the children born during these momentous times were inferior to that of their forefathers, and not only among urban dwellers, but also among the rural population both North and South. The thesis of this book is that the onset of market integration and nascent industrialization had a hidden cost – even in the resource-abundant United States. It would seem that the expansion of the market can be a two-edged sword, yielding both higher incomes but also a negative externality which has only recently been recognized.

This monograph explores the effect of economic change on the biological standard of living of antebellum Pennsylvanians. The conventional conceptualization of the standard of living is generally in terms of command over goods and services, typically measured by some variant of real per capita income. Yet, such a measure is incomplete for many reasons, including the fact that the distribution of income can change over time, and that income variability itself affects welfare. In addition, in a historical context, only aggregate estimates are available, and little is known about income by social class, its short-term variability over time, and its distribution within households themselves. The new conceptualization of well-being used in this volume enables an exploration of variation in welfare across social groups.

The United Nations has recognized that income, by itself, is far from a flawless indicator of welfare. It has begun to utilize a human development index incorporating measures of longevity, education, and of course, income. As a consequence of the acknowledged shortcomings of using income as the sole measure of living standards, economic historians have begun to consider biological aspects of well-being. The biological standard of living captures how well the human organism throve in its socio-economic and epidemiological environment. Medical research has found that physical stature is a good indicator of overall health status and may be linked to longevity in human populations.

Adult physical stature reflects cumulative net nutritional status (nutrient intake net of the demands of work and disease encounters) over the growth years. Stature, of course, is influenced by consumption, and hence by income, but income by itself does not determine consumption uniquely. It is affected by many other factors, including relative prices and how resources were distributed within the household. Height can be used to assess how well a population met its basic nutritional requirements.

Pennsylvania is the laboratory used to explore the extent to which economic processes differentially affected various segments of antebellum society. This study is based on a sample drawn from enlistment records of more than 20,000 Pennsylvania-born soldiers who fought in the Civil War. After examining the nature and course of economic development in Pennsylvania, the relationship between economic change and changes in the biological standard of living is documented. The effects of the spread of transportation networks, urbanization and early industrialization on the nutrition and health of Pennsylvanians are explored.

The analysis indicates that antebellum Pennsylvania-born males achieved an adult height between the 25th and 35th percentile of modern standards. Within every region of the state, farmers, who were closest to the source of nutrients, were consistently among the tallest. Men born in counties distant from markets for goods and services, removed from growing urban areas, and most nearly economically self-sufficient were significantly taller than were those born in regions which were experiencing modern economic growth. An inverse correlation is found between physical stature and a series of indicators of economic development and population density. Time trends show a slight and uneven decline in mean height from the 1820s through the 1840s, concentrated toward the end of this period especially among skilled and unskilled workers.

Population growth, urbanization, and market integration seem to have had a deleterious effect on the biological well-being of the working class population. Likely proximate causes are a combination of increased income inequality, increased disease exposure, declining per capita availability of protein-rich food, and intra-family decisions to substitute food consumption for manufactured goods.

The conclusion is warranted that, during the early stages of market integration and industrialization, progress was not uniform across all dimensions of human welfare. In some regards, the common men and women of the early industrial era were not as well-off as their parents. The human organism did not always thrive as well in the newly created socio-economic environment as the aggregate level purchasing power might imply. Thus, an examination of the biological standard of living affords a more nuanced view of the welfare of the populations living through the rapid structural changes accompanying the onset of modern economic growth.

Acknowledgements

According to a favorite colloquialism of the day, 'It takes a village to write a dissertation and turn it into a book.' The members of that village are many and their functions diverse. The completion of this monograph would not have been possible without the assistance of many academic village people.

Thanks are due to the many individuals who helped me to locate, collect, make machine-readable, code, and manipulate the stature data utilized in this study. They include Michael Meier (U.S. National Archives), Jonathan Stayer (Pennsylvania State Archives), Anne Leonard, Mark Pietrzyk, Dave Sherman, Ed Danielson, Christina Sherman, Eric Foltyn, Meredith Ridl, Matt Boccardi, Kristin Kronstain, Matthew Kurtz, Abigail Sumpter, Laura Cuff, Margaret Cuff, Carolyn Cuff, and Evann Garrison. Phil Sidel and Eileen S. Kopchik of the University of Pittsburgh's Social Science Computer Research Institute assisted me to manipulate the data and use SPSS and SAS to perform the analysis. Westminster College's Ann Throckmorton and Todd Fleckenstein worked their magic with Arcview software to ensure the production of maps in publishable form.

Financial support was provided by the University of Pittsburgh Faculty of Arts and Sciences through a doctoral studies research grant, Mellon Fellowship, and several travel grants. The University's Department of History also provided a series of travel grants which allowed me to attend national and international meetings in order to present early findings. Near the completion of the dissertation the Pennsylvania Historical and Museum Commission awarded me a position as a Resident Scholar which provided concentrated time to finalize the manuscript and begin collecting data for future extensions of this work. Jesse Mann and the Modern Language Department at Westminster College also provided me with a quiet office space in which I wrote Chapter Four.

Many friends and colleagues read all or portions of the manuscript. They include Eric Davin, Paul Riggs, Mike Naragon, Sue Corbesero, Sam Farmerie, Jim Hines, John Murray, Tom Weiss, Lee Craig, Joerg Baten, Farley Grubb, W. Peter Ward, Michael Haines, and Bernard Harris. Their thoughts and comments were extremely helpful in recasting ideas or raising questions about ideas which were not clearly expressed in earlier drafts. Special thanks are due to the chair and my colleagues in the Department of Religion, History, Philosophy, and Classics at Westminster College for their support; to Evann Garrison for her editorial assistance; to Sarah Charters, Thomas Gray, and the staff at Ashgate Publishing for their patience and assistance; and to Virginia Tomlinson for sharing her administrative and personal wisdom.

I was blessed by a thoughtful and congenial group of scholars who composed my dissertation committee. They willingly offered their time and added immeasurably to this project, from helping to establish a manageably-sized project at the outset, to providing leads and sources for various types of data, to giving both detailed and high-level critiques of early drafts which helped me to focus the work more tightly and improve its readability. In the best tradition of academe, they offered advice without seeking control, assistance without seeking to dominate, and encouragement when spirits were low. To each of them, Van Beck Hall, Ted Muller, Richard Steckel, and Jerome Wells, I will always be indebted.

My greatest professional appreciation, however, is reserved for John Komlos. He inspired, encouraged, promoted, and supported (emotionally and financially) my efforts to complete my thesis and turn it into this volume as well as to publish a series of related articles. At every turn he has opened doors which have literally enabled me to see the world. I am extremely grateful for his assistance and hope to be as good a mentor to my students as he has been to me.

Debts within the family are always difficult to denominate. Yet, without the support and love of my wife and children, my parents, and my siblings, this work would not have been completed. Many thanks are due to the members of my immediate and extended families for their patience, their understanding, and their smiles.

Chapter 1

The 'Antebellum Puzzle' in Pennsylvania

> As a general rule … it is better that the farmer should produce what he needs for home consumption. He may obtain more money from tobacco, hops or broom corn, than from breadstuffs, but taking all things into consideration will he be better off?[1]

The nineteenth-century American farmer quoted above questioned the ultimate value of the involvement in markets at a time when market participation, although nearly universal in some areas, was neither the basis for all consumption nor completely accepted by the populace. Theory and experience show that, over the long run, market participation certainly yielded higher material returns to most members of society than did autarky. Yet, when evaluating short- and medium-term effects, particularly when considering non-pecuniary rewards, the results were not always as clear-cut at the early stages of modern economic growth.

'To what degree did economic growth and its concomitant market integration provide short-term benefits to the American population during the antebellum period?' is a question of interest to economic and social historians, physical anthropologists, as well as to development economists concerned with trends in living standards. The ultimate answers have important policy implications.

The most controversial and longest-lived debate in this regard pertains to the impact on the 'standard of living' of the English working class during the early phases of the Industrial Revolution. The sometimes heated academic struggle between the 'optimists' and the 'pessimists' remains essentially unresolved. Academics are not alone in their interest in this complex of issues. From Bangkok to Brasilia political leaders and policy experts are concerned with welfare, though its definition is contested. There are multiple yardsticks by which well-being can be judged: real wages, mean life span, unemployment rates, average number of televisions per dwelling, suicides, telephones per household, food consumption levels, percentage of homes with indoor plumbing, to name just a few. While today's policy makers have the option of directing statistical bureaus to collect pertinent data, historians must be satisfied with records left behind by earlier generations of record keepers. With so little systematic extant evidence on wages, prices, diets, and housing conditions available for the social groups which experienced industrialization in Great Britain, it is hardly surprising that the debate over the secular changes in material welfare has continued for so long.

Over the course of the last quarter century, historians and economists have begun to utilize a type of data previously disregarded, namely those pertaining to the physical size of human populations, analyzed until then primarily by medical and biological researchers.[2] Adult physical stature reflects the cumulative net nutritional status of an individual over the course of his/her growth years. While at the individual level genes are an important co-determinant of final height attained, in large stable groups they do not determine short-term group variation either over time or cross-sectionally, in the absence of significant migration. Hence, the average height of a population can be used to assess how well a society was able, or chose, to meet its nutritional needs over time.[3] Since access to nutrition is related to, although not fully determined by, income, stature can also be used in some instances as an indicator of a society's general level of material welfare. More directly, stature is a measure of a biological rather than a material standard of living.

This study seeks to explore, in a regional geographic context, an aspect of a rather fundamental and long controversial question, 'What are the effects of rapid economic growth and development on the men, women, and children experiencing it?' Specifically within the antebellum American context, 'How did market integration in agricultural goods and the beginnings of industrialization affect the biological well-being of Pennsylvanians in the antebellum era?' Thus, the Keystone State is the geographic region of analysis, and the approach is that of historical anthropometrics. Mean human stature will be used to evaluate the physical well-being of this historical population.

The focus of this study, antebellum Pennsylvania, has some unusual, though not entirely unique, features. The process of market integration and early industrialization occurred in the first half of the nineteenth-century, at a time when settlement of much of North America by persons of European ancestry was still relatively recent. European methods of intensive cultivation had only recently been introduced across much of the land. The transportation revolution was also under way. The improved transportation system of canals and railroads not only traversed densely settled locales of long standing but also areas which had only recently been controlled by persons of European descent. In the 'west' a wilderness was being subdued coincident with, or only shortly before, the introduction of long-distance transport systems and the linking of these areas with distant agricultural markets.[4] Although generally thought of as a distinct phenomenon within the context of the contemporaneous Industrial Revolution across the ocean, these processes were actually an integral part of it in Pennsylvania.

Economic historians generally agree that early nineteenth-century per capita economic growth in the United States was substantial. There are debates over the exact rate of economic expansion, as well as about the timing of the upswing in economic activity,[5] but not over the direction of the trend. The antebellum years in the North, except in a few large metropolises which had already experienced these changes, were a time of market integration and expansion, of early industrialization and urbanization. The transportation network grew both denser and more extensive as the country east of the Mississippi and west of the Alleghenies was first settled and then linked to Atlantic coastal cities. Regional and city/hinterland specialization lead to increased output per head and increased opportunity to participate in markets for numerous goods.

However, there were hitherto unnoticed negative external effects. There is some evidence, not uncontested however, that the 1830s and 1840s were a period of increasing occupational wage differentials and wealth concentration.[6] Additionally, studies of numerous disparate populations, blacks and whites, Northerners and Southerners, show declines in mean adult physical stature over portions of the antebellum period. The timing of the decline varies slightly from group to group as does its size and intensity. However, its presence was almost universal. The only exception found hitherto is the case of slave men, whose productivity was so inextricably linked to their nutritional intake that their owners seemingly made certain that their nutritional status did not decline even at a time when the price of food was increasing. With the vast majority of early nineteenth-century Americans living in rural locales, the antebellum diminution in physical stature was to a considerable degree a rural phenomenon as well.[7] Limited data indicate that, as the decline continued into the middle and later decades of the century, its effect became concentrated among urban residents.[8] Though the trend in heights is clear, its causes are less so. This decline in heights at a time of obvious economic prosperity has become known as the 'antebellum puzzle' in the American context or as the 'early-industrial-growth puzzle' in the European context.[9]

While the biological sciences have identified the factors which influence final height, historians must determine the relative weight of the various forces and the *relationship* between nineteenth-century economic and social developments and their biological consequences.[10] In both the American and European contexts investigations and 'case-building' for the various factors have begun. Studies of European populations have shown that the initial stages of industrial development were accompanied by a series of collateral developments which had negative biological results for some subsets of the population most heavily involved in market activities.[11]

In the American case, a series of hypotheses have been developed and await further examination. Some authors believe that changes in the epidemiological environment were mainly responsible for declining average stature. Such a deterioration could have been caused by one or more of the following: 1) industrial and commercial expansion-related urbanization and subsequent crowding under unsanitary conditions, 2) the widening transportation network and the attendant increased movement of people and the infections they spread, and 3) the migration of people into areas more prone to harbor particular infections and their carriers.[12]

Another potential explanation is the tendency in the nineteenth-century toward rising levels of income and wealth inequality.[13] With growing inequality,[14] the upper classes, numerically only a small fraction of the population, benefited only marginally in physical stature and health from increased income. Their stature tended to be as high as their chosen diet structure and the disease environment would allow. In contrast, the lower classes, who tended to spend a significantly larger proportion of their income on food, had less money to spend on food; their nutritional status was reduced, and consequently their stature and health declined.[15]

Rapid population and labor force growth were also characteristic of nineteenth-century America. However, with rapid technological change in the industrial sector, a declining share of workers was employed directly in agriculture. If, as has been argued, agricultural productivity gains did not keep pace with population growth and the expansion of agricultural exports, per capita food availability would have declined.[16] The result would have been lower per capita food consumption leading to reduced average height levels.[17]

Others contend that the increasing availability of manufactured goods in the nineteenth-century may have induced some families to reduce their food consumption in order to market their crops more aggressively, especially high-protein meats and dairy products. While this might be a utility-increasing behavior, it would have a negative impact on the health of the children of the household. Such a change in the distribution of calories and high-protein foods from rural to urban consumption is also consistent with rural height declines.[18]

Only the initial shreds of evidence have been amassed in support of these hypotheses. To date, most large-scale anthropometric studies of U.S. whites have been national in scope.[19] More detailed studies of smaller localities with sample sizes large enough to bear the weight of detailed statistical analysis are needed to isolate the social, economic, and demographic factors most closely associated with the cycling in stature which has been identified both in Europe and the United States. A regional approach will show whether the local experience is identical to the national one, and help to determine how particular local economic and population characteristics were related to changes in physical well-being.

This work is an effort to begin to fill the knowledge gap noted above. It 1) seeks to confirm, at the local level, the existence of the 'antebellum puzzle' among U.S. males of European ancestry, 2) tests, within the setting of early nineteenth-century Pennsylvania, the hypothesis that distance from economic markets, i.e. relative economic self-sufficiency, provided a net nutritional advantage to early nineteenth-century Americans, 3) assesses the correlates of stature within this geographic and socio-economic context, and 4) adds to the body of literature which seeks to redefine economic well-being so as to include biological indicators and incorporate these types of costs and benefits into evaluations of economic development.

Several historical circumstances recommend Pennsylvania as a useful test environment for the hypothesis that economic development and the social changes related to it at least temporarily resulted in a decline in the biological well-being of the population. European settlement of the state occurred over several centuries with the last counties seeing settlement only in the fourth decade of the nineteenth-century, the middle of the period under consideration. As a result, the nature of economic activity differed greatly from locale to locale across the commonwealth.

The extent to which communities were part of local or regional trade networks also varied widely in 1800, as did the rate at which they entered into such systems. Early nineteenth-century Pennsylvania exhibited the entire gamut of economic orientations that existed in the United States at the time.[20] At one end of the continuum was Philadelphia, one of the major regional entrepôts and a major consumer of primary sector products.[21] However, such large urban agglomerations were the exception rather than the rule. In 1800, nearly 90 per cent of the state's population lived in rural areas or towns with fewer than 2500 inhabitants.[22] The Allegheny Mountains cut the state in two and made travel extremely difficult in the middle sections of the state, limiting land values there. Some counties were not even settled until the 1830s.[23] In such areas farmers were primarily engaged in subsistence-plus farming and local community exchange,[24] while many farmers in Southeastern Pennsylvania had already specialized in production to serve urban markets.

Over the course of the antebellum years the state as a whole experienced a relatively rapid process of economic development and urbanization. However, the integration of interior entrepôts with seaboard trading towns and the linking of more remote inland sites with regional cities did not occur uniformly across the land. Rather, topography, natural resource endowments, and transportation connections affected the speed with which locales became part of the antebellum trade network and made the transition from self-sufficient to interdependent communities.

Throughout this period approximately one-half of the state's population lived in the Southeastern Region (Figure 4.1).[25] Its indicators of market development, the dollar value of market gardening and the value of land, were the highest in the state, while the percentage of the work force in agriculture and level of home manufactures, indicators of separation from economic markets, were the lowest. The Southeastern Region was very well connected by transportation systems both internally and with regions outside of Pennsylvania.

On the other end of the spectrum of development were the Allegheny Forest, Northeastern, and Pocono Regions. With late settlement dates and low population densities, these regions, poorly linked by road, canal, or rail, with some of the highest levels of home manufacturing and agricultural employment and lowest urbanization rates, characterized early nineteenth-century Pennsylvanian self-sufficiency. Farmers dominated these regions, but they were without a feasible outlet for any substantial crop surplus. Many were situated on relatively poor agricultural soils. These regions did not have any towns with a population in excess of 2500 persons until the 1850 census. The difficult terrain and thin soil made producing sufficient crops to maintain one's family a difficult chore in the years immediately following settlement.[26]

In between these extremes of population density and economic development were three other regions, the Anthracite, the Ridge and Valley, and the Western parts of the state. With very different terrain and resource endowments, the three moved in rather different economic directions. The Anthracite region became, over the period, the second most urbanized region in the state, whose *raison d'être* was the 'black rock' beneath its soil. Tied to the Southeast and eventually to New York State by canal and railroad, the region was well integrated into the market, both internally and with the Southeastern Region.

The Ridge and Valley was similarly tied to other regions, in-state and out, by the exchange of agricultural produce. Serving as a source of swine for both the Philadelphia and Baltimore markets, the farmers there oriented themselves to one or both cities as outlets for pork and, to a lesser extent, market garden crops. The region was cut by long-distance road, canal, and railroad connections, but a dense network of internal routes did not exist.

While its population density and level of urbanization lay between the two previous regions, the Western Region was one of the last to receive fully effective transportation linkages to the rest of the state. Although relatively well served by rivers and streams, many of these were only navigable in the spring. Steamships traveled throughout the region, even far up the Allegheny River; however, most traffic of this sort was found downstream from Pittsburgh on the Ohio. With the exception of the Mainline, canal and rail services were late in spreading throughout and internally connecting the region. Erie had ties of long standing via the lake to many ports, especially Buffalo. By 1860 industrial development had begun to spread along the Ohio, Monongehela, and Allegheny Rivers and their tributaries but through most of the period the bulk of the region was characterized by mixed farming.

Antebellum Pennsylvania, with so many different initial levels of economic development, directions of change, and rates of growth is an ideal laboratory to test the effect of economic modernization on the biological welfare of the populations experiencing it. Cross-sectional and multivariate analysis of physical stature data for a large sample of Pennsylvanians who served in the Union Army will show that such variations in stature across sub-populations did exist during the antebellum years, and that they are consistent with earlier findings. Pennsylvanian men, on the whole, experienced a diminution in mean stature. Her farmers displayed a height advantage over men in most other occupations. After accounting for sample variation in numerous personal characteristics, regression analysis shows a strong positive correlation between many indicators of remoteness from markets and above average stature.

The results of this analysis offer support to the hypothesis that birth or residence in an area with extensive or increasing market involvement during a period of early economic integration is correlated with smaller stature. Another and potentially more important goal of the study is the presentation of evidence which adds to the growing literature seeking to conceptualize the notion of well-being in more nuanced ways than in purely material terms. Additionally, it should more completely explicate the history of antebellum Pennsylvania and through it, that of the northern United States, and the momentous impact the onset of modern economic growth had on the lives of the men and women who lived through those times, hopefully serving as a model for future research on the topic.

Notes

1 *Plough, Loom and Anvil* 4 (1852): 686 cited in Gavin W. Wright, *The Political Economy of the Cotton South: Households, Markets, and Wealth in the Nineteenth-century* (New York: W.W. Norton and Co., 1978), 71.

2 John Komlos and Timothy Cuff (ed.), *Classics of Anthropometric History: A Selected Anthology* (St. Katharinen, Germany: Scripta Mercaturae, 1998); John Komlos (ed.), *Stature, Living Standards, and Economic Development: Essays in Anthropometric History* (Chicago: The University of Chicago Press, 1994).

3 This is in relation to caloric needs based on work requirements and disease load.

4 This is one factor which differentiates the European and U.S. experiences of industrialization.

5 Paul David, 'The Growth of Real Product in the United States Before 1840: New Evidence, Controlled Conjectures,' *Journal of Economic History* 27 (1967): 151-197; Robert Gallman, 'The Statistical Approach: Fundamental Concepts as Applied to History,' in *Approaches to American Economic History*, edited by G.R. Taylor and L.R. Ellsworth (Charlottesville: University of Virginia Press, 1971), 87-105.

6 Jeffrey G. Williamson and Peter H. Lindert, *American Inequality: A Macroeconomic History* (New York: Academic Press, Inc., 1980), 36-46, 67-75; Robert A. Margo and Georgia C. Villaflor, 'The Growth of Real Wages in Antebellum America: New Evidence,' *Journal of Economic History* 47 (1987): 873-895.

7 John Komlos and Jörg Baten (ed.), *The Biological Standard of Living in Comparative Perspectives: Proceedings of a Conference Held in Munich January 18-23, 1997*, (Stuttgart: Franz Steiner Verlag, 1999); Richard Steckel, 'Stature and the Standard of Living,' *Journal of Economic Literature* 33 (1995): 1927.

8 Richard Steckel, 'Stature and Living Standards in the United States,' in *American Economic Growth and Standards of Living before the Civil War*, ed. Robert E. Gallman and J.J. Wallis (Chicago: National Bureau of Economic Research by University of Chicago Press, 1992), 265-310.

9 John Komlos, 'Shrinking in a Growing Economy? The Mystery of Physical Stature during the Industrial Revolution,' *Journal of Economic History* 58 (1998) 3: 779-802; John Komlos and Peter Coclanis 'On the "Puzzling" Antebellum Cycle of the Biological Standard of Living: the Case of Georgia,' *Explorations in Economic History* 34 (Oct. 1997) 4: 433-59; John Komlos, 'Anomalies in Economic History: Reflections on the "Antebellum Puzzle",' *Journal of Economic History* 56 (March, 1996): 202-214.

10 James C. Riley, 'Stature's Problems,' manuscript, Indiana University, 1993; Robert W. Fogel, 'Nutrition and the Decline in Mortality since 1700: Some Preliminary Findings,' in *Long-Term Factors in American Economic Growth*, ed. S. Engerman and R. Gallman (Chicago: University of Chicago Press for National Bureau of Economic Research, 1987), 506.

11 Roderick Floud, Kenneth Wachter, and Annabelle Gregory, *Height, Health, and History: Nutritional Status in the United Kingdom, 1750-1980* (Cambridge, England: Cambridge University Press, 1990); John Komlos, 'Height and Social Status in Eighteenth-Century Germany,' *Journal of Interdisciplinary History* 20 (1990): 607-621; Lars G. Sandberg and Richard H. Steckel, 'Soldier, Soldier, What Made you Grow so Tall? A Study of Height, Health and Nutrition in Sweden, 1720-1881,' *Economy and History* 23 (1980): 91-105.

12 C. Mosk and S.R. Johansson, 'Income and Mortality: Evidence from Modern Japan,' *Population and Development Review* 12 (1986): 417-428; Steckel, 'Stature and the Standard of Living,' 1929.

13 Williamson and Lindert. *American Inequality*; Richard Steckel, 'Height and Per Capita Income,' *Historical Methods* 16 (1983): 1-7.

14 This is not to imply that wealth or income was necessarily equally distributed in regions characterized by self-sufficiency. See for example Lee Soltow, 'Inequality Amidst Abundance: Land Ownership in Early Nineteenth-Century Ohio,' *Ohio History* 88 (1979): 133-151.

15 Fogel describes how differing demand elasticities and income limitations result in different responses to high food prices among different classes of a society. Robert W. Fogel, 'The Conquest of High Mortality and Hunger in Europe and America: Timing and Mechanisms,' in *Favorites of Fortune: Technology, Growth, and Economic Development Since the Industrial Revolution*, ed. P. Higonnet, D.S. Landes, and H. Rosovsky (Cambridge, MA: Harvard University Press, 1991), 33-71.

16 Timothy Cuff, 'A Weighty Issue Revisited: New Evidence on Commercial Swine Weights and Pork Production Trends in Mid-Nineteenth-Century America,' *Agricultural History* 66 (1982): 55-74; John Komlos, 'The Height and Weight of West Point Cadets: Dietary Change in Antebellum America,' *Journal of Economic History* 47 (1987): 897-927.

17 Parker (1957) has noted that a substantial portion of nineteenth-century American population growth was the result of immigration from Europe. Most of these individuals would have been accustomed to much lower per capita food consumption than those of native-born Americans. Parker hypothesizes that the influx of these individuals may have lowered per capita demand for food, and consequently the reduction of per capita food supply might not have resulted in increased prices. William N. Parker, 'Trends in Food Consumption in the United States, 1840-1910: An Experiment in Econometrical History' (Unpublished manuscript presented to the Econometrical Society, 1957).

18 Komlos, 'West Point Cadets;' Komlos, 'Shrinking in a Growing Economy.' Steckel thinks that this effect must have been weak. Steckel, 'Stature and the Standard of Living,' 1928-1929. This also raises the difficult issue of intra-family food distribution and control.

19 Steckel and Haurin's Ohio National Guard sample is an obvious exception. Richard Steckel and Donald Haurin, 'Health and Nutrition in the American Midwest: Evidence from the Height of Ohio National Guardsmen, 1850-1910,' in *Stature, Living Standards, and Economic Development: Essays in Anthropometric History*, ed. John Komlos (Chicago: University of Chicago Press, 1994), 117-128. See also Komlos and Coclanis, 'On the "Puzzling" Antebellum Cycle;' John Komlos and Peter Coclanis, 'Nutrition and Economic Development in Post-Reconstruction South Carolina: an Anthropometric Approach,' *Social Science History* 19 (1995): 91-116. A few studies of African-Americans with large samples from relatively small geographic areas have been carried out. John Komlos, 'Toward an Anthropometric History of African-Americans: The Case of the Free Blacks in Antebellum Maryland,' in *Strategic Factors in Nineteenth-Century American Economic History: A Volume to Honor Robert W. Fogel*, ed. C. Goldin and H. Rockoff (Chicago: University of Chicago Press, 1992), 267-329.

20 With the obvious exception of slave-based plantation agriculture.

21 Diane Lindstrom, *Economic Development in the Philadelphia Region, 1810-1850* (New York: Columbia University Press, 1978), 18-19.

22 John L. Andriot, *Population Abstract of the United States, Vol. 1* (McLean, VA: Andriot Associates, 1983), 670. The census-based definition of 'urban' at 2500 persons is somewhat arbitrary and understates the importance of many early nineteenth-century trading towns as centers of commerce. The 2,500 figure was first imposed in 1906 in a Census publication generated after the census of 1900. Early definitions had placed the urban threshold much higher. United States Bureau of the Census, *Historical Statistics of the United States: Colonial Times to 1970* (Washington, D.C., 1975), 2.

23 Dykstra notes that portions of the anthracite coal region of East Central Pennsylvania, as well as the Pocono and Allegheny Forest regions, remained unsettled until this relatively late date. Ann Dykstra, 'Region, Economy and Party: The Roots of Policy Formation in Pennsylvania,' (Ph.D. dissertation, University of Pittsburgh, 1988), pp. 46, 53, and 63.

24 Stevenson Whitcomb Fletcher, *Pennsylvania Agriculture and Country Life: 1840-1940* (Harrisburg: Pennsylvania Historical and Museum Commission, 1955), 1. See the following for descriptions of local community exchange: Robert E. Mutch, 'Yeoman and Merchant in Pre-industrial America: Eighteenth-century Massachusetts as a Case Study,' *Societas* 7 (1977): 279-302; James A. Henretta, 'Families and Farms: Mentalite in Pre-Industrial America,' *William and Mary Quarterly* 3rd series, 35 (1978): 3-32; Michael Merrill, 'Cash is Good to Eat: Self-Sufficiency and Exchange in the Rural Economy of the United States,' *Radical History Review* 3 (1977): 42-71.

25 See Chapter Four for regional definitions and descriptions as well as the sources of the population and agricultural production figures used in this chapter.

26 Stevenson Whitcomb Fletcher, *Pennsylvania Agriculture and Country* Life, 78.

Chapter 2

Historical Anthropometrics: Theory, Method, and the State of the Field

> Anthropometry is the technique of expressing quantitatively the form of the body.[1]

Historical anthropometrics, the study of longitudinal or cross-sectional patterns in human body size, is a fruitful new avenue of historical research which draws upon the disciplines of history, biology, anthropology, economics, and demography. While social welfare workers, public health specialists, and physical anthropologists have long utilized anthropometric measures as indicators of well-being, only relatively recently have historians begun to use such data to illuminate the historical experience of ordinary men and women of the past.[2]

Several rationales recommend the use of body size to investigate the human condition in a historical context. First, adult stature is a cumulative indicator of net nutritional status[3] over the growth years, and thus reflects the command over food and access to healthful surroundings. Since expenditures for these items comprised such a high percentage of family income for historical communities in the now developed world, as it still does in today's less developed countries (LDC), mean stature can be used to examine changes in a population's economic circumstances over time and to compare the well-being of different groups with similar genetic height potential. The World Health Organization describes stature as one of the best measures of overall health conditions within a society.[4]

'Conventional' measures of economic well-being such as per capita GNP, wage and price indices, and income inequality measures have been notoriously problematic to develop for historical communities. Price data often exist only for a few commodities in a handful of cities, while wages are similarly extant only for a few occupations. In contrast, anthropometric measures, especially height, are available for significant segments of many national populations as far back as the early 1700s, and thus can serve as complements to standard economic indicators. However, in some cases they provide the only means of assessing well-being within historical communities.[5]

While conventional economic indicators can be estimated for the early nineteenth-century only for infrequent intervals, anthropometric data are often available on an annual basis and are also extant for the pre-statistical period. The United States during the early and middle decades of the nineteenth-century is a case in point. If researchers only used U.S. census data, the existence of adverse biological developments for the American population in the 1830s and 1840s relative to those of the 1820s would not have been suspected. While the inter-decadal estimates of per capita GNP beginning with 1840 indicate ever-increasing levels, their shortcomings include the fact that they are unable to capture business cycle effects. While in the aggregate the material welfare of the American population undoubtedly improved, at least as evidenced by rising GNP,[6] the anthropometric evidence indicates unmistakably that the average adult height of males began to decline during the second half of the 1830s. These were apparently a hidden cost to economic modernization. Heights continued their descent until late in the nineteenth-century, during this same period of rising GNP.[7]

In addition, and potentially more importantly, historical anthropometrics broadens the understanding of 'well-being' beyond the one-dimensional 'ruler' of income, providing another lens through which the quality of life can be viewed in historical perspective. Stature, as a *net* measure of nutritional status, sums up the results of caloric inputs and the caloric demands of work and the disease environment. It reflects the actual physical outcomes of economic activity, rather than simply potential consumption as estimated by income.[8]

Although the sub-discipline is still relatively young, research findings have contributed to the scholarly debates over the nature of slavery, mortality trends, and the outcomes of industrialization and economic development.[9] Height has been the primary indicator utilized to date because it is the most commonly available for historical populations. Some authors have also utilized data on height-standardized weight indices and birth weight.[10] Age at which menarche is reached, while not a body measurement per se, is another biological proxy for net nutritional status, and historical studies of this indicator of female maturation have tended to be associated with the anthropometric approach. While many issues remain to be addressed, this line of research offers many new historical insights.

The Evolution of Body Measurement in Context[11]

The measurement and description of the human form date back to the classical civilizations of Greece and Rome. In these societies, through the Renaissance and into the early eighteenth-century, interest centered primarily on the determination of ideal body shapes and proportions rather than on absolute size.[12] As might be inferred, artists were most deeply interested in the proportional evolution of the human form throughout the life course. Even the first medical practitioner concerned with bodily measurement, and the man credited with the invention of the term 'anthropometrics,' German physician Johann S. Elsholtz was primarily interested in how 'out of balance' body proportions might increase disease susceptibility.[13]

The rationale for systematic, large-scale body measurement and record keeping came from neither artists nor doctors; rather,

> it was because of military requirements. Tall soldiers were regarded as preferable to short ones. Not only were they generally stronger; they could cover more ground on the march because of a greater length of stride, and in combat they could reach further with the bayonet and load more easily the long-barreled muskets of the time, in which the charge had to be rammed down the muzzle.[14]

The measurement of military recruits generally began by the mid-eighteenth-century. Not only did height provide a means for classifying men into military units, but it also provided a means of identifying them for the payroll or when they deserted.[15] After that time the reasons for height assessment and record keeping expanded enormously and included prisons, schools, passports, freedom certificates, and shipping manifests of slaves. However, the military's need to identify recruits provided the most measurements on young men.[16]

Scientific curiosity spurred the eighteenth-century development of the first textbooks on human growth.[17] These were more concerned with growth patterns throughout life than with stature differences across groups or trends over time. In the nineteenth century class differences in height were readily noted in England, because of their extreme nature.[18] The 'moral outrage' generated by the 'tiny children,' Dickens' 'Oliver Twists,' along with the view that medicine had a preventive as well as a curative function,[19] generated an interest in 'auxological epidemiology, the use of growth data to search out, and later to define, sub-optimal conditions of health.'[20] In particular, this meant anthropometry was directed primarily at the poor, especially children toiling in the factories of English and French industrial cities. Such investigations paved the way for legislation regulating the use of children's labor in factories.[21] Efforts to evaluate the welfare of working-class children continued in Europe throughout the nineteenth century. However, concern about the potential 'over-stressing' of children by the schools of the day led to more broadly based surveys of children's physical condition around 1900 in both North America and Europe as investigations into students' physical well-being were conducted to assess the impact of school attendance.[22]

In addition, fear in Britain over the 'degeneration' of its men and concern over their potential to form an effective fighting force provided motivation for large-scale anthropometric surveys, as did efforts evolving out of the child-welfare movement.[23] Thus, the early twentieth century saw the establishment of a series of longitudinal population surveys, first in North America and later in Europe. In some cases this work was directed toward the generation of growth standards, while other efforts evaluated social-class differences among children.[24] The world-wide economic depression of the 1930s led to further support for this research program, although the results of several long-term studies of children, begun well before the downturn, were also published during this time.[25] These studies, along with Bowles' 1932 work on several generations of Harvard families from the late nineteenth and early twentieth centuries can be seen as transitional steps between contemporary and historical anthropometrics.[26] Since the 1950s, anthropometry has been utilized for a variety of purposes in both the developed and underdeveloped world. Population groups, both in the 'modern' urban sector and in the 'traditional' rural regions, have been measured in order to develop standards, monitor nutritional status of individuals and populations, assess famines and evaluate the effectiveness of economic development programs.[27]

Anthropometric studies today can be classified as one of three types.[28] Auxologists perform basic research, collecting body measurements over the human life cycle to generate standards of physical development for twentieth-century populations against which individual development can be assessed. These data are used to investigate factors influencing growth processes, and to explore the relationship with subsequent morbidity and mortality. Identification of the 'ideal' body size is not the goal; rather, this work seeks to determine the range of sizes to be considered normal so that 'exceptional' cases of malnourishment can be identified, risks assessed and, if warranted, treatment undertaken.[29] In addition to its medical context, such basic research has application in the field of ergonomics or human factor engineering.[30]

The second focus of anthropometric research, a continuation of nineteenth-century work, pertains to the living standards of children. Such investigations often support regulatory legislation or government aid policies. In addition to 'in-country' use, international development practitioners use such measurement programs to determine current conditions as well as to evaluate the effectiveness of economic development interventions in third world societies.[31] As Bielicki notes,

> Students of growth have at their disposal a very sharp and reliable instrument with which they can measure the effectiveness of social policies practiced, or claimed to be practiced, by governments and ruling political parties.[32]

The third direction, and the concern of this work, is historical anthropometrics. Historians, anthropologists, and economists specializing in this field seek to assess, in physical terms, the well-being of previous societies and the factors which influence it. While historical anthropometric research is a relatively recent development, an extensive body of medical literature relating nutrition and epidemiological conditions to physical growth provides a strong theoretical underpinning for this line of analysis.

The Meaning of 'Nutritional Status'

The term 'nutritional status' is used to encompass more than simply diet, i.e. the intake of calories and nutrients, and is thus distinct from the more common term 'nutrition.' While nutrition refers to the quantity and quality of food *inputs* to the human biological system, it makes no reference to the amounts needed for healthy functioning. The latter varies with demands on the organism. For instance, two individuals with the same body size, one an accountant and the other a construction worker, might both receive the same amount of nutrition, yet the nutritional status of the latter, *ceteris paribus*, would be well below that of the accountant due to the vast differences in the caloric demands of his/her occupation. Thus, nutritional status refers to the balance between caloric and nutrient intake and the caloric demands placed on the body.[33]

While work intensity makes the most obvious demands on nutrient intakes, it is just one of many. Energy is required to resist infection,[34] so the epidemiological environment also influences nutritional status. Pregnancy adds caloric and nutrient demands, as does breast-feeding. Calories expended in any of these fashions are available neither for basal metabolism, the energy used to breathe, pump blood, and run other body systems in the rest state, nor for growth. Throughout this work the conceptual difference between nutritional intake and (net) nutritional status will be maintained.[35]

Human Growth and Development: The Medical Foundations of Historical Anthropometrics

As noted earlier, even nineteenth-century laymen were quite aware of the vast differences in the physical characteristics among the various social classes in Britain. While a few held the differences to be of ethnic or racial origin, many believed them to be caused by the advantages of wealth or the disadvantages of poverty. While much still remains to be learned in the field of human growth, medical knowledge of the factors influencing body size has advanced considerably.

In addition to final attained height, growth profiles during childhood and adolescence are matters of notable value. The duration of the growth period itself as well as the onset and intensity of the adolescent growth spurt are sensitive to nutritional status.[36] These all result from a complex interaction of nutritional intake, genetic endowment, and environmental effects.[37] At the level of the *individual*, genetics are a strong but not exclusive influence on the determination of final height and of growth patterns. Genetics are most important when net nutrition is optimal.[38] However, when evaluating differences between *groups* of people in sub-optimal nutritional circumstances, environmental influences predominate.[39]

The physical stature of a population does not reflect nutritional status at the time of measurement, but rather it indicates cumulative net nutrition over the growth period. It is a long-term indicator of relative biological well-being. Due to genetic variation, the same nutritional regime can result in different final stature for particular *individuals*, because of variation in the ability to continue growing in the face of adverse nutritional circumstances, or epidemiological and work environments.[40] However, the genetic height potential of most Europeans, Africans, and North Americans of European or African ancestry is comparable.[41]

Under equivalent environmental circumstances the *groups* have achieved nearly identical mean adult stature. In many parts of rural Africa, mean adult heights today are similar to those of Africans of 150 years ago, while well-fed urban Africans attain final heights similar to current-day Europeans and North Americans of European descent.[42] Further evidence of this genetic similarity is the fact that birth length for children born in the urban slums of the less developed countries are near the fiftieth centile standard for the developed world (they are taller than 50 per cent of other children their age) but quickly fall below the tenth percentile (they are taller than only 10 per cent of other children their age) as environmental factors begin to take their toll.[43] This is not to say that all physical differences have environmental origins. For example, as a result of evolutionary climatic adaptation, Africans are generally longer limbed and have less body fat than Europeans, but adult stature differences between these groups are not similarly determined.[44] Differences in nutritional intake result in wide variation in adult height even within populations of the same genetic make-up.[45] For example, individuals from higher socio-economic classes tend to be taller than their lower-class counterparts, whether in impoverished third-world countries or in the developed nations.[46]

Some racial/ethnic groups of Asian/Pacific origin may have a genetic height potential significantly below that of persons of European or African ancestry. These include Japanese, Chinese, Koreans, and several Indo-Malay groups.[47] Greulich's work on persons of Japanese ancestry, some reared in Japan and others in California, indicates that after several generations of living with a western dietary regime, mean stature did increase appreciably among both groups. However, those living in California were significantly taller than those who remained in Japan, and both groups were still shorter than the European and North American average.[48]

The growth profile is also an indicator of net nutritional status. The pattern of growth is remarkably similar for all individuals, although the timing of such events as the adolescent growth spurt and age at which terminal height is reached does vary. Among well-nourished modern populations, the absolute rate of linear growth, or growth velocity (increment in height), is fastest in the first two years of life. Growth velocity declines rapidly to about age three after which the rate of decline slows. At adolescence a marked acceleration in growth occurs. During this event, height velocity increases quickly, reaching about half the rate evident immediately following birth, but then falls just as rapidly and continues to fall until growth ceases entirely.[49] Environmental conditions, while affecting the timing of growth, do not affect the overall pattern.[50] Minor variations in the timing of major events are normal and some racial differences exist in this regard as well.[51] However, significant deviation from growth trajectory norms may indicate nutritional deprivation. The body seems to be self-stabilizing, postponing growth until caloric levels will support it, and maintaining genetically programmed body proportions more rigidly than size potential.[52] Under sub-optimal net nutrition regimes, the tempo of growth may be slower,[53] but might not necessarily result in permanent 'stunting.' Rather, if nutritional status improves within a reasonable length of time, height within the normal range can be achieved through 'catch-up' growth, increased growth velocity, and an elongation of the growth period.[54] Such extensions are not indefinite and, should nutritional status improvement be delayed too long, stunting, the permanent retardation of linear growth, will occur.[55] Hence, the process of growth can be thought of as 'target seeking.'[56]

The body's ability to keep open the window of opportunity for growth when experiencing inadequate nutritional conditions makes the mean age at which growth ceases a valuable indicator of a population's nutritional status. While final adult height and length of the growth period are not absolutely linked, populations which stop growing earlier usually, although not universally, end up being taller.[57] Late twentieth-century Europeans and North Americans cease growing, on average, at age 17.5 for boys and 15.5 years for girls.[58] Among eighteenth- and nineteenth-century Europeans, however, growth continued well into the early to mid-twenties.[59]

Height is the most common, but not the only, anthropometric indicator of nutritional status. Age at menarche, birth weight and weight for height are also useful. Age at menarche is not a measure of physical size but of sexual maturation.[60] Menarche generally occurs earlier among well-nourished women. The higher the socio-economic standing within the same culture, the earlier is menarche reached, though genetic variation also has an influence.[61] Average menarcheal age in the developed West is about 13 years,[62] while in the middle of the nineteenth century it was between 15 and 16 years among European women. During the twentieth century, most of the developed world has seen a decline in the age at menarche as well as a reduction in cross-class variation in this measure.[63] Nutritional differences seem to have a 'substantial effect'[64] but the evidence is indirect, based on socio-economic class differences and other anthropometric indicators rather than actual dietary assessment.[65] Areas which have not experienced nutritional improvement over the past century have not witnessed decreases in the age at menarche.[66]

For historians, birth weight is primarily a useful indicator of long-term maternal nutritional status.[67] A large number of factors influence birth weight, ranging from the mother's diet, work intensity, and quality of health care, to the sex of the child, maternal size and birth parity, as well as the mother's health practices. The level of economic inequality and social class are also correlated with birth weight variation, although these variables reflect some of the factors noted above.[68] However, because the mother's diet and health status are such strong influences on birth weight, it provides another useful means of monitoring women's well-being.[69]

Improvement in net nutritional status, both across wide segments of the population in developed countries and within urban areas of the LDCs, is generally accepted as the most salient influence on growth patterns and final stature. It is viewed as the most likely cause of the 'secular trend,'[70] a 'rather curious phrase [which] denotes both the tendency to get larger and the tendency to get more early maturing.'[71] This *unidirectional* trend toward greater stature and faster maturation has been apparent in most of the developed world only during the last century and more recently in the 'modern' sector of some LDCs. Before the twentieth century height cycling was the dominant pattern, without a secular trend. The 'secular trend,' it should be noted, has occurred only in areas in which economic and nutritional standards have been improving.[72] Two other sources of stature increase have been hypothesized but have garnered little support among the medical community.

Landauer posited in 1973 that the coincident increase in the practice of infantile smallpox vaccination and the upward secular trend in stature is evidence of the vaccination's prime influence in the U.S. He implicitly assumed a continuous upward trend in stature since 1800, rather than the pattern of cycling now known to have been the case. While the greater prevalence of vaccination has reduced the disease load carried by populations, and thus improved nutritional status, it is one among many rather than the primary cause of increased stature.[73]

Heterosis (hybrid vigor) describes varietal cross-breeding within a species which produces offspring larger or stronger than either parent. The increasingly widespread diffusion of mass transportation technology and the breakdown of human isolates over the past 200 years has created much greater variety in human mating pairs and the potential for heterosis-based stature increases. However, limited medical research has been carried out on the subject, and the results have been inconclusive.[74] Heterosis' effects, if any exist, are thought to be minor compared to environmental influences on stature.[75]

The genetic similarity in growth potential for ethnic groups which were significant components of the Western European and North American populations make stature an excellent vehicle for comparing nutritional status and health among and between these groups. As Tanner notes:

> height can indeed be used as a proxy for health, and not only in the nineteenth century and in developing countries. This is true, of course, only when comparing groups, not when comparing individuals, the variation between whom is overwhelmingly due to genetical causes except in the direst circumstances. But between social classes, urban and rural dwellers, educated and uneducated (provided we stay within a single ethnic group) height is a useful – perhaps the most useful – measure of healthiness.[76]

The Determination of Nutritional Status

Human biologists and medical scientists agree that within genetically similar populations net nutrition is the primary determinant of adult physical stature. While nutritional status is a biological term, the influences upon it are mostly environmental in origin. Bielicki stresses that, to a considerable degree, differences in height within a population are 'socially induced variation.'[77] Figure 2.1 (see page 20 and 21) indicates the numerous channels of influence on the final adult stature of any individual.

Nutritional status, as measured by anthropometric indicators, provides clues about access to nutrients net of the demands placed upon it by bodily functions, exertion, and disease encounters. The relationship between disease encounters, both endemic and epidemic, and nutritional status is synergistic. That is to say, nutritional status itself influences the extent to which disease pathogens impact the human organism. In general, anthropometric indicators reflect the relative ease or difficulty of acquiring sufficient nutrients to provide for growth in excess of the immediate needs of the body. Genetic make-up of an individual determines the general potential for growth and the sensitivity to the nutritional environment. Hence, it accounts for individual variation in stature, even if environmental conditions were identical for all members of the population. However, height variation across populations or sub-populations (within the European and North American gene-pool) is determined, in the main, not by genetic variation, but by such external factors as diet, disease exposure, and work intensity. In turn, these are influenced by the socio-economic environment and the ecological niche which the individual inhabits. Nutritional status and physical stature clearly are composite measures of well-being linked to economic processes. However, the link is mediated through a variety of social circumstances, some volitional, others not. Hence, anthropometric historians must evaluate each situation within its own economic, cultural, and historical context.

In earlier societies, and to some extent even in some less developed countries today, access to nutrients was determined not as much by money income as by the control over arable land. As markets for food developed and urban living became predominant, for increasing percentages of the population access to nutrients depended upon the ability to purchase food and shelter, i.e. on real income. Additionally, food allocation within the family is not determined by markets but by intra-household bargaining as well as by tastes and custom. For example, in order to maximize earning power, in some cultures households distribute food resources so as to ensure nutritional adequacy for those family members engaged in income- or resource-generating activity.[78]

The handful of studies which include historical anthropometric data for women reveal that stature trends by gender do not always move in concert. Rather, in periods of declining nutritional status, women often exhibited a reduction in stature levels before such changes appeared among males.[79] This is somewhat paradoxical because biologists generally argue that women's growth trajectories are more resistant to a diminution in nutritional status than are those of men.[80] Though too little research has been done on this issue to speak with certainty, the pattern might well imply that, in periods of nutritional stress, women bore the brunt of deprivation, at least initially.[81]

Other cultural practices, including the high status accorded to the use of certain foods, such as white flour, polished rice, tea or coffee, may promote greater consumption of nutritionally less valuable foods among those able to afford them. This would tend to *reduce* the resultant stature differences by income. It may also mean that increases in income might result in less nutritional improvement than was financially feasible.[82] Access to nutrients also depends upon other individual choices. A small landholder might decide to market much of the farm's high-value, high-protein meat and dairy products, reducing thereby his family's consumption of these nutritious food products in order to maximize money income. This would enable him to increase the purchase and consumption of manufactured goods. However, while material welfare might well increase, biological welfare, knowingly or unknowingly, might decrease at the same time.[83]

Disease-exposure variation occurs as a result of some factors under the individual's control, and other factors which are determined at the societal level. The extent of pathogen prevalence and potency and the level of community sanitation are critical factors, which are not directly affected by individual decision making. However, housing and occupation are individually chosen and do help to determine the extent of disease exposure. Housing quality influences stature both directly and indirectly via construction quality and location. The weather-tightness of a residence directly affects caloric expenditures involved in maintaining body temperature, and thus helps to determine calories available for growth.[84] Housing quality can also be viewed in terms of residence within an urban, rural, or a suburban location. Once transportation improvements allow housing segregation based on socio-economic status to occur within larger urban areas, residence can become an important factor of environmental influences. However, prior to such, for example in mid-nineteenth century United States, urban childhood mortality levels were more influenced by the number of children in a family than by parental occupation or socio-economic status. The close proximity of the homes of the wealthy and the poor created a common level of exposure to infectious agents and equally poor sanitary conditions for children of all economic classes.[85] Under such circumstances, wealthier families might have been at a biological advantage because of their ability to purchase more nutrients, but the common epidemiological environment created an equalizing force.[86]

Work intensity is another factor determining nutritional status. It is a function of the age at which youth entered the labor force, educational attainment, the physical exertion needed in a chosen occupation, and by the level of technology. There are obvious feedback effects from current nutritional status to future nutritional status. A low level of nutritional status today might hinder full-time labor-force participation, and result in low incomes, poor housing, and substandard food consumption in the subsequent period as well, thereby reinforcing the cycle of nutritional inadequacy.

Methodological Issues in Historical Anthropometrics

Issues of accuracy and representativeness are critical in evaluating the usefulness of any historical source materials, including anthropometric data. Physical measurements are effective proxy measures of nutritional status and comparable across social groups if they are recorded carefully using similar procedures. Modern auxologists have designed methods which minimize error and maximize intermeasurement consistency.[87] Without these techniques, historical records of

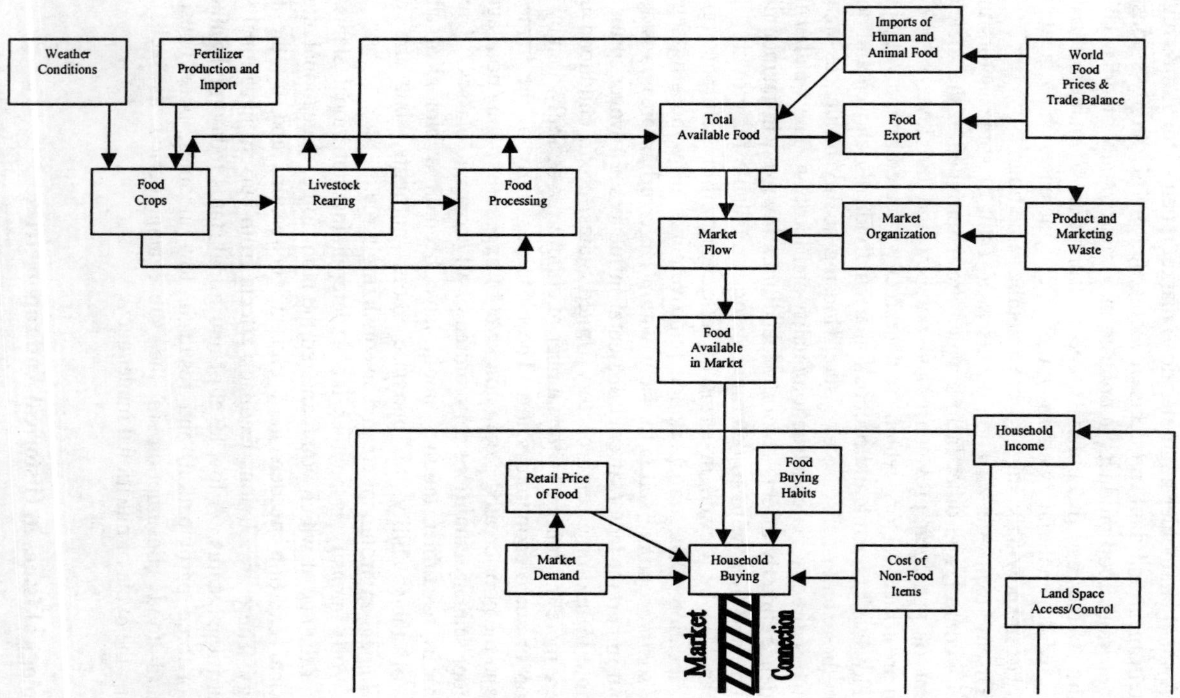

Weather Conditions
Fertilizer Production and Import
Imports of Human and Animal Food
World Food Prices & Trade Balance
Total Available Food
Food Export
Food Crops
Livestock Rearing
Food Processing
Market Flow
Market Organization
Product and Marketing Waste
Food Available in Market
Household Income
Retail Price of Food
Food Buying Habits
Market Demand
Household Buying
Cost of Non-Food Items
Land Space Access/Control
Market
Connection

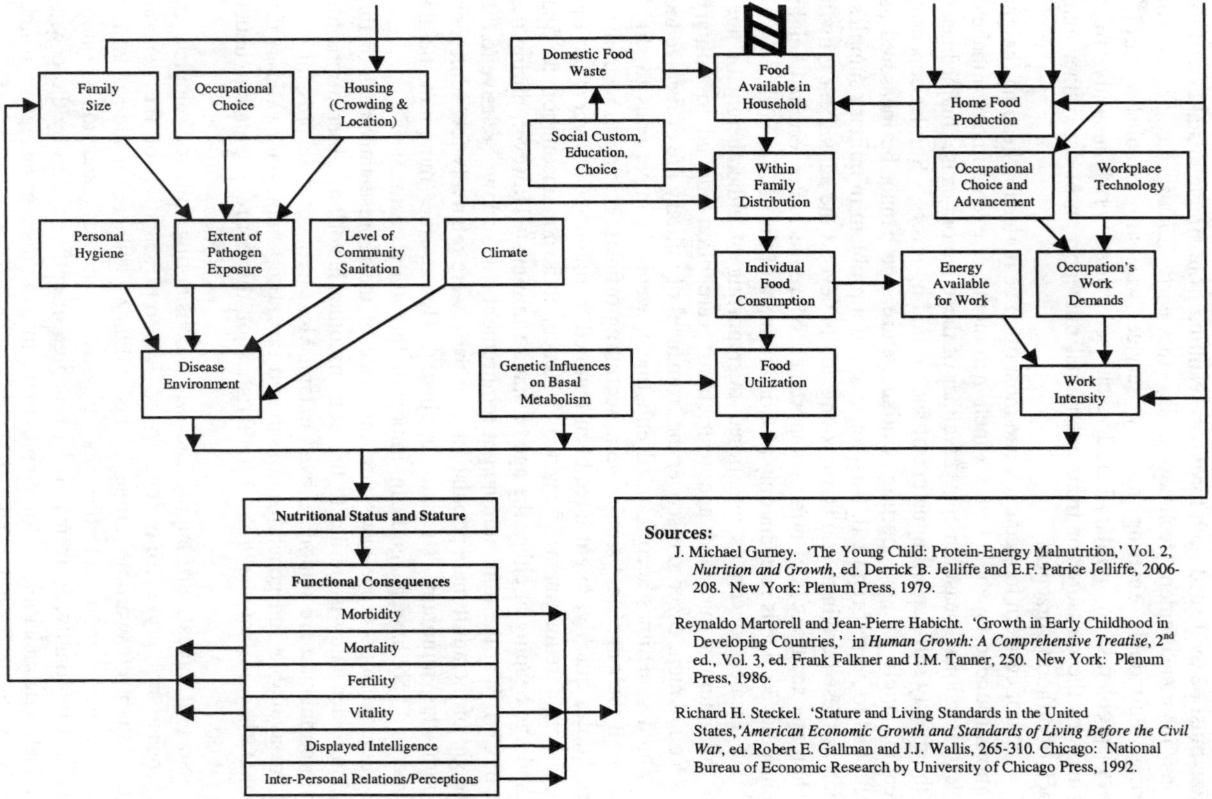

Sources:

J. Michael Gurney. 'The Young Child: Protein-Energy Malnutrition,' Vol. 2, *Nutrition and Growth*, ed. Derrick B. Jelliffe and E.F. Patrice Jelliffe, 2006-208. New York: Plenum Press, 1979.

Reynaldo Martorell and Jean-Pierre Habicht. 'Growth in Early Childhood in Developing Countries,' in *Human Growth: A Comprehensive Treatise*, 2nd ed., Vol. 3, ed. Frank Falkner and J.M. Tanner, 250. New York: Plenum Press, 1986.

Richard H. Steckel. 'Stature and Living Standards in the United States,' *American Economic Growth and Standards of Living Before the Civil War*, ed. Robert E. Gallman and J.J. Wallis, 265-310. Chicago: National Bureau of Economic Research by University of Chicago Press, 1992.

Figure 2.1 Influences on Human Stature in Market-Based Societies

body size must be evaluated both for errors resulting from simple mistakes and for variations in measurement techniques. By the early 1700s, the process of measuring individuals entering military service was an 'established art.'[88] Accuracy problems in military-based data sets arise predominantly from carelessness of the measurer or from intentional misreporting of data rather than from lack of orthodox practice.

Lack of concern for accuracy can most often be noticed in heaping (height observations rounded to whole feet, six inch increments, or even numbered inches) and lack of fractional measurements.[89] Neither of these factors cause major biases due to the mostly self-canceling nature of such rounding errors.[90] Similar concerns with heaping apply to age reporting. Unlike stature, age cannot be measured as such, and had to be self-reported. It is not much of a problem in military samples, inasmuch as these pertain to adults, or young adults beyond the adolescent growth spurt when age accuracy is of utmost importance. Moreover, after terminal height has been achieved, age is relevant only as a determinant of the year of birth.[91]

Of greater concern is intentional misreporting of either height or age, because minimum stature and age restrictions were often applied to military recruits. Young men, eager to discover the 'romance' of military life or receive the bounty which sometimes accompanied enlistment, were not impervious to slight fabrication of their age. In a similar vein, recruiting officers, hoping to meet their assigned quotas quickly, might have been tempted to round measurements to the minimum height requirement, if needed.[92] Hence, it is not uncommon to find height and age heaping at either the age or stature minima.[93] However, during the American Civil War the minimum height requirement was so low,[94] relative to the mean height of the adult male population, that there were relatively few adult men for whom the minimum standard applied.[95] Hence, the minimum height requirements do not have a significant impact on this study's estimates.[96]

For anthropometric historians, the issue of the representativeness of the population under study is similar to that for any other historian. Observations for the entire population are seldom, if ever, extant. Most frequently, records for sub-groups are available and generalizations based on these samples are valid to the extent that they reflect the true characteristics of the entire population under consideration.

Several caveats are appropriate when considering military samples. In time of peace military recruits tend to be less representative of the general population than do wartime armies. The military, with fewer demands for personnel, can be more selective and physical standards tend to be more stringent.[97] Additionally, there may exist a degree of self-selection by those who are physically fit and looking for employment in a military organization which involves both physical activity and bodily risk.

Other data sets also exhibit selectivity biases, although of different natures. Prison registers clearly do not provide a random sample of the population. The filter, however, is not based on size or desire for physical work – rather on the propensity for criminal activity and on the enforcement mechanism of the judicial system. If that system works in such a way that particular groups are over-represented in the prison population and a correlation exists between physical size and membership in such a group, the results based on such a sample might be misleading.[98] Inappropriate inferences are not always based on overrepresentation of persons at the lower end of the socio-economic ladder. Rather, data sets based on college students from the nineteenth- and early twentieth-centuries tend to pertain to members of the upper and upper-middle classes.[99]

The representativeness of a sample can also be affected by selection resulting not from individual decision, financial wherewithal, or policeman's whim, but from the actions of the Grim Reaper.[100] Within Afro-Caribbean slave populations in Trinidad, death rates were somewhat higher for shorter individuals (at all ages) than for the taller ones.[101] The result is that a select group of more robust and taller individuals remained alive for eventual measurement, and this sample provides a slightly overstated average height for that population. The extremely high death rates in Trinidad tend to exaggerate this phenomenon, but it might exist in other populations as well.[102]

As with all historical records, a clear understanding should exist about what height data represent, what biases are present, if any, and the extent to which results based on such samples can be generalized to larger segments of the society studied. As Sokoloff and Villaflor cogently state about military samples:

> … as long as the recruits are representative of their respective groups in the population, and we restrict our claims and results to well-defined categories of individuals, the seriousness of the military composition problem will be mitigated.[103]

The same can be said of samples drawn from other populations.

One difficulty faced by anthropometric historians is the association of this research, more imagined than real, with previous misuses of body measurement. Nineteenth-century American phrenologists used skull shape and size as a means of determining intelligence and as a way of justifying the enslavement of African-Americans because of their supposedly 'inferior' craniums.[104] The Bertillon approach to evaluating prison inmates included the measurement and classification of lips, ears, feet, nose, and limbs in an effort to discern a genetic or racial basis for criminality.[105] The Nazis attempted to breed the perfect race by eliminating all the physically 'inferior' peoples.[106] Each, appropriately, has made many squeamish in regard to the use of body measurements as an index of social development.

While the biological research which supports historical anthropometrics is scientifically well founded and fully justifies the approach, care must be exercised to ensure that the impression is not given that researchers either are searching for, or promoting, an 'aristocracy of the tall.' Being tall is not necessarily better in all circumstances.[107] However, for populations enduring an on-going sub-optimal net nutritional regime, an increase in mean height does signify improvement in the net nutritional level, and thus the general level of physical well-being. Height is a cumulative indicator of nutritional experiences, work intensity, and disease exposure over the growth years. Stature comparisons, across populations or across time, capture these experiences. As with any social science research, untangling the factors responsible for change in this social indicator is complicated. A recent critic stated that height is not a complete proxy for the quality of life.[108] Few anthropometric historians would claim that it is. However, it does provide a valuable means of assessing biological well-being in the past and the influence of social and economic developments on health.

Current State of the Field and Directions for Future Work

Le Roy Ladurie's studies of nineteenth century French soldiers in the late 1960s and early 1970s are recognized as the first publications in the spirit of historical anthropometrics. His studies revealed that stature among the French recruits varied with their socio-economic characteristics.[109] In America, the research was carried forward in the late 1970s. This research was based on nineteenth century records of the physical descriptions of U.S. slaves transported from the upper to the lower South. Studies of Caribbean slaves followed.[110]

In the 1980s many anthropometric studies were generated in connection with a National Bureau of Economic Research (NBER) directed study of American and European mortality trends from 1650 to the present, coordinated by Robert W. Fogel.[111] Motivated in great part by the desire to evaluate McKeown's hypothesis that improvements in nutrition were the critical component in mortality declines in the seventeenth- through the nineteenth-centuries,[112] the project has generated numerous large anthropometric data bases. These have been the starting point for the analysis of trends in physical stature and net nutritional status on both sides of the Atlantic. While most historical anthropometric studies published in the U.S. during the early and mid-1980s were either outgrowths of the NBER project or were conducted by students of Robert Fogel,[113] such as Richard Steckel and John Komlos, mortality trends were no longer the sole focus of historical anthropometrics. Anthropometric statistics were used to analyze the effect of industrialization on the populations experiencing it, as well as the characteristics of slavery in the United States.[114] The data sources were primarily military records or documents relating to slaves.[115] As the 1980s became the 1990s several developments expanded the field's focus. The geographic range of stature studies moved beyond Europe and North America to include Asia, Australia, and Africa. Other data sources were utilized. These included records from schools, utopian communities, English convict records, certificates of freedom for manumitted slaves, voter registration cards, runaway slave and indentured servant advertisements and prison inmate registers.[116]

While some of the findings remain tentative, due to the limited number of samples which have been analyzed, results have already proven worthy of the large investments required for the analysis. These achievements include 1) the determination of the main outlines of the trend in physical stature in Europe and North America between the eighteenth and twentieth centuries and 2) the emergence of several hypotheses pertaining to the relationship between height and economic and social development accompanying modern economic growth in these centuries.

The early finding, that there was not a unidirectional upward trend in stature since the 1700s, at first startled researchers,[117] whose expectations were based on recent experience. Extrapolating backward, Floud, Wachter, and Gregory note that, if the twentieth-century's rate of increase in height had been occurring for several centuries, medieval Europeans would have been dwarfs or midgets.[118] Instead, both in Europe and in the United States, cycles in height, reminiscent in some ways of business cycles, were evident.

Though smaller in amplitude than in Europe, cycling in height was a feature of American experience as well. At the time of the Revolution, the Civil War, and World War II, the mean height of adult, native-born white males was a fraction over 68 inches (Table 2.1), but there was significant variation in between these periods.[119] In the eighteenth-century the height of white men peaked at 68.3 inches for the birth cohorts of the 1780s.[120] Those born in the 1790s exhibited a slight decline in mean stature, with subsequent recovery to 1790 levels by the 1820s. Subsequent cohorts exhibited declining stature from after the Civil War through the depression of the 1890s.[121] Near the turn of the century, mean stature began its relatively uninterrupted increase which continues to the present day.[122] These findings are based primarily on military records drawn from the early national army, the Civil War forces, West Point Cadets, and the Ohio National Guard,[123] although other data sets show similar trends.[124]

There is now evidence that the free black population experienced a downturn in physical stature very similar to that of whites.[125] However, an exception to the antebellum diminution in nutritional status has been found among slave men.[126] The time trend in slave women's stature differs from that of men in that it adheres to the free pattern by showing a slight diminution in the antebellum period.[127]

In addition to the cycling in height, anthropometric historians have documented that heights differ systematically across nations with the level of economic development. Within societies, stature differences also occur along the urban–rural gradient, as well as across occupational categories and social class.

The intuitively anticipated positive correlation between mean height and per capita income holds at the national level in the twentieth-century.[128] Steckel has shown that, in cross-national comparison, the correlation between height and per capita income is as high as 0.84 to 0.90. However, since per capita income is highly correlated with a series of other variables that also affect height, the exact pathway through which income affects height is not fully clear.[129] Among the factors which help to explain the variation are better diet, medicine, improvements in sanitary infrastructure, longer schooling, more sedentary life, and better housing. Intense work regimes and psycho-social stress, both of which affect growth negatively, might also be mitigated by greater per capita income.

However, in prior centuries the relationship between height and income was not monotonic. U.S. troops during the American Revolution were nearly as tall as U.S. soldiers sent to Europe and Japan in the 1940s, despite the fact that per capita income in the earlier period was substantially below that in the latter.[130] Similarly, while per capita income in the U.S. in the late 1770s was below that of the British, the American troops had a height advantage of several inches over their British counterparts in the War of Independence.[131]

Table 2.1 Mean Heights of Adult Males (in inches)

North America					Europe		
European Ancestry			African Ancestry		Hungary	England	Sweden
1775-1783	1861-1865	1943-1944	1811-1861	1943-1944	1813-1835	1816-1821	1843-1886
68.1	68.5	68.1	67.0	67.9	64.2	65.8	66.3

Sources: U.S. whites, 1775-1783: Sokoloff and Villaflor, 'Early Achievement,' 458. U.S. whites, 1861-65: Margo and Steckel, 'Height of Native-Born Whites,' 168. U.S. whites and blacks, 1943-44: Karpinos, 'Height and Weight of Selective Service Registrants,' Table 5, 302. U.S. blacks, 1811-1861: Margo and Steckel, 'Height of American Slaves,' Table 1, 518. Hungary: Komlos, *Nutrition and Economic Development*, Table 2.1, 57. Britain: Floud, Wachter, and Gregory, *Height, Health, and History*, Table 4.1, 148. Sweden: Sandberg and Steckel, 'Overpopulation and Malnutrition,' Table 2, 7.

Note: Dates refer to dates of measurement.

The level of income inequality also has a powerful influence on mean heights. Steckel's analysis of data for the twentieth-century indicates that a 0.1 increase in the Gini coefficient (indicating greater income equality) is associated with a gain in mean stature of about 3.7 cm (1.5 inches).[132] In societies with high inequality, increases in per capita income have little effect on average stature if the gains accrue primarily to the wealthier segments of the society. In all likelihood, wealthy parents already have provided a perceived optimal food intake for their children. Increased income for those at the bottom of the income pyramid would be more likely to produce gains in height and health. Even without changes in average national per capita income, a reduction in inequality can have similar positive impact upon the stature and health of those at the lower rungs of the income ladder.[133]

The high level of social inequality at the onset of modern economic growth in England is exemplified by the substantial disparity between the height of students of the Sandhurst Royal Military Academy, an elite institution, and the Marine Society, a home for destitute boys in London. The difference in mean height at age fourteen exceeded three inches in favor of the gentry. In some years the gap was even greater.[134] Komlos has documented similar findings elsewhere: regardless of location, boys from 'prestigious military schools in England, France, and Germany were much taller than the population at large.'[135] A similar pattern existed in the nineteenth century U.S., but on a smaller scale: recruits into the regular Army were somewhat shorter than West Point cadets of the same age, who generally were drawn from higher socio-economic groups. However, the social gap in the U.S. was miniscule compared to that prevailing in the Old World.[136] Stature varied also by occupational groups. In eighteenth- and nineteenth century Europe and North America, white collar and professional workers tended to be significantly taller than laborers and unskilled workers.[137] However, farmers, being close to the source of nutrients, tended to be the tallest, though their advantage disappeared by the twentieth century.

Floud, Wachter, and Gregory have shown that, in early nineteenth century Britain, regional variation in stature dwarfed occupational differences.[138] In 1815, Scotsmen, rural and urban, as well as the Irish, were about one-half an inch taller than the non-London urban English of the day. The rural English were slightly shorter, on average, than Englishmen born in small and medium sized towns. Londoners, however, had a mean height almost one-third of an inch less than other urban dwellers in England and more than three-quarters of an inch below the Irish or the Scots.[139] A similar pattern held among convicts transported to New South Wales, Australia, except that the stature of the rural English was well above the average for all other English transported convicts.[140] Floud, Wachter, and Gregory show a trend of convergence in height among these groups after 1800. The tendency for low-population-density rural areas in the nineteenth century to be home to the tallest individuals was apparent from the Habsburg Monarchy to Scotland, and in the remote northern regions of late nineteenth century Sweden and Japan as well.[141]

In colonial America the rural–urban gradient did not exist. As cities grew, a divergence between the mean stature of the rural- and urban-born became evident, with the rural population displaying an advantage of some 0.45 inches among birth cohorts in the late 1700s.[142] The divergence persisted into the nineteenth century, and disappeared in the early twentieth century, when the urban-born gained a height advantage.[143]

Research on slave heights has provided important insight on the living standards of these deprived people. Large differences in stature have been documented between slaves on the North American mainland and those in the Caribbean. Adult mainland slaves, both women and men, were approximately two inches taller than those in the West Indies throughout the eighteenth and nineteenth centuries. This disparity reflects the differing work regime, food supply, and disease environment for the two groups.[144] Steckel argues that the growth pattern and infant mortality rates of U.S. slave children indicate that they were moderately to severely malnourished. In his analysis of slave transport manifest records, the mean heights of slave children aged four to nine were below the second percentile of modern growth standards. Their mortality rates were twice those estimated for the United States as a whole.[145] When young slaves entered the plantation work force, however, they began to eat in the fields with the rest of the hands. Steckel reasons that between age eight and twelve, caloric and protein intake increased enough to provide the large energy requirement needed for field work and to fuel growth at a rate sufficient for catch-up growth.[146] Although below the fifth percentile throughout childhood, these slaves grew to be relatively tall by nineteenth century standards, reaching about the twenty-fifth percentile of today's height distribution.[147] As adults, they were taller than most European populations of the time.[148]

Work in historical anthropometrics has also shed light on the extent of 'slave breeding,' the practice of forcing young slave women to bear children for the purpose of creating a larger stock of slave capital.[149] Trussell and Steckel argue that available evidence makes it unlikely that 'slave breeding' was a common practice in the antebellum South. They hold that the poor treatment received by the newly created capital, as indicated by infant and child growth curves, speaks against 'breeding' as a widespread practice on Southern plantations.[150] While age at first birth data are available for slave women, records of the ages at which slaves reached menarche are not. However, the height-by-age profile can be used to estimate the age at which menarche was reached, insofar as it occurs a little more than a year after the peak of the adolescent growth spurt.[151] This evidence and this relationship enabled Trussell and Steckel to argue that the average interval between a female slave reaching menarche and the birth of her first child was greater than five years. While the biology of reproductive capacity development posits a three year average delay between the two events, under the assumption of unrestricted sexual activity, the additional two years is evidence that slave owners did not routinely seek to maximize the 'output' of slave babies.[152]

Historical research on human height has indicated how much healthier the New World environment was compared to that of Europe. Europeans who immigrated to North America, on average, obtained a net nutritional status far better than that which was possible for them to attain in their place of birth. In the eighteenth century, the population of North America attained a mean height which was not achieved by Europeans until the twentieth century.[153] The combination of lower population density, lower levels of income inequality, and greater food resources bestowed a great benefit upon those growing up in North America (Table 2.1). This advantage is evident not only in adult heights but also in the earlier timing of the adolescent growth spurt among North Americans, as well as the relatively early attainment of final height.[154]

The evaluation of McKeown's hypothesis that much of the modern decline in mortality rates could be traced to improvements in nutrition (food intake) was one of the early rationales for the modern study of historical stature. The research conducted in association with Fogel's project has presented evidence for the parallel cycling of height and life expectancy at age ten in the United States during the nineteenth century.[155] Fogel presented a preliminary estimate that nutritional improvement accounted for 'four tenths' of the decline in mortality since the 1700s.[156] Furthermore, the analysis of Union Army enlistment and pension records has uncovered a negative relationship between height and rejection rates, on account of infirmity. The relationship between the body-mass index (weight in kilograms divided by height in meters squared), morbidity, and mortality risk within historical populations has also been documented.[157] Along a similar line, Sandberg and Steckel's data on Sweden have pointed out the parallel nature of stature trends and childhood mortality rates in the mid-nineteenth-century.[158]

Economic and social history are not the only two fields on which historical anthropometrics' impact has been felt. North American slave height-by-age profiles developed by Steckel have been used by auxologists to exemplify the range of possible growth patterns among humans.[159] Based on findings within the biological sciences, historical studies of stature have come full circle and are providing those same sciences with new data on human physical potential.

Conclusion and Future Directions

Historical anthropometrics is maturing. Over the past several years a series of 'state of the field' articles have been written, summarizing past accomplishments, consolidating isolated findings into more generalized conclusions, and pointing out the next steps for researchers.[160] However, acceptance is not complete. Skepticism remains about the approach. To combat this, researchers must be careful to stress repeatedly what stature describes, what its limits are, and how knowledge of stature trends can influence our understanding of economic and social history.

Anthropometric historians have drawn the basic pattern of the development of human stature from the eighteenth- through the twentieth-centuries for Europe, North America, and to some extent even for Africa, Asia, and Australia. Of course, still much work remains.[161] Findings to date have primarily been drawn from military samples and are subject to the vagaries of the recruitment process, especially in peacetime. It would be desirable to obtain greater diversity in the sources of future data. Expansion of the number and type of samples are important steps in the confirmation and consolidation of early results. Continued investigations will add to our understanding of economic processes and of the adjustments in response to social and economic change, while at the same time expanding our definition of human well-being.

One of the field's on-going frustrations is that, except for slave records, few data sets contain physical measurements for large numbers of females. To date, female slaves and ex-slaves, some late nineteenth-century U.S. college women, along with some female convicts, are the only women for whom historical stature data have been analyzed. Generalizations of research findings to entire populations are hindered by the small amount of data on females and the knowledge, from that data which are extant, that stature trends for the two sexes do not mimic each other.[162] Similarly, upper class samples of either sex are not common.[163] Future efforts should be directed at locating samples which contain data on these two understudied groups.

As Riley notes, the problem which anthropometric historians seek to resolve is not the identification of likely influences on stature. The biological sciences have provided that theoretical framework. The task at hand is to determine the relative weight of the various influences or, in Fogel's terms, to perform 'an accounting exercise of particularly complicated nature, which involves measuring not only the direct effect of particular factors but also their indirect effects and their interactions with other factors.'[164] While in both the American and British contexts 'case-building' for the various factors involved in the mid-nineteenth-century decline in mean stature has begun, no consensus has emerged. A series of potential explanations has been identified. These include a worsening of the disease environment caused by increased movement of people and pathogens via the expanded transportation network.[165] Transportation improvement played a role in another potential source of stature decline, the process of market integration. This development opened urban markets to a more diversified range of products from the hinterlands. However, it may have led some farmers to market a greater proportion of their produce than they had previously. Potentially, in exchange for newly available manufactured goods, farmers knowingly or unknowingly reduced their children's biological well-being. Another explanation is that food production did not keep pace with burgeoning American population growth and increased food exports.[166] Increasing income and wealth concentrations may also have played a significant role, as they do in international comparisons. The task of untangling these influences will be challenging. The pertinent developments are closely interrelated, identifying them separately in a non-experimental setting is not an easy task.

More localized studies, with ample sample sizes for adequate statistical analysis, are needed. These will allow the determination of the social, economic, and demographic factors most closely associated with trends in human height which have been identified on both sides of the Atlantic. Other key areas of future investigation include the functional consequences of height differences, including differences in life expectancy and their effect on labor productivity.[167] Some work in progress has called for the development of terms and methods for describing a historical 'biological standard of living.'[168]

The research presented here will fill some of the gaps noted above. The data base to be analyzed is large and geographically concentrated. Linking these data to county level economic and demographic data provides a more detailed picture of the relationship between economic development and changes in physical stature than has been produced by previous studies. The economic theory which helps to explain their relationship follows.

Notes

1 Noel Cameron, 'The Methods of Auxological Anthropometry,' in *Human Growth: A Comprehensive Treatise*, 2nd ed., Vol. 3, ed. F. Falkner and J.M. Tanner, (New York: Plenum, 1986), 263-281.

2 John Komlos (ed.), *The Biological Standard of Living in Europe and America 1700-1900. Studies in Anthropometric History* (Aldershot, England: Variorum Press, 1995); John Komlos (ed.), *The Biological Standard of Living on Three Continents: Further*

Essays in Anthropometric History (Boulder: Westview Press, 1995); Bernard Harris, 'Health, Height, and History: An Overview of Recent Developments in Anthropometric History,' *Social History of Medicine* 7 (1994): 297-320.

3 Net nutritional status signifies total caloric intake minus the caloric demands of basal metabolism, disease resistance and physical exertion. Remaining calories are available to fuel growth. Robert W. Fogel, 'Nutrition and the Decline in Mortality Since 1700: Some Preliminary Findings,' in *Long-Term Factors in American Economic Growth*, ed. Stanley Engerman and Robert Gallman (Chicago: National Bureau of Economic Research, 1987), 446-447.

4 WHO Expert Committee on Maternal and Child Care, 'New Trends in the Delivery of Maternal and Child Care in Health Services,' Who Technical Report Series, #600 (Geneva: World Health Organization, 1976), 95; Tadeusz Bielicki, 'Physical Growth as a Measure of the Economic Well-Being of Populations: The Twentieth century,' in *Human Growth: A Comprehensive Treatise*, 2nd ed., Vol. 3, ed. F. Falkner and J.M. Tanner (New York: Plenum, 1986), 283. However, unlike contemporary researchers in the LDCs, who can collect new data pertaining to their respective populations, historians must be content with extant data from the past.

5 David Eltis, 'Welfare Trends Among the Yoruba in the Early Nineteenth century: The Anthropometric Evidence,' *Journal of Economic History* 50 (1990): 522; Robert W. Fogel, S. Engerman, R. Floud, G. Friedman, R. Margo, K. Sokoloff, R. Steckel, J. Trussell, G. Villaflor and K. Wachter, 'Secular Changes in American and British Stature and Nutrition,' *Journal of Interdisciplinary History* 14 (1983): 445-447.

6 Robert Gallman, 'The Statistical Approach: Fundamental Concepts as Applied to History,' in *Approaches to American Economic History*, ed. George Rogers Taylor and L.R. Ellsworth (Charlottesville, University of Virginia Press, 1971), pp. 87-105; Paul David, 'The Growth of Real Product in the United States Before 1840: New Evidence, Controlled Conjectures,' *Journal of Economic History* 27 (June 1967): 151-197; Robert Gallman, 'The Pace and Pattern of American Economic Growth,' in *American Economic Growth: An Economist's History of the United States,* ed. Lance Davis, Richard Easterlin, and William N. Parker (New York: Harper and Row, 1972), 15-60; Thomas Weiss, 'Long Term Changes in U.S. Agricultural Output Per Worker, 1800-1900,' Working Paper 23, National Bureau of Economic Research Series on Historical Factors in Long Run Growth, 1991.

7 Dora Costa, 'Height, Wealth, and Disease among the Native-Born in the Rural Antebellum North,' *Social Science History* 17 (1993): 355-383.

8 R. Floud, K. Wachter, and A. Gregory, *Height, Health, and History: Nutritional Status in the United Kingdom, 1750-1980* (Cambridge, England: Cambridge University Press, 1990), 286-287. As Steckel has noted, using stature as an indicator of economic well-being is congruent with Sen's recent emphasis on functionings and capabilities as the basis for evaluating the efficacy of an economic system, as well as with Adelman and Morris' basic needs approach to living standards. Richard Steckel, 'Height, Living Standards, and History,' *Historical Methods* 24 (1991): 183-187.

9 John Komlos, 'Stature and Nutrition in the Habsburg Monarchy: The Standard of Living and Economic Development in the Eighteenth century,' *American Historical Review* 90 (1985): 1149-1161; for recent contributions see the special issue, 'Historische Anthropometrie,' Guest Editor, John Komlos, *Jahrbuch für Wirtschaftsgeschichte*, 2000, no. 1.

10 Dora L. Costa, 'Height, Weight, Wartime Stress, and Older Age Mortality: Evidence from the Union Army Records,' *Explorations in Economic History* 30 (1993): 424-449; Robert W. Fogel, 'The Conquest of High Mortality and Hunger in Europe and America: Timing and Mechanisms,' in *Favorites of Fortune: Technology, Growth, and Economic Development Since the Industrial Revolution*, ed. P. Higonnet, D.S. Landes, and H. Rosovsky (Cambridge, MA: Harvard University Press, 1991), 33-71; Timothy Cuff, 'The Body Mass Index Values of Nineteenth-Century West Point Cadets: A Theoretical Application of Waaler's Curves to A Historical Population,' *Historical Methods* 26 (1993): 71-83; Thomas E. Jordan, 'Linearity, Gender, and Social Class in Economic Influences on Heights of Victorian Youth,' *Historical Methods* 24 (1991): 116-123; W. Peter Ward, and Patricia C. Ward, 'Infant Birth Weight and Nutrition in Industrializing Montreal,' *American Historical Review* 89 (1984): 324-345; W. Peter Ward, *Birth Weight and Economic Growth: Women's Living Standards in the Industrializing West* (Chicago: University of Chicago Press, 1993).

11 This section draws upon James M. Tanner's comprehensive book on this topic, *A History of the Study of Human Growth* (Cambridge: Cambridge University Press, 1981).

12 Tanner, *Study of Human Growth*, 32-33, and 65.

13 Tanner, *Study of Human Growth*, 45-49.

14 Tanner, *Study of Human Growth*, 98.

15 Tanner, *Study of Human Growth*, 99; and private communication with Michael Meier, Military Reference Branch, U.S. National Archives, Washington, D.C.

16 The earliest systematic military records date from the early 1700s. Tanner, *Study of Human Growth*, 100-101, 142-4.

17 Tanner notes Bergmuller's book of growing children's proportions (1723), Buffon's publication of the first fetal and early childhood growth measurements (1749), Stoller's textbook on human growth (1729) and Jampert's valuable, but seldom referenced, table on human growth from age 1-25 (1754). Tanner, *Study of Human Growth*, 49-52, 73-74, 79-83, 88-89.

18 Floud, Wachter and Gregory, *Height, Health, and History*, 3.

19 Villerme's comments in 1829 sound like calls in the late twentieth-century United States for more focus on the ambient conditions which result in ill-health and less on curing illness. L. R. Villerme, 'Memoire sur la Taille de L'homme en France,' *Annales d'Hygiene Publique* 1 (1829): 551-99, cited in Tanner, *Study of Human Growth*, 162-163.

20 Auxology is the study of human growth, auxologists those who study it. Tanner, *Study of Human Growth*, 142.

21 Tanner, *Study of Human Growth*, 147-153, and 163-164.

22 Such evaluations were conducted in England, Denmark, Sweden, Norway, Germany, Russia, Switzerland, and the United States. Tanner, *Study of Human Growth*, 202-215.

23 Roderick Floud and Kenneth Wachter 'Poverty and Physical Stature, Evidence on the Standard of Living of London Boys, 1770-1870,' *Social Science History* 6 (1982): 426.

24 Tanner, *Study of Human Growth*, 299-301. Some of these continued well into the recent period ending only in the 1960s and 1970s.

25 Tanner, *Study of Human Growth*, 312.

26 Tanner, *Study of Human Growth*, 228-229; Bowles notes height variation between generations. G. T. Bowles, *New Types of Old Americans at Harvard and at Eastern Women's Colleges* (Cambridge, MA: Harvard University Press, 1952).

27 See James M. Tanner, 'Growth and Physique in Different Populations of Mankind: A Proposal for the Establishment of an International Bureau of Growth Studies,' in *The*

Biology of Human Adaptability, ed. P.T. Baker and J.S. Weiner (Oxford: Clarendon Press, 1966), 44-66, for a description of the proposal to begin collection of such data on a worldwide basis.

28 Tanner identifies three impulses for anthropometry, 'the social, the medical, and the intellectual.' Tanner, *Study of Human Growth*, 397.

29 Tanner, *Study of Human Growth*, 380.

30 This work seeks to match the design characteristics of furniture, tools, vehicles, and machinery to the shape, proportion, and range of motion of the human body as well as providing data to fashion and interior designers. For a fascinating review of anthropologist Albert Damon's contribution to the ergonomics of World War II bombers and an example of the importance of human factor engineering to the success of machine design, see H.T.E. Hertzberg, 'Albert Damon's Contributions to Engineering Anthropology,' *American Journal of Physical Anthropology* 42 (1975): 455-460.

31 See for example, R. Biaragi, 'A Comparison of Five Anthropometric Indices for Identifying Factors of Malnutrition,' *American Journal of Epidemiology* 126 (1987): 258-267; World Health Organization 'Use and Interpretation of Anthropometric Indicators of Nutritional Status,' *Bulletin of the World Health Organization* 64 (1986): 929-941; Lincoln C. Chen, A.K.M. Alauddin Chowdhury, and Sandra L. Huffman, 'Anthropometric Assessment of Energy-Protein Malnutrition and Subsequent Risk of Mortality Among Preschool Aged Children,' *American Journal of Clinical Nutrition* 33 (1980): 1836-1845.

32 Bielicki, 'Physical Growth as a Measure,' 301.

33 Cameron notes that 'nutriture' is a 'functional concept involving the dynamic process of 'intake' and 'expenditure,' nutritional status describes the physical outcome. Noel Cameron, 'Measurement Issues Related to Anthropometric Assessment of Nutritional Status,' in *Anthropometric Assessment of Nutritional Status*, ed. John H. Himes (New York: Wiley-Liss, Inc., 1991), 348.

34 Disease exposure reduces growth through a variety of mechanisms, some by choice, others not: 1) dietary restrictions imposed upon the ill, 2) diversion of energy from other uses to fighting infection, 3) direct energy loss via fever, 4) poor nutrient absorption by the body during illness, 5) vomiting, 6) infection spurs the release of hydrocortisone from the adrenal glands. Hydrocortisone impedes growth processes. Reynaldo Martorell and Jean-Pierre Habicht, 'Growth in Early Childhood in Developing Countries,' in *Human Growth: A Comprehensive Treatise*, 2nd ed., Vol. 3, ed. F. Falkner and J.M. Tanner (New York: Plenum, 1986), 251; James M. Tanner, *Foetus into Man: Physical Growth from Conception to Maturity* rev. and enl. ed. (Cambridge, MA: Harvard University Press, 1990), 95.

35 Nutritional status is also sometimes known as 'net nutritional status' to make explicit the idea that this term encompasses both the in-flow of calories and the demands placed upon them.

36 Such information can be gathered either from data collected longitudinally, that is from a series of measurements of single individuals taken over the course of his/her life, or cross-sectionally, measurements of many individuals each of whom is at a different point in the aging process. The former type would be most useful and is preferable, however, it is the latter type which is the most abundant in historical records. The data type available also influences the type of standards which should be used in evaluating stature and net nutrition. Phyllis B. Eveleth and James M. Tanner, *Worldwide Variation in Human Growth* (Cambridge: Cambridge University Press, 1976), 5-10.

37 Phyllis Eveleth, 'Population Differences in Growth: Environmental and Genetic Factors,' in *Human Growth: A Comprehensive Treatise,* 2nd ed., Vol. 3, ed. F. Falkner and J.M. Tanner (New York: Plenum, 1986), 221; Tanner, *Foetus into Man*, 117.

38 Tanner, *Foetus into Man*, 163.

39 For example, correlation between parents' and children's final height generally range between 0.25 and 0.50, but the correlation between brothers is higher, an indicator of the relatively larger importance of environmental factors. William H. Mueller, 'The Genetics of Size and Shape in Children and Adults,' in *Human Growth: A Comprehensive Treatise*, 2nd ed., Vol. 3, ed. F. Falkner and J.M. Tanner (New York: Plenum, 1986), 147 and 157-59. The decreasing range of variation in height between unrelated adult males (25 cm.), adult brothers (16 cm.), and monozygotic twins (1.6 cm.) points to the influence of genetic factors. Tanner, *Foetus into Man*, 123-124, 163 and 211; Eveleth, 'Population Differences,' 221, 244; Richard Steckel, 'Slave Height Profiles from Coastwise Manifests,' *Explorations in Economic History* 16 (1979): 369.

40 Napoleon Wolanski, 'Biological Reference Systems in the Assessment of Nutritional Status,' in *Nutrition and Malnutrition: Identification and Measurement*, ed. A.E. Roche and F. Falkner (New York: Plenum Press, 1974), 231-233; Thomas K. Landauer, 'Infantile Vaccinations and the Secular Trend in Stature,' *Ethos* 1 (1973): 499-503.

41 Tanner, *Foetus into Man*, 163 and 239.

42 Eltis, 'Welfare Trends Among the Yoruba,' 522; T. Prazuck, A. Fisch, E. Pichard, and Y. Sidibe, 'Lack of Secular Change in Male Adult Stature in Rural Mali (West Africa),' *American Journal of Physical Anthropology* 75 (1988): 471-475.

43 Martorell and Habicht, 'Growth in Early Childhood,' 255-257; J. P. Habicht, R. Martorell, C. Yarbrough, R.M. Malina, and R.E. Klein, 'Height and Weight Standards for Pre-School Children: How Relevant are Ethnic Differences in Growth Potential,' *The Lancet* 7858 (April 6, 1974): 612-614.

44 Tanner, *Foetus into Man*, 143-145.

45 Eveleth and Tanner, *Worldwide Variation*, 241-261. This variation is generally rather uniform, and, in fact, adult human height distributions provided one of the first examples of normal distributions.

46 Martorell and Habicht's Figure 2 demonstrates that height differences across socio-economic classes dwarf genetic differences. Martorell and Habicht, 'Growth in Early Childhood,' 244.

47 Eveleth and Tanner, *Worldwide Variation*, 119 and 273-274; Eveleth, 'Population Differences,' 225; Tanner, *Study of Human Growth*, 399; Martorell and Habicht, 'Growth in Early Childhood,' 242-3. Of late some anthropologists are beginning to question the assumption of genetic shortness of Asians.

48 W.W. Greulich, 'Some Secular Changes in the Growth of American-born and Native Japanese Children,' *American Journal of Physical Anthropology* 45 (1976): 553-568; W.W. Greulich, 'A Comparison of the Physical Growth and Development of American Born and Native Japanese Children,' *American Journal of Physical Anthropology* 15 (1957): 489-515.

49 The growth curve of different individuals with good nutritional status may look different in its timing vis-à-vis birth, but if centered around the timing of the peak of the adolescent growth spurt (PHV, the peak height velocity) the curves will appear nearly identical. Tanner, *Study of Human Growth*, 230; Michael J.R. Healy, 'Statistics of Growth Standards,' in *Human Growth: A Comprehensive Treatise*, 2nd ed., Vol. 3, ed. F. Falkner and J.M. Tanner (New York: Plenum, 1986), 53-54.

50 L.A. Malcolm, 'Ecological Factors Relating to Child Growth and Nutritional Status,' in *Nutrition and Malnutrition: Identification and Measurement,* ed. A.E. Roche and F. Falkner (New York: Plenum Press, 1974), 348; Richard Steckel, 'Stature and Living Standards in the United States,' in *American Economic Growth and Standards of Living Before the Civil War,* ed. R.E. Gallman and J.J. Wallis. (Chicago: University of Chicago Press for National Bureau of Economic Research, 1992), 265-310; Tanner, *Foetus into Man*, 112.

51 Tanner, *Foetus into Man*, 140-142; Eveleth and Tanner, *Worldwide Variation*, 224-229.

52 M.T. Newman, 'Nutritional Adaptation in Man,' in *Physiological Anthropology*, ed. Albert Damon (New York: Oxford University Press, 1975), 234; Tanner, *Foetus into Man*, 138; Tanner, 'Growth and Physique,' 49.

53 The World Health Organization indicates that children's growth patterns, when compared to norms for the developed countries, comprise one of the best indicators of health and nutritional status within a community. WHO Expert Committee, 'Delivery of Maternal and Child Care,' 95; Bielicki, 'Physical Growth as a Measure,' 283. See also Tanner, *Foetus into Man*, 283; Eveleth and Tanner, *Worldwide Variation*, 275.

54 Tanner, *Foetus into Man*, 166.

55 Martorell and Habicht, 'Growth in Early Childhood,' 245; Stunting can be seen as the body's adaptation to sub-optimal nutrition. Smaller persons have lower basal metabolic requirements. Fogel, 'Conquest of High Mortality,' 50. Psychological adaptation may also occur to restrict activity under poor nutritional circumstances. Herman Freudenberger and Gaylord Cummins, 'Health, Work, and Leisure Before the Industrial Revolution,' *Explorations in Economic History* 13 (1976): 1.

56 James M. Tanner, 'Growth as a Target-Seeking Function, Catch-up and Catch-down growth in Man,' in *Human Growth: A Comprehensive Treatise*, 2nd ed., Vol. 1, ed. F. Falkner and James M. Tanner (New York: Plenum, 1986), 167 and 176. Final height is independent of the timing of growth spurts. Tanner, *Study of Human Growth*, 280.

57 James M. Tanner, 'The Potential of Auxological Data for Monitoring Economic and Social Well-Being,' *Social Science History* 6 (1982): 575; Tanner, *Foetus into Man*, 122 and 129-131. Auxologists define growth as having stopped when its rate falls below 1 cm per year and when 98 per cent of final adult height has been achieved. Tanner, *Study of Human Growth*, 118.

58 With a standard deviation of two years. Tanner, *Foetus into Man*, 19.

59 A. Theodore Steegmann, Jr., 'Eighteenth-Century British Military Stature: Growth Cessation, Selective Recruiting, Secular Trends, Nutrition at Birth, Cold and Occupation' *Human Biology* 57 (1985): 80.

60 Tanner, *Study of Human Growth*, 298.

61 John Bongaarts, 'Does Malnutrition Affect Fecundity? A Summary of the Evidence,' *Science* 208 (1980): 565-566; Eveleth and Tanner, *Worldwide Variation*, 217 and 245.

62 It is 12.5 years for African-American women, and 12.8 for American women of Northwest European descent. Eveleth, 'Population Differences in Growth,' 229-231. Women of comparable economic and nutritional status in Southeastern Europe experience menarche slightly sooner than Northwest European women.

63 Eveleth and Tanner, *Worldwide Variation*, 217-219; J.E. Brudevoll, K. Liestol, and L. Walloe, 'Menarcheal Age in Oslo during the Last 140 Years,' *Annals of Human Biology* 6 (1979): 412; James M. Tanner, 'Trend towards Earlier Menarche in London, Oslo, Copenhagen, the Netherlands, and Hungary,' *Nature* 243 (1973): 95-96; Bongaarts, 'Does Malnutrition Affect Fecundity,' 565. Komlos' work on early twentieth-century Viennese

women indicates a similar range. John Komlos, 'The Age of Menarche in Vienna,' *Historical Methods* 22 (1989): 158-163.

64 Bongaarts, 'Does Malnutrition Affect Fecundity?' 565; Brudevoll, Liestol, Walloe, 'Menarcheal Age in Oslo,' 407-416.

65 Bongaarts, 'Does Malnutrition Affect Fecundity?' 565-566; D.F. Roberts, L.M. Rozner, and A.V. Swan, 'Age at Menarche, Physique and Environment in Industrial North East England.' *Acta Paediatrica Scandinavica* 60 (1971): 159-60.

66 For example, women in rural Bangladesh achieve menarche at age 16 and in various tribes in New Guinea at just over age 18. Jane Menken, James Trussell, and Susan Watkins, 'The Nutrition Fertility Link: An Evaluation of the Evidence,' *Journal of Interdisciplinary History* 11 (1981): 431.

67 It may take up to two generations for the stature effect of a severe case of lifelong maternal malnutrition to be overcome in the adult height of a woman's offspring and their children. However, brief periods of even intense malnutrition seem to leave little 'mark' on the children exposed *in utero* to such conditions. Tanner, *Foetus into Man*, 43; Zena Stein, Mervyn Susser, Gerhart Saenger, and Francis Marolla, *Famine and Human Development: The Dutch Hunger Winter of 1944-45* (New York: Oxford University Press, 1975). Public health officials currently use the percentage of low birth weight babies (<2500 g) as a national measure of social and economic development. Ward, *Birth Weight and Economic Growth*, 12. The optimal range of birth weights in the developed world today is between 3500 and 3900 grams. Ward's recent work indicates that birth weights in lying-in hospitals in three large European cities averaged well below 3300 grams for the last half of the nineteenth and early twentieth-century as compared to weights near 3500 grams in Boston and Montreal during the same period. Ward attributes this, in great part, to the better nutritional environment in North America. There was, however, considerable variation over the course of the seventy-five years covered by his study. Ward, *Birth Weight and Economic Growth*, 114-116.

68 Even in Scandinavia, where the socio-economic differences are small, a gradient of birth weight by socio-economic class is still quite obvious. Ward, *Birth Weight and Economic Growth*, 16.

69 Ward and Ward, 'Birth Weights in Industrializing Montreal,' 325-327. The mother's body shields the fetus and absorbs much of the impact of short-term nutritional deficits. Birth weights may be affected depending upon the timing and intensity of the deprivation. Stein, Susser, Saenger, and Marolla, *Famine and Human Development,* 120. Body length at birth is not as useful an indicator because of the negative correlation between birth length and height gain in the first year. Restricted *in utero* growth, due to uterus size, is overcome in the first year of life and does not affect adult stature. Tanner, *Study of Human Growth*, 321.

70 Brinkman, Drukker, and Slot show that DeWijn was the first to use the term in a 1954 article. Henk Jan Brinkman, J.W. Drukker, and Brigitte Slot, 'Height and Income: A New Method for the Estimation of Historical National Income Series,' *Explorations in Economic History* 25 (1988): 227-264.

71 Tanner, *Study of Human Growth*, 116. This getting larger has been concentrated in increased leg length rather than purely proportional increases throughout the body. J.C. van Wieringen, 'Secular Growth Changes,' in *Human Growth: A Comprehensive Treatise*, 2nd ed., Vol. 3, ed. F. Falkner and J.M. Tanner (New York: Plenum, 1978), 308.

72 Bielicki, 'Physical Growth as a Measure,' 297-98.

73 Landauer, 'Infantile Vaccinations,' 499-503.

74 Much of the research conducted has been based on birthplace rather than the inbreeding coefficient. Mueller, 'Size and Shape,' 159-160.

75 Eveleth and Tanner, *Worldwide Variation*, 237 and 239; Mueller, 'Size and Shape,' 159-160. Studies of the issue often do not exercise sufficient control over socio-economic variables. Van Wieringen, 'Secular Growth,' 323-324. Some research has indicated that more heterogeneous individuals (the result of greater cross-breeding) may have growth patterns and potential which are more susceptible to environmental forces. Napoleon Wolanski, 'Heterosis and Homosis in Man,' in *Physical Anthropology of European Populations*, ed. Ilse Schwidetzky, B. Chiarelli, and Olga Necrasov (The Hague: Mouton Publishers, 1980), 222-224.

76 Tanner, *Foetus into Man*, 163.

77 It should be noted that stature variation across social classes has been eliminated in some countries, notably in Scandinavia. Bielicki, 'Physical growth as a measure,' 291; Floud, Wachter, and Gregory, *Height, Health, and History*, 135; Martorell and Habicht, 'Growth in Early Childhood,' 284.

78 Steckel argues that the feeding practices of plantation owners produced a pattern of severely delayed growth among the slave population. Richard Steckel, 'A Peculiar Population: The Nutrition, Health, and Mortality of American Slaves from Childhood to Maturity,' *Journal of Economic History* 46 (1986): 734-36, 739-40. For an economic model explaining this strategy, see Ray Rees, John Komlos, Ulrich Woitek, and Ngo Van Long, 'Slave Prices, Food Allotments, and Heights,' unpublished manuscript, University of Munich, 2000.

79 John Komlos, 'Toward an Anthropometric History of African-Americans: The Case of the Free Blacks in Antebellum Maryland,' in *Strategic Factors in Nineteenth-Century American Economic History: A Volume to Honor Robert W. Fogel*, ed. by Claudia Goldin and Hugh Rockoff (Chicago: University of Chicago Press, 1992), 267-329; Paul Riggs, 'The Standard of Living in Scotland, 1800-1850,' in *Stature, Living Standards, and Economic Development: Essays in Anthropometric History*, ed. John Komlos (Chicago: University of Chicago Press, 1994), 60-75; John Murray, 'Stature Among Members of a Nineteenth-Century American Shaker Commune,' *Annals of Human Biology* 20 (1993): 121-129; Jialu Wu, 'The Anthropometric History of Pittsburgh and Allegheny County, Pennsylvania, 1890-1945,' *Annals of Human Biology* 19 (1992): 79-86; Stephen Nicholas and Deborah Oxley, 'The Living Standards of Women during the Industrial Revolution, 1795-1820,' *Economic History Review* 46 (1993): 723-749.

80 Tanner, *Study of Human Growth*, 337 and 365. This generally accepted view has recently come under question. Harris, 'Health, Height and History,' 302-303.

81 Komlos, 'Anthropometric History of African-Americans,' 328-329.

82 John Komlos, *Nutrition and Economic Development in the Eighteenth-Century Habsburg Monarchy* (Princeton: Princeton University Press, 1989), 31.

83 John Komlos, 'The Height and Weight of West Point Cadets: Dietary Change in Antebellum America,' *Journal of Economic History* 47 (1987): 921.

84 Steegmann found an inverse relation between mean winter temperature and stature among eighteenth-century British males. This may be due to the effect of cold on disease transmission and not caloric requirements for temperature maintenance. Steegmann, 'Eighteenth-Century British Military Stature,' 86.

85 Richard Steckel, 'The Health and Mortality of Women and Children.' *Journal of Economic History* 48 (1988): 339-40; Eric L. Davin, 'The Era of the Common Child: Egalitarian Death in Antebellum America,' *Mid-America* 75 (1993): 135-163.

86 The initial efforts at the provision of clean water for urban residents were private ones whose impact was limited to families with the means to pay for such a 'luxury' and thus were of limited success. See Stanley K. Schultz, *Constructing Urban Culture: American Cities and City Planning, 1800-1920* (Philadelphia: Temple University Press, 1989), 163 and Howard P. Chudacoff, *The Evolution of American Urban Society* (Englewood Cliffs, N.J.: Prentice-Hall, Inc., 1975), 36-37.

87 Noel Cameron, 'The Methods of Auxological Anthropometry,' in *Human Growth: A Comprehensive Treatise*, 2nd ed., Vol. 3, ed. F. Falkner and J.M. Tanner (New York: Plenum, 1986), 263-281; and Cameron, 'Measurement Issues,' 347-364.

88 Steegmann, 'Eighteenth-Century British Military Stature,' 79.

89 Whether measurement took place with or without shoes is always an issue. Fogel's investigations indicate that 'The proportion of men in the Union Army that may have been measured with shoes was too small' to affect the results of his investigations. Fogel, 'Secular Changes in American and British Stature,' 456-457, fn 13.

90 Fogel and Engerman, 'Secular Changes in American and British Stature,' 456; Bernard D. Karpinos, 'Height and Weight of Selective Service Registrants Processed for Military Service During World War II,' *Human Biology* 40 (1958): 292-321. Analysis of the records of WW II soldiers shows that rounding which involved dropping fractional portions of inches resulted in a 0.2 inch height understatement. Robert W. Fogel, Stanley Engerman, et al. 'Changes in American and British Stature Since the Mid-Eighteenth-Century: A Preliminary Report on the Usefulness of Data on Height for the Analysis of Secular Trends in Nutrition, Labor Productivity, and Labor Welfare,' NBER Working Paper #890 (1982): 46.

91 Above age 50, physical shrinkage becomes noticeable, however soldiers of this age are not present in our sample.

92 Floud, Wachter, and Gregory, *Height, Health, and History*, 153. Baxter notes that Union officers who organized units for the Civil War often sought to fill them as quickly as possible. Once the units had begun to organize, but prior to their formal acceptance by the government, the organizing officer had a degree of financial responsibility for the pay/upkeep of the men he had enrolled. This may have encouraged some bending of the rules relative to age and stature. Only a man's oath was required as proof of age. J. H. Baxter, *Statistics, Medical and Anthropological of the Provost-Marshall-General's Bureau* (Washington: G.P.O., 1875), 14.

93 Fogel, 'Changes in American and British Stature,' 46.

94 Union Army height minima varied from 5'4.5" just prior to the Civil War, falling to 5'3" in August 1861, and falling still lower, to 5'0", in 1864. Baxter, *Statistics, Medical and Anthropological*, xlix; U.S. War Department, 'General Order #59,' August 17, 1861, in *General Orders of the War Department Embracing the Years 1861, 1862, and 1863. Adapted Specially for the Use of the Army and Navy of the United States* by Thomas O'Brien and Oliver Diefendorf (New York: Derby and Miller, 1864), 102.

95 Prison data are less likely to contain such aberrations, because there is little benefit to either convict or jailor in misreporting stature.

96 Two studies have found that the use of maximum likelihood estimates does not improve upon ordinary least square regressions. John Komlos, 'On the Biological Standard of Living of African-Americans: the Case of the Civil War Soldiers,' in Komlos and Baten (ed.), *The Biological Standard of Living in Comparative Perspective* (1998): 236-249. Brian A'Hearn, 'The Antebellum Puzzle Revisited: A New Look at the Stature of Union Army Recruits during the Civil War,' in *The*

Biological Standard of Living in Comparative Perspective, Vol. I, The Americans, Asia, and Australia, ed. John Komlos and Joerg Baten (Stuttgart: Steiner Verlag, 1999).

97 Steegmann, 'Eighteenth-Century British Military Stature,' 81.

98 Such situations might arise if the criminal justice system is more likely to convict the poor or the new immigrant. Riggs, 'Standard of Living in Scotland,' 73.

99 Wu's results in 'Anthropometric History of Pittsburgh' show how, with the GI Bill, the influx of middle- and lower-class men into colleges resulted in a decline in average stature among college students after WW II.

100 Fogel, Engerman, et al., 'Secular Changes in American and British Stature,' 471-472.

101 The shortest quintile of non-adult males had a death rate twice as great as the tallest quintile. Females in the lowest height quintile, a one and one-half greater risk of dying as the tallest women. Gerald C. Friedman, 'The Heights of Slaves in Trinidad,' *Social Science History* 6 (1982): 482-515.

102 Fogel, Engerman, et al., 'Secular Changes in American and British Stature,' 471-472. Tanner notes that greater death rates for shorter individuals also has been noted in two recent studies of African children. Tanner, *Foetus into Man*, 163.

103 John Komlos, 'The Biological Standard of Living of Eighteenth-Century Americans: Taller, Richer, and Healthier,' unpublished manuscript, University of Munich. Kenneth L. Sokoloff and Georgia C. Villaflor, 'The Early Achievement of Modern Stature in America,' *Social Science History* 6 (1982): 454.

104 For instance Chapter Three in William Stanton, *The Leopard's Spots: Scientific Attitudes toward Race in America, 1815-1859* (Chicago: University of Chicago Press, 1960).

105 Bertillon's system was a method designed to uniquely identify individuals, primarily criminals, developed prior to, but later used in conjunction with, fingerprinting. Henry T.F. Rhodes, *Alphonse Bertillon: Father of Scientific Detection* (New York: Abelard-Schuman, Inc., 1956): 89-95 and 110-118.

106 A German colleague once related to me, after I had briefly explained my work to him, that he did not feel he could carry out such work in Germany due to the negative reaction to anything which smacked of earlier efforts in this regard.

107 Bielicki, 'Physical Growth as a Measure,' 300-301.

108 Riley, 'Stature's Problems.'

109 Emmanuel Le Roy Ladurie, N. Bernageau, and Y. Pasquet, 'Le Conscrit et l'ordinateur. Perspectives de recherches sur les Archives Militaries du XIXieme siecle Francais,' *Studi Storici* 10 (1969): 260-308; Emmanuel Le Roy Ladurie, 'The Conscripts of 1868: A Study of the Correlation between Geographical Mobility, Delinquency and Physical Stature and other Aspects of the Situation of the Young Frenchmen called to do Military Service that Year,' Chapter in *The Territory of the Historian*, translated by Ben and Sian Reynolds (Chicago: University of Chicago Press, 1979). Recently, Steckel has argued that this work did not take hold because early publications neither built a strong theoretical context for the research nor connected it to on-going historical debates. Richard Steckel, 'Strategic Ideas in the Rise of the New Anthropometric History and Their Implications for Interdisciplinary Research,' *Journal of Economic History*, 1998. Another reason is that the early work in anthropometric history was written in French, and therefore was not easily accessible to American scholars.

110 Steckel, 'Slave Height Profiles,' 363-380; Barry W. Higman, 'Growth in Afro-Caribbean Slave Populations,' *American Journal of Physical Anthropology* 50 (1979): 373-385. While Engerman's compilation of slave heights from the coastwise manifests was

published in 1976, it interestingly contained no substantive analysis of the data. Stanley Engerman, 'The Height of U.S. Slaves,' *Local Population Studies* 16 (1976): 45-50.

111 The project was first described in Robert W. Fogel, Stanley L. Engerman, James Trussell, Roderick Floud, Clayne L. Pope, and Larry T. Wimmer, 'The Economics of Mortality in North America, 1650-1910: A Description of a Research Project,' *Historical Methods* 11 (1978): 75-108. The evolution and progress of the project has been documented in a series of interim reports generated throughout the 1980s and early 1990s. Robert W. Fogel, 'New Sources and New Techniques for the Study of Secular Trends in Nutritional Status, Health, Mortality, and the Process of Aging,' *Historical Methods* 26 (1993): 5-43.

112 Fogel, et. al., 'Economics of Mortality,' 83-84; Harris, 'Health, Height and History,' 299.

113 It continued with Costa's recent work, 'Height, Wealth, and Disease.'

114 Komlos, 'Stature and Nutrition in the Habsburg Monarchy.'

115 Richard Steckel, 'Birth Weights and Infant Mortality among American Slaves,' *Explorations in Economic History* 23 (1986): 173-198; Richard Steckel, 'Growth Depression and Recovery: The Remarkable Case of American Slaves,' *Annals of Human Biology* 14 (1987): 111-132; Robert W. Fogel, *Without Consent or Contract: The Rise and Fall of American Slavery* (New York: W.W. Norton Co., 1989); A. Theodore Steegmann, Jr. and P. A. Haseley, 'Stature Variation in the British American Colonies: French and Indian War Records, 1755-1763,' *American Journal of Physical Anthropology* 75 (1988): 413-421.

116 John Komlos, 'Patterns of Children's Growth in East-Central Europe in the Eighteenth-Century,' *Annals of Human Biology* 13 (1986): 33-48; John Komlos, 'Stature and Nutrition in the Habsburg Monarchy: The Standard of Living and Economic Development in the Eighteenth-Century,' *American Historical Review* 90 (1985): 1149-1161; Lars G. Sandberg and Richard H. Steckel, 'Overpopulation and Malnutrition Rediscovered: Hard Times in 19th-Century Sweden,' *Explorations in Economic History* 25 (1988): 1-19; Lars Sandberg and Richard Steckel, 'Heights and Economic History: The Swedish Case,' *Annals of Human Biology* 14 (1987): 101-110; Brinkman, Drukker, and Slot, 'Height and Income;' Komlos, *Nutrition and Economic Development*; Komlos, 'Height and Social Status;' Komlos, 'Anthropometric History of African-Americans;' John Komlos, J. Tanner, P.S.W. Davies and T. Cole, 'Growth of Boys in the Stuttgart Carlschule, 1771-1793,' *Annals of Human Biology* 19: 139-152; Eltis, 'Welfare Trends Among the Yoruba;' Stephen Nicholas and Richard Steckel, 'Heights and Living Standards of English Workers During the Early Years of Industrialization, 1770-1815,' *Journal of Economic History* 51 (1991): 937-957; Murray, 'American Shaker Commune;' Wu, 'Anthropometric History of Pittsburgh;' Riggs, 'Standard of Living in Scotland;' John Komlos, 'The Stature of Runaway Slaves in Colonial America,' in Komlos (ed.) *Stature, Living Standards, and Economic Development: Essays in Anthropometric History* (Chicago: University of Chicago Press, 1994), pp. 93-116; John Komlos, 'A Malthusian Episode Revisited: The Height of British and Irish Servants in Colonial America,' *Economic History Review* 46 (Nov. 1993): 768-82.

117 Steckel, 'Stature and Living Standards,' 285.

118 Floud, Wachter, and Gregory, *Height, Health, and History*, 134.

119 Kenneth Sokoloff 'Heights of Americans in Three Centuries,' in *Further Essays in Anthropometric History*, ed. John Komlos (Boulder, CO: Westview Press, 1995) 133-150.

120 Komlos, 'The Biological Standard of Living of Eighteenth-Century Americans.'

121 John Komlos and Peter Coclanis, 'Nutrition and Economic Development in Post-Reconstruction South Carolina: an Anthropometric Approach,' *Social Science History* 19 (1995): 91-116.

122 Potential explanations for this fall in mean stature include disease transmission through improved transport, unsanitary conditions in growing urban centers, population growth and food exports which outran agricultural production increases, and greater income inequality.

123 Richard Steckel and Donald R. Haurin, 'Health and Nutrition in the American Midwest: Evidence from the Height of Ohio National Guardsmen, 1850-1910,' in John Komlos, *Stature, Living Standards, and Economic Development: Essays in Anthropometric History* (Chicago: University of Chicago Press, 1994), 117-128; Robert Margo and Richard Steckel, 'Heights of Native-Born Whites During the Antebellum Period,' *Journal of Economic History* 43 (1983): 167-174.

124 Komlos, 'West Point Cadets'; Murray, 'American Shaker Commune.'

125 Komlos, 'Toward an Anthropometric History of African-Americans.'

126 Komlos and Coclanis, 'On the "Puzzling" Antebellum Cycle;' Ray Rees, John Komlos, Ulrich Woitek, and Ngo Van Long, 'Slave Prices, Food Allotments, and Heights,' Unpublished Manuscript, University of Munich 1998.

127. Steckel, 'Slave Height Profiles,' 376-377; Komlos, 'Anthropometric History of African-Americans,' 304-316.

128 van Wieringen, 'Secular Growth Changes.'

129 Steckel, 'Height and Per Capita Income,' 1, 3-4.

130 Steckel and Haurin, 'Ohio National Guardsmen,' 117.

131 Sokoloff and Villaflor, 'Early Achievement,' 456-459.

132 Steckel, 'Height and Per Capita Income,' 5.

133 Steckel, 'Stature and Living Standards,' 277-284.

134 Final adult heights, as Floud, Wachter, and Gregory note, probably did not differ as much as the boys'. In all likelihood, the Marine Society boys continued to grow well after the Sandhurst boys had stopped. As noted earlier in this chapter, lower nutritional status delays growth, not just reduces it. See Chapter Four in Floud, Wachter, and Gregory, *Height, Health, and History*.

135 Komlos, *Nutrition and Economic Development*, 95.

136 Komlos, 'West Point Cadets,' 902-903.

137 Floud, Wachter, and Gregory, *Height, Health, and History*, Chapter Five; Komlos, 'West Point Cadets.'

138 Floud, Wachter, and Gregory, *Height, Health, and History*, 200-225.

139 Floud, Wachter, and Gregory, *Height, Health, and History*, 201-204.

140 Nicholas and Steckel, 'Living Standards of English Workers,' 944-945.

141 Komlos, *Nutrition and Economic Development*, 114; Sandberg and Steckel, 'Overpopulation and Malnutrition,' 7-8; Riggs, 'Standard of Living in Scotland'; Ted Shay, 'The Level of Living in Japan, 1885-1938: New Evidence,' in *Further Essays in Anthropometric History*, ed. John Komlos (Boulder, CO: Westview Press, 1995), 173-201. Among twentieth-century populations, the urban-born tend to display a stature advantage over their rural counterparts. This would seem to be a function both of higher incomes in urban areas, enabling greater food purchases, but also better medical care and housing. The size differential varies considerably from situation to situation. For a more complete exposition see Bielicki, 'Physical growth as a measure,' 292-296.

142 Sokoloff and Villaflor, 'Early Achievement.'

143 Bielicki, 'Physical Growth as a Measure,' 293-295. Bielicki notes however that, in the late twentieth-century, the size of the rural/urban gradient tends to be inversely related to the overall wealth of the nation.

144 Higman, 'Afro-Caribbean Slave Populations;' Friedman, 'Slaves in Trinidad,' 486; Margo and Steckel, 'Height of American Slaves.' Some of this difference might also result from the greater proportion of slaves on the islands who were born in Africa than was the case on the mainland. Steckel, 'Slave Height Profiles,' 378.

145 Steckel, 'Growth Depression and Recovery,' 113; Steckel, 'A Peculiar Population,' 733.

146 Steckel, 'Growth Depression and Recovery,' 130.

147 Steckel, 'A Peculiar Population,' 724-725. Prichett and Freudenberger argue that Steckel's analysis overestimates the position of the average slave child vis-à-vis modern growth standards, while Komlos argues it may underestimate it and questions the homogeneity of the sample. Jonathan B. Prichett and Herman Freudenberger, 'A Peculiar Sample: The Selection of Slaves for the New Orleans Market,' *Journal of Economic History* 52 (1992): 125-126; Komlos, 'Anthropometric History of African-Americans,' 321-325.

148 Steckel, 'Growth Depression and Recovery,' 115.

149 James Trussell and Richard Steckel, 'The Age of Slaves at Menarche and Their First Birth,' *Journal of Interdisciplinary History* 8 (1978): 504. The practice can be defined in various ways, the most common is fertility maximization, especially in times of high slave prices. See Robert W. Fogel and Stanley Engerman, 'The Slave Breeding Thesis,' in *Without Consent or Contract: The Rise and Fall of American Slavery. Conditions of Slave Life and the Transition to Freedom: Technical Papers*, Vol. II, ed. Robert W. Fogel (New York: W.W. Norton and Co., 1991), 455-472.

150 Steckel, 'A Peculiar Population,' 734, 736-741.

151 Menarche on average occurs sixteen months after a woman has achieved peak height velocity during her adolescent growth spurt. William A. Marshall and James M. Tanner, 'Puberty,' in *Human Growth: A Comprehensive Treatise*, 2nd ed., Vol. 2, ed. F. Falkner and J.M. Tanner (New York: Plenum, 1986): 174.

152 This is not an argument that such behavior on the part of slave owners never occurred, nor an argument that it was not damaging to the individuals who were forced into such behaviors. However, the evidence available on the mean timing of events in the physical maturation and life cycle of female slaves indicates that it was not a routine practice. Trussell and Steckel, 'Age of Slaves at Menarche.'

153 Komlos, 'The Biological Standard of Living of Eighteenth-Century Americans.'

154 Steckel, 'Stature and Living Standards,' 292-298.

155 Thomas McKeown, *The Modern Rise of Population* (New York: Academic Press, 1976); Fogel, 'Nutrition and the Decline in Mortality,' 464-466; Clayne L. Pope, 'Adult Mortality in America before 1900: A View From Family Histories,' in *Strategic Factors in Nineteenth-Century American Economic History: A Volume to Honor Robert W. Fogel*, edited by C. Goldin and H. Rockoff (Chicago: University of Chicago Press, 1992), 267-296.

156 Such effects were concentrated in decline in infant and small child mortality. Fogel, 'Nutrition and the Decline in Mortality,' 507.

157 Such work has at its base the work of Swedish medical researcher Hans Th. Waaler who has examined the relationship between height and mortality rates as well as body mass indices and mortality rates. Hans Th. Waaler, 'Height, Weight, and Mortality: The Norwegian Experience,' *Acta Medica Scandinavica*, supplement 679, 1984. Early extensions of this work include Costa, 'Height, Weight, and Wartime Stress'; Costa,

'Height, Wealth and Disease'; Cuff, 'Body Mass Index Values'; Robert W. Fogel, 'The Relevance of Malthus for the Study of Mortality Today: Long-Run Influences on Health, Mortality, Labor Force Participation, and Population Growth,' NBER Working Paper Series on Historical Factors in Long Run Growth, Working Paper #54, Cambridge, MA, 1994; Dora L. Costa, 'Health, Income, and Retirement Behavior: Evidence from Nineteenth-Century America,' Cambridge, MA: NBER, 1993, Working Paper #4537; John Murray, 'Standards of the Present for People of the Past: Height, Weight, and Mortality among Men of Amherst College, 1834-1949,' *The Journal of Economic History* 57 (1997): 585-606.

158 A series of unique applications for stature data includes such wide ranging topics as Murray's argument for adverse selection in American utopian communities, Costa's research on the effect which income levels and health, proxied by height, have on retirement behavior, as well as attempts to directly estimate per capita income from height series. John Murray, 'Human Capital in Religious Communes: Literacy and Selection Among the Shakers,' *Explorations in Economic History* 32 (1995): 217-235; Brinkman, Drukker, and Slot, 'Height and Income.'

159 Cameron, 'Measurement Issues,' 354-355.

160 John Komlos, 'Anthropometric History: What Is It?' *Journal of Social and Biological Structures* 14 (1991): 353-356; Richard H. Steckel, 'Heights and Health in the United States, 1710-1950,' in *Stature, Living Standards, and Economic Development: Essays in Anthropometric History*, ed. John Komlos (Chicago: University of Chicago Press, 1994).

161 Fogel, 'Nutrition and the Decline in Mortality,' 464; Steckel, 'Stature and Living Standards,' 291.

162 Murray's works on members of the Shaker and Oneidan utopian communities have provided some of the few historical analyses of antebellum white women in the U.S., although his sample sizes are very small. Murray, 'American Shaker Commune'; John Murray, 'A New Anthropometric Look at the Status of Women and Children in Oneida Community, 1848-1881,' in *The Biological Standard of Living on Three Continents: Further Explorations in Anthropometric History*, ed. John Komlos (Boulder, CO: Westview Press, 1995), 105-122. For other studies including data on women's stature see Riggs, 'The Standard of Living in Scotland,' 72; Komlos, 'Anthropometric History of African-Americans,' 304-316; Steckel, 'Slave Height Profiles,' 372-377.

163 The Civil War samples, however, do include some adult men from the upper classes of the nation although not proportionate with their representation in the general population. Studies of upper class youth, who have not yet completed their growth process, such as Komlos' West Point Cadets and Stuttgart Carlschule students, as well as Floud, Wachter, and Gregory's Sandhurst Military Academy students, are somewhat more common.

164 Riley, 'Stature's Problems'; Fogel, 'Nutrition and the Decline in Mortality,' 506.

165 Fogel, 'Nutrition and the Decline in Mortality,' 498-503; Steckel, 'Stature and Living Standards,' 291-298.

166 Komlos argues for the latter in 'West Point Cadets,' 911-919, 922-927. Cuff has shown that, even with very favorable commercial-home slaughter weight ratios, pork availability, especially pork protein, did not keep pace with internal population growth in the middle decades of the nineteenth-century. Timothy Cuff, 'A Weighty Issue Revisited: New Evidence on Commercial Swine Weights and Pork Production Trends in Mid-Nineteenth-Century America,' *Agricultural History* 66: 55-74.

167 Costa, 'Height, Wealth, and Disease.' This is also clear from Figure 2.1.

168 The concept of the biological standard of living was first proposed in Komlos, 'Stature and Nutrition in the Habsburg Monarchy.' Steckel proposes a way of measuring it throughout the life course based on the concept of the 'quality adjusted life-year.' 'Stature and the Standard of Living,' *Journal of Economic Literature* 33 (1995): 1903-1940. In a sense, this would be a return to the more inclusive definition of living standards favored by Kuznets when the U.S. national income accounting system was being developed in the early 1930s. Steckel, 'Stature and Living Standards,' 268-270.

Chapter 3

Trade, Economic Restructuring, and Physical Stature Variation

> They had been at one accord not to hurry through life, not to be always skimping and saving. They saw their neighbours buy more land and feed more stock than they did, without discontent. Once when the creamery agent came to the Rosickys to persuade them to sell him their cream, he told them how much money the Fasslers, their nearest neighbours, had made on their cream last year.
>
> 'Yes,' said Mary, 'and look at them Fassler children! Pale, pinched little things, they look like skimmed milk. I'd rather put some colour into my children's faces than put money into the bank.'[1]

Introduction

There were only minor differences in mean height across social and occupational groups in colonial America.[2] However, with the onset of modern economic growth this pattern changed and by the late antebellum years substantial divergence in mean heights had appeared. These were apparent across the urban–rural divide, by state of birth, as well as by occupational groups. As a concomitant of modernization, the population experienced a deterioration in biological well-being, reflected in reduced adult physical stature across the United States, and among Pennsylvanians. Americans were still the tallest in the world but, obviously, something had changed in the intervening decades. Economic theory can explain these shifts in the biological welfare of nineteenth-century Pennsylvanians, and why modernization had a different impact on the various social classes. Industrialization and urbanization led to changes in the socio-economic environment, which ultimately affected the biological standard of living of the population.

Pennsylvanians, and most residents of the northern antebellum United States, were participants in one of the most far-ranging developments of the nineteenth century: they were experiencing the beginnings of 'modern economic growth.' This period, which saw both population and per capita material product increase substantially, resulted in great part from increased efficiency due to technological change. The process was characterized by an acceleration in the production of industrial goods, which meant that the share of GNP originating in the agricultural sector was declining.[3]

Transportation services, one of the critical factors in modernization, improved considerably. As will be described in Chapter Four, wide-ranging investments in the transportation network took place in Pennsylvania, as elsewhere, throughout the young nation.[4] The spread and improvement of roadways, the construction of short and long distance canals, increased and improved steamboat navigation on rivers made more navigable by early engineering works, as well as the early growth of railroads were all parts of an increasingly dense transportation system which began to cover a greater proportion of the northern half of the country.[5]

Eastern Pennsylvania was already quite well integrated by the turn of the nineteenth century, but parts of the state further west consisted, in large part, of hard to reach, newly settled subsistence farms. With the expansion of transportation infrastructure, opportunities increased for farmers in the west to market their foodstuffs in regional urban centers, while at the same time gaining access to manufactured goods not readily available earlier. Farmers west of the Alleghenies could send goods to markets regularly, rather than just once a year by flatboat or pack trail, and thus could move out of subsistence or near-subsistence agriculture, an opportunity long 'enjoyed' by eastern Pennsylvanians.[6] Greater product specialization and associated gains in productivity were thus becoming possible.

Yet, not everyone was sanguine about these developments.[7] Some questioned whether participation in the growing agricultural markets would have positive consequences for farmers and their families. Historians today are similarly interested in determining the effects which market integration and related antebellum socio-economic developments had on the population's standard of living, including the ways in which the associated costs and benefits of the transition were distributed across the population.[8]

Mainstream economic theory of long standing emphasizes that economic integration and market development invariably have a net positive impact on material well-being. More recent considerations present a more nuanced view of the differential effects of trade and specialization on the participating economic actors.[9] The following section describes the theory's central tenets and possible ramifications of market integration on the biological standard of living.[10] In addition, the effects of trade expansion upon social and family structure are considered. The role of the individual in the process of trade expansion, and the extent to which participants can control the impact of such changes on their family's welfare is also examined.

The Theory of Interregional Trade

Economic integration, a process which characterized much of early nineteenth-century Pennsylvania, is the means by which geographic and political subdivisions become a unified market for goods, services and factors of production. It implies easy mobility throughout the integrated area, non-discrimination in sale or purchase based on place of origin, and a division of labor, i.e. at least partial specialization in the region's most efficiently produced goods and services.[11] Economic integration can be measured both in terms of geographic range and in terms of its depth. The latter refers to the extent of integration throughout product and factor markets and across all economic sectors.[12] The 'criteria' for the existence of economic integration are the near equality of prices (net of transportation costs) for goods and services of equivalent quality, and their free movement throughout the integrated area.[13] 'Trade is usually regarded as the quintessence of economic integration,'[14] and theory explains why regional, national, and international economic integration occurs, and how its material benefits and costs are distributed. International trade is basically just interregional trade with a national boundary between the regions.[15]

The concepts of comparative advantage and trade barriers are applicable to the nineteenth-century Pennsylvanian economy. According to classical theory, trade occurs between regions if one of them has a comparative advantage in producing some goods, i.e., whenever the relative price of goods differs in the two regions by an amount that exceeds the cost of any trade barriers (e.g. transport costs, tariffs, information costs).[16] Thus, each region specializes, at least partially, in the production of those goods in which it is most efficient, and imports goods which it produces less efficiently.

The classical or Ricardan theory of international trade and comparative advantage assumes a labor theory of cost, constant returns to scale, and fixed factor proportions. Prior to beginning to trade, the two regions produce under conditions of autarky. When comparative advantage exists, trade benefits both sides by enabling each to consume beyond the limits of its own production possibilities. Rather than utilizing its factors of production in the creation of all goods, including those it produces inefficiently, trade enables a region to specialize in the goods it produces most efficiently. A share of the efficiently produced goods in excess of internal consumption needs is traded for those goods the region produces relatively inefficiently. In other words, the factor costs of reaching the greater consumption level with trade is less than those that obtained in autarky.

The classical theory assumes that productivity differences exist between geographic units, explains why trade occurs, and assesses the gains obtained through exchange. The Heckscher-Ohlin extension[17] is concerned with explaining why these productivity differences exist in the first place, and how such differences influence who benefits and who loses in this interaction.[18] Its primary focus is on factor endowments, and how they affect product cost and thus exchange.[19]

As the level of trade increases, the relative price for the exported good rises with its scarcity. Meanwhile, the relative price for the imported good falls, as it is now available at a cost below that associated with internal production.[20] Wages per unit time are equal to the value of the marginal product of labor (VMP), or labor's marginal productivity times the price of the good being produced. The higher average VMP of labor resulting from improved productivity across the trading region, due to partial specialization in both nations, means that real wages rise. Inasmuch as labor is homogeneous and provides all factor inputs in this model, it garners all the gains from trade. Further, since it is assumed that all labor is mobile within the nation, these gains are equally distributed across the society, assuming identical tastes between the two nations.[21] As trade expands, relative prices in both locations approach equality, although full equality may never be reached.[22] Trading partners share similar benefits, assuming that the level of trade relative to each country's output of the imported good is not inconsequential.

The Heckscher-Ohlin version postulates that trade is beneficial for both partners, as does its classical predecessor. However, the latter is more concerned with the causation of product cost and price differences.[23] Heckscher-Ohlin assumes that relative factor endowments are the major determinant of which good a nation produces most efficiently.[24] These endowments also have important consequences on the distribution of economic gains and losses which result from increased trade. In sum, though, gains outweigh losses.

Trade, under the latter framework, results from an internal comparative advantage generated by the relative abundance of either of the two factors of production. Goods produced with extensive utilization of the relatively abundant factor will be exported while those produced using the scarce factor intensively will be imported. Within each country, 'indirect' exports of the abundant factor will cause demand and prices for the abundant factor to rise, while 'indirect' imports lower demand for the scarce factor.[25] Returns will be reduced on the factor used intensively in the production of the imported good (on the scarce factor), but returns will be increased on the factor used intensively in the production of the export good (on the abundant factor).[26] The associated factor price equalization theorem holds that, as trade continues, returns to the factors of production will move toward equality across the national border.[27] In addition, in the long run total real incomes increase beyond levels prevailing in autarky, and product prices are equalized.

None of the above occurs, however, if sufficiently large tariffs or transport costs mitigate any comparative advantage. The existence of trade barriers has several consequences. The price of goods on which the tariff has been levied increases for consumers in the importing country, and the internal production of the good increases. Yet, since these goods are the ones which are less efficiently produced, total national output declines. The returns to those factors used intensively in the production of the tariff-bearing good rises.[28] In some cases a 'factor flow effect' may result. That is to say, the factors necessary to produce a given good may move into an area in which the flow of goods themselves is restricted.[29] In the exporting country, without an outlet for the good on which the tariff was placed, production falls (assuming a two-country world) and specialization declines in order to make up for the loss of imports from the tariff-imposing country. Returns to the owners of the various factors would tend to return to their pre-trade levels, differentially benefiting some and injuring others, but again total income falls.[30]

An international border is not necessary for trade barriers to exist. Transportation costs large enough to obliterate the price differences between goods produced in different regions, 'nature's way of providing protection for local industries,'[31] can be sufficient to make locally produced goods cheaper for the consumer. This may be true even though, relative to goods produced in economically inaccessible locations, such goods are inefficiently produced. In cases of extremely high transport costs, the flow of nearly all goods may be precluded.[32] Nations or regions can be trapped in local self-sufficiency, with resultant income levels lower than those possible with trade.[33]

What are the implications of these theoretical considerations for antebellum Pennsylvania and its inhabitants? In such a rural frontier environment, land must be considered as a third factor of production. Rather than using only capital and labor, it would be more useful to think of the factors as complex bundles of resources which either were, or were not, intensively utilized in food production. This would allow the two factor model to be maintained while dealing with the more complicated situation in which large amounts of both land and labor are required in the production of agricultural goods, and which more accurately reflects local factor intensities. Land is not a major input into the production of industrial goods. Thus, it is possible for two regions, one of which is well endowed with nutrient-producing resources but poorly endowed with factors needed for producing all other goods (an isolated rural region, for example), and a second with the opposite factor intensities (i.e., urban areas and their hinterlands), to increase their level of trade as barriers diminish due to transport-cost reductions. The Heckscher-Ohlin theory holds that, without barriers, the outcome will be a function of the relative resource endowment between the two regions. As trade begins, specialization between the regions should become evident. Individuals and sub-regions should begin to move out of self-sufficiency and begin to specialize in the production of that good for which they have comparative advantage based upon their factor endowments. For the rural region, this means a decline in the production of home manufactures and local crafts and greater emphasis on the production of agricultural products for the newly accessible market. Farm owners experience income gains, while the income of manufacturers (craftsmen) in these areas erodes. In contrast, for urban residents, the new trading opportunities imply an influx of cheaper agricultural products and the growth of a wider market for their manufactured wares. Owners of non-nutrient-producing factors in the urban areas see their incomes rise. Agricultural workers and farm owners in and around towns experience a decline in their incomes, as their products must compete with cheaper foodstuffs from the more distant rural regions. Over time they either move out of agriculture entirely and into industrial endeavors, or change their product mix to take advantage of their proximity to the urban markets.

Chapter Four describes just such a development in antebellum Pennsylvania. Total and per capita output began to rise in response to the opportunities provided by interregional specialization and the associated greater efficiencies in the utilization of various factors of production. However, as will be demonstrated in Chapter 5, the gains were not distributed equally between the residents of the two types of regions, as measured by nutritional status, and symptoms of short-run dislocations were evident. Farmers and residents of outlying districts, as well as urban business owners and professionals, were able to maintain their nutritional status, while unskilled workers and craftsmen in both rural and urban areas experienced a diminution in physical stature. Associated environmental changes probably exacerbated these trends in urban areas.

Trade and 'Modern Economic Growth'

Both short and long distance trade has existed ever since the dawn of civilization primarily but not exclusively in goods with a high value to weight ratio, undertaken most frequently on behalf of local elites.[34] Thus, the existence of trade preceded the onset of modern economic growth by millennia.[35] Though advantageous, as outlined above, trade by itself was not a panacea for all economic challenges. Often developing countries which rely on a limited number of agriculture or natural resource exports do so without widespread structural change that would lead to sustained growth in per capita product.[36] However, the development of large scale and dense transportation networks has the potential of providing large segments of the population with consumption goods which were previously unavailable to them. This is a recent development, and one with the potential for altering the nature of production within and across the trading region.

Trade occurs because it is possible for individuals to increase their total consumption through specialization. However, this is not the only effect at the aggregate level. According to Kuznets' theoretical considerations, subsequently confirmed by development economists Chenery and Syrquin, a series of other changes take place as economic integration and specialization proceed. Such changes become evident across economic sectors as well as within social structure. Each has the potential for creating conditions conducive to the alteration of physical well-being.

Shifts across economic sectors occur both in the types of goods produced and in the proportion of the work force involved in their production, as increased income modifies demand structure and productivity growth alters labor requirements.[37] Historically, as trade networks developed involving large proportions of the populace, the proportion of persons working in the primary sector[38] tends to decline, while, secondary- and tertiary-sector employment proportions grow. Productivity gains in agriculture, along with the effects of Engel's law, free up individuals to shift into activities other than food production. Trade may also mean specialization within, not just across, regional or sectoral boundaries as resource endowments and transportation constraints make production and shipment of some goods easier than others.[39]

Kuznets' 'inverted U' model of income distribution is also associated with the beginning of 'modern economic growth.' According to this hypothesis, levels of economic inequality increase during the early phases of modern economic growth, only to decrease subsequently.[40] Lindert and Williamson argue for just such a course of events in the nineteenth-century U.S.[41] Chenery and Syrquin also document this tendency in developing countries.[42]

The effects of expanded transportation networks and regional specialization are not limited to income-related phenomena, however. As manufacturing and service firms grow, they tend to cluster geographically, in order to take advantage of the positive externalities associated with agglomerations. Established cities expand and new urban centers arise.[43] While greater levels of urbanization can lead to a reduction in transaction costs and efficiency gains in production and distribution, other externalities, some of them negative, also accompany these processes. Rapid urban growth can lead to an overburdened infrastructure. Housing demand can outrun supply, leading to excessive crowding and an increased share of income used for shelter.[44] Water and sewer facilities, to the extent that they even exist, often prove inadequate to the needs of growing populations. Combined with the greater density of human interaction, these conditions mean greater exposure to disease. Urbanization can proceed only so long as agricultural production and imports provide basic nutritional needs.[45] While in resource-abundant America urbanization was not constrained by the availability of food supplies per se, the other factors mentioned above – increased inequality, rising housing prices, urban crowding, and lack of adequate sanitary systems (drinking water and sewers) – seemingly did have a negative impact on the human organism. In addition, perishable foods, such as milk, were more expensive in towns, and hence their consumption likely was not comparable to rural levels. These issues probably account for the fact that urban populations were markedly shorter than rural ones until the end of the nineteenth century.

The beginning of modern economic growth transforms many basic social structures. The economic roles of the two sexes change. The rise of factory labor and the decline of household manufacturing associated with urbanization can lead to a reduction in women's role in the generation of household income and the production of consumables such as garden fruits and vegetables, butter, and clothing.[46] The potential benefit of children's labor to the family was also transformed. All these social changes are captured only inadequately by indexes of real wages, which as a rule pertain only to male breadwinners, neglecting other changes in family labor and production which might be equally strong influences on well-being within the family.[47] Anthropometric measures, therefore, are appropriate complements to real wage indexes, particularly good in capturing welfare changes of children and youth, whose well-being can only be inferred indirectly from their father's wages.

Economic Development, Choice, and Change in Physical Stature

The development of trade and the start of 'modern economic growth' mean much more to the people who live through the transition than simply increased consumption potential. Many of the basic structures of social and economic life are radically altered. In addition, families encounter social reorganization and new environmental circumstances over which they have little or no control. Family wealth and income levels constrain the range of responses to such changes.

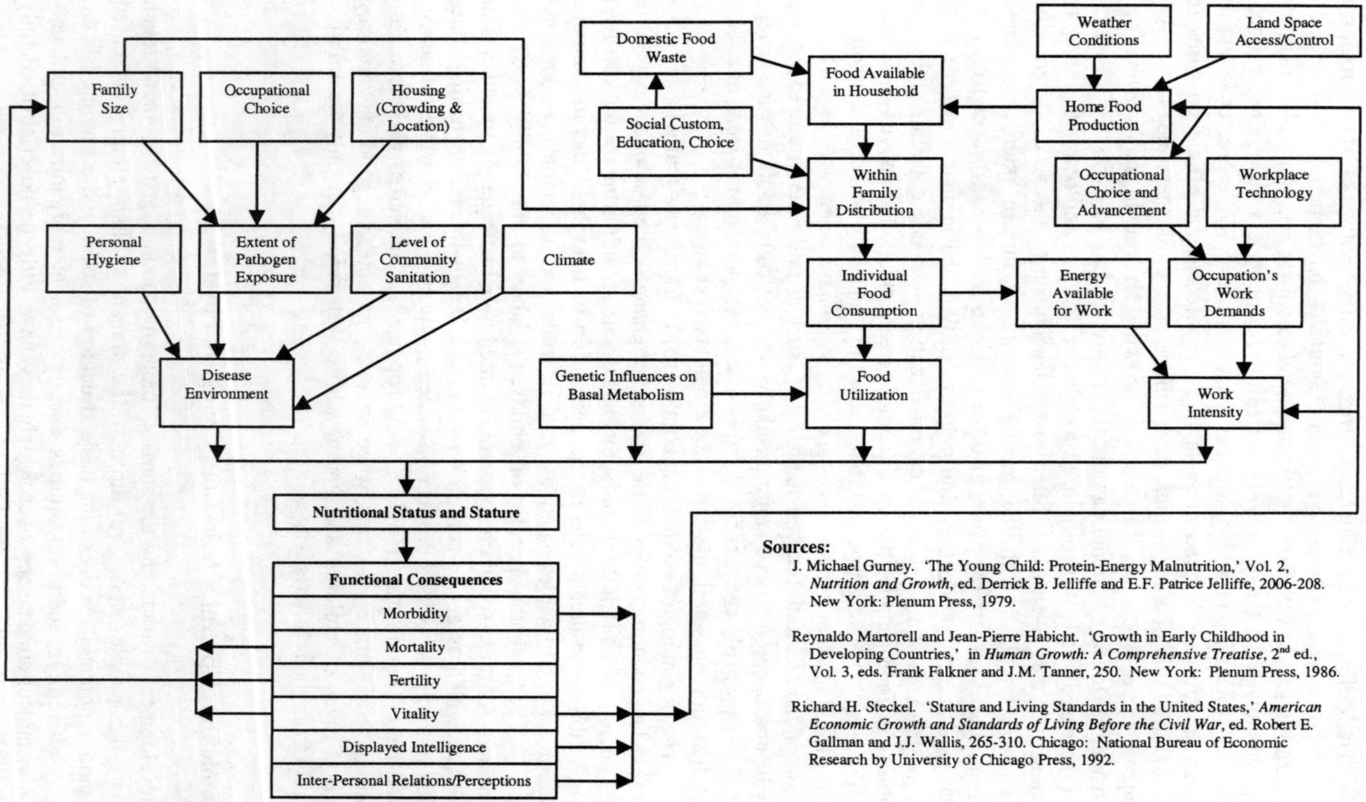

Sources:

J. Michael Gurney. 'The Young Child: Protein-Energy Malnutrition,' Vol. 2, *Nutrition and Growth*, ed. Derrick B. Jelliffe and E.F. Patrice Jelliffe, 2006-208. New York: Plenum Press, 1979.

Reynaldo Martorell and Jean-Pierre Habicht. 'Growth in Early Childhood in Developing Countries,' in *Human Growth: A Comprehensive Treatise*, 2nd ed., Vol. 3, eds. Frank Falkner and J.M. Tanner, 250. New York: Plenum Press, 1986.

Richard H. Steckel. 'Stature and Living Standards in the United States,' *American Economic Growth and Standards of Living Before the Civil War*, ed. Robert E. Gallman and J.J. Wallis, 265-310. Chicago: National Bureau of Economic Research by University of Chicago Press, 1992.

Figure 3.1 Influences on Human Stature in Societies *without* Integrated Markets

However, almost no level of wealth could fully isolate anyone from the multitudinous effects of nineteenth-century economic transformation. The growth of a small village into a town on a transport route was a situation over which the original residents had little say. Yet, they had to contend with the consequences of an intensified disease environment, more commercialized markets for foodstuffs, and changes in labor markets. Each resulted from increased specialization and growing numbers of persons moving into or through the area.

Individuals living in societies undergoing the initial stages of 'modern economic growth' also have a series of new choices confronting them. Farmers need to choose between continuing to practice self-sufficiency, or to increase market-directed production through product specialization. While microeconomic theory makes the move to market involvement an almost 'natural' reaction based upon increased income potential, the theory formally assumes that individuals seek to maximize utility, not just income or consumption. Mary Rosicky's comments at the beginning of this chapter highlight a critical point. Market participation occurs if individuals perceive that their utility, and not just their consumption/income, will be increased by such participation. Obviously, utility includes the consideration of aspects of the human condition other than simply material goods. The relative values of leisure *vs* consumption, health *vs* consumption (to the extent that these are even recognized), long-term economic security *vs* consumption,[48] and the welfare of the children *vs* the utility of the adults all influenced a typical nineteenth-century Pennsylvanian's decisions as they do that of his twenty-first-century counterpart.[49]

While the antebellum landholding yeoman farmer may have had the financial independence to remain aloof from the market, the urban wage laborer, or rural day laborer, did not have the resources necessary to do so. In the newly structured economic environment, he was constantly buffeted by changes in the level of demand for his services, as well as by shifting price levels for the food and manufactured goods which he purchased. While some Americans may have resisted these changes,[50] it is clear that eventually the vast majority, by their own choice or against their will, embraced or were embraced by the increasingly dense markets for goods and services that wove themselves throughout the nation.

Even with increased income resulting from labor specialization and market integration, the biological consequences could have been negative for those entering into the market for foodstuffs. Komlos argues that the antebellum rise in food prices relative to manufactured goods may well have induced consumers to maximize their utility by purchasing greater quantities of manufactured goods and a similar quantity of food. While food quantity in terms of food weight may have remained stable, the diet, he argues, became less healthy. Food buyers may well purchase more grain and less meat and dairy products in order to physically satisfy hunger, although this would not compensate for the reduction in protein consumption. Komlos and Coclanis suggest that with both real incomes and the relative price of food rising, consumer expenditures shift, in monetary terms, toward greater purchases of manufactured goods and smaller purchases of nutrient-rich food items.[51] A higher indifference curve is reached with higher incomes (i.e.

the level of utility achieved is greater), but protein consumption nonetheless declines, and the physical stature of children is reduced (assuming the disease environment and caloric expenditures for work are constant). The reduction in height during periods of market integration and the early stages of modern economic growth, in Komlos and Coclanis' view, are not necessarily a 'natural' result, but are easily explained by standard economic theory.[52]

Additionally, individuals who live through the transitional period, during which specialization and extensive trade develop, also have to contend with the problems associated with new trade networks and new market structures. Efficient market 'institutions' do not spring up fully formed and fully functioning. Rather, it took time for them to emerge and spread.[53] Individuals living through the transition did not necessarily obtain the full benefits which the new institutions were capable of eventually providing. Various frictions reduced the positive returns of market participation.

This project seeks to evaluate the biological impact of this massive socio-economic transformation. Figures 2.1 and 3.1 present graphically the differences in the social and economic environments before and after market integration. In the subsistence economy (Figure 3.1) the opportunity for increased income through specialized production and market exchange is nearly absent. In contrast, Figure 2.1 indicates both the new opportunities for trade but also the negative externalities associated with it. These include potential disease exposure increases due to urbanization, loss of nutrients in commercialized agricultural processing, and the increased transactions costs and price variability associated with increased market activity.

The onset of 'modern economic growth' across nineteenth-century Pennsylvania meant that disparate regions of the commonwealth were becoming economically integrated with Philadelphia, New Orleans, and New York City. New inland towns within the state were increasingly linked to growing regional centers. Output per capita was growing considerably and sectoral shifts in output and employment were beginning. New intermediary institutions were developing to handle long distance trade. Yet, all the outcomes can not be termed positive. These developments were not necessarily beneficial to the physical welfare of all Pennsylvanians. Before exploring the secular trend in the biological well-being of Pennsylvanians, it is necessary to examine more completely the social and economic changes that accompanied the onset of modern economic growth during the antebellum decades in the Keystone State.

Notes

1 Willa Cather, 'Neighbor Rosicky,' in *Obscure Destinies* (New York: Alfred A. Knopf, 1941), 24-25. I am indebted to Jerome Wells for pointing out this anecdote within Cather's short story.

2 Kenneth L. Sokoloff, 'The Heights of Americans in Three Centuries: Some Economic and Demographic Implications,' in *The Biological Standard of Living on Three*

Continents: Further Explorations in Anthropometric History, ed. John Komlos (Boulder, CO: Westview Press, 1995), 136-138.

3 Kuznets dates the beginning of the transition to 'modern industrialization' in the U.S. to the 'later 1830s.' Simon Kuznets, *Modern Economic Growth: Rate, Structure and Spread* (New Haven: Yale University Press, 1966), 473, 490-500.

4 Clearly, not all improvements critical to Pennsylvania actually occurred within the state's borders. Regional developments, such as the Erie Canal, also were key. Philip S. Klein and Ari Hoogenboom, *A History of Pennsylvania*, 2nd ed. (University Park, PA: Pennsylvania State University Press, 1980), 202-211.

5 George Rogers Taylor, *The Transportation Revolution, 1815-1860*, Vol. 4, *The Economic History of the United States* (New York: Rinehart and Company, Inc., 1962), 15-103.

6 Solon J. Buck and Elizabeth H. Buck, *The Planting of Civilization in Western Pennsylvania* (Pittsburgh: University of Pittsburgh Press, 1939), 288-298; Klein and Hoogenboom, *A History of Pennsylvania*, 199; Stevenson Whitcomb Fletcher, *Pennsylvania Agriculture and Country Life, 1640-1840* (Harrisburg: Pennsylvania Historical and Museum Commission, 1950), 285-288; James T. Lemon, *The Best Poor Man's Country: A Geographical Study of Early Southeastern Pennsylvania* (New York: W.W. Norton & Co., Inc., 1972), 216.

7 See the quote from an 1850s farmer which begins Chapter One.

8 In the American context, the recent historiography of markets primarily includes debates over the existence of, or lack of, a 'market mentality' among late colonial and early antebellum farmers in the North and the 'desire' of northern farmers to access and come under the rule of agricultural and industrial markets. There was an extended debate in the late 1970s and throughout the 1980s between Rothenberg, who argued, consistent with Bidwell, that the Northern farmer was constrained from market participation by the lack of adequate transport, and a series of historians who, with a view of economic change similar to Polanyi's, argued for the existence of an agricultural community in the late 1700s and early 1800s which was unwittingly destroyed by the emergence of extensive market relations. While the debate poses interesting questions as to the ability to extract 'intent' and 'interest' from historically observable activities, its focus is somewhat outside that of this work. There is no debate, however, about the fact that market-directed activity increased, growing in intensity and expanding in geographic reach in the antebellum period. See Percy W. Bidwell and John I. Falconer, *History of Agriculture in the Northern United States, 1620-1860* (Washington, D.C.: Carnegie Institution of Washington by The Lord Baltimore Press, 1925), 164-166, for descriptions of the hindrance posed by poor transportation infrastructure to the market participation of antebellum northern farmers. Rothenberg's arguments are contained in Winifred B. Rothenberg, *From Market-Places to a Market Economy: The Transformation of Rural Massachusetts, 1750-1850* (Chicago: University of Chicago Press, 1992). For the debate over the nature of orientation of antebellum agriculture see Christopher Clark, 'Household Economy, Market Exchange and the Rise of Capitalism in the Connecticut Valley, 1800-1860,' *Journal of Social History* 13 (1979): 169-189; Robert E. Mutch, 'Yeoman and Merchant in Pre-industrial America: Eighteenth-Century Massachusetts as a Case Study,' *Societas* 7 (1977): 279-302; James A. Henretta, 'Families and Farms: Mentalite in Pre-Industrial America,' *William and Mary Quarterly* 3rd series, 35 (1978): 3-32; Michael Merrill, 'Cash is Good to Eat: Self-Sufficiency and Exchange

in the Rural Economy of the United States,' *Radical History Review* 3 (1977): 42-71; Bettye Hobbs Pruitt, 'Self-Sufficiency and the Agricultural Economy of Eighteenth-Century Massachusetts,' *William and Mary Quarterly* 3rd. series, 41 (1984): 333-364; J. Ritchie Garrison, 'Farm Dynamics and Regional Exchange: The Connecticut Valley Beef Trade, 1670-1850,' *Agricultural History* 61 (1987): 1-17.

9 Classical theory dates to the early 1800s, while the 'modern' version of Heckscher and Ohlin was first formulated about a century later. A. Myrick Freeman, *International Trade: An Introduction to Method and Theory* (New York: Harper and Row, 1971), 23 and 60.

10 The efficacy of models is judged by, quoting Freeman, 'their usefulness, on their ability to provide order out of chaos, and on their power to explain and predict important phenomena.' The utility of the theory of international trade is not its complete agreement with reality, but its ability to generally describe certain developments and put them within an understandable context. Freeman, *International Trade*, 10.

11 The concept includes integration within and across regions, within and across national borders, and even within particular sectors of an economy. Fritz Machlup, *A History of Thought on Economic Integration* (New York: Columbia University Press, 1977), 15-17.

12 For example, in the first two decades of the nineteenth century in Pennsylvania, transportation cost barriers meant that geographically large markets existed for only a few goods (e.g. salt, iron wares), but not for many agricultural products. Deeply integrated markets involve the exchange of large numbers of products in all sectors.

13 Bertil Ohlin, *Interregional and International Trade* (Cambridge, MA: Harvard University Press, 1967), 24-27; Machlup, *Economic Integration*, 58.

14 Machlup, *Economic Integration*, p. 43.

15 Ohlin, *Interregional and International Trade*, 49. While the terms 'country' or 'nation' will be used in this description of trade theory, it should be remembered that the terms 'region' or 'area' could be substituted without any loss of explanatory power. This definition obviously ignores exchange rate issues and frictional problems of international factor markets.)

16 Limits on resource migration are also a factor.

17 Freeman, *International Trade*, 60.

18 William R. Allen, *International Trade Theory: Hume to Ohlin* (New York: Random House, 1965), 5; Richard E. Caves, Jeffrey A. Frankel, and Ronald W. Jones, *World Trade and Payments: An Introduction*, 5th ed. (Scott, Foresman and Co.: 1990), 126-138.

19 The Ricardan version assumes technology differences as the basis for trade. Caves, Frankel, and Jones, *World Trade*, 84. Other theories hold that demand differences can also help to determine the pattern of trade. Caves, Frankel, and Jones, *World Trade*, 118-120.

20 Ohlin, *Interregional and International Trade*, 24-25.

21 Freeman, *International Trade*, 35-37.

22 Ohlin, *Interregional and International Trade*, 26-27.

23 Allen, *International Trade*, 5.

24 Numerous assumptions underlie this theory and include 1) a 2 x 2 x 2 good/factor/country matrix, 2) constant returns to scale, 3) factor quality equivalence, 4) fixed factor quantities, 5) the two goods production functions must differ, 6) no

factor intensity reversals, 7) fully competitive factor and product markets, 8) goods, but not factors, flow freely across 'borders,' and 9) no complete product specialization. The role of demand is assumed to be negligible. Caves, Frankel, and Jones, *World Trade*, 135.

25 Caves, Frankel, and Jones, *World Trade*, 136.

26 Freeman, *International Trade*, 73-77.

27 O'Rourke and Williamson have recently documented the occurrence of factor price equalization in the American and English economies as a result of increased grain trade in the late nineteenth century. Kevin O'Rourke and Jeffrey Williamson, 'Late Nineteenth-Century Anglo-American Factor-Price Convergence: Were Heckscher and Ohlin Right?' *Journal of Economic History* 54 (December 1994): 892-916.

28 Ohlin, *Interregional and International Trade*, 196.

29 This is population migration if the factor is labor.

30 This entire scenario obviously is based on a two-good, two-country model. While the results in a more complex situation are more difficult to specify, the general principles would hold.

31 Caves, Frankel, and Jones, *World Trade*, 157.

32 It should be noted, however, that access to markets via reasonably priced transportation routes will not automatically produce market integration. Weiman's study of two Georgia counties in the antebellum period indicates that the presence of investment in commercial infrastructure (e.g. warehousing facilities) is also important in market development. David F. Weiman, 'Farmers and the Market in Antebellum America: A View from the Georgia Upcountry,' *Journal of Economic History* 47 (1987): 629.

33 Evaluations of the Heckscher-Ohlin trade theory have not validated it completely. Empirical work indicates that all the assumptions needed for the theory are not inherent in real world situations and that actual results of trade and product specialization diverge somewhat from the hypothesized ones. Leontief's paradox describes this anomaly. The Heckscher-Ohlin framework, however, has great explanatory power and is the dominant theoretical framework within which trade is viewed, even as others seek to refine it. Caves, Frankel, and Jones, *World Trade*, 138-143.

34 Karl Polanyi, *The Great Transformation: The Social and Economic Origins of Our Time* (Boston: Beacon Press, 1944), 42-45.

35 In the eighth century, the Grand Canal in China was used to transport great quantities of rice across the continent, allowing specialized labor and the increased size of urban centers. William H. McNeill, *A History of the Human Community* (Englewood Cliffs, N.J.: Prentice-Hall, 1993), 249-251.

36 Some economic historians have described the antebellum South in such terms. See Morton Rothstein, 'The Antebellum South as a Dual Economy: A Tentative Hypothesis,' *Agricultural History* 41 (1967): 373-382.

37 Hollis Chenery and Moises Syrquin, *Patterns of Development, 1950-1970* (New York: Oxford University Press, 1975, reprint 1977), 48-53.

38 Absolute numbers do not necessarily decline depending upon the rate of population growth.

39 The regional specialization of U.S. agriculture (Old Northwest: corn and hogs; New England: fruits and dairy) during the antebellum period is an excellent example. Stanley Lebergott, *The Americans: An Economic Record* (New York: W.W. Norton and Co., 1984), 202-208.

40 The inverted 'U' represents a graph with the level of development plotted on the x-axis and the level of inequality on the y-axis. Under this scenario, the level of inequality first rises and then falls during the early phases of modern economic growth. This plots the inverted 'U.'

41 Jeffrey Williamson and Peter Lindert, *American Inequality: A Macroeconomic History* (New York: Academic Press, 1980), 95, 102-103, 109.

42 It should be noted that this relationship is found in cross-sectional rather than longitudinal data. Chenery and Syrquin, *Patterns of Development*, 60-63.

43 In the nineteenth-century U.S., where levels of agricultural productivity per capita were relatively low, even small towns and cities would require fairly large agricultural hinterlands to supply the non-farming population with food.

44 Recent work on antebellum New York City finds rising rents throughout the period and a subsequent overestimation of real wage gains. Robert Margo, 'The Price of Housing in New York City, 1830-1860,' National Bureau of Economic Research Working Paper on Historical Factors in Long Run Economic Growth, #63, 1994.

45 An extensive literature on this topic exists in the field of development economics. Wells' concept of Johnston-Mellor adequacy (JMAD) stresses that increased food availability, resulting from productivity increases and food imports, must expand at a rate equal to population growth multiplied by food demand increases resulting from gains in income by urban residents. Without such expansion the continued development of secondary sector production can be choked off. Jerome Wells, 'On the Agricultural Performance of Developing Nations, 1950-1985,' *Food Research Institute* 21 (1989): 165-191.

46 While native-born women were among the first factory operatives in the United States, they were later replaced by immigrant laborers. Thomas Dublin, *Women at Work: The Transformation of Work and Community in Lowell, Massachusetts, 1826-1860*, 132-144. See Sara Horrell and Jane Humphries, 'Women's Labor Force Participation and the Transition to the Male Breadwinner Family, 1790-1865,' *Economic History Review* 48 (1995): 89-117, for a description of the British situation. Cohen's study of nineteenth-century Ontario during the development of agricultural markets and early industrialization is the study which most closely reflects the situation in Pennsylvania. She argues that, in less developed frontier regions, initial local market development enabled women's production, which had previously been confined to consumption within the family, to be marketed and increasingly, rather than decreasingly, used as a source of cash income rather than for self-sufficiency. Marjorie Griffin Cohen, *Women's Work: Markets, and Economic Development in Nineteenth-Century Ontario* (Toronto: University of Toronto Press, 1988), 157-158.

47 Horrell and Humphries, 'Women's Labor Force Participation,' 90.

48 Danhof emphasizes, and Wright reiterates, the great importance of capital accumulation (i.e. increased farm size and improvements) to nineteenth-century American farmers. Clarence Danhof, *Change in Agriculture: The Northern United States, 1820-1870* (Cambridge, MA: Harvard University Press, 1969), 16-25; Gavin Wright, *The Political Economy of the Cotton South: Households, Markets, and Wealth in the Nineteenth century* (New York: W.W. Norton and Co., 1978), 69-73. Bateman and Atack also point out that, in spite of higher returns in other occupations/investments, antebellum individuals chose to be farmers. Apparently the security and non-pecuniary rewards of the agricultural life were of greater utility to large numbers of individuals. Fred Bateman and Jeremy Atack, *To Their Own Soil:*

Agriculture in the Antebellum North (Ames, IA: University of Iowa Press, 1987), 262-266. John Murray has suggested to me that job-specific human capital investments in the techniques of farming would also have been an influencing factor.

49 Due to differences in anticipated lifespan, the risks inherent in nineteenth-century life and the average material living standard, time preferences might well be considerably different between the two groups.

50 For an argument which puts economic dislocation as the prime motive for upswings in utopian activity, see Brian J. Berry, *America's Utopian Experiments: Communal Havens from Long-Wave Crises* (Hanover, N.H.: University Press of New England, 1992), 15-26. Kesten's view is of more eclectic causation, Seymour R. Kesten, *Utopian Episodes: Daily Life in Experimental Colonies Dedicated to Changing the World* (Syracuse, N.Y.: Syracuse University Press, 1993), 27-40.

51 John Komlos and Peter Coclanis, 'On the Puzzling Cycle in the Biological Standard of Living: The Case of Antebellum Georgia,' *Explorations in Economic History* 34 (1997): 433-459.

52 Komlos and Coclanis, 'Puzzling Cycle;' John Komlos, 'Shrinking in a Growing Economy? The Mystery of Physical Stature during the Industrial Revolution,' *Journal of Economic History* 58 (1998): 779-802.

53 For example, middlemen must arise who will serve as conduits for farm produce, replacing the western farmer's once a year trip to Louisville or New Orleans. See Fred Mitchell Jones, 'Middlemen in the Domestic Trade of the United States, 1800-1860,' *Illinois Studies in the Social Sciences* 21 (1937): 1-81; Stuart Bruchey, 'The Business Economy of Marketing Change, 1790-1840: A Study of the Sources of Efficiency,' in Darwin P. Kelsey, *Farming in the New Nation: Interpreting America's Agriculture, 1790-1840* (Washington, D.C.: The Agricultural History Society, 1972), 211-226. See Douglass C. North, *Structure and Change in Economic History* (New York: W.W. Norton and Co., 1981) for examples of social and institutional change in economic history.

Chapter 4

Antebellum Pennsylvania: A Test Environment for the Biological Effects of Market Integration

> It was now possible to start from Philadelphia in a shower of soot and cinders; change from railroad to canal packet at Columbia on the Susquehanna; be pulled majestically by mules along the Pennsylvania Canal to Hollidaysburg; transfer there to the Portage Railroad for the abrupt rise over the Allegheny Front; change back to packet boat again at Johnstown; and arrive in Pittsburgh five days after starting ...[1]

Introduction

Early nineteenth-century Pennsylvania is a useful 'laboratory' for testing the hypothesis that market integration can, at least temporarily, lead to a decline in average physical well-being for the population experiencing it. Pennsylvania's value is based both on the diverse nature of its economy at the beginning of the nineteenth century and the spatial variability in the extent of market integration and level economic development in the antebellum years. The wide range of economic orientations resulted from differences in the length of settlement, the level of accessibility of the region, and natural resource endowments. While Pennsylvania had some of the oldest communities of the new nation in 1800, there were also areas that had only recently been settled by persons of European descent. Yet other locales were not to be settled for another twenty or thirty years.[2]

The physical properties of the land across the state varied and were influential. Terrain ranging from flat lakeside plains and fertile valley bottoms contrasted with the wild mountainous areas in the center and north central portions of the commonwealth. Land fertility and sub-soil natural resource endowments differed greatly from region to region.[3] The state was a near textbook example of an area economically segmented by transportation barriers. The Allegheny Mountains, which had served as the western boundary of colonial settlement, posed a serious hindrance to the transport of goods from the seaboard to the interior after the Revolution.[4] Pennsylvania is almost cut in half by this range of geologically 'old' mountains. They divided the state naturally into regions which, in the early nineteenth century, 'faced' in opposite directions in terms of their primary trade orientation.[5] Even common roads were lacking in much of the state, making travel extremely difficult. With such hindrances the economic value of much of the state's land was limited.

Philadelphia in 1800 was one of the country's dominant centers of commerce and manufacturing.[6] One of the largest cities in the nation,[7] Philadelphia served as a regional entrepôt for raw materials, as well as being an important consumer of the same. As the 1700s ended it was a commercial city, but early in the new century a transition began which resulted in manufacturing becoming its economic cornerstone.[8] Most of the state's population, over 70 per cent, resided in Philadelphia and its hinterland, the Southeastern Region.[9] Farmers there had already specialized production for the urban markets of both Philadelphia and Baltimore. However, outside of this region most farmers were engaged in subsistence farming with only occasional forays into market activity.[10] Much of the land outside of the Southeastern Region remained close to the frontier stage of development.[11] The indigenous inhabitants had not farmed the land in the European manner, and vast tracts remained heavily forested and required clearing before intensive agriculture could begin. With low population densities throughout much of the state, the 'new world' system of agriculture, with the extensive use of land and low yields per acre, but high yields per worker, characterized farming.[12]

Over the course of the following six decades, the state, as a whole, experienced a relatively rapid process of economic development and urbanization, as did much of the new nation. Between 1820 and 1860 the proportion of the work force involved in manufacturing rose from 29 to 36 per cent,[13] while agricultural employment fell from 68 to 37 per cent. The urban share of the population almost doubled from 22.5 per cent in 1810 to 40.5 per cent in 1860.[14] Like settlement itself, the integration of interior trade centers with seaboard markets and the linking of more remote inland sites with early internal cities did not occur uniformly across the landscape. Terrain, natural resource endowments, and access to viable transportation routes determined the rapidity with which localities became part of the intraregional, and later the interregional, trade system. These factors also influenced the speed with which they made the transition from nearly self-sufficient agricultural communities to those based on specialized production for the market.

As this summary makes clear, numerous types of economic activity developed across the state throughout the 60 years in question. By 1860, Philadelphia and Pittsburgh were large industrial centers. However, many pockets of semi-subsistence agriculture persisted.[15] The 'full range' of economic activity present in the United States existed within the state's borders throughout the period.[16] Great changes occurred in some areas and more modest ones elsewhere. The state's heterogeneity makes it a promising laboratory for analysis of the effect of the onset of modern economic growth on the biological standard of living.

Social and Economic Characteristics

There is no detailed economic history of the commonwealth for the early nineteenth century. Existing literature tends to be tightly focused either on particular regions, particular sectors, or even selected industries.[17] As a result, an economic context for the examination of patterns and trends in mean physical stature to be presented in Chapter Five must be built here. Drawn from census data, contemporary descriptions, and secondary sources it will not be a comprehensive economic history of the state. Rather, this chapter presents a region-by-region overview of the state's economy between 1800 and 1860 focused on the transition to market-based, specialized agriculture and the social and economic developments which accompanied it. Four types of indicators will be of particular concern. These include 1) the extent to which a region exhibited production patterns reflective of self-sufficiency or regional economic integration,[18] 2) the extent to which a region was connected to distant locales via transport routes, 3) the extent of urban growth, and 4) the level of land prices.[19]

When nearly all individuals in a region are engaged in agriculture, but few in the production, marketing, and distribution of its products or by-products, it is highly probable that the extent of market activity is rather limited. The censuses of 1820 and 1840 provide county-level employment figures for the state. Some sense of the extent of movement into commercialization can be obtained by tracing the percentage of workers in agriculture between these dates. This information can be augmented by other available indicators: the dollar values of market gardening and orchard production and the number of swine and milch [sic] cows in stock.[20] Data on cheese and butter production become available in 1850. Comparing these data at the regional level on a per capita basis provides a measure of the extent of market based agriculture. Extremely high or extremely low values can be used as a sign of the existence or absence of commercial orientation, respectively.

The other side of this situation, the extent to which the region depended on the importation of manufactured goods, can be represented by the extent of home manufacturing. These data, available for 1840, 1850, and 1860, provide evidence of the presence or lack of trade linkages with developing urban industrial centers. Since self-sufficiency implies that all goods consumed within the household were produced within it, or that exchange was at most a local phenomenon, a decline in this type of home production implies an increase in market involvement.

The development of a transportation system was clearly critical because the linkages enabled the less expensive produce of specialized agriculture to reach consumers in urban centers. Without that connection, surplus agricultural output would have had no outlet and the impact of higher productivity in agriculture would have remained limited. Farmers could justify neither the added expenses associated with high productivity methods, nor the increased risks if their crops had difficulties reaching receptive markets. The extension of the antebellum transportation network between 1800 and 1860 will be reviewed in order to gauge how effectively particular regions were connected to the outside world.[21] However, canal boats left more than just manufactured goods in their wake, and railroads more than just their smoke. They also had the potential to bring disease carriers into the towns on their routes. They indicate economic development, but they also signify a potential negative impact on net nutritional status.

Another indicator of effective and expanding agricultural markets is the growth of urban centers. Without connection to an agricultural hinterland, the size of urban agglomerations is limited. The presence and expansion of urban areas is *prima facie* evidence of such a linkage. Several measures of urban growth will be utilized.[22] The percentage of the population living in towns with more than 2500 residents will be documented, as will population density (persons per square mile, psm), and population growth rates.[23] Population density and city residence may also affect stature through a greater likelihood of contagion.

Writing about the nineteenth-century United States, Craig, Palmquist and Weiss note that 'land prices reflected the net discounted value of expected future income generated from the property. The pertinent income stream was net of transport costs, and so would have been affected by canal and railroad access.'[24] Thus, land values capture many aspects of the *perceived* worth of land including its locational value, fertility and valuable mineral content. In antebellum Pennsylvania, as in much of the U.S., land prices were in great part determined by the ability to move crops to market.[25] Though most of the land in early nineteenth-century Pennsylvania could support a family at a decent level of subsistence,[26] lands linked to distant markets commanded higher prices.[27] Hence, county mean land valuations for 1815 and 1845 collected by the commonwealth are used to describe development levels in this regard.[28]

Regional descriptions have been developed to make the presentation of economic information manageable, but no attempt has been made to calculate a single index of market integration or economic development at the regional level. Even within geographically small regions, there was considerable inter-county variation in the various indicators.[29] Additionally, since the regression analysis technique used in the following chapter can adjust for variation in these indicators throughout the more than sixty counties, neither larger aggregations of data at the regional level nor a single index of development are necessary.

The Regions

Needless to say, the idea of a 'region' is a slippery concept. Bigger than a city, but potentially crossing national boundaries, regions can be defined in many ways. For purposes of analysis the state was divided into seven regional units.[30] This level of geographic aggregation allows for the development of spatial analysis which is detailed enough to be of value while general enough to be manageable. These regions are: Southeastern, Pocono, Northeastern, Anthracite, Ridge and Valley, Allegheny Forest, and Western (see Figure 4.1 and Table 4.1). The cities of Philadelphia (Philadelphia County) in the Southeastern Region and Pittsburgh (Allegheny County) in the Western Region were rather atypical for the time, due to their large urban populations. Until the 1840 census, they were the only towns with more than 10,000 residents, and in 1860 they alone had inhabitants in excess of 25,000. Hence, Philadelphia and Allegheny Counties will, in some instances, be

Table 4.1 Counties by Region

Southeastern
Philadelphia*
Delaware*
Chester*
Montgomery*
Bucks*
Northampton
Lehigh*
Berks*
Lancaster*
York*
Adams*
Cumberland*
Franklin*

Anthracite
Montour
Dauphin
Lebanon
Northumberland*
Schuylkill*
Columbia
Luzerne
Carbon

Pocono
Monroe
Wayne*
Pike

Northeastern
Tioga*
Bradford*
Susquehanna*
Wyoming

Ridge and Valley
Snyder
Centre
Bedford
Huntingdon
Mifflin
Juniata
Perry*
Union
Blair
Fulton

Allegheny Forest
Forest
Warren
McKean
Potter*
Venango
Jefferson
Clearfield
Lycoming
Clinton
Clarion
Elk
Sullivan

Western
Erie*
Crawford*
Mercer
Beaver
Washington*
Greene*
Butler*
Fayette*
Armstrong
Westmoreland*
Indiana*
Cambria*
Somerset*
Lawrence
Allegheny*

Source: These county grouping are based on Dykstra's *Region, Economy, and Party*, 1988, 37-38.

Note: * denotes county without border changes between 1820 and 1860

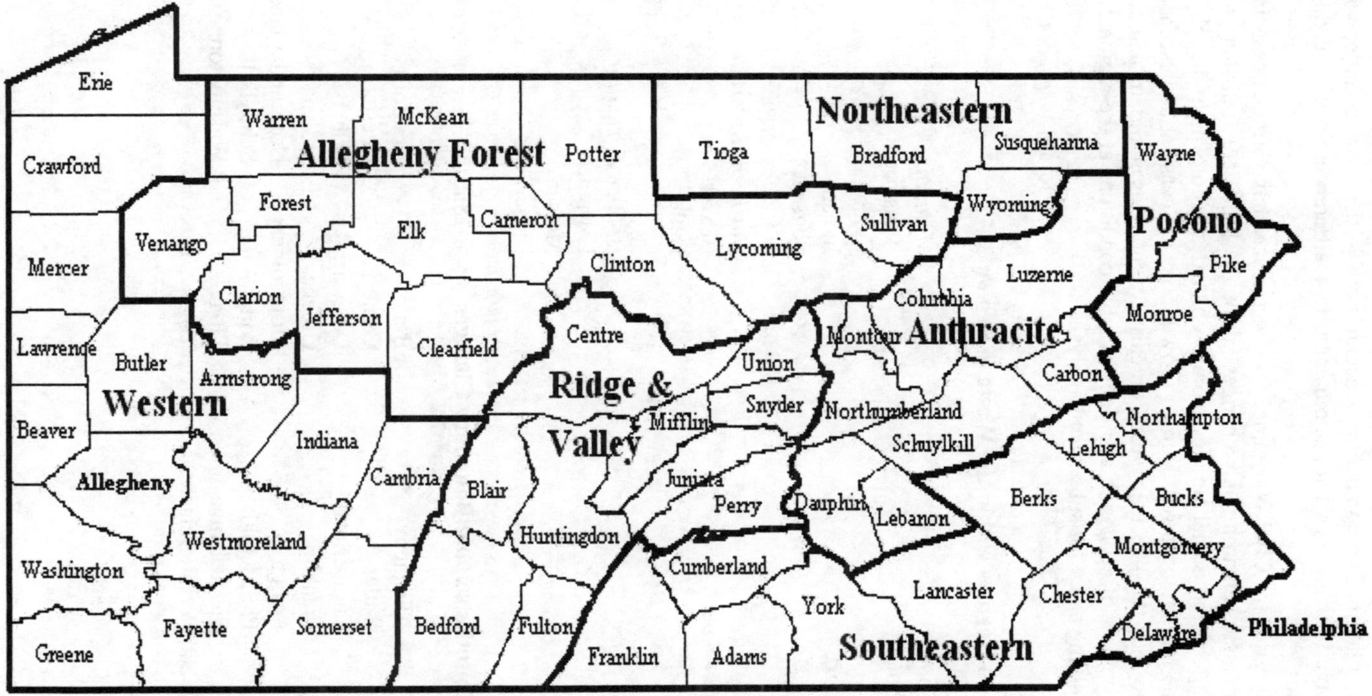

Figure 4.1 Regions of Pennsylvania

analyzed in isolation. The population concentrations in these two counties will be shown to have been the basis for some important differences in their economic characteristics.

As men in the Civil War samples to be analyzed have birth dates as late as 1849,[31] economic environment changes through 1860 are relevant to an understanding of the social and economic context within which the physical growth of the recruits occurred. Human growth does not cease at adolescence but can continue into the late teen years or early twenties as it did in antebellum America. A review of economic and demographic conditions at the regional level is a basic building block for subsequent analysis.

Table 4.2 Sub-Regions within the Western Region

Allegheny County	*Mountain/Mineral*
Allegheny County	Armstrong
	Cambria
Lake Transport	Indiana
Crawford	Somerset
Erie	
	Northern Hinterland
Southern Hinterland	Beaver
Fayette	Butler
Greene	
Washington	*Isolated Agricultural*
Westmoreland	Lawrence
	Mercer

Table 4.3 Counties *without* Boundary Changes, 1820-1860

Adams	Allegheny	Berks	Bradford
Bucks	Butler	Cambria	Chester
Crawford	Cumberland	Delaware	Erie
Fayette	Franklin	Greene	Indiana
Lancaster	Lehigh	Montgomery	Northumberland
Perry	Philadelphia	Potter	Schuylkill
Somerset	Susquehanna	Tioga	Washington
Wayne	Westmoreland	York	

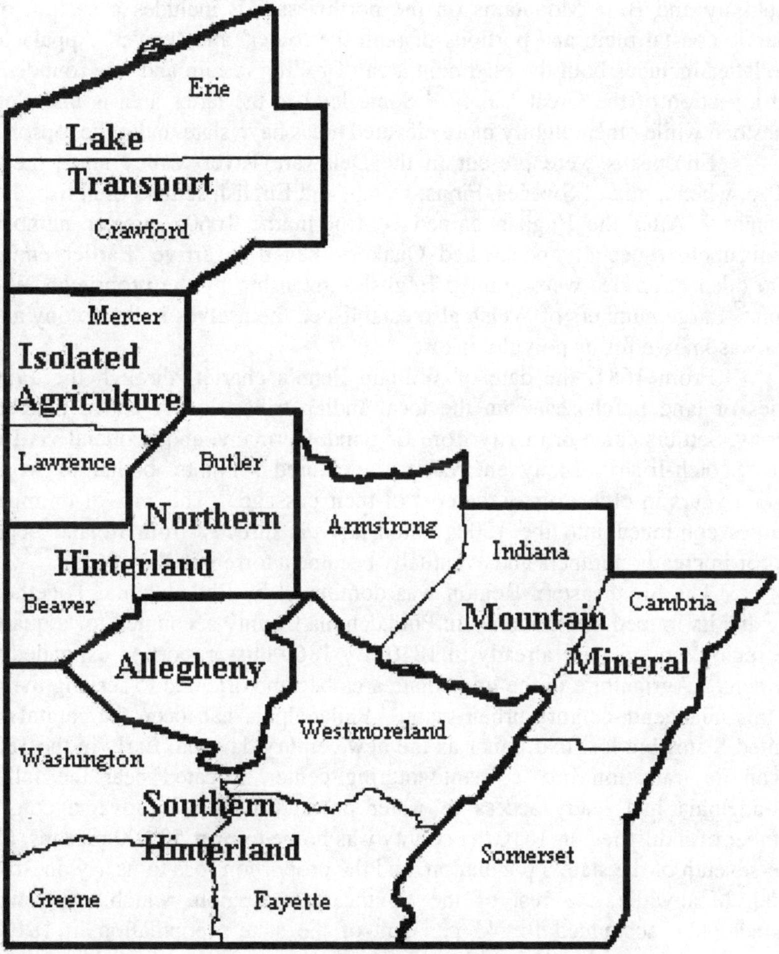

Figure 4.2 Western Sub-Regions

Southeastern Region

The Southeastern Region of the state consisted of 13 counties.[32] Its borders are defined by Maryland and Delaware in the south, New Jersey in the east and by the Kittatinny and Blue Mountains on the northwest.[33] It includes a section of the Atlantic coastal plain and portions of both the 'older' and 'newer' Appalachians. The latter includes both the piedmont area of rolling terrain and low rounded hills and a section of the Great Valley.[34] Some land in the latter area is underlain by limestone while other slightly more elevated areas have slate under the topsoil.[35]

Europeans were present in the Delaware River Valley since the early 1600s, when a mix of Swedes, Finns, Dutch, and English settlers established small colonies.[36] After the English gained control in the 1660s, greater numbers of Englishmen, especially persecuted Quakers, began to arrive. Earlier emigrants from other countries were granted English citizenship by the proprietor, William Penn.[37] Large numbers of Welsh also established themselves in the colony and the area was known for its polyglot nature.[38]

From 1681, the date of William Penn's charter, through the 1730s, a series of land purchases from the local Indian tribes slowly added land to the colony. Settlers came primarily from England, Germany, and Scotland via Ireland (the 'Scotch-Irish'). Many entered as indentured servants, bound to work for several years in order to pay the cost of their passage.[39] This mix of immigration sources continued into the 1800s when arrivals directly from Ireland began to appear in greater numbers and eventually became a torrent in the 1840s.

The Southeastern Region was dominated by Philadelphia. Together, the city and its immediate suburbs[40] in Philadelphia County accounted for a quarter of the region's population already in 1810. By 1860 this proportion expanded to 44 per cent.[41] Agriculture in the immediate area became oriented to serving the needs of this nineteenth-century urban giant.[42] Philadelphia had been the capital of the United States but lost that honor as the new century dawned. Early in the 1800s it began its transition into a manufacturing center. Located near the fall line, Philadelphia had ready access to water power which was advantageous to a number of industries. In 1810 the county was home to over 50,000 persons, almost one-seventh of the state's population, and the proportion rose to nearly one-fifth by 1860. Meanwhile, the rest of the Southeastern Region, which, even without Philadelphia, accounted for 43 per cent of the state's population in 1810, lost population share and contained less than a quarter of the state's residents in 1860. Growth in the remainder of the region did not keep pace with the urban hub, which saw its population density quintuple (to 4189.1 psm) over the fifty year span, while that for the rest of the region only doubled (to 98.2 psm).

The Southeastern Region had the highest urban share of any region of the state, increasing from 1810 (33.8 per cent) to 1860 (63.4 per cent) (Table 4.7). Urbanization was not confined to Philadelphia, however. Even without it, the region's urban population proportion was still the highest until 1840. Thereafter, it fell to second place, behind the Anthracite Region.

Table 4.4 Regional Population Proportions (%), 1810-1860

		Southeastern								Western		
Decade	State Average	Without Philadelphia	Philadelphia	Entire Region	Anthracite	Ridge & Valley	Pocono	Northeastern	Allegheny Forest	Without Allegheny	Allegheny	Entire Region
1810	100	43.0	13.7	56.7	10.7	6.6	0.5	0.2	2.0	20.2	3.1	23.3
1820	100	39.2	13.1	52.3	9.8	9.6	0.7	2.4	2.3	19.5	3.3	22.8
1830	100	35.1	14.0	49.1	9.8	9.4	0.9	3.4	3.1	20.5	3.7	24.2
1840	100	30.6	15.0	45.6	9.8	8.7	1.5	4.0	4.6	21.1	4.7	25.8
1850	100	26.5	17.7	44.2	10.8	7.6	1.8	4.6	6.0	19.2	6.0	25.2
1860	100	24.8	19.5	44.3	11.9	7.0	1.9	4.4	6.7	17.7	6.2	23.9

Sources: United States, *Returns of The Whole Number of Persons within the Several Districts of the United States According to 'An Act Providing for the Second Census...'*, Second Decennial Census, 1800 (Washington: Duane, 1801); United States Treasury Department, *Aggregate Amount of each description of persons within the United States of America and the Territories thereof, agreeably to actual enumeration made according to law in the Year 1810*, Third Decennial Census, 1810 (Washington, 1811); United States Census Office, *Census for 1820*, Fourth Decennial Census, 1820 (Washington: Gales and Seaton, 1821); United States Census Office, *Fifth Census; or, Enumeration of the Inhabitants of the United States, 1830* , Fifth Decennial Census, 1830 (Washington: Duff Green, 1832); United States, *Compendium of the Enumeration of the Inhabitants and Statistics of the United States as obtained at the Department of State from the returns of the Sixth Census*, Sixth Decennial Census, 1840 (Washington: Thomas Allen, 1841); United States, *The Seventh Census of the United States: 1850*, Seventh Decennial Census, 1850 (Washington: Robert Armstrong, 1853); United States, *Population of the United States in 1860; Compiled from the Original Returns of the Eighth Census*, Eighth Decennial Census, 1860 (Washington: G.P.O., 1864); United States, *Agriculture of the United States in 1860; Compiled from the Original Returns of the Eighth Census*, Eighth Decennial Census, 1860 (Washington: G.P.O., 1864); Inter-University Consortium for Political and Social Research, *Historical Demographic, Economic and Social Data: The United States, 1790-1970*, ICPSR Data Set 0003 (Ann Arbor: ICPSR, 1992).

Table 4.5 Population Growth Rate (%), 1810-1860

		Southeastern								Western		
Decade	State Average	Without Philadelphia	Philadelphia	Entire Region	Anthracite	Ridge & Valley	Pocono	Northeastern	Allegheny Forest	Without Allegheny	Allegheny	Entire Region
1810/20	29.6	18.1	23.3	19.4	19.4	88.9	70.2	1413.6	50.5	25.5	37.9	27.1
1820/30	28.5	15.0	37.7	20.6	28.2	26.3	78.1	78.2	70.6	35.0	44.8	36.4
1830/40	27.9	11.3	36.7	18.6	28.2	17.4	104.4	52.6	92.5	31.7	60.7	36.2
1840/50	34.1	16.1	58.4	30.0	46.8	17.0	60.6	52.8	73.0	22.0	70.2	30.8
1850/60	25.7	17.6	38.4	25.9	39.4	16.8	36.8	21.1	41.1	15.4	29.3	18.7

Sources: United States, *Returns of The Whole Number of Persons within the Several Districts of the United States According to 'An Act Providing for the Second Census...'*, Second Decennial Census, 1800 (Washington: Duane, 1801); United States Treasury Department, *Aggregate Amount of each description of persons within the United States of America and the Territories thereof, agreeably to actual enumeration made according to law in the Year 1810*, Third Decennial Census, 1810 (Washington, 1811); United States Census Office, *Census for 1820*, Fourth Decennial Census, 1820 (Washington: Gales and Seaton, 1821); United States Census Office, *Fifth Census; or, Enumeration of the Inhabitants of the United States, 1830*, Fifth Decennial Census, 1830 (Washington: Duff Green, 1832); United States, *Compendium of the Enumeration of the Inhabitants and Statistics of the United States as obtained at the Department of State from the returns of the Sixth Census*, Sixth Decennial Census, 1840 (Washington: Thomas Allen, 1841); United States, *The Seventh Census of the United States: 1850*, Seventh Decennial Census, 1850 (Washington: Robert Armstrong, 1853); United States, *Population of the United States in 1860; Compiled from the Original Returns of the Eighth Census*, Eighth Decennial Census, 1860 (Washington: G.P.O., 1864); United States, *Agriculture of the United States in 1860; Compiled from the Original Returns of the Eighth Census*, Eighth Decennial Census, 1860 (Washington: G.P.O., 1864); Inter-University Consortium for Political and Social Research, *Historical Demographic, Economic and Social Data: The United States, 1790-1970*, ICPSR Data Set 0003 (Ann Arbor: ICPSR, 1992).

Table 4.6 Population Density (Persons/Square Mile), 1810-1860

		Southeastern								Western		
Decade	State Average	Without Philadelphia	Philadelphia	Entire Region	Anthracite	Ridge & Valley	Pocono	Northeastern	Allegheny Forest	Without Allegheny	Allegheny	Entire Region
1810	18.0	44.0	823.8	68.1	—	10.9	—	1.5	0.7	15.0	34.7	16.2
1820	23.2	54.7	1015.5	73.0	17.9	16.8	5.5	8.2	1.5	18.8	47.8	20.6
1830	29.9	59.5	1398.5	81.9	29.5	21.2	8.2	14.5	2.2	25.4	69.2	28.1
1840	38.3	69.9	1911.4	105.0	37.8	26.0	12.2	22.2	8.1	33.4	111.3	38.3
1850	51.3	83.5	3027.9	136.8	53.4	29.6	21.6	30.1	13.5	41.8	189.4	51.3
1860	64.5	98.2	4189.1	172.3	76.3	34.0	29.6	36.4	17.5	48.2	245.0	60.8

Sources: United States Treasury Department, *Aggregate Amount of each description of persons within the United States of America and the Territories thereof, agreeably to actual enumeration made according to law in the Year 1810*, Third Decennial Census, 1810 (Washington, 1811); United States Census Office, *Census for 1820*, Fourth Decennial Census, 1820 (Washington: Gales and Seaton, 1821); United States Census Office, *Fifth Census; or, Enumeration of the Inhabitants of the United States, 1830*, Fifth Decennial Census, 1830 (Washington: Duff Green, 1832); United States, *Compendium of the Enumeration of the Inhabitants and Statistics of the United States as obtained at the Department of State from the returns of the Sixth Census*, Sixth Decennial Census, 1840 (Washington: Thomas Allen, 1841); United States, *The Seventh Census of the United States: 1850*, Seventh Decennial Census, 1850 (Washington: Robert Armstrong, 1853); United States, *Population of the United States in 1860; Compiled from the Original Returns of the Eighth Census*, Eighth Decennial Census, 1860 (Washington: G.P.O., 1864); United States, *Agriculture of the United States in 1860; Compiled from the Original Returns of the Eighth Census*, Eighth Decennial Census, 1860 (Washington: G.P.O., 1864); Inter-University Consortium for Political and Social Research, *Historical Demographic, Economic and Social Data: The United States, 1790-1970*, ICPSR Data Set 0003 (Ann Arbor: ICPSR, 1992). Square mileage for each county was obtained from Thomas F. Gordon, *A Gazetteer of the State of Pennsylvania* (Philadelphia: T. Belknap, 1833), 34; Thomas Burrowes, *State-book of Pennsylvania* (Philadelphia: Uriah Hunt and Son, 1846), 8; A. Howry Espenshade, *Pennsylvania Place Names* (State College: The Pennsylvania State College, 1925), 350-351; United States. Bureau of the Census, *Sixteenth Census of the United States: 1940, Agriculture*, Vol.1 (Washington, D.C.: G.P.O., 1942), 348-353.

Table 4.7 Percentage of Population in Towns of 2500+ (%), 1810-1860

		Southeastern								Western		
Decade	State Average	Without Philadelphia	Philadelphia	Entire Region	Anthracite	Ridge & Valley	Pocono	Northeastern	Allegheny Forest	Without Allegheny	Allegheny	Entire Region
1810	22.5	16.4	88.3	33.8	16.7	0.0	0.0	0.0	0.0	2.1	34.9	6.5
1820	24.4	19.8	91.5	37.8	16.0	2.5	0.0	0.0	0.0	7.0	45.2	12.6
1830	29.4	25.4	94.2	45.0	21.8	9.9	0.0	0.0	0.0	11.2	52.3	17.6
1840	31.0	27.9	96.1	50.3	24.4	1.7	0.0	0.0	0.0	13.3	58.6	1.5
1850	34.8	26.6	95.9	54.3	30.4	3.1	6.3	0.0	2.0	17.3	63.1	28.2
1860	40.5	34.7	100.0	63.4	39.6	5.6	15.3	2.3	4.6	12.7	72.0	28.0

Sources: United States Treasury Department, *Aggregate Amount of each description of persons within the United States of America and the Territories thereof, agreeably to actual enumeration made according to law in the Year 1810*, Third Decennial Census, 1810 (Washington, 1811); United States Census Office, *Census for 1820*, Fourth Decennial Census, 1820 (Washington: Gales and Seaton, 1821); United States Census Office, *Fifth Census; or, Enumeration of the Inhabitants of the United States, 1830*, Fifth Decennial Census, 1830 (Washington: Duff Green, 1832); United States, *Compendium of the Enumeration of the Inhabitants and Statistics of the United States as obtained at the Department of State from the returns of the Sixth Census*, Sixth Decennial Census, 1840 (Washington: Thomas Allen, 1841); United States, *The Seventh Census of the United States: 1850*, Seventh Decennial Census, 1850 (Washington: Robert Armstrong, 1853); United States, *Population of the United States in 1860; Compiled from the Original Returns of the Eighth Census*, Eighth Decennial Census, 1860 (Washington: G.P.O., 1864); United States, *Agriculture of the United States in 1860; Compiled from the Original Returns of the Eighth Census*, Eighth Decennial Census, 1860 (Washington: G.P.O., 1864); Inter-University Consortium for Political and Social Research, *Historical Demographic, Economic and Social Data: The United States, 1790-1970*, ICPSR Data Set 0003 (Ann Arbor: ICPSR, 1992).

Table 4.8 Agricultural Employment as Per cent of Total, 1820 and 1840

		Southeastern									Western	
Entire Allegheny	State Decade Region	Without Average	Philadelphia	Entire Philadelphia	Region	Ridge & Anthracite	Valley	Pocono	Allegheny Northeastern	Without Forest		Allegheny
1820	67.7 (73.0)*	66.0	18.1	57.1	70.0	76.5	84.5	94.8	83.2	80.9	62.9	78.6
1840	60.2 (69.5)*	62.2	8.1	45.1	62.3	68.0	66.3	82.5	78.4	77.1	38.7	71.6
Per cent Change 1820 to 1840	-7.5% (-3.5%)*	-3.8%	-10.0%	-12.0%	-7.7%	-8.5%	-18.2%	-12.3%	-4.8%	-3.8%	-24.2%	-7.0%

Sources: United States Census Office, *Census for 1820*, Fourth Decennial Census, 1820 (Washington: Gales and Seaton, 1821); United States, *Compendium of the Enumeration of the Inhabitants and Statistics of the United States as obtained at the Department of State from the returns of the Sixth Census*, Sixth Decennial Census, 1840 (Washington: Thomas Allen, 1841); Inter-University Consortium for Political and Social Research, *Historical Demographic, Economic and Social Data: The United States, 1790-1970*, ICPSR Data Set 0003 (Ann Arbor: ICPSR, 1992).

Note: *Numbers in parentheses represent statewide averages after having eliminated data for Philadelphia and Allegheny Counties.

Table 4.9 Swine Stocks Per Capita, 1840-1860

		Southeastern								Western		
Decade	State Average	Without Philadelphia	Philadelphia	Entire Region	Anthracite	Ridge & Valley	Pocono	Northeastern	Allegheny Forest	Without Allegheny	Allegheny	Entire Region
1840	0.87	0.98	0.05	0.67	0.74	1.53	0.67	0.74	1.08	1.19	0.43	1.05
1850	0.45	0.56	0.02	0.35	0.42	0.67	0.33	0.40	0.51	0.68	0.25	0.58
1860	0.35	0.48	0.01	0.28	0.33	0.62	0.32	0.30	0.42	0.53	0.16	0.43
Per Cent Change 1840 to 1860	-60.0%	-50.7%	-76.0%	-58.2%	-54.9%	-59.8%	-52.9%	-59.4%	-61.6%	-55.5%	-62.2%	-59.0%

Sources: United States, *Compendium of the Enumeration of the Inhabitants and Statistics of the United States as obtained at the Department of State from the returns of the Sixth Census*, Sixth Decennial Census, 1840 (Washington: Thomas Allen, 1841); United States, *The Seventh Census of the United States: 1850*, Seventh Decennial Census, 1850 (Washington: Robert Armstrong, 1853); United States, *Population of the United States in 1860; Compiled from the Original Returns of the Eighth Census*, Eighth Decennial Census, 1860 (Washington: G.P.O., 1864); United States, *Agriculture of the United States in 1860; Compiled from the Original Returns of the Eighth Census*, Eighth Decennial Census, 1860 (Washington: G.P.O., 1864); Inter-University Consortium for Political and Social Research, *Historical Demographic, Economic and Social Data: The United States, 1790-1970*, ICPSR Data Set 0003 (Ann Arbor: ICPSR, 1992).

Table 4.10 Milch Cow Stocks Per Capita, 1850-1860

		Southeastern								Western		
Decade	State Average	Without Philadelphia	Philadelphia	Entire Region	Anthracite	Ridge & Valley	Pocono	Northeastern	Allegheny Forest	Without Allegheny	Allegheny	Entire Region
1850	0.23	0.31	0.02	0.19	0.16	0.25	0.23	0.39	0.26	0.33	0.11	0.28
1860	0.23	0.32	0.01	0.19	0.15	0.25	0.28	0.42	0.27	0.36	0.10	0.30
Per Cent Change 1850 to 1860	0.0%	3.2%	-50.0%	0.0%	-6.3%	0.0%	17.9%	7.7%	3.8%	9.1%	-10.0%	7.1%

Sources: United States, *The Seventh Census of the United States: 1850*, Seventh Decennial Census, 1850 (Washington: Robert Armstrong, 1853); United States, *Population of the United States in 1860; Compiled from the Original Returns of the Eighth Census*, Eighth Decennial Census, 1860 (Washington: G.P.O., 1864); United States, *Agriculture of the United States in 1860; Compiled from the Original Returns of the Eighth Census*, Eighth Decennial Census, 1860 (Washington: G.P.O., 1864); Inter-University Consortium for Political and Social Research, *Historical Demographic, Economic and Social Data: The United States, 1790-1970*, ICPSR Data Set 0003 (Ann Arbor: ICPSR, 1992).

Table 4.11 Butter Production (Pounds) Per Capita, 1850-1860

		Southeastern								Western		
Decade	State Average	Without Philadelphia	Philadelphia	Entire Region	Anthracite	Ridge & Valley	Pocono	Northeastern	Allegheny Forest	Without Allegheny	Allegheny	Entire Region
1850	17.3	27.5	1.6	17.1	12.3	14.9	16.2	33.4	15.9	21.1	7.0	17.8
1860	16.8	29.6	0.6	16.9	12.5	17.3	26.8	42.3	20.4	32.8	7.8	26.3
Per Cent Change 1850 to 1860	-2.9%	7.9%	-63.6%	-1.5%	1.7%	16.3%	65.4%	26.7%	27.9%	55.6%	10.5%	48.3%

Sources: United States, *The Seventh Census of the United States: 1850*, Seventh Decennial Census, 1850 (Washington: Robert Armstrong, 1853); United States, *Population of the United States in 1860; Compiled from the Original Returns of the Eighth Census*, Eighth Decennial Census, 1860 (Washington: G.P.O., 1864); United States, *Agriculture of the United States in 1860; Compiled from the Original Returns of the Eighth Census*, Eighth Decennial Census, 1860 (Washington: G.P.O., 1864); Inter-University Consortium for Political and Social Research, *Historical Demographic, Economic and Social Data: The United States, 1790-1970*, ICPSR Data Set 0003 (Ann Arbor: ICPSR, 1992).

Table 4.12 Cheese Production (Pounds) Per Capita, 1850-1860

		Southeastern								Western		
Decade	State Average	Without Philadelphia	Philadelphia	Entire Region	Anthracite	Ridge & Valley	Pocono	Northeastern	Allegheny Forest	Without Allegheny	Allegheny	Entire Region
1850	1.1	0.1	0.0	0.1	0.4	0.1	0.6	2.9	0.4	4.3	0.0	3.3
1860	0.9	1.4	0.0	0.8	0.2	0.1	0.4	2.0	0.5	1.9	0.2	1.5
Per Cent Change 1850 to 1860	-11.1%	897.3%	—	831.8%	-42.6%	6.7%	-35.6%	-29.6%	22.9%	-56.1%	660.9%	-5.8%

Sources: United States, *The Seventh Census of the United States: 1850*, Seventh Decennial Census, 1850 (Washington: Robert Armstrong, 1853); United States, *Population of the United States in 1860; Compiled from the Original Returns of the Eighth Census*, Eighth Decennial Census, 1860 (Washington: G.P.O., 1864); United States, *Agriculture of the United States in 1860; Compiled from the Original Returns of the Eighth Census*, Eighth Decennial Census, 1860 (Washington: G.P.O., 1864); Inter-University Consortium for Political and Social Research, *Historical Demographic, Economic and Social Data: The United States, 1790-1970*, ICPSR Data Set 0003 (Ann Arbor: ICPSR, 1992).

Table 4.13 Value of Home Manufactures Per Capita, 1840-1860 (1821-25 Dollars)

		Southeastern								Western		
Decade	State Average	Without Philadelphia	Philadelphia	Entire Region	Anthracite	Ridge & Valley	Pocono	Northeastern	Allegheny Forest	Without Allegheny	Allegheny	Entire Region
1840	0.75	0.39	0.00	0.26	0.76	0.52	0.62	2.01	1.04	1.71	0.14	1.42
1850	0.42	0.20	0.00	0.12	0.31	0.32	0.52	1.20	0.80	1.00	0.11	0.79
1860	0.21	0.12	0.00	0.07	0.27	0.15	0.12	0.42	0.28	0.52	0.03	0.39
Per Cent Change 1840 to 1860	-72.0%	-69.2%	—	-73.1%	-64.5%	-71.2%	-80.6%	-79.1%	-73.1%	-70.6%	-78.6%	-72.5%

Sources: United States, *Compendium of the Enumeration of the Inhabitants and Statistics of the United States as obtained at the Department of State from the returns of the Sixth Census*, Sixth Decennial Census, 1840 (Washington: Thomas Allen, 1841); United States, *The Seventh Census of the United States: 1850*, Seventh Decennial Census, 1850 (Washington: Robert Armstrong, 1853); United States, *Population of the United States in 1860; Compiled from the Original Returns of the Eighth Census*, Eighth Decennial Census, 1860 (Washington: G.P.O., 1864); United States, *Agriculture of the United States in 1860; Compiled from the Original Returns of the Eighth Census*, Eighth Decennial Census, 1860 (Washington: G.P.O., 1864); Inter-University Consortium for Political and Social Research, *Historical Demographic, Economic and Social Data: The United States, 1790-1970*, ICPSR Data Set 0003 (Ann Arbor: ICPSR, 1992).

Table 4.14 Value of Market Garden Produce Per Capita, 1840-1860 (1821-25 Dollars)

		Southeastern								Western		
Decade	State Average	Without Philadelphia	Philadelphia	Entire Region	Anthracite	Ridge & Valley	Pocono	Northeastern	Allegheny Forest	Without Allegheny	Allegheny	Entire Region
1840	0.13	0.02	0.54	0.19	0.08	0.00	0.01	0.00	0.00	0.06	0.51	0.15
1850	0.39	0.14	1.39	0.64	0.21	0.07	0.11	0.01	0.06	0.23	0.45	0.28
1860	0.52	0.33	1.38	0.79	0.38	0.10	0.11	0.03	0.02	0.15	1.42	0.48
Per Cent Change 1840 to 1860	33%	1550.0%	155.5%	23.4%	375.0%	—	1000.0%	—	—	150.0%	178.4%	71.4%

Sources: United States, *Compendium of the Enumeration of the Inhabitants and Statistics of the United States as obtained at the Department of State from the returns of the Sixth Census*, Sixth Decennial Census, 1840 (Washington: Thomas Allen, 1841); United States, *The Seventh Census of the United States: 1850*, Seventh Decennial Census, 1850 (Washington: Robert Armstrong, 1853); United States, *Population of the United States in 1860; Compiled from the Original Returns of the Eighth Census*, Eighth Decennial Census, 1860 (Washington: G.P.O., 1864); United States, *Agriculture of the United States in 1860; Compiled from the Original Returns of the Eighth Census*, Eighth Decennial Census, 1860 (Washington: G.P.O., 1864); Inter-University Consortium for Political and Social Research, *Historical Demographic, Economic and Social Data: The United States, 1790-1970*, ICPSR Data Set 0003 (Ann Arbor: ICPSR, 1992).

Table 4.15 Value of Orchard Produce Per Capita, 1840-1860 (1821-25 Dollars)

		Southeastern								Western		
Decade	State Average	Without Philadelphia	Philadelphia	Entire Region	Anthracite	Ridge & Valley	Pocono	Northeastern	Allegheny Forest	Without Allegheny	Allegheny	Entire Region
1840	0.35	0.39	0.04	0.28	0.39	0.39	0.31	0.62	0.32	0.48	0.20	0.43
1850	0.41	0.73	0.04	0.45	0.37	0.34	0.13	0.21	0.21	0.49	0.36	0.46
1860	0.56	0.88	0.03	0.51	0.48	0.85	1.02	0.98	0.22	0.63	0.43	0.58
Per Cent Change 1840 to 1860	60.0%	125.6%	-25.0%	82.1%	23.1%	117.9%	229.0%	58.1%	-31.3%	31.3%	115.0%	34.9%

Sources: United States, *Compendium of the Enumeration of the Inhabitants and Statistics of the United States as obtained at the Department of State from the returns of the Sixth Census*, Sixth Decennial Census, 1840 (Washington: Thomas Allen, 1841); United States, *The Seventh Census of the United States: 1850*, Seventh Decennial Census, 1850 (Washington: Robert Armstrong, 1853); United States, *Population of the United States in 1860; Compiled from the Original Returns of the Eighth Census*, Eighth Decennial Census, 1860 (Washington: G.P.O., 1864); United States, *Agriculture of the United States in 1860; Compiled from the Original Returns of the Eighth Census*, Eighth Decennial Census, 1860 (Washington: G.P.O., 1864); Inter-University Consortium for Political and Social Research, *Historical Demographic, Economic and Social Data: The United States, 1790-1970*, ICPSR Data Set 0003 (Ann Arbor: ICPSR, 1992).

Table 4.16 Real Estate Valuations Per Acre, 1815 and 1845 (1821-25 Dollars)

		Southeastern								Western		
Decade	State Average	Without Philadelphia	Philadelphia	Entire Region	Anthracite	Ridge & Valley	Pocono	Northeastern	Allegheny Forest	Without Allegheny	Allegheny	Entire Region
1815	6.79	18.33	330.15	22.43	7.60	5.04	0.83	1.44	1.10	2.19	3.96	2.30
1845	18.48	39.38	1847.17	68.64	15.01	11.06	3.58	3.99	2.42	8.04	39.02	10.13
Per Cent Change												
1815 to 1845	172.2%	114.8%	459.5%	206.0%	97.6%	119.4%	331.4%	178.2%	119.4%	267.7%	885.8%	341.0%

Sources: Pennsylvania Senate, 'Report of the Board of Revenue Commissioners, transmitted to the Governor, in pursuance of an act of the 29th of April 1844,' *Journal of the Senate 1845*, Vol. II, Document 53 (Harrisburg: J. M. G. Lescure, 1845), 303-320; Pennsylvania Senate, 'Communication from the State Treasurer, enclosing Tables of the Valuation fixed on the Several Counties of the Commonwealth,' by the Board of Revenue Commissioners, *Journal of the Senate 1845*, Vol. II, Document 54 (Harrisburg: J. M. G. Lescure, 1845), 321-326; 'An Abstract of the Returns made by the Commissioners of the City of Philadelphia and the Several Counties of the Commonwealth of Pennsylvania,' *Hazard's Register* July 1828, 12-13.

Population growth in the Southeastern Region ranged between 19 per cent and 30 per cent per decade, compared to 25 to 34 per cent for the state. It was most rapid in the 1840s and 1850s.[43] However, even including Philadelphia's population growth, which was two to three times faster than the rest of the region and significantly higher than the state as a whole, the Southeastern Region's growth rates were among the lowest, only once (1850/60) exceeding the statewide average (Table 4.5).

In an area as densely populated as Philadelphia County, the agricultural labor force was small and declining. Eighteen per cent of Philadelphia County residents reported their occupation as agricultural in 1820 and the figure declined to eight per cent by 1840. The Southeastern Region's 1840 agricultural employment proportion of 45 per cent, including Philadelphia County, and 62 per cent excluding it, were both the lowest in the state in 1840.[44]

While the agricultural sector was relatively small, it was also extremely productive. In 1840, the Southeast produced 49 per cent of the state's wheat, 36 per cent of its corn, and had 35 per cent of its hogs. Lindstrom has demonstrated the region's dynamic nature by noting that, over the period 1810 through 1840, the region increasingly evolved to serve the large Philadelphia food market, developing 'rings' of agricultural specialization consistent with the theory first put forth by von Thünen.[45] In the areas closest to Philadelphia, farmers specialized in dairying, livestock fattening and market gardening. The second ring, slightly more distant, emphasized the production of cord wood and some lumbering,[46] while the third ring, even more distant from the center city, saw intensive grain cultivation. Von Thünen's fourth and fifth rings, specialization in 'grain with fallow' and 'butter, cheese and distilling' were not apparent in Philadelphia's hinterland,[47] in part due to variation in soil quality and the presence of great mineral wealth suitable for mining industry.[48] However, a distant ring of stock raising was apparent in Wayne, Susquehanna, and Bedford Counties.[49] Local farmers also sent considerable produce south toward the Baltimore markets.

Specialization in the provisioning of Philadelphia is also evident in census data. The region had the highest per capita dollar value of market gardening in 1840, 1850 and 1860. Very little of this was produced within Philadelphia County. Excluding Philadelphia County, the Southeast produced the second most butter per capita in 1850 and ranked third in 1860. Swine and milch cow stocks per capita were just above the state average in the three census years, if Philadelphia County's figure is excluded, just below if included.[50] In both cases, Philadelphia County's share is negligible. The situation is similar with the dollar value of orchard produce.[51] With transport distances short, a rich and increasingly productive agricultural hinterland supplied Philadelphia with abundant foodstuffs.

Philadelphia County residents specialized in commerce and manufacturing, using the wages and profits so obtained to purchase nutrients, and became intensively market integrated. Home manufactures were not produced within Philadelphia County. The entire Southeastern Region produced home manufactures at a rate only 50 per cent of the state mean if Philadelphia County is excluded, but there was great county-by-county variation. Southeastern Region counties distant from Philadelphia generated home manufactures at or above the state average for all three years. Those closer to the city generated very small amounts of these goods.

Buyers and sellers were connected over an extensive and rapidly developing system of transportation in the Southeastern Region. Channel clearing on the Lehigh and Schuylkill Rivers, both of which flowed from the Anthracite Region toward the southeast, was under way by 1800. On the Susquehanna, a short canal had already bypassed the impediment to travel posed by the falls at Conewago by then, and construction had begun on a canal which would link the Susquehanna and Schuylkill Rivers via Tulpehoken Creek.

A series of turnpikes also cut the region in 1810. The most famous, the stone paved turnpike from Philadelphia to Lancaster, completed in 1794, provided an effective road for commerce between this highly productive agricultural district and Philadelphia. It was, however, only one among many state chartered turnpikes with at least one terminus in the Southeastern Region. These included toll roads from Lancaster to Harris Ferry, completed in 1815, and other routes from Easton to Wilkes-Barre, Sunbury to Reading, Germantown to Reading, Lancaster to Wright's Ferry, and Philadelphia to Trenton. All were chartered and/or built in the first decades of the 1800s. Turnpike construction across the state was most heavily concentrated in the southeast.[52]

Toll road construction and channel clearing efforts continued after 1815, but canal construction became the most important activity and remained so through the mid-1840s. The Legislature's authorization to build the Main Line system in 1826, partially in an effort to help Philadelphia compete with New York City in the western trade, began a burst of canal construction.[53] By the late 1830s, a combination of private and state canals linked the Southeastern Region internally and with other regions in-state and out. The new canals made the Anthracite Region's coal fields much more accessible. By 1831, both the Lehigh Coal and Navigation Company's canal to Mauch Chunk and the Schuylkill Navigation Company's canal to Port Carbon were complete, providing two routes between the southern anthracite fields and the Southeastern Region. The Delaware Division of the State Works reached New Hope by 1828 and Easton in 1847. Interior towns also obtained new canal service. Reading, on the west bank of the Schuylkill, was connected to the Susquehanna by the Union Canal in 1822, while York obtained a similar connection via the Codorus in 1829. The Susquehanna and Tidewater Canal Company built its channel along the western bank of the lower Susquehanna from Wrightsville to the Maryland line.

Authorization of the Main Line also expanded railroad construction in the Southeastern Region. The building of the Philadelphia-Columbia Railroad, part of the State Works between Philadelphia and Pittsburgh, began in 1828 and was completed in 1834. The mid and late 1830s saw the completion of a series of relatively long distance rail lines designed 1) to connect trading towns within southeastern Pennsylvania and 2) to link these towns, especially Philadelphia, with points outside the state.[54] Many of these followed existing canal or river courses while others provided new overland links between points previously joined only by turnpikes or other roads. Several short-distance rail lines in the Philadelphia area were also constructed.

No new canals were built in the Southeastern Region after 1845 and many existing ones were sold to railroad companies. Two additional rail lines were built to service the coal fields, the Allentown and the Lehigh Valley railroads. Much of the other new rail service connected small towns in the region with one another.[55] The system of transportation which tied Philadelphia and its nearby hinterland together and sufficiently large local agricultural surpluses enabled extensive specialization of production to occur and created an inter-dependent regional economy.

Increasingly connected to the interior of the state via road, canal and eventually railroad,[56] Philadelphia was a center of local and regional commerce.[57] Manufacturing also took root and, by the end of the antebellum period, had become dominant. Hence, in both the Southeastern Region as a whole and especially within Philadelphia County, real estate values increased rapidly between 1815 and 1845, much faster than population growth could account for.[58] Valuation increases were not evenly distributed.[59] In the region as a whole real estate values increased by 206 per cent, from $22/acre to $69/acre. In contrast, Philadelphia County's valuations grew by more than 450 per cent, to $1847/acre. Values rose 115 per cent in the rest of the region, similar to the increases of the Anthracite, Ridge and Valley, and Allegheny Forest Regions.[60] Developments both within and without the region were increasing the value of real property in the southeast. Lindstrom notes that the financial benefits of specialization throughout eastern Pennsylvania, western New Jersey, and northern Delaware were concentrated in the lower portion of the Southeastern Region and especially in Philadelphia County.[61]

Anthracite Region

Named for the 'black rock'[62] which lay beneath much of the land in this eight-county region and which eventually determined the nature of its economic life, the Anthracite Region is bordered on the west by the Susquehanna River. Its southern boundary is marked by the irregular line of the Blue and Kittatinny Mountains. No above ground features denote its eastern and northern flanks, but its range is delimited by the extent of the anthracite coal fields of the north central portion of the state. The region lies in the northeastern edge of the 'newer' Appalachians, in the east-central part of the commonwealth.[63]

Except for the portion of present day Dauphin and Lebanon Counties, southeast of the Blue Mountain, very little settlement occurred in the Anthracite Region before 1750.[64] The region was populated by a mix of peoples not unlike that which occurred in the southeast. Englishmen, Irishmen, Scotch-Irish, and people of German ancestry filled the region, the first three groups predominating until the 1840s. Germans were concentrated in the southern areas with the highest soil fertility and the best opportunities for agriculture.[65] With the anthracite boom in the late 1820s and 1830s, large numbers of Irish and Welsh miners arrived to meet the labor demand.[66]

The presence of valuable mineral deposits as well as considerable stands of timber resulted in settlement and development patterns which were rather different from those elsewhere in the state. Population concentration occurred early on and agriculture did not dominate the region's early history.[67] By 1810, 17 per cent of the region's population lived in urban areas, second only to the Southeastern Region. The level of urbanization increased throughout the period until by 1860 it reached 40 per cent. The region's relative standing as the second most urban continued, even exceeding the Western Region which included Pittsburgh.[68] In 1850 and 1860 the Anthracite's urbanization level exceeded that of the Southeastern Region, without Philadelphia County, but its population density was only one-half to two-thirds of that of the former, closer to that of the Western Region. Unlike the Southeastern Region, the Anthracite was characterized by dense clusters of population and vast open tracts of land.[69] Prior to the expansion of coal production, the rate of population increase was only equal to the state average. However, it became particularly rapid in the 1840s and 1850s as miners flocked to the region. By 1860, the Anthracite's population share increased to 12 per cent of the state total.

The sectoral distribution of employment was similar to that of its neighbor to the southeast. In 1820, 70 per cent of the Anthracite Region's inhabitants were in agriculture, second lowest in the state. This share fell to 62 per cent in 1840, still second to the Southeast, but only by a negligible margin. For a relatively urbanized area, the Anthracite Region had a rather high level of home manufacturing in 1840: 76 cents per capita. Only the sparsely populated Northeastern, Allegheny Forest, and Western Regions (without Allegheny County) had higher values. The fall in home manufacturing production between 1840 and 1850 was greatest in this region, a reduction of almost two-thirds to 31 cents per capita. Meanwhile, the level of market gardening increased from eight cents per person in 1840 to 38 cents in 1860, placing it on a level similar to that of the Southeastern Region, Philadelphia County excluded. Swine stocks on a per capita basis were near the commonwealth average and declined from 1840 to 1860 at a rate similar to that of the state's. However, milch cow stocks per capita were lower here than in any other region. Only Philadelphia and Allegheny Counties had lower per capita levels. There is a fairly consistent relationship between the indicators of market participation and mining in this region. The counties with the most extensive mining operations, Schuylkill and Carbon, had the region's lowest levels of home manufacturing and general farming and the highest level of market gardening. The other counties, with less coal production, were much higher, close to the state average on all these measures.

The divergence can be explained by the region's topology. Much of the mountainous section was too rugged and infertile to provide a good base for farming, but many small valleys were quite productive in mixed agriculture of grain and livestock.[70] The colliers provided a demand for agricultural goods, which was in great part met by local farmers who were presented with a 'ready market, at good prices in the mining district.'[71] This is evident in the high level of market gardening in some of the region's counties. Farmers elsewhere in the region sent their excess crops either to Philadelphia or Baltimore.[72] The emergence of iron mining and manufacture in Columbia County eventually created another local market for agricultural products.[73]

Some of the earliest transportation improvements in the commonwealth, apart from turnpikes, took place in the Anthracite Region. In 1797, the completion of a canal enabled Susquehanna River traffic to continue unimpeded around the falls at Conewago.[74] Between 1800 and 1845 a series of river clearings were undertaken along the region's main waterways: the Susquehanna, the Lehigh and the Schuylkill Rivers. Efforts were made to connect the Schuylkill and the Susquehanna Rivers between Reading and Middletown via canal. By 1830 this link was established and the southern anthracite fields were reached by short-distance railroads which provided a connection to canals carrying the coal to points down river. Four years later, the North Branch Division of the State Works was completed to the northern fields. By 1845 a network of canals and railroads crisscrossed the Anthracite Region, allowing coal, iron, and lumber to be shipped out. Railroads were no longer relegated to short-distance hops to canal terminals. The number of short-distance feeder rail lines increased and many had connections to the Reading Railroad linking the region to Philadelphia. Numerous additional canals and railways were under construction. They eventually cut across the region, linked the northern and southern fields, and tied the fields into canals along the Susquehanna, the Lehigh, and the Delaware rivers. After 1845, such railways as the Philadelphia and Reading, and the Schuylkill and Susquehanna were built. They first competed with, and increasingly replaced, the canals. In many cases, the rails followed almost the identical route as the canals, while a few took more direct paths to the fields.[75] Rail and canal lines were so common that by 1860 there was no spot in the region which was more than 20 miles removed from the new transportation system.[76] By the period's end the Anthracite counties were tightly linked via many different routes to the Southeastern Region.

In spite of great mining and transport development activity, the Anthracite Region had the smallest percentage increase in land valuation of any region.[77] Although population density almost quadrupled,[78] real estate values only doubled. This still sufficed to keep land values the second highest in the state. Only the Southeastern Region (and Philadelphia and Allegheny Counties individually) were higher.

Ridge and Valley Region

The Ridge and Valley Region, named for its folded and undulating topography, had borders defined by similarly striking geological features. Its ten counties arched to the right, shaping one-quarter of a wide ring. Its southern edge was formed by the state's border with Maryland. The inner circumference was defined by the Tuscarora and Blue Mountains, while the Susquehanna River formed the eastern edge. The outer circumference followed the line of the Tuscarora and Blue Mountains but transposed about forty to fifty miles to the west or northwest.

Only a few localities were established before 1760, but by 1790 many settlements had been founded by a mix of German, Irish, and Scotch-Irish.[79] Following rapid population growth between 1810 and 1820, the region grew more slowly than the rest of the state between 1820 and 1860 and hence, its population share declined. The region was sparsely urbanized with the percentage of the urban population only doubling between 1810 and 1860, to a meager six per cent. It was the third most densely settled region in the state at the start of the period with 11 psm. Like urbanization, regional population density increased slowly, more slowly than the state's. By 1860, it stood at 34. Only the Pocono and Allegheny Forest Regions had lower densities. Even the Western Region without Allegheny County had more people per square mile.

The Ridge and Valley played the role of a stock raising region for the Philadelphia and Baltimore markets. Producing meat and other foodstuffs employed three-quarters of those employed in these counties in 1820, and just over two-thirds in 1840. In both cases, this level of agricultural employment was several percentage points above the statewide average. Swine levels per capita were the highest in the state, although they fell between 1840 and 1860, as was the case across Pennsylvania. Milch cow stocks per capita were about equal to the state average, and did not change between 1850 and 1860. The Ridge and Valley increased its butter production per capita modestly over this ten year span. It was slightly below the state average in 1850 and slightly above it in 1860.

Supplying other regions with their primary 'white meat,' the Ridge and Valley was not unconnected from the rest of the state. The medium-low level of home manufactures, which it produced between 1840 and 1860, and its level of market garden production, which was neither as high as those regions close to the large urban centers of Pittsburgh and Philadelphia, nor as low as those of the distant and difficult-to-reach Allegheny Forest and Northeastern Regions, give evidence of this. Orchard produce per capita was near the state average in 1840 and 1850, but by 1860 it stood at 150 per cent of the state mean.

Just as the rivers and streams, the transportation network accommodated itself to the ridges which gave the region its name. Both the 'northern' and 'southern' turnpike routes from Philadelphia to Pittsburgh traversed the Ridge and Valley. Cut out of the forest along old Indian trading paths, these two routes were first used as pack horse trails. Eventually they were widened and improved in the early 1800s.[80]

Canal building began in the late 1820s, primarily as an operation of the state government. The entire Juniata Division of the State Works was built in the region, completed by 1832. Portions of the Eastern and Susquehanna Divisions lay on the region's eastern border. Only the Bald Eagle and Spring Creek Canal, which eventually connected Williamsport with Bellefonte, began as a private initiative. No other canals were built in the region, but a series of river navigation improvements and clearings were carried out along the Juniata and Little Juniata Rivers, as well as on the Raystown branch of that stream. The connection of the region to the west continued via the Allegheny Portage Railroad which met the Juniata Division at Hollidaysburg. The portage railroad, begun in 1831 and completed two years later, carried cargo over the Allegheny Front and to the Conemaugh River at Johnstown.

As was the case in the Southeastern and the Anthracite Regions, the late 1840s and 1850s saw the construction of new rail lines which competed with existing canals. The Pennsylvania Railroad built a line parallel to the Juniata Division Canal between 1847 and 1862. It also replaced the less efficient inclined planes of the Allegheny Portage with the New Portage Railroad. A few small feeder or connector rail lines were built which provided transport access to many areas of the region for the first time.[81] Previously, transport systems either literally ran around the edges of the region, or simply cut it in half. While providing non-agricultural employment in the towns through which it passed, and an improved through route for cross-state travel, the Main Line did not provide improved transportation services to many areas within the region.

Its most rapid population increases having occurred by 1820, with the lowest rates of increase of any region thereafter, real estate values in the Ridge and Valley increased at a pace well below the state average. In 1845 they settled at $11 an acre. As was noted above, most transportation improvements, with the exception of the Main Line, went around the region's edges. Without a dense network of feeders, access to the region was limited, and so was the economic value of the land.

Pocono Region

Three counties made up the Pocono Region with the Delaware River forming its eastern flank. The Blue and Kittatinny Mountains formed the region's southern edge with Wayne and Monroe Counties' western borders defining the region's western extent. It was a 'high, rolling, glaciated tableland' with a 'thin and rocky' soil.[82] With only the extreme eastern lip of the region settled by 1750 and the majority of the land not settled until the 1790s,[83] the hilly Pocono Region was sparsely populated in 1810.

Originally claimed by Connecticut, and the site of armed hostilities between settlers with disputed land claims, most residents had their roots in New England or New York State.[84] Population growth was rapid throughout the antebellum years, more than double the state's mean rate between 1810 and 1840. Fueled by the arrival of Irish and German immigrants, especially in Pike County, population growth exceeded 150 per cent of the state's rate from 1840 through 1860. Even in 1860, though, the region contained only two per cent of the commonwealth's population. It had Pennsylvania's second lowest population density (5.5 psm in 1810 rising to 30 psm in 1860). Only the tardily settled Allegheny Forest region had fewer residents per square mile. Until 1850, this region did not have a town with more than 2500 inhabitants, but by 1860 15 per cent of the population of the region was urban.

By 1840, after the most rapid growth of the antebellum period, just over 25,000 persons lived in the region. Most were settled along the Delaware River or its tributaries.[85] Lumbering and agriculture were the two primary forms of employment. Almost 85 per cent of the labor force was engaged in the agricultural sector in 1820. As throughout the state, this proportion fell in the following years, but it fell more here than in any other region. The relatively cold climate meant that potatoes, buckwheat, and rye, and not corn or wheat, were the primary crops. Most farming took place in the valleys adjacent to streams and rivers.[86] Maple sugaring and stock raising were important, both more appropriate to the weather and landscape.[87]

Most of the timber which was readily accessible had already been felled and sent down river by 1840, but some logging continued.[88] Prior to the building of canals through the region, most lumber was sent as whole logs downstream with the spring's high water.[89] However, in Monroe County a series of sawmills had been constructed by the mid-1840s to process some of the timber locally. Canal connections with Wilkes-Barre made this a financially feasible investment.[90] Small quantities of iron were manufactured in Monroe County along with some glass, the latter based on the availability of some excellent sand in Wayne County.[91]

Swine stocks were similar to those in other regions without effective transport linkages, about two-thirds of a hog per person in 1840. The reduction of more than 50 per cent in per capita levels between 1840 and 1860 was not far from the state average. Milch cow stocks per capita were very similar to those of other regions in the central and northeastern portions of the state, hovering near the state average. Butter output per capita rose in the 1850s by more than two-thirds. This indicates the benefits which resulted from specialization, and, in light of the slower growth of cow stocks, greater productivity. The Pocono Region in 1840 had a lower level of home manufacturing than might be expected for a region without good transportation linkages. However, the level of market gardening was quite low, consistent with inaccessibility to large urban areas.[92]

Cut off by Kittatinny Mountain, only the Delaware Water Gap, Wind Gap, and Smith's Gap allowed access to the Pocono Region from the south. Connections were better with New York than with other areas of the Keystone State. Until 1823, channel clearing on the Delaware and Lackawaxen Rivers were the only transport infrastructure improvements undertaken in the region. With the construction of the Delaware and Hudson Canal in 1823 and the beginning of the Delaware and Hudson Canal Company Railroad in 1829,[93] the center of this region was linked to the Delaware River and, eventually, to the Hudson. A few improvements to the navigability of Bushkill Creek were initiated, but there were few other projects until 1850, when the Pennsylvania Coal Company built two additional rail lines into the northern anthracite fields near Scranton. In the same year a rail link from Scranton to Stroudsburg was begun by the Delaware, Lackawanna and Western Railroad. Turnpikes emanating out of Easton and Milford tied the region together, both internally and with towns outside of the region's borders.

Between 1815 and 1845, land prices in the Pocono Region rose by 331 per cent. While the rate is impressive, initial land prices were very low, less than a dollar an acre. Land price increases were greater than increases in population density. In 1845 Pocono Region real estate was the state's second cheapest. Farm real estate values were almost unchanged in Wayne and Pike County after the introduction of railroads in the 1850s, although Monroe County's farm land values increased by more than 50 per cent between 1850 and 1860.[94]

Northeastern Region

Four counties, three of which abut the Pennsylvania border with New York State, and a fourth, Wyoming County, which was created only in 1842, made up the Northeastern Region. Topographical features do not define its boundaries. The counties form a unit because of their proximity and the nature of their agricultural production. Isolated from the rest of Pennsylvania by the rugged terrain to the south, residents of these counties oriented their economic activities northward toward New York State.

As another portion of Pennsylvania originally claimed by Connecticut, the region was settled predominantly by New Englanders and New Yorkers. However, they did not arrive in significant numbers before the 1770s. Through the early decades of the nineteenth century, the area was lightly settled, with portions of Bradford County not having an established settlement until the 1830s.[95] Still, population grew at rates much higher than the state average, and between 1820 and 1860[96] the region almost doubled its share of the state's population. Settlement, however, was widely dispersed. No single town in the region had a population in excess of 2500 until 1860, when one such town existed. While it began as one of the state's most sparsely populated areas, the Northeastern Region also witnessed relatively rapid growth in population density reaching 36 psm by 1860.

As might be expected of such a thinly settled and isolated region, the occupational distribution was heavily tilted toward agriculture: 95 per cent in 1820, and still 82.5 per cent in 1840. At both times these were the state's highest values.

With few neighbors and few effective transportation routes, residents of this region were highly self-sufficient: the level of home manufactures was the highest in the state in 1840, 1850, and 1860.[97] Moreover, the region had one of the two lowest levels of market garden production. However, the self-sufficiency was not complete, and farmers in the Northeastern Region were beginning to orient themselves toward wider markets for primary sector goods as early as the 1840s. The region was heavily forested and sent large amounts of timber downstream. By 1843, there were 213 sawmills in Bradford County alone[98] (one sawmill for every 154 residents). The terrain and climate of the region were not favorable to wheat growing, although some was produced. Rather, oats and potatoes seemed best suited to this hilly and chilly clime.[99] Cattle and sheep production, which utilized the steep contours of the land, were also important, and by the 1840s herds were driven into New York and New Jersey for sale.[100]

Contemporary sources note that farmers in this area marketed dairy products mostly into New York, using a growing network of transportation routes.[101] Especially striking are the milch cow stock per capita. They were the highest of any region in 1850 and 1860, even higher than the Southeastern Region (excluding Philadelphia), which had specialized in the production of dairy products very early on. Not surprisingly, the Northeastern Region produced the most butter per capita of any region and shared the lead in cheese production with the Western Region.[102] Swine stocks in 1840 were at the low end of the state spectrum, and the region experienced per capita declines consistent with the reductions elsewhere.

With the exception of some turnpikes which cut through Susquehanna County, there were no major improvements in transport routes in this region until 1836. In that year the Tioga Navigation Company built a railroad from the New York State line to Blossburg, Tioga County. In the other direction, this train operated to Corning, N.Y. Construction also began in that same year on the North Branch Extension to the Main Line Canal. Designed to run from Pittston to the state line, where it would connect with the New York State system, it was not completed for twenty years. The canal then provided access through the center of the region to Elmira and Binghamton, N.Y.

With so little canal mileage and its late arrival, railroads did not so much compete with, or replace, canals as supplant them as the main mode of transportation of marketable goods. New lines begun in 1839 and 1851 cut through the region. They served locals to some degree, but were more important for carrying goods and people from more southerly portions of Pennsylvania into New York State and vice versa. Two feeder lines, one connecting with the North Branch Extension Canal, the other with the Tioga Railroad, did enable coal to be shipped more easily out of the region's mines.

By 1845 real estate values in the Northeastern Region had risen to 178 per cent of the 1815 level of $1.4/acre. Population density, however, increased twice as fast. Much of the land was not perceived to be exceedingly valuable.

Allegheny Forest Region

Sprawling over 10,083 square miles of heavily forested stream-cut tableland, the Allegheny Forest was the last region in the state to be settled.[103] Its southeastern edge is defined by the Allegheny Front, the western boundary by the Western Region, while the Northeastern Region defined its eastern limit. On the north was New York State. In 1800 it was still a wilderness with a population density below one person per square mile. Only 16,100 persons resided in the seven counties of the region in 1810. Speaking of Jefferson County in particular, Day writes 'for many years after its establishment this county was little better than a hunting ground for whites and Indians.'[104] Settlers came from New York, New England, and other parts of Pennsylvania. Most of this land was opened up after 1800.[105] Only Clinton and Lycoming Counties had significant settlement activity before this date.[106]

The overall population growth rate was high, anywhere from 150 per cent to 300 per cent of the state rate, and the Allegheny Forest Region grew from two per cent to seven per cent of the state's population between 1810 and 1860. Even so, in 1860 this vast land only had 17.5 psm and three counties still had densities below three psm. As in the Northeastern Region, towns appeared late; the first was recorded in 1850. In 1860 only five per cent of the region's population was urban.

The work force in this rural and difficult-to-reach region was highly agricultural. In 1820, 83 per cent of the labor force was involved in producing food, and it remained at that high level. By 1840 the proportion had fallen a little and was still at 78 per cent. Lumbering was the region's only major industry, with vast rafts of logs sent southward on the French Creek, the Allegheny, Clarion, and Susquehanna Rivers.[107]

Without easy connection either to the rest of the state or with its neighbors to the north, the Allegheny Forest Region did not participate extensively in trade early in the century. It had the third highest per capita level of home manufactures ($1/person) in 1840. It retained this position even though the absolute level fell by 73 per cent in the following twenty years. The lack of access to urban centers is also apparent in the very low level of market garden produce grown in the region. Contemporary sources consistently complained about the region's remoteness.[108] Farmers raised slightly more than the state per capita average of swine and milch cows.

With the exception of the construction of a crushed stone road which cut the southwest corner of the region between Clearfield and Franklin on the way to Erie, river channel clearing was the type of transportation improvement most prominent in the Allegheny Forest Region. As elsewhere in the state, waterway improvements were carried out late in the eighteenth century on French Creek in the extreme western portion of the region and early in the nineteenth century on Bald Eagle Creek in the east. Both the West Branch of the Susquehanna and the Allegheny Rivers saw stream clearance efforts, as did several other major creeks. Canal construction started in 1828. When completed, the West Branch Division Canal along the West Branch of the Susquehanna provided residents in the eastern portion of the region with more consistent access to the rest of the state via the Susquehanna River. When this project was completed, work began on the Bald Eagle and Spring Creek Navigation Company Canal, a private extension which joined the West Branch Division at Lock Haven. During the years between 1830 and 1860, a series of navigational improvements and clearings were made between Clearfield and Cherry Tree farther up the West Branch.

Railroads made their first appearance in the region in 1834 when construction started on a rail line from Williamsport to Elmira, N.Y.,[109] though it was not completed until 1854. Construction of the Sunbury & Erie (incorporated 1837), which eventually traversed the entire region, began in 1853 but was likewise not completed until much later, in 1864.[110] Work did not begin in earnest before 1860, although a series of small feeders were added near the eastern terminus even before completion. In the western section of the region several rail lines were under construction as the period closed. These included the Atlantic and Great Western as well as the Buffalo, Bradford, & Pittsburgh.[111]

Land values in the region increased slightly less than the state average, increasing by 119 per cent between 1815 and 1845, reflecting the presence of few valuable resources and very limited transportation improvements.[112] With very low population densities at the start, and only 13.5 psm in 1850, there was not much pressure on land prices from population growth.

Western Region

The Western Region is composed of fifteen counties[113] at the western edge of the state. Bounded by Lake Erie on the north, Ohio on the west and Virginia on the south and west, the region's southeastern edge is defined by the southern quarter of the Allegheny Front[114] and the northeastern by its curving border with the Allegheny Forest Region. It is largely a 'desiccated plain' of rolling hills created by numerous well-watered streams which have cut, to varying depths, into the plateau, providing its rolling terrain. Covering the entire western portion of the state, this region has much variation in both soil conditions and topography.[115] The southeastern section, which includes both Laurel Hill and Chestnut Ridge, was a relatively mountainous, forested region. Farmers in that area had to contend with less fertile and hilly lands and colder temperatures than farmers farther to the west closer to the Ohio or Virginia borders, where the land is rolling and somewhat more productive.[116] Initial settlers were met with a heavily forested terrain throughout. Buck notes that the forest was so omnipresent that the region was practically silent because songbirds had few clearings in which to nest.[117] Northern Erie County lies on a section of the Lake Erie Plain.[118]

The Western Region was obtained by the state in the Purchases of 1768 and 1784[119] and the Erie Triangle Purchase from the federal government (1792). The legislature cut the region's land into counties between 1773 and 1845.[120] Present-day Greene County in the 1750s was the site of the first European agricultural (as opposed to military or trading) settlement.[121] Settlers were primarily of English, Scotch-Irish, and German extraction with each group present throughout the region in varying concentrations.[122] Somerset and Cambria Counties' populations were most heavily of German descent, many of whom had moved from eastern areas of the state.[123] In the counties west of Chestnut Ridge and Laurel Hill and south of the Ohio and Allegheny Rivers, where most early settlement occurred, in-migrants from Virginia and Maryland were in the majority, giving the southwestern corner of the state a heavily Scotch-Irish flavor.[124] Yankee immigrants from New England and western New York populated the extreme northwest portion of the state, mixing with the Scotch-Irish coming from the Great Valley.[125] Prior to 1794, settlement in the Western Region was confined almost exclusively to lands south of the Ohio River and east of the Allegheny. Lands 'beyond' the rivers were settled more densely after the cessation of hostilities with the Indians; the latter initiated by the 'ratification' of previous land sessions following the Battle of Fallen Timbers in Ohio (1794) and the Treaty of Greenville (1795).[126] The wide range of levels of economic development that existed in 1810 is expected, given the wide variety of settlement dates.

The total population of the region in 1810 was 189,000, or 23 per cent of the state's. Over the next fifty years population grew rapidly, although not uniformly either temporally or geographically. It slightly outpaced growth statewide, growing most rapidly (more than 36 per cent per decade) in the 1820s and 1830s. Pittsburgh, the region's main urban hub, grew fastest in the 1830s and 1840s, increasing in population by more than 60 per cent in each of those decades.

Western Pennsylvania contained about a quarter of the state's residents throughout the period.

Within the region, Pittsburgh was dominant and becoming more so. Early in the century its preeminence was based on its strategic location at the forks of the Ohio and its status as provisioner of the Ohio Valley. Later growth was spurred by expanded manufacturing. In 1790, the city could only claim 376 souls, but by 1860 had almost 50,000 residents, 78,000 if Allegheny City, a 'sister' city across the river, is included. Allegheny County, for which Pittsburgh was the seat, increased its share of the Western Region's population from a little more than one-seventh to over one-quarter between 1810 and 1860. Outside of Allegheny County, however, fewer than one in fourteen western Pennsylvanians lived in towns in 1810. This share increased to 17 per cent in 1850, before falling below 13 per cent in 1860. Allegheny County's percentage increased at a similar rate, but already in 1810 over one-third of Allegheny County's residents were urbanites, so that by 1860 more than seven in ten were. While Pittsburgh was growing and becoming a manufacturing town rather than just a trading outpost for western settlement, few other small urban centers emerged. Other than the cities of Pittsburgh and Allegheny City, no single place in western Pennsylvania had more than 10,000 residents in 1860.[127] Outside of Allegheny County only two places, Erie and Mill Creek (twin towns in Erie County) and Hempfield (Westmoreland County), had populations of more than 5000.

Beginning in 1810, Erie County experienced phenomenal growth, although it had no large town at its center.[128] Its average population increase was more than 100 per cent per decade through 1830. Crawford County, just to its south, followed a similar growth trajectory with rapid increases in the 1820s and 1830s but smaller ones later. This was probably a reflection, in both cases, of the early success of Erie as a Great Lakes port connected via the lake to the terminus of the Erie Canal at Buffalo and with easy access to Pittsburgh via turnpike and much later by canal and railroad. All of these transport 'lines' eventually traversed Crawford County. Erie and Crawford were not among the region's most densely populated counties. Erie County had a density only one-quarter of that of Allegheny County, Crawford even less.

Erie and Crawford are the most prominent examples of the tendency in the Western Region for the areas least populated in 1810 to experience the highest rates of population growth thereafter.[129] Counties in the area of oldest settlement, the southwest corner, experienced the slowest rates of population expansion between 1810 and 1860. Population spread across the region in a fashion which tended to equilibrate population densities, so that, with the exception of Allegheny County at the high end and Somerset at the low, the rest of the counties in 1860 had population densities between 40 and 66 psm. Some counties did see rapid population growth due to increased demand for labor. Cambria County grew rapidly throughout this period, consistently exhibiting growth rates above 55 per cent per decade. This was a reflection of the labor demands of the growing transportation industry and the beginning of bituminous coal mining.[130]

Census statistics show the results of both increased market integration and specialization and increased agricultural productivity. Between 1820 and 1840, the percentage of workers employed in agriculture declined slightly, from 79 per cent to 72 per cent, a reduction proportionate to the statewide one. The reduction was most concentrated in Allegheny County where the agricultural work force fell from 63 to 39 per cent. Over the same period, the other counties in the region experienced only a slight diminution in the proportion of agricultural workers. Except for Allegheny County, only Fayette had fewer than two-thirds of its workers in agriculture in 1840.

Throughout the period, the nature of agriculture varied significantly. In 1810, in some of the more remote areas in the north near-subsistence agriculture prevailed. Efforts were directed toward providing food for the family and clearing and improving land.[131] Trade was episodic and involved only a few essential items. Extra foodstuffs, when available, were sold for salt, iron products, and some other household needs.[132] However, in the areas which had been settled longest, especially those along the Monongehela River, a more mature and more specialized agricultural regime prevailed.[133] Only one-third of the farmers were yeoman, and not renting, their lands.[134] A large group of landless agricultural workers already existed. In this more developed area they comprised up to 20 per cent of the work force.[135]

The hilly nature of the terrain and only fair soil quality also induced many farmers in the southwestern part of the state, especially Greene County, to begin specializing in sheep and cattle.[136] Similar conditions, along with short summers, motivated Somerset County farmers to move in the same direction. While in the 1840s the southern part of Mercer County (and what is now Lawrence County) was viewed as good grain land, northern Mercer County had lands suitable for grass and pasturage, as did Crawford and Erie Counties.[137]

Throughout the entire Western Region from 1840 to 1860, per capita swine stocks diminished at a rate similar to the state's average. This was the case in all counties in the region, with reductions as high as 75 per cent.[138] As cheaper hogs and packed pork from the west flooded into Pennsylvania, many farmers succumbed to the competition and moved into other crops or other endeavors. Even with these changes, Reiser notes that, in 1850 in Pittsburgh 'city life had not yet developed to the extent that it was impossible to supply the table needs from one's own garden, or from the surrounding farms.'[139] At that point Pittsburgh was 'not an importer of agricultural products by way of the Pennsylvania Canal but rather a distributor of products gathered from other agricultural areas.'[140]

The other side of this transition can be seen not so much in the per capita milch cow ratios, which stayed relatively stable across the region and the state between 1850 and 1860, but in the level of butter production. Prior to the availability of refrigerated train cars, local farmers had a comparative advantage in butter production, in contrast to swine raising, and they increased their production by more than 50 per cent between 1850 and 1860. Farmers in the Western Region increasingly moved into dairy production as a market niche in which they could still compete.

Even with Allegheny County, the Western Region had the second highest level of home manufacturing in the state from 1840 through 1860.[141] Without Allegheny County, in 1860 the region produced the most home manufactures per capita of any region. This pattern, in combination with declining swine stocks, serves to highlight a characteristic of the Western Region, its ability to move goods (e.g. pork) to urban markets on major transport routes, and its difficulty in moving goods elsewhere in the region.

Transportation routes in the early nineteenth century were not well developed. Wagons did not become the dominant form of transport over the Allegheny Front until the 1790s. Prior to that, occasional pack trains traveled east over the Forbes and Braddock Roads carrying goods with price-to-weight ratios high enough to make the journey profitable.[142] In 1800, most goods involved in long distance trade were sent downstream during the one or two times a year when water levels were high enough to move flatboats on the secondary watercourses.[143] Any farmer could become a trader by building a boat, loading it with surplus wheat, pork and whiskey, and piloting it on spring freshets at least as far as Pittsburgh, and maybe to Natchez or New Orleans.[144] This initial means of marketing crops was confining both in the quantity of goods which could be shipped and in the timing of arrival at market.[145]

The combination of roads and canals developed between 1800 and the 1840s augmented an extensive network of natural waterways. The Monongehela, Youghigheny, lower Allegheny and Ohio Rivers served as the main arteries of water transportation in the southern section of the region. The Allegheny and its tributaries were naturally navigable upstream all the way to Waterford in Erie county[146] and served to connect the northern portions of the region with Pittsburgh and intermediate points. However, many of its feeders were only navigable during the spring. Prior to their improvement, or until canals were constructed, they served as a means of moving bulk goods downstream in that rainy season alone.

Improved land transport, although expensive, was available through the southern portion of the region. The Forbes Road, the Braddock Road, and their later respective incarnations as turnpikes along with the National/Cumberland Road all provided routes to the east.[147] In 1804 a turnpike from Waterford to Erie was constructed. This served as an early tie between Lake Erie and the most northerly point of navigability on French Creek, one of the Allegheny River's tributaries. By the 1840s, Erie was also connected to the east by turnpike via Harrisburg.[148] These routes generally carried manufactured goods from the east, but there was little return traffic except for ginseng, furs, and whiskey. The Western Region could produce little needed in the east that was not produced more cheaply in Philadelphia's hinterland, after accounting for transport costs.[149]

Water-based transport improvement until 1826 was comprised only of a series of stream clearings on the Kiskiminetas, Conemaugh, Monongehela, and Youghigheny Rivers as well as on French Creek. However, in that year, construction on the Western Division of the State Works between Pittsburgh and Johnstown began. A year later work on the French Creek Feeder Canal also started. Both were complete by 1834, by which time the building of the Beaver Division of the State Works had begun. The 1830s and early 1840s saw continued river improvements on the Ohio, the Beaver, the Monongehela, and the Allegheny. Further enhancements to what had been the Beaver Division and the French Creek Feeder of the State Works were completed between 1843 and 1845 by the Erie Canal Company, which had purchased both. This created a 'network' of canals which spanned the western portion of the state from Erie to Beaver, Pittsburgh to Johnstown (Beaver to Pittsburgh traffic traveled directly on the Ohio River), and Pittsburgh to New Geneva (Fayette County). The Pennsylvania system linked up with canals in the Buckeye State via the Ohio-Pennsylvania Canal just west of New Castle.

These routes were augmented by steamboat travel after 1811 which made the shipment of goods into and out of Western Pennsylvania easier and more consistent, particularly upriver. While this traffic was concentrated down the Ohio from Pittsburgh, steamers also operated on the Monongehela and Allegheny Rivers and even some of the smaller tributaries.[150] As with keelboats, steamboat operations were subject to the vagaries of water depth.

In the late 1840s, railroad construction began in earnest in the Western Region. Prior to that, the only railroad operating was a portion of the western end of the Allegheny Portage Railroad. Many railroads had been chartered in the 1840s and some in the 1830s. Only a few saw construction begin before 1850, however. Many followed the watercourses so prominent in the west and either traced the paths of existing canals or displaced canals that were planned but never constructed. Pittsburgh became linked by rail in all directions. The Pennsylvania Railroad followed a more southerly route out of Pittsburgh than the Main Line Canal had, but it joined the path of the canal just east of Blairsville, following the canal and then the original portage railroad. Rail lines toward Wheeling and into Ohio (on the way to Fort Wayne and Chicago) were also planned and at least partially constructed by 1860. Erie and Pittsburgh were not yet connected by rail, but some track had been laid following the Erie Canal Company's route.

Numerous new railroads developed around Pittsburgh with track completed to Connellsville and Uniontown and up the valley of the Allegheny to Kittanning. By 1860 tracks to Butler were being laid. Additionally, lines were built which cut across the region, without necessarily intersecting its largest city. Rail lines from Wheeling, Virginia, to Washington, Pennsylvania, were begun in 1856. The Erie and Northeast Railroad connected Erie with Cleveland and Buffalo. Around Pittsburgh and Sharon, as well as in other smaller towns, a series of small railroad lines (in many cases only a few miles of track) were built to connect raw material sources with manufacturing facilities, canals, or other rail lines.

A vast and increasingly dense transportation network, valuable and accessible mineral resources, and a growing population eager to purchase land all led to rapidly rising real estate prices in the Western Region of the state. If Allegheny County is included, the Western Region had the largest gain in land values of any region (341 per cent). Even without Allegheny County, where land values increased by 885 per cent over the period, the region experienced a 268 per cent gain between 1815 and 1845. Land prices in Allegheny County increased much more rapidly than did population.

Conclusion

Men and women living in antebellum Pennsylvania experienced a wide variety of changes in the organization of economic life. Agricultural employment fell from 68 per cent in 1820 to 37 per cent in 1860.[151] The population increasingly lived in cities and worked in jobs that did not exist at the beginning of the period. By 1860 the state was a veritable checkerboard, crisscrossed by transportation systems of all types. The trip from Philadelphia to Pittsburgh took weeks in 1800, but only a day via the Pennsylvania Railroad.[152] Primary products and manufactured goods moved as easily as people, and the days of the pack train were gone. Transportation improvements increasingly provided a more consistent and faster means of supplying Pennsylvania's cities with foodstuffs. Interregional parts of this system exposed Pennsylvania, and all the east, to Midwestern competition in grain and pork. Unable to compete with these more efficiently produced goods, Pennsylvania farmers, like those throughout the east,[153] eventually had to move out of the production of small grains and swine and reconfigure their production toward a mix of dairying, fruits and vegetables.[154] This search for comparative advantage, although a reluctant one on the part of many farmers,[155] can be seen in the shifting nature of livestock holdings, market garden crops, and home manufacturing production as captured in the censuses of 1840, 1850, and 1860.

Families produced less and less of what they consumed and instead became enmeshed in the market for necessities as well as luxuries. As early as 1840, homespun was no longer produced, even in the most remote localities.[156] Not only did the proportion of the work force engaged in agriculture decline, but farmers increasingly produced a more limited range of crops. The extent and timing of the changes were not uniform across the state. Philadelphia and its near hinterland had experienced some of these developments late in the eighteenth century, while portions of the Allegheny Forest Region were still extremely isolated as the period ended.

Developments in Pennsylvania were the result of multiple processes occurring simultaneously across the state. While some lands had been occupied by Europeans since the mid-1600s, much of the land in 1800 had been under their control for less than fifty years. Some regions would not be settled for three more decades. Settlement and land clearing were initial concerns and so too was the establishment of effective transportation between rural communities and their urban hubs. This process of local market connection and intra-regional linkage was occurring at the same time as interregional ties were being developed and interregional agricultural specialization was taking place.[157] Since the first process began even before canal and railroad technology was available,[158] the two processes were reciprocally influential in shaping the nature and direction of agricultural market development in Pennsylvania. The next chapter will evaluate the relationship between these variations in the level of economic development and the biological well-being of the population, investigating the working hypothesis that remoteness from markets provided some net nutritional advantages to the self-sufficient families of Pennsylvania.

Notes

1 Raymond E. Murphy and Marion Murphy, *Pennsylvania: A Regional Geography* (Harrisburg: The Pennsylvania Book Service, 1937), 113.

2 John William Florin, *The Advance of Frontier Settlement in Pennsylvania, 1638-1850: A Geographic Interpretation* (University Park, PA: Pennsylvania State University, 1977), 9-10. Florin's definition for 'settlement' was the date of the first permanent settlement in a minor civil division (townships, towns, boroughs). He obtained his data from county histories.

3 Murphy and Murphy, *Regional Geography*, 67; Stevenson Whitcomb Fletcher, *Pennsylvania Agriculture and Country Life, 1640-1840* (Harrisburg: Pennsylvania Historical and Museum Commission, 1950), 5; Florin, *Frontier Settlement*, 28.

4 George Rogers Taylor, *The Transportation Revolution, 1815-1860*, Vol. 4, *The Economic History of the United States* (New York: Rinehart and Company, Inc., 1951), 158.

5 Susan P. Lee and Peter Passell, *A New Economic View of American History* (New York: W.W. Norton and Company, 1979), 64. This was not simply the result of transportation difficulties however, but also the inability of western Pennsylvanians, at that stage of development, to produce goods for Philadelphia and other eastern seaboard communities which residents of these areas could not obtain more cheaply, after factoring in transportation costs, from their own hinterlands. Solon J. Buck and Elizabeth H. Buck, *The Planting of Civilization in Western Pennsylvania* (Pittsburgh: University of Pittsburgh Press, 1939), 291-292.

6 Diane Lindstrom, *Economic Development in the Philadelphia Region, 1810-1850* (New York: Columbia University Press, 1978), 18-19.

7 Donna Andriot, *Population Abstract of the United States* (McLean, VA: Documents Index Inc., 1993), 272, 295, 304, 461, 570. While Andriot places Philadelphia second, a review of the 1800 census indicates that Philadelphia, per se, is smaller than New York City per se, but the latter's home county population is smaller than that of Philadelphia County. United States, *Returns of The Whole Number of Persons within the Several Districts of the United States According to 'An Act Providing for the Second Census...*,' Second Decennial Census, 1800 (Washington: Duane, 1801).

8 Lindstrom, *Economic Development*, 40-44.

9 This is an area east of Kittatinny Ridge/Blue Mountain or an imaginary line drawn from just west of Allentown through Harrisburg to Chambersburg. Murphy and Murphy, *Regional Geography*, 98 and 108.

10 Stevenson Whitcomb Fletcher, *Pennsylvania Agriculture and Country Life: 1840-1940* (Harrisburg: Pennsylvania Historical and Museum Commission, 1955), 1.

11 Florin's maps indicate that by 1810 less than 50 per cent of the Allegheny Forest Region's minor civil divisions had seen the establishment of initial settlements. In 1830 a significant fraction of the region still exhibited that pattern. Even areas as close to Philadelphia as Cumberland and Adams Counties were described in this period as being peopled by 'scattered farmers' with few small towns. Florin, *Frontier Settlement*,

see Figures 6-9, 11, 12, 14-24 on pages 34, 39, 40, 42, 46, 49, 53, 59, 60, 66, 74, 75, 80, 83-86.; *History of Cumberland and Adams Counties, Pennsylvania* (Chicago: Warner, Beers & Co., 1886), 109.

12 Yujiro Hayami and Vernon W. Ruttan, *Agricultural Development: An International Perspective*, rev. ed (Baltimore: Johns Hopkins University Press, 1985), 69-71. Ethnic composition of the farmers was an important variable in that regard with Scotch-Irish farmers generally being seen as more likely to run the land down and move on than German farmers who tended to invest heavily in fertility maintenance and improvement. Philip S. Klein and Ari Hoogenboom, *A History of Pennsylvania*, 2nd ed. (University Park, PA: Pennsylvania State University, 1980), 191-193.

13 Changes in the nature of data collected by the census takers prevent a further direct comparison with 1860 figures. The 36.2 per cent figure was calculated by classifying individual occupations in the 1860 census into a manufacturing category.

14 The urban population is defined as those living in towns or cities of more than 2500 inhabitants. The 2500 cut-off figure is one not based on the importance of a city/town of that size but on later Census Office convention. During the antebellum period urban places of smaller size would have been important trading centers and points around which economic production was organized.

15 Fletcher notes that, as late as 1930, 25 per cent of the farms in Clearfield County were still self-sufficient as defined by the census (50 per cent or more of production consumed on the farm itself). 'They are most common on rough and poor land, especially in the coal regions and in areas remote from markets.' Fletcher, *Country Life, 1840-1940*, 8.

16 Obviously, slave based plantation agriculture was an exception.

17 The following list will provide some idea of the situation. *Agriculture, Its Early History and Development in Pennsylvania, and its Present Status* (Harrisburg: Bureau of Industrial Statistics, 1875); Frederick Moore Binder, *Coal Age Empire: Pennsylvania Coal and its Utilization to 1860* (Harrisburg: Pennsylvania Historical and Museum Commission, 1974); Buck and Buck, *Planting of Civilization*; Kuan-I Chen, 'Agricultural Production in Pennsylvania, 1840-1950' (Unpublished Ph.D. Dissertation, Pennsylvania State University, 1954); Fletcher, *Country Life, 1640-1840*; Louis C. Hunter, *Factors in the Early Pittsburgh Iron Industry* (Cambridge, MA: Harvard University Press, 1932); Louis C. Hunter, 'Influence of the Market upon Techniques in the Iron Industry in Western Pennsylvania up to 1860,' *Journal of Economic and Business History* 1 (1929): 241-281; H. F. James, *Agricultural Industry of Southeastern Pennsylvania: A Study in Economic Geography* (Ph.D. dissertation, University of Pennsylvania, 1927); Pennsylvania Department of Agriculture, 'Agriculture in Pennsylvania: A Study of Trends, County and State Since 1840,' by George Fiske Johnson, *General Bulletin* No. 484 (Harrisburg: Department of Agriculture, 1929); Chester Lloyd Jones, *The Economic History of the Anthracite-Tidewater Canals* (Philadelphia: University of Pennsylvania Press, 1908); Theodore B. Klein, *The Canals of Pennsylvania and the System of Internal Improvements* (Harrisburg: William Stanley Ray, State Printer, 1901); James T. Lemon, *The Best Poor Man's Country: A Geographical Study of Early Southeastern Pennsylvania* (New York: W.W. Norton & Co., Inc., 1972); Diane Lindstrom, *Economic Development in the Philadelphia Region, 1810-1850* (New York: Columbia University Press, 1978); James W. Livingood, *The Philadelphia-Baltimore Trade Rivalry, 1780-1860* (Harrisburg: Pennsylvania History and Museum Commission, 1947); Paul F. Paskoff,

Industrial Evolution: Organization, Structure and Growth of the Pennsylvania Iron Industry, 1750-1860 (Baltimore and London: Johns Hopkins University Press, 1983); Thomas Peter Pavick, 'An Economic History of Southwestern Pennsylvania, 1850-1860' (Unpublished Ph.D. dissertation, West Virginia University, 1973); Catherine Elizabeth Reiser, *Pittsburgh's Commercial Development, 1800-1850* (Harrisburg: Pennsylvania Historical and Museum Commission, 1951); Donald F. Schaefer, 'A Quantitative Description and Analysis of the Growth of the Pennsylvania Anthracite Coal Industry, 1820 to 1865' (Ph.D. dissertation, University of North Carolina, 1967); Leighton P. Stradley, *Early Financial and Economic History of Pennsylvania* (New York: Commerce Clearing House, Inc., 1942); William A. Sullivan, *The Industrial Worker in Pennsylvania, 1800-1840* (Harrisburg: Pennsylvania Historical and Museum Commission, 1955).

18 This 'indicator' will be represented by several data series including agricultural employment proportions, the per capita level of swine and milch cow stocks, the per capita level of dairy (butter and cheese) production, and the per capita value of home manufactures, market gardening, and orchard production.

19 Measuring the extent to which a state or region was producing goods for agricultural markets is difficult for a time period in which production and distribution records are sketchy, at best. Less direct measures must be used. U.S. Census data, the best figures available, come with their own difficulties. The definitions of various categories of data changed between the decennial collections. Long-term series are not available as certain categories of data were not collected continuously. Regardless of this familiar litany of regret, these are the data available and they will be put to their best uses. These shortcomings will require a degree of flexibility in interpretation. Such data generally will be presented on a per capita basis. It should also be noted that primarily it will be the *level* of an indicator or variable which is examined, not their rates of change. In the process of market integration and more differentiated economic activity, the speed at which changes occur might also be influential in stature change. Later continuations of this research agenda should address that issue.

20 Dollar valuations of agricultural goods and lands reported in this chapter have been adjusted to a 1821-25 base year dollar value using Bezanson's price indices for Philadelphia for this period. A. H. Cole, *Wholesale Commodity Prices in the United States, 1700-1861* (Cambridge: Harvard University Press, 1938; reprint, New York: Johnson Reprint Co., 1969), 142-143.

21 This transportation improvement summary is derived from the maps generated for 1800 (#1), 1815 (#2), 1830 (#3), 1845 (#4), and 1860 (#5) by Christopher T. Baer, *Canals and Railroads of the Mid-Atlantic States, 1800-1860* (Wilmington, DE: Regional Economic History Research Center, Eleutherian Mills-Hagley Foundation, 1981.) A transparent overlay map containing county and regional boundaries was constructed and used to determine in which regions various developments took place.

22 The U.S. Census, beginning in the early twentieth century, defined urban areas as settlements with over 2500 residents. Early census reports had a higher cut-off. U.S. Bureau of the Census, *Historical Statistics of the United States, Colonial Times to 1970, Part 1* (Washington, D.C.: G.P.O., 1975), 2.

23 It may be that, as urban places grow, it is not only the size of the place which matters but the rate at which it is growing. Institutions, including agricultural markets, take time to develop. During the transition their full benefits may not materialize.

24 Lee A. Craig, Raymond B. Palmquist, and Thomas Weiss, 'Transportation Improvements and Land Values in the Antebellum United States: A Hedonic Approach,' Manuscript #95-2-5 (North Carolina State University, 1997), 3.

25 Lebergott notes similar effects in the eighteenth century as well, with land having water transport access 50 per cent more costly than land without. Stanley Lebergott, *The Americans: An Economic Record* (New York: W.W. Norton and Co., 1984), 93.

26 This was especially true when members of local communities had complementary by-employments.

27 Inasmuch as land valuations are the result of both personal expectation and political maneuvering, there is a degree of subjectivity to them. However, they provide an indication of the extent to which particular locales were viewed as worthy of economic investment.

28 In the early nineteenth century the Commonwealth of Pennsylvania, for purposes of assessing taxes, had the various counties provide returns of mean real estate valuations. The valuations of 1815 and 1845 were particularly useful in that a legislative committee in each case adjusted the valuations to account for under-reporting by some counties. Pennsylvania Senate, 'Report of the Board of Revenue Commissioners, transmitted to the Governor, in pursuance of an act of the 29th of April 1844,' *Journal of the Senate*, 1845, Vol. II, Document 53 (Harrisburg: J. M. G. Lescure, 1845), 303-320; Pennsylvania Senate, 'Communication from the State Treasurer, enclosing Tables of the Valuation fixed on the Several Counties of the Commonwealth,' by the Board of Revenue Commissioners, *Journal of the Senate*, 1845, Vol. II, Document 54 (Harrisburg: J. M. G. Lescure, 1845), 321-326; 'An Abstract of the Returns made by the Commissioners of the City of Philadelphia and the Several Counties of the Commonwealth of Pennsylvania,' *Hazard's Register* (July 1828): 12-13.

29 If the data were available for even smaller political sub-divisions within counties, it would probably show considerable intra-county variation as well.

30 The regional division of Pennsylvania used in this study is drawn essentially from the work of Murphy and Murphy as modified by Dykstra. Dykstra used the Murphys' regional breakdown from 1840, which was based on physical geography and economic development, and modified the regional division to match county political borders in order to link economic and political data. Murphy and Murphy, *Regional Geography*, 98-112; Anne Dykstra, 'Region, Economy and Party: The Roots of Policy Formation in Pennsylvania' (Unpublished Ph.D. dissertation, University of Pittsburgh, 1988), 22-84. While regions with natural boundaries in some cases would be more appropriate as a basis for describing an individual's environment during the growth years, few nineteenth-century political entities kept records by regions defined by natural boundaries unless they were associated with political ones.

31 Most analysis will focus on those born between 1810 and 1845.

32 Throughout this chapter, the number of counties referred to in a region pertains to the number which existed in 1860. Between 1800 and 1860 the number of counties in Pennsylvania increased from 35 to 66. Klein, *History of Pennsylvania*, 585.

33 Portions of Dauphin and Lebanon counties 'protrude' south of these mountains, but will be considered as part of the Anthracite Region for purposes of this analysis.

34 Murphy and Murphy, *Regional Geography*, 18-26.

35 Murphy and Murphy, *Regional Geography*, 26-27.

36 Klein and Hoogenboom, *History of Pennsylvania*, 9-14.

37 Klein and Hoogenboom, *History of Pennsylvania*, 25.

38 Klein and Hoogenboom, *History of Pennsylvania*, 41.
39 Klein and Hoogenboom, *History of Pennsylvania*, 44-45.
40 Primary among these suburbs, all eventually annexed into the city, were the Northern Liberties, Spring Garden, Southwark, Kensington, and Moyamensing.
41 Unless otherwise noted, population figures, occupational proportions, agricultural and manufacturing production totals are drawn from the decennial U.S. Censuses from the date noted. Per capita values were calculated from these figures and are found in Tables 4.4 through 4.16. The sources of the data were the printed volumes of the various censuses as well as an ICPSR data file containing selected decennial census information. United States, *Returns of The Whole Number of Persons within the Several Districts of the United States According to 'An Act Providing for the Second Census...,'* Second Decennial Census, 1800 (Washington: Duane, 1801); United States Treasury Department, *Aggregate Amount of each description of persons within the United States of America and the Territories thereof, agreeably to actual enumeration made according to law in the Year 1810*, Third Decennial Census, 1810 (Washington, 1811); United States Census Office, *Census for 1820*, Fourth Decennial Census, 1820 (Washington: Gales and Seaton, 1821); United States Census Office, *Fifth Census; or, Enumeration of the Inhabitants of the United States, 1830*, Fifth Decennial Census, 1830 (Washington: Duff Green, 1832); United States, *Compendium of the Enumeration of the Inhabitants and Statistics of the United States as obtained at the Department of State from the returns of the Sixth Census*, Sixth Decennial Census, 1840 (Washington: Thomas Allen, 1841); United States, *The Seventh Census of the United States: 1850*, Seventh Decennial Census, 1850 (Washington: Robert Armstrong, 1853); United States, *Population of the United States in 1860; Compiled from the Original Returns of the Eighth Census*, Eighth Decennial Census, 1860 (Washington: G.P.O., 1864); United States, *Agriculture of the United States in 1860; Compiled from the Original Returns of the Eighth Census*, Eighth Decennial Census, 1860 (Washington: G.P.O., 1864); Inter-University Consortium for Political and Social Research, *Historical Demographic, Economic and Social Data: The United States, 1790-1970* [computer file], ICPSR Data Set 0003 (Ann Arbor: ICPSR [producer and distributor], 1992).
42 Lemon, *Best Poor Man's Country*, 216. This statement applied in 1790 only to the immediate vicinity of Philadelphia where dairying, truck farming, and stock fattening were directed to the metropolis.
43 Growth rates here, as through the rest of this work, refer to inter-decadal rates based on the U.S. Censuses.
44 These and all occupational proportion summaries are based on the census reports. It should be noted that, with these as with so much census data, the results rely on the statements of the enumerated and their perception of their employment. Sectional proportions are based on the total number of persons noted as having occupations, not the total population.
45 Lindstrom, *Economic Development*, 140-145.
46 This was most prominent to the southeast in New Jersey rather than in Pennsylvania. Lindstrom, *Economic Development*, Table 5.8.
47 Lindstrom, *Economic Development*, 140. Lindstrom's definition of Philadelphia's hinterland extends beyond the bounds placed on the 'Southeastern Region' defined in this work.
48 Efforts to extract anthracite eventually created additional agricultural market centers other than Philadelphia and disrupted assumptions upon which von Thünen's theory

was based. Johann H. von Thünen, *Von Thünen's Isolated State: An English Edition of Der Isolierte Staat* edited by Peter Hall, translated by Carla M. Wartenberg (Oxford: Pergamon Press Ltd., 1966).

49 Lindstrom, *Economic Development*, 142-145. A contemporary local observer noted in 1843, that 'there is, perhaps, no city in the world which exceeds Philadelphia in the abundance, excellence, and cheapness of the provisions furnished by its markets.' Trego, *Geography of Pennsylvania*, 324.

50 In 1840 swine but not milch cows were reported in the U.S. Census. Milch cow totals first appeared in 1850.

51 In 1850 the region's average orchard production was not pulled down sufficiently by Philadelphia County's value to go below the state average.

52 Fletcher, *Country Life, 1640-1840*, 253-255.

53 Swank, *The Amazing Pennsylvania Canals*, 14, Julius Rubin, 'Canal or Railroad?: Imitation or Innovation in the Response to the Erie Canal in Philadelphia, Baltimore, and Boston,' *Transactions of the American Philosophical Society* 51 (1961).

54 These included the Philadelphia & Trenton, the Philadelphia, Wilmington, & Baltimore, the Cumberland Valley, the Wrightsville, York, & Gettysburg, the Harrisburg, Portsmouth, Mount Joy, & Lancaster, as well as the Philadelphia and Reading. Baer, *Canals and Railroads*, maps 1-5. For a description of the three 'batches' of railroad construction in the early nineteenth century see Lance Davis, Richard Easterlin, and William Parker, ed., *American Economic Growth: An Economist's History of the United States* (New York: Harper and Row Publishers, 1972), 492.

55 Examples would be the East Pennsylvania Railroad, the Northern Central (which also linked Adams County with Baltimore), the Chester Valley Railroad and the West Chester Railroad. Baer, *Canals and Railroads*, maps 1-5.

56 Much development will evolve out of the location of many of the anthracite railroad termini within thc Southeastern Region.

57 As Lindstrom argues, it is regional rather than interregional or foreign trade which was the dominant endeavor for Philadelphia merchants. Lindstrom, *Economic Development*.

58 Land valuations include the value of land and improvements (i.e. real estate). Pennsylvania Senate, 'Report of the Board of Revenue Commissioners,' 303-320; Pennsylvania Senate, 'Communication from the State Treasurer, enclosing Tables of the Valuation,' 321-326; 'An Abstract of the Returns,' *Hazard's Register* (July 1828): 12-13.

59 The comparison for population density is with figures from 1810 and 1850, making the disparity even greater than an 1815-1845 comparison would.

60 It should be noted, however, that land values in these later regions were only one-half to one-twentieth of that in the Southeastern Region. See Table 4.16.

61 Lindstrom, *Economic Development*, 173.

62 At first discovery, this coal was unmarketable. The first load of anthracite taken to Philadelphia could not be sold due to difficulties potential customers had in believing that it would burn. Day, *Historical Collections*, 604.

63 Murphy and Murphy, *Regional Geography*, 18.

64 Florin, *Frontier Settlement*, see Figures 6-9, 11, 12, 14-24 on pages 34, 39, 40, 42, 46, 49, 53, 59, 60, 66, 74, 75, 80, 83-86.

65 Charles B. Trego, *A Geography of Pennsylvania* (Philadelphia: Edward C. Biddle, 1843), 235, 276, 525, 603.
66 Sherman Day, *Historical Collections of the State of Pennsylvania* (Philadelphia: G.W. Gorton, 1843; reprint, Long Island, N.Y.: Ira J. Friedman, Inc., 1969), 447; Trego, *Geography of Pennsylvania*, 346 and 603.
67 Murphy and Murphy, *Regional Geography*, 126.
68 These figures probably understate the extent of 'urban' living which existed in the region. While many mining camps would not have reached the 2500 person threshold, living conditions in these camps were, by most common understandings, urban. I thank Van Beck Hall for pointing this out to me.
69 In 1840 most of this was concentrated near Mauch Chunk, Carbondale, and Pottsville. Murphy and Murphy, *Regional Geography*, 125-126.
70 Trego, *Geography of Pennsylvania*, 206 and 221; Day, *Historical Collections*, 524.
71 Trego, *Geography of Pennsylvania*, 346.
72 Trego, *Geography of Pennsylvania*, 274.
73 Trego, *Geography of Pennsylvania*, 222.
74 This canal, located on the Susquehanna River (the border between the Anthracite and Southeastern Regions), is assumed to have been of benefit to both regions, and thus is mentioned in both regional summaries.
75 For example, the Schuylkill and Susquehanna Railroad which cut between these two rivers via the southern anthracite field enabled coal to be routed in either direction. Baer, *Canals and Railroads*, maps 3 (1830), 4 (1845), and 5 (1860).
76 This would be 'as the crow flies' not necessarily via roads. Baer, *Canals and Railroads*, Map 5 (1860).
77 This may indicate that the land prices of 1815 ($7.6/acre) already anticipated much of the value of the land.
78 This population density estimate is made somewhat ambiguous due to the fact that 1) Carbon County, taken from land in the Southeastern Region, was created and was classified as part of the Anthracite Region and 2) Wyoming County was cut out of Luzerne County and became part of the Northeastern Region. Klein, *History of Pennsylvania*, 586.
79 Florin, *Frontier Settlement*, see Figures 6-9, 11, 12, 14-24 on pages 34, 39, 40, 42, 46, 49, 53, 59, 60, 66, 74, 75, 80, 83-86.
80 This was done both by companies chartered to make turnpikes out of them or via direct state aid. Fletcher, *Country Life, 1640-1840*, 253-255.
81 These included the Bellefonte & Snowshoe Railroad, the Tyrone & Clearfield Railroad, and Pennsylvania Railroad lines from Lock Haven to Tyrone, Hollidaysburg to Altoona, Hollidaysburg to Tyrone and Huntingdon to Tyrone. Baer, *Canals and Railroads*, maps 1-5.
82 Murphy and Murphy, *Regional Geography*, 126.
83 Florin, *Frontier Settlement*, see Figures 6-9, 11, 12, 14-24 on pages 34, 39, 40, 42, 46, 49, 53, 59, 60, 66, 74, 75, 80, 83-86.
84 Day, *Historical Collections*, 676.
85 Murphy and Murphy, *Regional Geography*, 127.
86 Trego, *Geography of Pennsylvania*, 367.
87 Day, *Historical Collections*, 676.
88 Murphy and Murphy, *Regional Geography*, 127.
89 Trego, *Geography of Pennsylvania*, 340.

90 Trego, *Geography of Pennsylvania*, 300.
91 Day, *Historical Collections*, 472; Trego, *Geography of Pennsylvania*, 368.
92 Pike County displays an extremely high, and then extremely low, level of home manufacturing in 1840 and 1850, respectively. It may be that the overall average was unduly influenced by what may have been incorrect or inconsistent data collection.
93 The first seventeen miles of track, from Carbondale to Honesdale, were laid in 1829. No further track was laid until the 1840s. Baer, *Canals and Railroads*, unnumbered appendix.
94 Thomas J. Pressley and William H. Scofield (ed.), *Farm Real Estate Values in the United States, 1850-1959* (Seattle: University of Washington Press, 1959), 26.
95 Florin, *Frontier Settlement*, see Figures 6-9, 11, 12, 14-24 on pages 34, 39, 40, 42, 46, 49, 53, 59, 60, 66, 74, 75, 80, 83-86.
96 The figure for 1810-1820 growth is distorted by changes in land area due to county creation.
97 In 1860 the Western Region without Allegheny County had a higher figure but not the Western Region as a whole.
98 Day, *Historical Collections*, 194.
99 Trego, *Geography of Pennsylvania*, 194 and 353.
100 Trego, *Geography of Pennsylvania*, 353.
101 Murphy and Murphy, *Regional Geography*, 127; Trego, *Geography of Pennsylvania*, 353.
102 The Western Region was the highest in 1850, the Northeastern in 1860. While both dairy goods were produced in all four counties, dairying was concentrated in Bradford and Susquehanna.
103 See Florin, *Frontier Settlement*, 87-97.
104 Day, *Historical Collections*, 380.
105 Florin, *Frontier Settlement*, see Figures 6-9, 11, 12, 14-24 on pages 34, 39, 40, 42, 46, 49, 53, 59, 60, 66, 74, 75, 80, 83-86.
106 Day, *Historical Collections*, 112, 458, 702; Trego, *Geography of Pennsylvania*, 291.
107 Day, *Historical Collections*, 228, 381, 458; Trego, *Geography of Pennsylvania*, 292, 342, 363.
108 See for example Day's extensive quotation from Benjamin Birt, Esq. for a statement about the difficulty of obtaining supplies and foodstuffs. Day, *Historical Collections*, 599.
109 It took fifteen years to connect these two cities. Baer, *Canals and Railroads*, tabular supplements.
110 Roger B. Saylor, *The Railroads of Pennsylvania* (University Park, PA: Penn State University Press, 1964), 123.
111 This line connected with the Sunbury and Erie at Wayne. Baer, *Canals and Railroads*, map 5 (1860).
112 After large scale commercial extraction of oil began in 1859, land prices in at least one Allegheny Forest county rose rapidly.
113 Fifteen counties made up the western region in 1860 after the creation of Lawrence County in 1845. Until then only fourteen counties existed in this region. It should also be noted that the region 'lost' some territory when, in 1839, Clarion County was created, partially from lands previously part of Armstrong County. Klein, *History of Pennsylvania*, 585-586.
114 Murphy and Murphy, *Regional Geography*, 34-35.

115 Murphy and Murphy, *Regional Geography*, 34.
116 Florin, *Frontier Settlement*, 29. See his Figure 4. Day, *Historical Collections*, 178-179 and 615-616.
117 Buck and Buck, *Planting of Civilization*, 10.
118 Murphy and Murphy, *Regional Geography*, 18.
119 In the two Treaties of Fort Stanwix (1768 and 1784) the natives were forced to cede land to the Pennsylvanians. Buck and Buck, *Planting of Civilization*, 114 and 200.
120 Klein, *History of Pennsylvania*, 586. All but Lawrence County was created by 1804.
121 Buck and Buck, *Planting of Civilization*, 139.
122 There has been some dispute within the last decade over the proportions of the various ethnic groups which settled in the region, although not about the various groups which were present. See Harper for a description of this clash over naming classification methodology. R. Eugene Harper. *The Transformation of Western Pennsylvania: 1770-1800* (Pittsburgh: University of Pittsburgh Press, 1991), 5-7.
123 Buck and Buck, *Planting of Civilization*, 222.
124 Florin, *Frontier Settlement*, 67.
125 Buck and Buck, *Planting of Civilization*, 224; Day, *Historical Collections*, 173.
126 Buck and Buck, *Planting of Civilization*, 204-206.
127 Erie came closest with 9419. The town of Mill Creek, part of a small urban agglomeration around Presque Isle, was a close neighbor to Erie and, if viewed together, like Pittsburgh and Allegheny City would have had a combined population in 1860 of 14,489.
128 The town of Erie did not even have more than 2500 residents recorded in a census until 1840.
129 Allegheny County is an exception. Pittsburgh attracted great numbers of individuals during the period of heavy immigration in the 1830s and 1840s.
130 Day, *Historical Collections*, 178-179; Trego, *Geography of Pennsylvania*, 205.
131 Buck and Buck, *Planting of Civilization*, 288-290.
132 Murphy and Murphy, *Regional Geography*, 105
133 Buck and Buck, *Planting of Civilization*, 288-290.
134 Harper, *Transformation of Western Pennsylvania*, 172-73.
135 Harper, *Transformation of Western Pennsylvania*, 58.
136 Murphy and Murphy, *Regional Geography*, 131. Murphy and Murphy go so far as to describe the area surrounding Allegheny County as the 'Western Livestock Farming Region.' Day, *Historical Collections*, 358.
137 Day, *Historical Collections*, 461.
138 The per capita hog stock reductions across counties were about proportional, so that intraregional rankings changed little.
139 Reiser, *Commercial Development*, 100.
140 Reiser, *Commercial Development*, 101.
141 In the 1850 census the Allegheny Forest and Western Regions 'tied' for second place with $0.80 and $0.79 per capita.
142 Buck and Buck, *Planting of Civilization*, pp. 230-231; Catherine Elizabeth Reiser, *Pittsburgh's Commercial Development, 1800-1850* (Harrisburg: Pennsylvania Historical and Museum Commission, 1951), 70.
143 Erik F. Haites, James Mak, Gary M. Walton, *Western River Transportation: The Era of Early Internal Development, 1810-1860* (Baltimore: Johns Hopkins University Press, 1975), 14.

144 Reiser, *Pittsburgh's Commercial Development*, 177.
145 Men who made these arduous journeys often faced glutted markets and low prices. Fletcher, *Country Life, 1640-1840*, 288.
146 Baer, *Canals and Railroads*, Map 1 (1815).
147 Rates were high, $5 per hundredweight for Philadelphia to Pittsburgh cartage in the early 1800s. Buck and Buck, *Planting of Civilization*, p. 240; Fletcher notes a $3 per barrel charge for the same journey. *Country Life, 1640-1840*, 262.
148 Trego, *Geography of Pennsylvania*, p. 381.
149 Buck and Buck, *Planting of Civilization*, 291-292.
150 The Monongehela was navigable for sixty miles upriver from Pittsburgh, the Allegheny 200 miles. Fletcher, *Country Life, 1640-1840*, pp. 242-243.
151 This figure for 1860 was calculated from the state aggregate occupational distribution published in the compendium. County level figures are not available in published form. United States, *Population of the United States in 1860; Compiled from the Original Returns of the Eighth Census*, Eighth Decennial Census, 1860 (Washington: G.P.O., 1864). Agricultural employment was calculated by summing the total number of workers in agricultural jobs in the 1860 Census and adding to that total 59.5 per cent of those workers who simply identified themselves as laborers. Agricultural job classification was based upon the detailed listing of 'agricultural' jobs in the 1870 Census. Fifty-nine and one-half per cent is the proportion of the population which lived in rural areas around the state in 1860.
152 Buck and Buck, *Planting of Civilization*, p. 240; Fletcher, *Country Life, 1640-1840*, 262.
153 Lee and Passell, *New Economic View*, 134-135.
154 After 1810 swine were driven east into Pennsylvania from Ohio and Indiana. Fletcher, *Country Life, 1640-1840*, 190-191.
155 Fletcher notes the reluctance of many farmers to move out of general farming into more specialized production. Fletcher, *Country Life, 1840-1940*, 98.
156 Fletcher, *Country Life, 1640-1840*, 427.
157 The growth of interregional markets for pork and wheat products is the prime example. Pennsylvania's swine levels per capita peaked in 1840 and fell thereafter as a result of this development. Fletcher, *Country Life, 1840-1940*, 261.
158 This was not the case in areas farther west in which the improved transportation technology existed at the time of settlement.

Chapter 5

Variation and Trends in the Stature of Antebellum Pennsylvanians

> The tendency has been to employ real wages not just as a measure (or even as the principal measure) of the standard of living but sometimes to convert it into a synonym for the standard of living.
>
> The point is not that real wage measures should be discarded ... We may be able to obtain a deeper understanding of the changing standard of living of workers, develop a subtler appreciation of the manifold dimensions of the phenomenon, if the information embodied in both real wage indexes and measures of per capita income is reviewed in the light of the information contained in anthropometric measures. [1]

Introduction

The results of economic change are not always uniformly positive across the spectrum of economic actors nor across all aspects of human well-being. Development, while increasing total output and the level of output per capita, seldom results in an equal distribution of income or other material benefits. Similarly, the biological results of economic development and related social changes are not necessarily equally distributed.

Antebellum Pennsylvanians experienced the often wrenching transition from a rural agricultural society to one increasingly urban and industrial. Material welfare was affected, but as this chapter's description of height levels and height trends for the native-born male population[2] will show, so was physical well-being. A description of the data samples upon which this work is based begins this chapter. Having identified the sources of these data and the samples which were drawn, the analysis will proceed in three steps. An initial review will briefly examine the data from the perspective of the Civil War military, providing a portrait of the Pennsylvanians who fought in the War of the Rebellion. Height variation across the personal characteristics of age, occupation, and migrant status will individualize the picture of the physical well-being of early nineteenth-century Pennsylvania men. The heights of these men will then be placed in a national and international context to evaluate this sample's congruence with earlier anthropometric research. Occupational and temporal patterns of stature will be identified and regression analysis used to verify that these patterns are not simply artifacts of the sample's composition.[3] Lastly, the data will be evaluated in light of regional and county level economic characteristics. In particular, the relationship between stature and indicators of market involvement and urbanization will be assessed.

Sample Construction

The height and personal data for individual soldiers were drawn from the regimental and company descriptive books[4] of Pennsylvania units which served the Union Army during the U.S. Civil War.[5] As described more fully in the Appendix, two samples were extracted from these documents. A statewide sample was constructed in order to assess stature trends across Pennsylvania and provide a context for a second geographically smaller regional sample. This second sample was drawn from the same sources, but was limited to men from units raised in fifteen 'western' counties (Tables 4.1 and 4.2, Figures 4.1 and 4.2).

The statewide sample includes 11,953 observations of men born in Pennsylvania and enlisted in her Civil War regiments.[6] Of these, 2330 are from the Union Army sample collected as part of Robert Fogel's Nutrition and Mortality project.[7] The western sample contains 7357 observations. As Chapter Three described, the western region of the state was settled relatively late by persons of European descent, had a much lower population density, and was much less economically developed in the antebellum period than were the southeastern portions of the state. Set within the larger statewide context, this western sample enables an examination of trends in physical stature at a very early stage in the process of market integration, yet with sufficient observations to make refined statistical analysis possible.

Much of the later analysis within this chapter will be based upon a soldier's county of birth. This is done under the biologically supported assumption that net nutritional conditions in the first years of life are of great importance in determining final height.[8] While geographic proportionality was obtained relative to the units of enlistment which were drawn for inclusion into the sample(s), simply because a company was primarily raised from a particular county does not mean that all the men in that unit were necessarily born there. This resulted in a certain amount of randomness in the final breakdown of birthplaces and a distribution of birthplaces which does not exactly match the regional population in 1860.[9] Randomness in this regard is increased because although each company had a primary recruitment county many units also contained significant numbers of men from other, often distant, regions of the state. As a consequence, neither the distribution of birthplaces nor of residence in the sample matches exactly the regional population in 1860.[10] (Table 5.1) While many non-Pennsylvania-born men were found in the various regiments, only the Pennsylvania-born were included in

Table 5.1 State Regional Population Proportions in 1860 and Sample Regional Population Proportions

	Proportion of State's 1860 Population by Residence	Proportion of Statewide Sample by Birth Place	Proportion of Statewide Sample by Enlistment Place
Southeastern Region			
with Philadelphia Co.	44.3%	34.0%	32.6%
without Philadelphia Co.	24.8	24.6	20.5
Philadelphia Co.	19.5	9.3	12.1
Anthracite Region	11.9	13.0	22.5
Pocono Region	1.9	0.7	0.2
Northeastern Region	4.4	5.6	5.7
Ridge and Valley Region	7.0	15.8	9.5
Allegheny Forest Region	6.7	5.0	4.9
Western Region			
with Allegheny County	23.9	25.9	24.5
without Allegheny County	17.7	21.3	17.0
Allegheny County alone	6.2	4.7	7.5

either sample. Initial reviews of the data will proceed using these two, relatively geographically proportional, samples. Later regression-based analysis will use data sets constructed by merging all or portions of these samples.

The use of data originating in military personnel records raises the question of the extent to which the men for whom data was recorded were subject to height minima or maxima. Enlistment requirements varied before the Civil War with several different height minimums imposed on recruits. Limits changed with manpower needs. In order to enlist in the army in 1825, a man had to be at least 18 years old and be 5'6" tall for the infantry, and 5'8" for the artillery.[11] At the time of the Mexican War, the limit was decreased to 5'3".[12] Baxter documents two minimums during the Civil War period, 5'3" in 1861 (down from an antebellum limit of 5'4.5", established in 1854) and 5'0" in 1864. No height minimums existed for drafted men.[13] No orders or regulations specifying different height limits for infantry, cavalry, or artillery units during the War of the Rebellion have been found.[14] However, some later analysis of the sample will omit cavalry, artillery, and Reserve Corps (infantry) units because of their somewhat different height levels, a function in all likelihood of some size preference on the part of those recruiting for these units and the fact that such units were not equally recruited throughout Pennsylvania.[15]

Visual inspection of the height distributions by age, rank, and enlistment year reveal little evidence of left-tail truncation, i.e. the effective imposition of height minimums. Truncated regressions, progressively eliminating from the data set any cases below 5', 5'3", 5'4.5", and 5'6" (Tables A.10 and A.11) show that neither the time trend nor any other pattern in the regression results is affected by removal of the left-tail cases.[16] Analysis will proceed under the assumption that left-tail truncation did not affect the data.[17] The Appendix describes in greater detail efforts taken to evaluate possible left-tail truncation.

Stature Trends

Mean stature levels of Pennsylvania soldiers in these samples are congruent with previous scholarship. Variation within the samples meets expectations based on medical and historical research. The two unadjusted means for the statewide and western samples are 67.49 and 67.96 inches, respectively. The statewide figure is almost identical to the average value of 67.47 presented by Baxter for a sample of 43,798 men from Pennsylvania examined by Union army surgeons (these included rejected men as well).[18] These means include the height of youth who had not yet completed the growth process. The mean value for adult men, age 25-49, is 67.99 inches in the statewide sample and 68.48 inches in the western sample. These are comparable with Margo and Steckel's reported mean value of 68.5 inches for a nationwide sample of 25-49 year old Civil War soldiers. The lower value for the statewide Pennsylvania-born sample is consistent with Baxter's finding that the mean height of soldiers from Pennsylvania units was about two-tenths of an inch below the mean height of Union soldiers generally.[19]

Stature Variation Across Military Components

Enlistment year, enlistment type, and rank As the initial enthusiasm for the war evaporated, the U.S. government instituted a draft and various bounty systems. The social status of the men who entered the military declined and increasingly shorter men were drawn into the regiments. The mean height of adults in the statewide sample who enlisted in 1861 and 1862 was between one-half and three-quarters of an inch above that of men who enlisted in the following three years. The situation in the western sample was similar. Table 5.2 and Figures 5.1, 5.2, and 5.3 show the pattern of height-by-age for each enlistment year and indicate that variation was not simply a function of younger men being enlisted as the war dragged on.

Further examination of the data reveals that men enlisting for the war during 1861 and 1862 were slightly more likely to have indicated that they were professionals, proprietors, and also more likely to provide only a work-site description,[20] than those who enlisted in the following three years. For the statewide sample, 6.3 per cent and 7.6 per cent of enlistees in 1861 and 1862, respectively, indicated themselves as professionals, proprietors, or only indicated a work site. Only 4.7, 4.9, and 5.0 per cent did so in 1863, 1864, and 1865. The western sample provides similar results: 8.1 and 8.5 per cent for 1861 and 1862, only 5.0, 3.9, and 5.0 per cent during the war's last three years. Appendix Tables A.7, A.8, and A.9 present this breakdown by enlistment year. Regression results confirm the direction and approximate extent of stature differences across enlistment years (Tables 5.3 and 5.4).[21]

As noted in the Appendix, determining which members of the sample were drafted, which were substitutes, and which simply joined out of a desire to fight for

Table 5.2 Adult Height by Year of Enlistment (in inches)

Year of Enlistment	Western Sample	Statewide Sample
1861	68.62 (1395)	68.24 (1843)
1862	68.69 (1310)	68.16 (1430)
1863	67.92 (223)	67.58 (481)
1864	68.09 (1317)	67.79 (2930)
1865	68.21 (498)	67.51 (931)

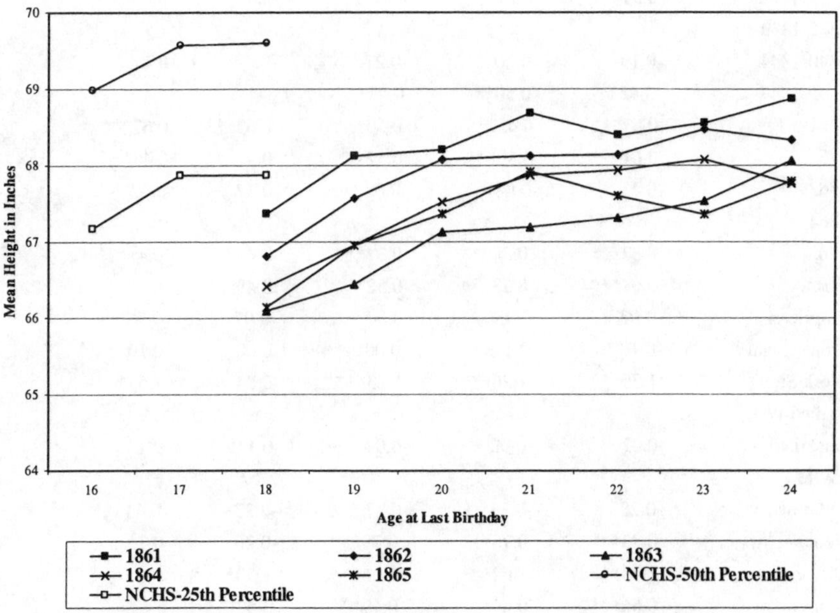

Figure 5.1 Height by Age by Enlistment Year: Merged Sample, Values via Regression

Table 5.3 Determinants of the Height of Soldiers – Western Sample

	(A)	(B)	(C)	(D)	(E)
Constant	67.39***	67.68***	67.76***	67.61***	67.68***
15 & Below	-4.24***	-4.22***	-5.30***		
16	-2.60***	-2.60***	-2.98***		
17	-1.63***	-1.56***	-1.68***		
18	-1.14***	-1.12***	-1.21***		
19	-0.37*	-0.36*	-0.43**		
20	-0.12	-0.11	-0.14		
21	0.20	0.21	0.21		
22	0.07	0.07	0.08		
23	0.09	0.10	0.11		
24	0.29*	0.30*	0.31*		
25-49					
50 & Above	-0.83	-0.89	-0.96		
1815-1819	0.16*	0.48**	0.46*	0.45*	0.42
1820-1824	0.38**	0.38**	0.37**	0.40**	0.46**
1825-1829	0.25*	0.26*	0.25	0.22	0.11
1830-1834	0.51***	0.51***	0.52***	0.50***	0.41**
1835-1839					
1840-1844	-0.19	-0.20	-0.21	-0.02	0.14
1845-1849	-0.42*	-0.50**	-0.48**		
1861	0.57***	0.45***	0.50***	0.62***	0.62***
1862	0.61***	0.50***	0.52***	0.42***	0.48**
1863	-0.12	-0.08	-0.08	0.17	-0.42
1864					
1865	0.37***	0.34***	0.37***	0.45**	0.41*
Farmer	0.62***	0.53***	0.52***	0.49***	0.40**
Proprietor	-0.02	-0.03	0.04	-0.07	0.56
Professional	-0.17	-0.17	-0.00	0.08	0.10
Work Site	1.35***	1.26***	1.23***	0.84	1.57*
Skilled Wrkr					
Unskilled Wrkr	0.02	-0.00	-0.04	0.11	0.13
Unknown	-0.28	-0.26	-0.27	-0.23	-0.44
None	0.83***	0.76***	0.79***	-0.20	0.73
Officer	1.48**	1.62***	1.64**	1.50*	
Non-comm	0.66***	0.64***	0.49***	0.52***	
Private					
Artisan	0.27	0.23	0.07	-0.36	
Musician	-2.44***	-2.45***	-0.15	-0.63	

Table 5.3 (continued)

	(A)	(B)	(C)	(D)	(E)
'Standard'					
Drafted	0.33	0.33	0.29		
Substitute	-0.37	-0.33	-0.35		
Recruit	0.58*	0.49	0.49		
Bounty Rcpnt	-0.31	-0.32	-0.36*		
Infantry					
Cavalry	0.29***	0.32***	0.33***	0.37**	
Artillery	0.45***	0.32***	0.36***	0.56***	
Reserve Inf.	0.51***	0.42**	0.34**	0.50	
Stayer					
Migrant	0.15**	0.13**	0.12*	0.11	0.09
Largest City Size in Enlistment County					
Under 5K					
5K to 10K	-0.42***	-0.44***	-0.37**	-0.49***	
10K to 25K	-0.67***	-0.68***	-0.40	-0.21	
25K+	-0.08	-0.11	-0.01	0.03	
Largest City Size in Birth County					
Under 5K					
5K to 10K-0.16	-0.16	-0.29	-0.45		
10K to 25K	-0.12	-0.12	-0.22	-0.48*	
25K+	-0.74***	-0.71***	-1.13***	-0.98**	
N	6580[a]	6580[b]	6580[c]	2052[d]	1339[e]
Adjusted R^2	0.12	0.13	0.12	0.04	0.04
F	23.9***	22.1***	22.2***	3.6***	2.9***

*** significant at the 0.01 level

** significant at the 0.05 level

*significant at the 0.10 level

[a] Intercept represents a 25-49 year old private, a standard enlistee in 1864, who enlisted in the infantry in the same county in which he was born, who was a skilled worker born between 1835 and 1840.

[b] Intercept represents a 25-49 year old private, a standard enlistee in 1864, who enlisted in the infantry in the same county in which he was born, a county which had no town larger than 5000 persons either at his birth or at the time of enlistment, and who was a skilled worker born between 1835 and 1840.

[c] Intercept represents a 25-49 year old, a standard enlistee in 1864, who enlisted in the infantry in the same county in which he was born, a county which had no town larger than 5000 persons either at his birth or at the time of enlistment, and who was a skilled worker born between 1835 and 1840.

[d] Intercept represents a private, a standard enlistee in 1864, who enlisted in the infantry in the same county in which he was born, a county which had no town larger than 5000 persons either at his birth or at the time of enlistment, and who was a skilled worker born between 1835 and 1840. This regression only included standard enlistees aged 25-49.

[e] Intercept represents a private, a standard enlistee in 1864, who enlisted in the infantry in the same county in which he was born, a county which had no town larger than 5000 persons either at his birth or at the time of enlistment, and who was a skilled worker born between 1835 and 1840. This regression only includes standard enlistees in the infantry, aged 25-49.

Table 5.4 Determinants of the Height of Soldiers – Statewide Sample

	(A)	(B)	(C)	(D)	(E)
Constant	68.25***	68.35***	68.44***	68.55***	68.54***
15 & Below	-6.02***	-6.06***	-6.74***		
16	-3.80***	-3.81***	-4.01***		
17	-1.73***	-1.69***	-1.79***		
18	-1.52***	-1.51***	-1.60***		
19	-0.94***	-0.93***	-0.99***		
20	-0.57***	-0.58***	-0.61***		
21	-0.18	-0.20	-0.21		
22	-0.30**	-0.31**	-0.31**		
23	-0.19	-0.19	-0.19		
24	-0.16	-0.16	-0.15		
25-49					
50 & Above	0.56	0.46	0.44		
1815-1819	-0.11	-0.12	-0.16	0.03	0.09
1820-1824	0.28**	0.27**	0.23*	0.24	0.24
1825-1829	0.23**	0.22**	0.21*	0.20	0.09
1830-1834	0.15	0.16*	0.15	0.19	0.14
1835-1839					
1840-1844	0.04	0.04	0.04	-0.37	-0.52
1845-1849	-0.10	-0.16	-0.13		
1861	0.50***	0.53***	0.54***	0.42***	0.51***
1862	0.15*	0.17**	0.19**	0.09	0.03
1863	-0.24*	-0.20	-0.23	0.19	0.28
1864					
1865	-0.18**	-0.16**	-0.16*	-0.05	0.02
Farmer	0.31***	0.28***	0.26***	0.08	0.23
Proprietor	-0.06	-0.05	-0.01	-0.03	-0.09
Professional	0.40	-0.36	0.43	0.12	-0.05
Work Site	-0.03	-0.04	-0.10	0.02	0.13
Skilled Wrkr					
Unskilled Wrkr	0.01	-0.01	-0.04	0.02	-0.01
Unknown	0.02	0.01	-0.04	0.19	0.39
None	0.55**	0.51**	0.55**	1.64	1.63
Officer	0.30	0.26	0.24	0.27	
Non-comm	0.58***	0.58***	0.49***	0.49***	
Private					
Artisan	-0.49	-0.54	-0.85	-0.20	
Musician	-1.75***	-1.75***	-1.24*	-1.58*	
'Standard'					
Drafted	-0.00	0.09	0.01		

Table 5.4 (continued)

	(A)	(B)	(C)	(D)	(E)
Substitute	-0.18	0.28	0.22		
Recruit	-0.07	-0.04	-0.08		
Bounty Rcpnt	-0.12	-0.06	-0.11		
Infantry					
Cavalry	0.29***	0.31***	0.27***	0.23	
Artillery	0.08	0.11	0.06	0.11	
Reserve Inf.	-0.18	-0.37*	-0.41**	-0.75*	
Stayer					
Migrant	-0.04	-0.08	-0.07*	-0.17	-0.12
Southeast	-1.13***	-1.03***	-1.02***	-0.97***	-1.02***
Anthracite	-1.06***	-1.06***	-1.06***	-0.84***	-0.87***
Pocono	-0.16	-0.16	-0.13	-0.88	-1.39**
Northeast	-0.23**	-0.29**	-0.30***	-0.31	-0.38
Ridge & Valley	-0.31***	-0.38***	-0.35***	-0.45***	-0.50***
Allegheny Forest	-0.28**	-0.32***	-0.28**	-0.11	0.12
West					
Largest City Size in Enlistment County (Under 5K omitted)					
5K to 10K		-0.19***	-0.18**	-0.36**	-0.39**
10K to 25K		-0.10	0.09	-0.04	-0.04
25K+		-0.08	-0.09	-0.13	-0.25
Largest City Size in Birth County (Under 5K omitted)					
5K to 10K		-0.12	-0.13	-0.32*	-0.27
10K to 25K		-0.25*	-0.27*	-0.45	-0.15
25K+		-0.47***	-0.46***	-0.62***	-0.54**
N	9945[a]	9945[b]	9945[c]	2574[d]	2134[e]
Adjusted R^2	0.14	0.15	0.14	0.06	0.07
F	36.3***	33.0***	34.5***	5.6***	5.7***

***significant at the 0.01 level, **significant at the 0.05 level, *significant at the 0.10 level

[a] Intercept represents an 25-49 year old private, a standard enlistee in 1864, who enlisted in the infantry in the same county in which he was born, who was a skilled worker born between 1835 and 1840 in the Western Region

[b] Intercept represents an 25-49 year old private, a standard enlistee in 1864, who enlisted in the infantry in the same county in which he was born, a county which had no town larger than 5000 persons either at his birth or at the time of enlistment, and who was a skilled worker born between 1835 and 1840 in the Western Region.

[c] Intercept represents an 25-49 year old, a standard enlistee in 1864, who enlisted in the infantry in the same county in which he was born, a county which had no town larger than 5000 persons either at his birth or at the time of enlistment, and who was a skilled worker born between 1835 and 1840 in the Western Region.

[d] Intercept represents an private, age 25-49, a standard enlistee in 1864, who enlisted in the infantry in the same county in which he was born, a county which had no town larger than 5000 persons either at his birth or at the time of enlistment, and who was a skilled worker born between 1835 and 1840 in the Western Region. This regression only contains standard enlistees age 25-49.

[e] Intercept represents an 25-49 year old private, a standard enlistee in 1864, who enlisted in the infantry in the same county in which he was born, a county which had no town larger than 5000 persons either at his birth or at the time of enlistment, and who was a skilled worker born between 1835 and 1840 in the Western Region. This regression only contains standard infantry enlistees age 25-49.

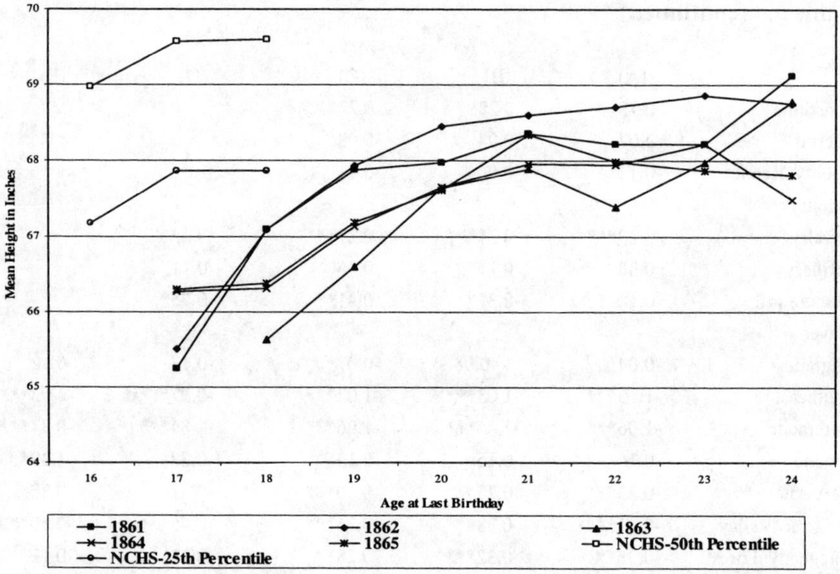

Figure 5.2 Height by Age by Enlistment Year: Western Sample, Civil War Pennsylvanians

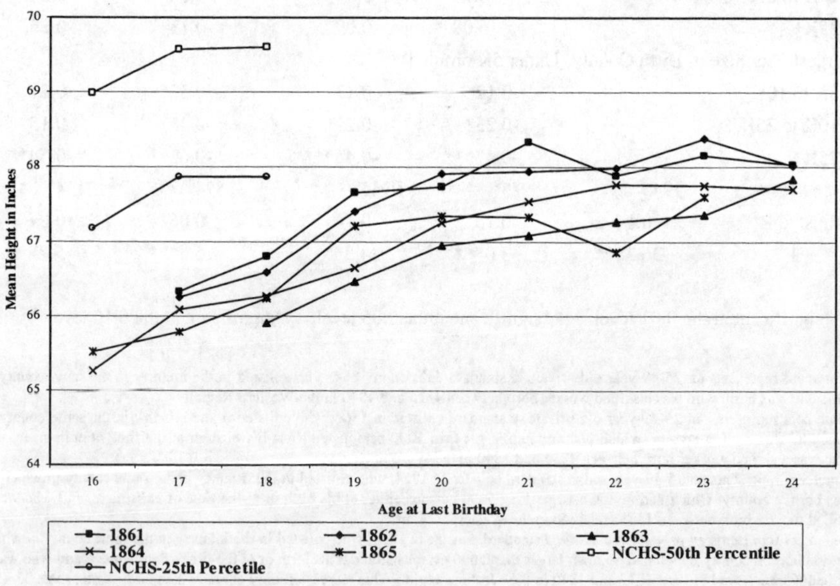

Figure 5.3 Height by Age by Enlistment Year: Statewide Sample, Civil War Pennsylvanians

the Union was an inexact process.[22] It should be assumed that some of the men whose records in the descriptive books did not note their enlistment status[23] may have been either drafted, substitutes, or bounty recipients. Stevens notes with some pride the relatively low 10 per cent figure for Pennsylvania soldiers who were either drafted or substitutes during the conflict.[24] The proportion in these samples is somewhat different: 5.7 per cent in the statewide sample and 2.5 per cent in the west. This is an indication of probable under-reporting. In both the statewide and western samples, the standard enlistees and the draftees have heights which are nearly identical, differing by less than one-tenth of an inch. Bounty recipients in both samples were, on average, between one-quarter and two-thirds of an inch shorter than standard enlistees and/or draftees, while the average substitute in both samples was more than an inch shorter than the standard enlistee. There is great age variation, however, across the enlistment categories. Drafted men in both samples were 4.5 to 5 years older than the average enlistee, while substitutes were 2.5 to 3.5 years younger. Evaluation of these differences indicates that much of the substitutes' height deficit was a function of this age disparity. Few statistically significant stature differences are found between these categories in the multiple regression analyses.

The variation in stature by military rank (see the Appendix for classification details) indicates that height rose in tandem with rank[25] (see Table 5.5). Officers in the statewide sample were on average just under an inch taller than privates, although the difference in the western sample was more than an inch and a half.[26] Sergeants in the statewide sample were, on average, 0.76 inch taller than privates, and the difference in the western sample was 0.53 inch.[27] The election process by which some officers and non-comms were chosen might itself have been influenced by the social power which height tends to confer upon those

Table 5.5 Adult Height by Rank at Enlistment of Pennsylvania-born Civil War Soldiers (in inches)

Rank at Enlistment	Western Sample	Statewide Sample
Captain	69.63 (4)	68.57 (15)
Lieutenant	69.39 (11)	68.33 (30)
Sergeant	69.09 (267)	68.41 (333)
Corporal	68.99 (318)	68.31 (461)
Private	68.33 (4105)	67.88 (5152)
Musician	67.03 (13)	66.64 (26)
Artisan	68.84 (25)	67.44 (27)

Note: The statewide sample, by including the units from Fogel's sample, includes men whose rank is not known. The bulk of them would be privates, however, all Fogel's cases have been omitted from the data in this table.

Table 5.6 Determinants of the Height of Soldiers – Merged Sample

	(A)	(B)	(C)	(D)	(E)
Constant	67.95***	68.09***	68.18***	68.15***	68.15***
15 & Below	-5.08***	-5.09***	-5.93***		
16	-3.38***	-3.38***	-3.63***		
17	-1.70***	-1.66***	-1.77***		
18	-1.37***	-1.37***	-1.45***		
19	-0.71***	-0.71***	-0.77***		
20	-0.39***	-0.39***	-0.42***		
21	-0.03		-0.03		-0.04
22	-0.16		-0.17		-0.16
23	-0.06		-0.06		-0.06
24	0.02		0.03		0.03
25-49					
50 & Above	0.13		0.08		0.06
1815-1819	0.17	0.16	0.13	0.26	0.24
1820-1824	0.34***	0.33***	0.30***	0.34***	0.34**
1825-1829	0.25***	0.25***	0.23***	0.23**	0.11
1830-1834	0.29***	0.30***	0.30***	0.33***	0.24**
1835-1839					
1840-1844	-0.06	-0.05	-0.05	-0.25	-0.31
1845-1849	-0.23*	-0.27*	-0.25*		
1861	0.49***	0.47***	0.49***	0.47***	0.56***
1862	0.33***	0.30***	0.32***	0.24**	0.25**
1863	-0.19*	-0.17	-0.19	0.16	0.20
1864					
1865	0.03	0.03	0.04	0.16	0.21
Farmer	0.40***	0.37***	0.35***	0.24***	0.27**
Proprietor	-0.04	-0.03	0.02	-0.05	0.11
Skilled Wrkr					
Unskilled Wrkr	0.02	-0.00	-0.03	0.05	0.03
Work Site	0.55**	0.53**	0.49**	0.24	0.41
None	0.68***	0.66***	0.69***	0.20	0.96
Professional	0.18	0.17	0.27	0.13	0.00
Unknown	-0.02	-0.03	-0.07	0.13	0.29
Non-comm	0.61***	0.61***		0.49***	0.50***
Officer	0.60*	0.56*		0.57	0.61
Private					
Artisan	-0.10	-0.10		-0.32	-0.22
Musician	-1.98***	-1.99***		-0.97	-1.32*
Unknown	0.12**[1]	0.13**			
'Standard'					
Drafted	0.02	0.12	0.05		
Substitute	0.02	0.13	0.08		
Recruit	0.12	0.09	0.06		
Bounty Rcpnt	-0.21*	-0.16	-0.21*		

[1] Unknown rank signifies a man from Fogel's sample. The positive, and significant coefficient, may be further evidence of the inclusion of non-comms in the sample, as their greater stature would explain the significantly positive coefficient.

Table 5.6 (continued)

	(A)	(B)	(C)	(D)	(E)
Infantry					
Artillery	0.21***	0.22***	0.20**	0.29**	
Reserve Inf.	0.10	0.04	-0.02	-0.10	
Cavalry	0.31***	0.33***	0.31***	0.31***	
Stayer					
Migrant	0.07*	0.04	0.04	0.01	0.01
Southeast	-1.03***	-0.97***	-0.95***	-0.93***	-0.90***
Anthracite	-0.91***	-0.90***	-0.90***	-0.65***	-0.64***
Pocono	-0.16	-0.18	-0.15	-0.58*	-0.69*
Northeast	-0.22**	-0.29***	-0.30***	-0.27	-0.29
Ridge & Valley	-0.23***	-0.29***	-0.27***	-0.30**	-0.29**
Allegheny Forest	-0.06	-0.11	-0.09	-0.04	0.17
West					
Largest City Size in Enlistment County					
Under 5K					
5K to 10K		-0.30***	-0.30***	-0.40***	-0.45***
10K to 25K		-0.02	-0.03	-0.14	-0.06
25K+		-0.07	-0.09	-0.03	-0.13
Largest City Size in Birth County					
Under 5K					
5K to 10K		-0.02	-0.02	-0.11	-0.16
10K to 25K		-0.26***	-0.26***	-0.39**	-0.40*
25K+		-0.36***	-0.36***	-0.55***	-0.51**
N	16525[a]	16525[b]	16525[c]	4626[d]	3473[e]
Adjusted R^2	0.14	0.15	0.14	0.06	0.06
F	60.4***	54.8***	56.8***	9.5***	8.2***

*** significant at the 0.01 level
** significant at the 0.05 level
* significant at the 0.10 level

[a] Intercept represents a 25-49 year old private, a standard enlistee in 1864, who enlisted in the infantry in the same county in which he was born, who was a skilled worker born between 1835 and 1840 in the Western Region.

[b] Intercept represents a 25-49 year old private, a standard enlistee in 1864, who enlisted in the infantry in the same county in which he was born, a county which had no town larger than 5000 persons either at his birth or at the time of enlistment, and who was a skilled worker born between 1835 and 1840 in the Western Region.

[c] Intercept represents a 25-49 year old, a standard enlistee in 1864, who enlisted in the infantry in the same county in which he was born, a county which had no town larger than 5000 persons either at his birth or at the time of enlistment, and who was a skilled worker born between 1835 and 1840 in the Western Region.

[d] Intercept represents a private, age 25-49, a standard enlistee in 1864, who enlisted in the infantry in the same county in which he was born, a county which had no town larger than 5000 persons either at his birth or at the time of enlistment, and who was a skilled worker born between 1835 and 1840 in the Western Region. This regression contains only standard enlistees aged 25-49.

[e] Intercept represents a private, age 25-49, a standard enlistee in 1864, who enlisted in the infantry in the same county in which he was born, a county which had no town larger than 5000 persons either at his birth or at the time of enlistment, and who was a skilled worker born between 1835 and 1840 in the Western Region. This regression contains only standard enlistees aged 25-49 from infantry units.

whose stature is above the norm. From this point of view, rank would be a function of height rather than an input into height variation. As such, it will not be utilized as an independent explanatory variable in later analysis.

Musicians, even after accounting for their young age, were much shorter than privates, generally more than 1.5 inches shorter in the regressions. Artisans (blacksmiths, saddlers, artificers) comprised only a very small percentage of the sample; in the statewide sample, they are somewhat shorter and older than the privates, while in the western sample they are also older but tend to be a bit taller. In neither case is the difference statistically significant, probably due to the small number of observations.

Type of unit There were significant differences among men enlisted in the various types of units: infantry, cavalry, artillery and the Reserve Corps (infantry).[28] Regression analysis of the statewide sample finds that the cavalry were about a third of an inch taller than infantrymen, however, the men in artillery units were not significantly taller than the infantry. In the western sample the differences between the infantry and all three other unit types were positive and statistically significant, ranging from one-quarter to two-thirds of an inch (Tables 5.3 and 5.4). Subsequent analysis will concentrate on the infantry units so as not to complicate interpretation due to variations in the size of the sample in various military units.

Variation in Height by Personal Characteristics

Variation in mean height also existed across the characteristics of age, occupation, and migrant status. Each comparison provides insight into antebellum society.

Age Mean height at various ages, for both the western and the statewide samples, follows the standard pattern described in the biological literature with moderate growth over the late teen years and then a tailing off with final height attainment in the early twenties.[29] The process of growth ended by the age 21 in both the statewide and western samples (Figure 5.1 and Table 5.7). This is not far from the age of growth cessation in modern well-nourished populations, 18 years of age,[30] and is consistent with the level of adult stature in the western sample, a mean height equivalent to the 35th percentile of current American standards. The statewide mean only reached the level of the 25th percentile of modern American standards.[31]

Occupation There are clear occupational differences in height across both the statewide and western samples.[32] Other studies have shown that farmers and rural residents had a substantial advantage in height over most other men during the early stages of industrialization.[33] This pattern is quite evident in these data sets as well (Tables 5.8 and 5.9, Figures 5.4 and 5.5). Such variation did not exist in the colonial period. Changes in the American antebellum social and economic environment seemingly helped to create a stature gap between occupational groupings.

Farmers from both the statewide and western samples were 0.4-0.6 inch taller than their contemporaries who were proprietors, skilled or unskilled workers. They were not the tallest, however, being about a half-inch shorter than professionals. In the western sample, farmers had only a negligible height advantage over professionals: 0.1 inch, but they were more than 0.75 inches shorter than soldiers who noted only a work site as a place of employment. In both samples, skilled and unskilled workers show only a slight stature difference as skilled workers were just over two-tenths of an inch taller.

Regression analysis indicates the height advantage of farmers over both skilled and unskilled workers are robust and consistent across several formulations of the model (Tables 5.3 and 5.4). Few other differences across occupations were statistically significant, either because there were few observations available, or because the variation was of negligible size. The propinquity to nutrients and distance from disease centers seems to have conferred a net nutritional advantage to farmers.[34] The stature advantage of farmers over most other men is also consistent across regions so that, regardless of a farmer's birthplace, he was likely to be taller than most other workers[35] (Figures 5.6, 5.7, and 5.8).

Migrant/non-migrant status Economic and social historians interested in the nature of migration and its effect on economic development have long examined the characteristics of the persons who left one place bound for settlement elsewhere in order to assess the differences between those who migrated and those who stayed behind. Sokoloff and Villaflor's study of French and Indian War and

Table 5.7 Height by Age of Pennsylvania-born Civil War Soldiers and West Point Cadets

Age	Civil War Soldiers		West Point	NCHS-50th
	Western	Statewide	Cadets	Percentile
16	64.93 (30)	64.04 (56)	66.06 (22)	68.98
17	66.03 (113)	65.99 (228)	66.92 (101)	69.57
18	66.70 (1171)	66.36 (1799)	66.84 (74)	69.61
19	67.56 (796)	66.99 (1215)	67.15 (68)	
20	67.92 (665)	67.46 (1016)	67.34 (48)	
21	68.35 (842)	67.82 (1184)	67.84 (27)	
22	68.25 (573)	67.77 (786)		
23	68.38 (480)	67.86 (725)		
24	68.49 (352)	67.86 (593)		
25-49	68.48 (2496)	67.99 (4327)		

Table 5.8 Mean Height and Age by Category – Western Sample

	N	%	Mean Height	SD	Mean Age	SD
Entire Sample	7537	100	67.96	2.54	24.14	6.77
Birth Cohort						
1815-1819	145	1.9	68.89	2.62	44.58	2.75
1820-1824	314	4.2	68.57	2.53	40.84	2.06
1825-1829	441	5.9	68.50	2.42	35.80	1.98
1830-1834	698	9.3	68.68	2.57	30.37	2.07
1835-1839	1577	20.9	68.38	2.41	24.90	1.98
1840-1844	3230	42.9	67.91	2.45	20.35	1.70
1845-1849	1132	15.0	66.56	2.41	18.26	0.92
Enlistment Year						
1861	2217	29.4	68.19	2.57	23.99	6.80
1862	1932	25.6	68.34	2.54	23.74	6.09
1863	298	4.0	67.58	2.55	25.20	6.59
1864	2173	28.8	67.58	2.47	24.58	7.24
1865	917	12.2	67.59	2.41	23.94	6.86
Occupation						
Farmer	2919	38.7	68.24	2.49	23.64	6.62
Proprietor	402	5.3	67.75	2.65	22.97	5.18
Professional	42	0.6	68.11	2.31	27.64	7.06
Work Site Only	50	0.7	69.09	2.17	22.10	5.10
Skilled Worker	2252	29.9	67.87	2.48	25.33	7.05
Unskilled Worker	1675	22.2	67.62	2.64	23.98	6.92
None (Student)	100	1.3	68.11	2.53	19.96	2.42
Unknown	97	1.3	67.47	2.44	22.90	6.24
Rank						
Officer	16	0.2	69.58	1.80	28.00	5.95
Non-comm	691	9.1	68.89	2.44	25.37	6.05
Private	6763	89.7	67.87	2.51	24.01	6.82
Musician	37	0.5	64.56	3.77	19.62	4.00
Artisan	30	0.4	68.59	2.54	28.53	7.96
Enlistment Status						
'Standard'	7132	94.6	67.99	2.54	24.17	6.77
Drafted	83	1.1	67.94	2.46	28.69	7.10
Substitute	97	1.3	66.65	2.27	20.74	5.03
Recruit	63	0.8	67.72	2.86	22.41	5.92
Bounty Recipient	162	2.1	67.35	2.29	23.26	6.80

Table 5.8 (continued)

	N	%	Mean Height	SD	Mean Age	SD
Type of Unit						
Infantry	5131	68.1	67.88	2.53	24.05	6.84
Cavalry	1617	21.5	68.06	2.55	24.03	6.55
Artillery	541	7.2	68.14	2.53	25.62	7.08
Reserve Inf.	248	3.3	68.49	2.48	23.33	5.41
Age						
Under 15	12	0.2	62.73	5.12		
16	30	0.4	64.93	3.15		
17	113	1.5	66.03	2.41		
18	1171	15.5	66.70	2.29		
19	796	10.6	67.56	2.50		
20	665	8.8	67.92	2.33		
21	842	11.2	68.35	2.32		
22	573	7.6	68.25	2.52		
23	480	6.4	68.38	2.42		
24	352	4.7	68.49	2.41		
25-49	2496	33.1	68.48	2.50		
50+	7	0.1	67.89	3.51		
Largest town in county of birth (at closest census)						
< 5,000	6315	83.8	67.98	2.54	24.03	6.82
5,000-10,000	286	3.8	67.79	2.67	29.13	8.23
10,000-25,000	797	10.6	67.99	2.43	23.04	6.97
25,000+	139	1.8	67.24	2.42	25.24	6.87
Regional[a]						
Allegheny Co.	1520	18.9	67.77	2.58	23.04	6.01
Mntn/Mineral	1973	24.6	68.07	2.42	24.35	6.83
Southern Hinterland	2144	26.7	68.30	2.47	24.52	6.80
Northern Hinterland	878	10.9	68.35	2.57	23.93	6.46
Lake Transport	609	7.6	67.61	2.57	23.10	6.05
Isolated Agric.	910	11.3	68.51	2.52	22.82	5.91

[a] This section is based not on the western sample but rather from all observations (statewide and western sample) for men born in the western region. See Table 4.1 for definitions of these regions.

Table 5.9 Mean Height and Age by Category – Statewide Sample

	N	%	Mean Height	SD	Mean Age	SD
Entire Sample	11953	100.0	67.49	2.51	24.52	6.96
Birth Cohort						
1815-1819	198	1.7	68.05	2.26	45.02	3.14
1820-1824	501	4.2	68.15	2.37	41.20	2.11
1825-1829	873	7.3	68.06	2.41	35.97	1.97
1830-1834	1232	10.3	68.08	2.46	30.64	2.08
1835-1839	2339	19.6	67.93	2.42	25.23	2.03
1840-1844	4754	39.8	67.48	2.43	20.58	1.81
1845-1849	2056	17.2	66.21	2.49	18.27	0.85
Enlistment Year						
1861	2936	24.6	67.83	2.65	23.99	6.68
1862	2166	18.1	67.80	2.43	24.10	6.46
1863	640	5.4	67.27	2.44	25.17	6.23
1864	4661	39.0	67.34	2.44	24.92	7.28
1865	1550	13.0	66.97	2.48	24.65	7.29
Occupation						
Farmer	3543	29.6	67.84	2.56	23.85	6.68
Proprietor	564	4.7	67.25	2.51	23.72	6.21
Professional	69	0.6	68.35	2.36	29.25	7.25
Work Site Only	58	0.5	67.92	2.54	26.16	6.96
Skilled Worker	3882	32.5	67.43	2.39	25.66	7.24
Unskilled Worker	3458	28.9	67.22	2.54	24.12	6.93
None (Student)	95	0.8	67.59	2.84	20.04	3.05
Unknown	284	2.4	67.44	2.79	23.72	6.09
Rank						
Officer	46	0.4	68.38	2.07	30.09	6.55
Non-comm	976	8.2	68.27	2.40	25.10	5.81
Private	6741	71.1	67.41	2.50	24.31	7.00
Musician	67	0.6	65.22	3.12	21.39	6.18
Artisan	31	0.3	67.33	1.88	26.61	5.95
Unknown	2331	19.5	67.50	2.51	25.01	7.16
Enlistment Status						
'Standard'	8629	72.2	67.52	2.52	24.30	6.80
Drafted	337	2.8	67.57	2.28	29.33	7.47
Substitute	209	1.7	66.50	2.44	21.50	6.71
Recruit	61	0.5	67.73	2.48	22.66	6.48
Bounty Recipient	387	3.2	67.26	2.66	24.13	6.82
Unknown	2330	19.5	67.51	2.48	25.01	7.16

Table 5.9 (continued)

	N	%	Mean Height	SD	Mean Age	SD
Type of Unit						
Infantry	9800	82.0	67.47	2.52	24.75	7.09
Cavalry	1187	9.9	67.72	2.45	23.29	6.17
Artillery	711	5.9	67.40	2.50	23.81	6.42
Reserve Inf.	255	2.1	67.44	2.61	23.35	5.59
Age						
Under 15	9	0.1	61.36	3.72		
16	56	0.5	64.04	3.97		
17	228	1.9	65.99	2.51		
18	1799	15.1	66.36	2.35		
19	1215	10.2	66.99	2.49		
20	1016	8.5	67.46	2.38		
21	1184	9.9	67.82	2.33		
22	786	6.6	67.77	2.41		
23	725	6.1	67.86	2.52		
24	593	5.0	67.86	2.47		
25-49	4327	36.2	67.99	2.41		
50+	15	0.1	68.45	1.83		
Largest town in county of birth (at previous census)						
< 5,000	9606	80.4	67.54	2.54	24.39	7.08
5,000-10,000	1164	9.7	67.25	2.30	24.92	6.32
10,000-25,000	366	3.1	68.01	2.65	23.84	5.03
25,000+	817	6.8	66.93	2.30	25.80	6.88
By Statewide Regions[a]						
Southeastern						
with Phila Co.	3659	34.0	66.99	2.41	24.89	7.14
w/out Phila Co.	2654	24.6	67.13	2.38	25.04	7.19
Phila. Co.	1005	9.3	66.63	2.46	24.50	7.00
Anthracite	1401	13.0	67.01	2.52	23.82	6.55
Pocono	73	0.7	68.23	2.20	25.88	7.15
Northeastern	603	5.6	68.01	2.49	24.22	7.12
Ridge & Valley	1704	15.8	67.82	2.37	25.36	7.26
Allegheny Forest	535	5.0	67.98	2.40	24.36	6.30
Western						
with Algny Co.	2794	25.9	68.13	2.52	23.57	6.31
w/out Algny Co.	2291	21.3	68.22	2.48	23.70	6.40
Algny Co.	503	4.7	67.72	2.66	22.95	5.84

[a] Summed percentages do not total 100% because of double listing of Philadelphia and Allegheny Counties. Percentages based on the number of cases with valid county codes.

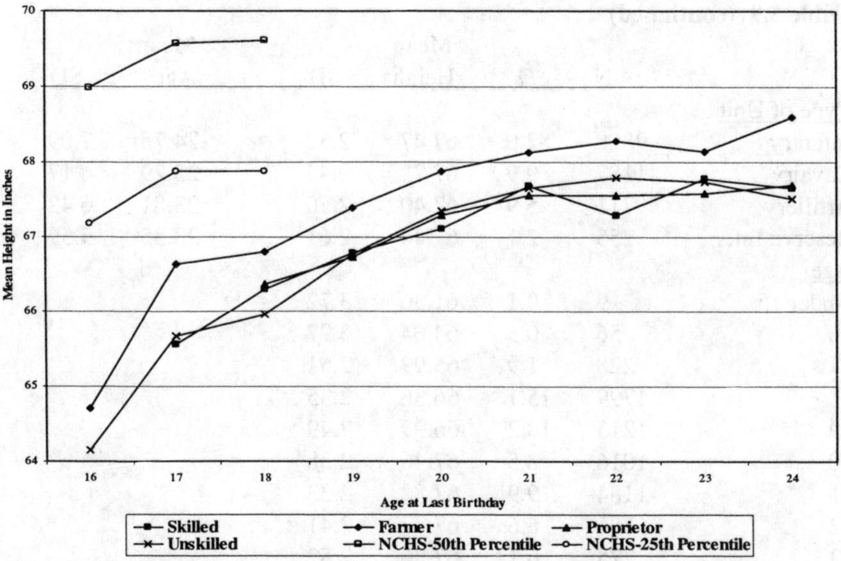

Figure 5.4 Height by Age by Occupation: Civil War Soldiers, Statewide Sample & NCHS Standards

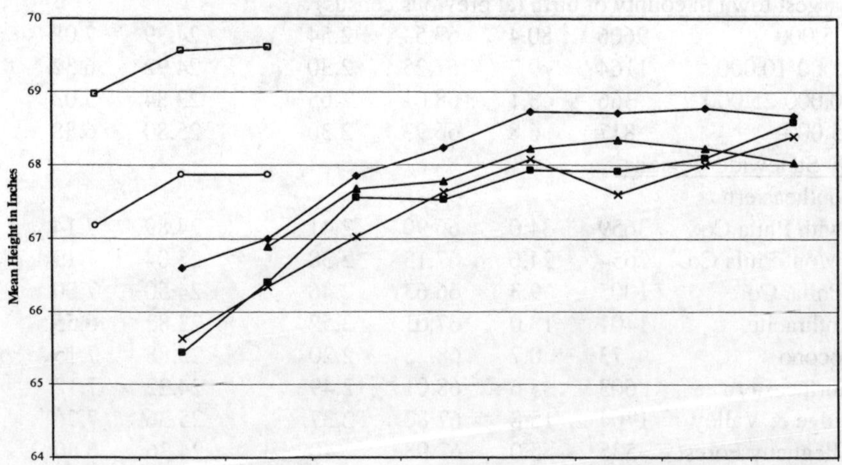

Figure 5.5 Height by Age by Occupation: Civil War Soldiers, Western Sample & NCHS Standards

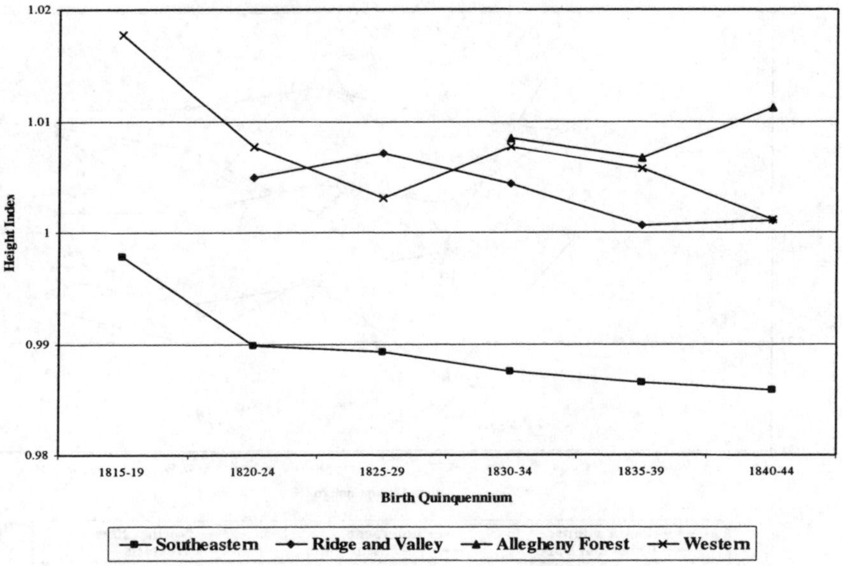

Figure 5.6 Age Standardized Height by Region: Unskilled Workers

Revolutionary War soldiers found that men who migrated across county lines but within a single state, during the years between birth and enlistment, exhibited no difference in final adult height, whereas those crossing state boundaries did.[36] The latter had a height advantage of 0.45-0.85 inches over their less mobile counterparts, after accounting for other variables. Margo and Steckel note that, in their analysis of Fogel's national sample of Civil War soldiers, short-distance migrants (which they defined as men moving within census-based regions) exhibited no difference in stature over non-migrants. However, long-distance migrants moving into the West were 'significantly taller (0.7-0.9 inches).[37]

This study's samples include only Pennsylvania-born men, therefore, they can only be used to evaluate in-state migration. The height of migrants, men who enlisted in a county other than the one in which they were born, were not consistently different from those of non-migrant men. The height difference in the western sample, while statistically significant, is small, less than two-tenths of an inch. Statewide, however, an opposite pattern is evident. Stayers are taller than leavers, but again by a very small and statistically insignificant amount (Tables 5.3 and 5.4). These findings are, in the main, consistent with the results reported by Sokoloff and Villaflor, and Margo and Steckel. Men who migrated short distances were not particularly different from men who did not.

However, the pattern is strikingly different among men born in Philadelphia and Allegheny Counties (Figure 5.9). From 1815 through 1844, the

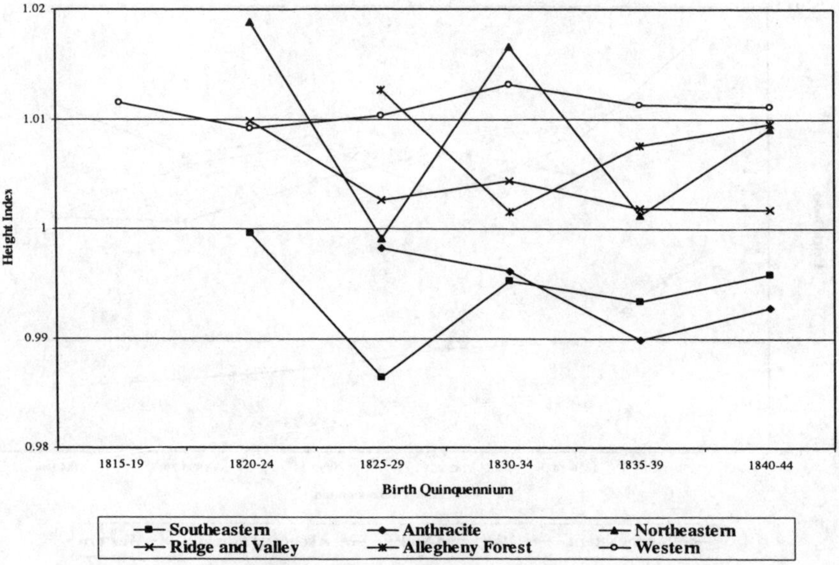

Figure 5.7 Age Standardized Height by Region: Farmers

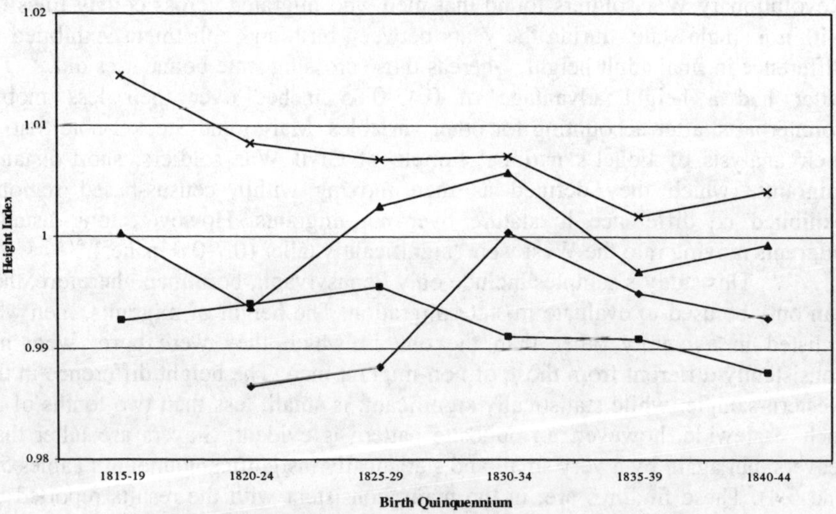

Figure 5.8 Age Standardized Height by Region: Skilled Workers

mean height of men born and enlisted in Philadelphia County fell slowly, while the mean height of those men born in Philadelphia but who later migrated out of it slowly rose. Apparently, as time went on, the cost, in biological terms, of staying in the state's largest urban area, became increasingly high, both relatively and absolutely. The pattern in Allegheny County, the West's urban center, is rather different. Post 1830 birth cohorts of stayers and migrants had nearly identical physical stature. This indicates that the impact of the small but growing Pittsburgh area did not have such a severe negative impact on men growing up there as in Philadelphia.[38]

National and International Comparisons

Early anthropometric research has established the very significant net nutritional and stature advantage which eighteenth- and nineteenth-century North Americans enjoyed over their European contemporaries.[39] This difference is also evident between Pennsylvania Civil War soldiers and several nineteenth-century European military samples (Table 5.10). The mean adult heights of the Pennsylvanians are two and one-half to four inches greater than those of the European soldiers.

However, Pennsylvania Union soldiers were not as tall as those born in other parts of the United States (Table 5.11). There was a half inch deficit in height between the statewide sample of Pennsylvanians and the national sample of Civil War soldiers.[40] This is consistent with Baxter's summary of the heights of men by state of enlistment during the Civil War which showed Pennsylvanians to be below the national mean. This variation is also consistent with Sokoloff's finding that in the antebellum period men from the Mid-Atlantic Region tended to be shorter than U.S. males generally.[41] The mean adult height for the western sample of 68.5 inches is equivalent to the national average of Civil War soldiers calculated by Sokoloff and much closer to the 68.8 inch level of Union men from the Midwest/West.[42] The lower mean values for Pennsylvanians statewide may reflect the relatively greater level of urbanization and market involvement in the state and the Mid-Atlantic Region generally than was the case nationwide. Western Pennsylvanians had a mean stature between that of the statewide sample and that of Midwestern soldiers, congruent with a level of economic development situated between the national and Midwestern levels.

The West Point cadets born in Pennsylvania were taller than the Union sample at younger ages, but the mean stature of the soldiers exceeded that of the cadets by age 18 in case of the Western sample and at age 19 in the statewide sample[43] (Figures 5.10 and 5.11). After age 19 the cadets were markedly shorter than the soldiers from the western sample.[44] Cadets were drawn in much greater proportion from urban areas than was the case for the Civil War soldiers.[45] The West Pointers' advantage of being from higher socio-economic class families possibly was counteracted by the fact that the cadets were to a large extent of urban

Table 5.10 Mean Heights of Adult Males (in inches)

Pennsylvania European Ancestry 1861-1865		Europe		
Western Sample	Statewide Sample	Hungary 1813-1835	England 1816-1821	Sweden 1843-1886
68.5	68.0	64.2	65.8	66.3

Sources: Hungary: Komlos, *Nutrition and Economic Development*, Table 2.1, 57 (using QBE); Britain: Floud, Wachter, and Gregory, *Height, Health, and History*, Table 4.1, 148 (using RSMLE); Sweden: Sandberg and Steckel, 'Overpopulation and Malnutrition,' Table 2, 7 (using QBE).

Note: Dates refer to dates of measurement.

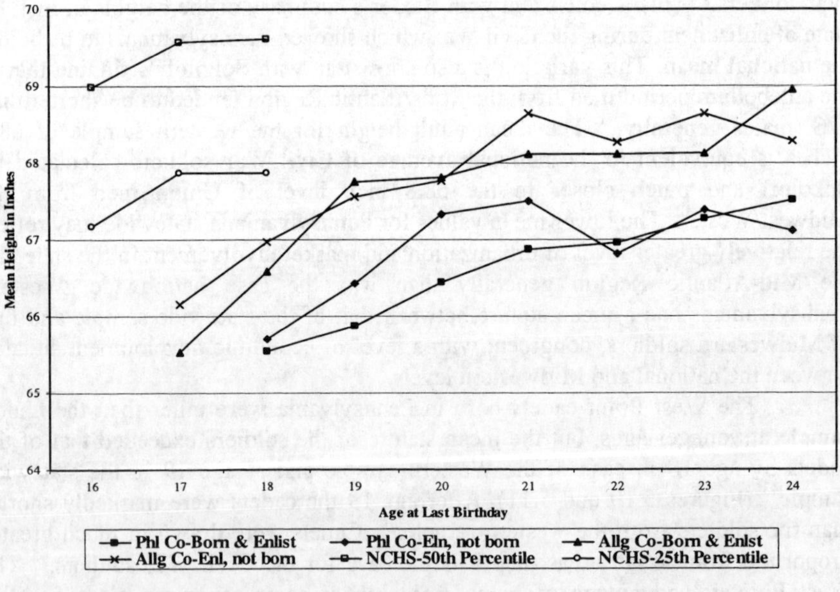

Figure 5.9 Height by Age: Urban Enlistment County

origin. This finding is consistent with the hypothesis that distance from markets yielded a net nutritional status advantage in the antebellum United States. A more detailed examination of this relationship follows.

Statewide Variation in Height

An analysis of spatial variation in mean heights provides insights into the relationship of economic development and net nutritional status. Raw means present an overview of the stature trends and patterns while multiple regression analysis accounts for sample composition variation.

Birth Cohort and Regional Stature Patterns

The antebellum stature time trends in the statewide and western samples are consistent with the trend in other studies of the antebellum United States. From the 1820-24 through the 1840-44 quinquennia, a slight and uneven fall in mean stature of about two-thirds of an inch occurred in both samples (Tables 5.8 and 5.9).[46] The mean data show an upward 'blip' of two-tenths of an inch in the western sample in the 1830-34 cohort and a much smaller jump statewide. Regression analysis reveals that, after adjusting for other variables, this general trend – a decline between 1820 and 1844 with a one quinquennium upward jump in the 1830-34 cohort – is still present in the western sample but a somewhat slower, steadier

Table 5.11 Mean Heights of Adult Males, U.S. (in inches)

North America					Pennsylvania	
European Ancestry			African Ancestry		European Ancestry 1861-1865	
1775-1783	1861-1865	1943-1944	1811-1861	1943-1944	Western Sample	Statewide Sample
68.1	68.5	68.1	67.0	67.9	68.5	68.0

Sources: U.S. whites, 1775-1783: Sokoloff and Villaflor, 'Early Achievement,' 458 (using QBE); U.S. whites, 1861-65: Margo and Steckel, 'Height of Native Born Whites,' 168; U.S. whites and blacks, 1943-44: Karpinos, 'Height and Weight of Selective Service Registrants,' Table 5, 302; U.S. blacks, 1811-1861: Margo and Steckel, 'Height of American Slaves,' Table 1, 518.

Note: Dates refer to dates of measurement.

decline occurred statewide. The stature differences in the statewide sample between the earlier quinquennia and the omitted one (1835-39) are only weakly statistically significant and on the order of one-quarter inch.

The same time trend is apparent across the occupational spectrum. If the samples are disaggregated by occupational category the mean height for each of the categories follows a trend similar to the one described above (Figures 5.12 and 5.13). While there is a degree of variability, especially in the early quinquennia in which there are relatively few observations, the trend is rather consistent with falling mean height evident over the entire period, although again, not monotonically. Just as forces had produced an occupational gradient in height by the early nineteenth century, so they caused mean average stature to fall in the later antebellum years. One small, but important, exception is the height of the professionals in the statewide sample, which do not decline in the second half of the 1830s. This might well have been a general pattern, insofar as Komlos has already noted that the height of those West Point cadets who had middle-class parents did not decline in the second half of the 1830s,[47] although decline in heights among the cadets in general was, indeed, evident (Table 5.12).[48]

Regional analysis of height variation reveals patterns that support the view that men in areas least involved in markets benefited biologically from their separation[49] (Figures 5.14 and 5.15). An aggregate view of age standardized height by county for men born between 1815 and 1844 is presented in Figure 5.16.[50] The overall east-west and north-south gradients in height are immediately evident moving away from Philadelphia.[51] Philadelphia County never had a mean height above 99.25 per cent of the state average over the 1815-1844 period. However, the relatively low stature levels exhibited by Philadelphia County's birth cohorts are not restricted to that county hard on the banks of the Delaware River. Short soldiers were found across the whole of the southeastern corner of the state.

Table 5.12 West Point Cadets: Age Standardized Height by Birth Decade

Birth Decade	Cadets from Pennsylvania	All Cadets
1820s	1.003	1.005
1830s	1.002	1.003
1840s	0.997	1.000
1850s	0.994	0.996
1860s	1.003	0.999
1870s	1.005	1.005

Note: Age standardization was calculated by dividing the height of each Pennsylvania cadet by the mean height of all Pennsylvania cadets of his same age. A similar process was carried out for the national sample of cadets using national mean heights by age.

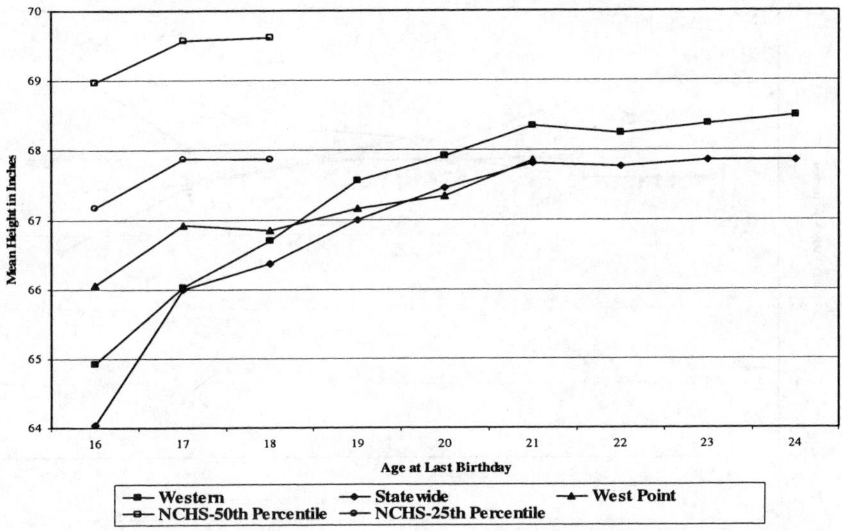

Figure 5.10 Height by Age: Civil War Soldiers, West Point Cadets, & NCHS Standards

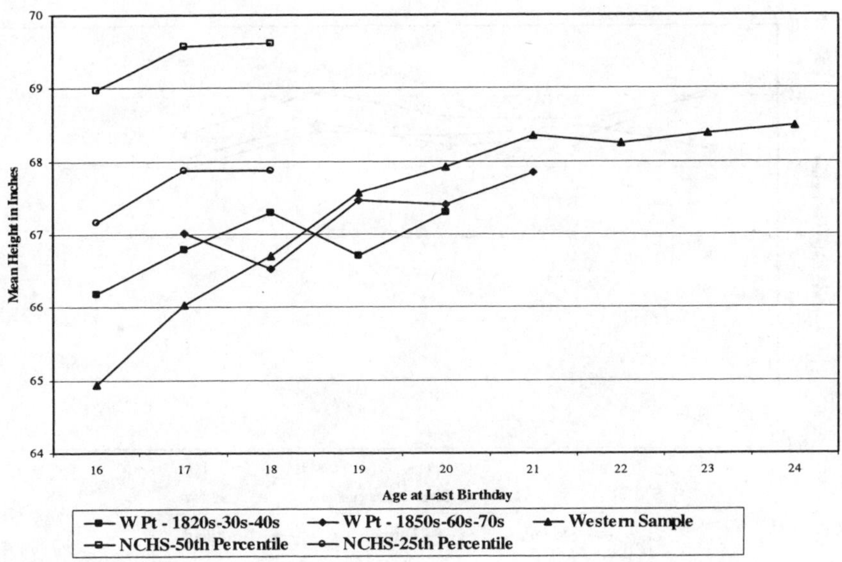

Figure 5.11 Height by Age: Civil War Soldiers, West Point Cadets, & NCHS Standards

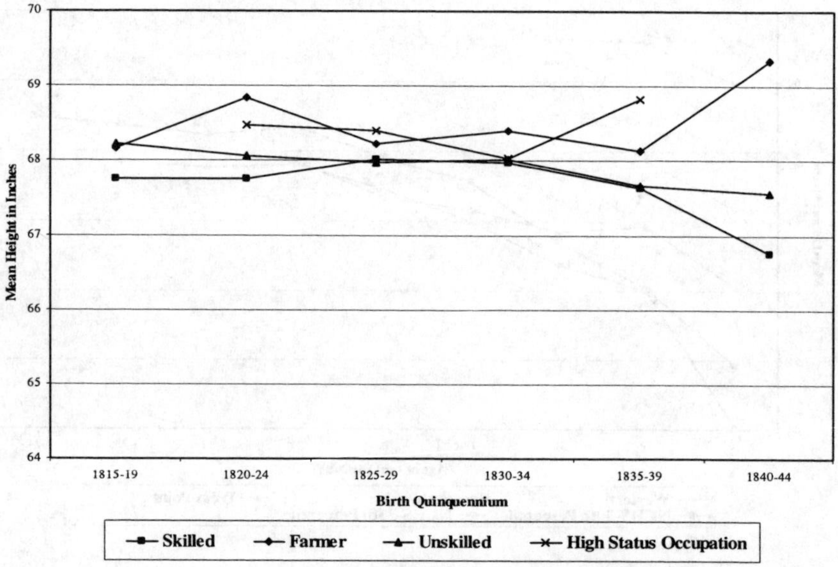

Figure 5.12 Adult Height by Occupation: Statewide Sample

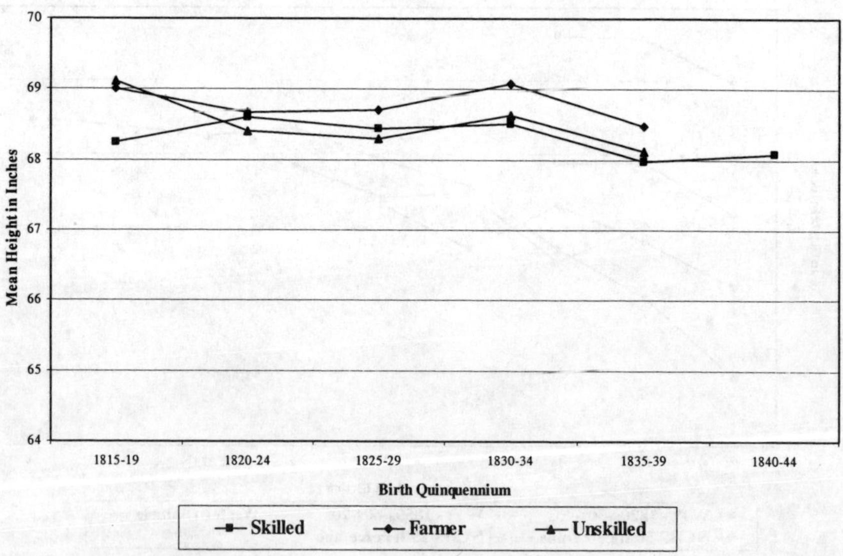

Figure 5.13 Adult Height by Occupation: Western Sample

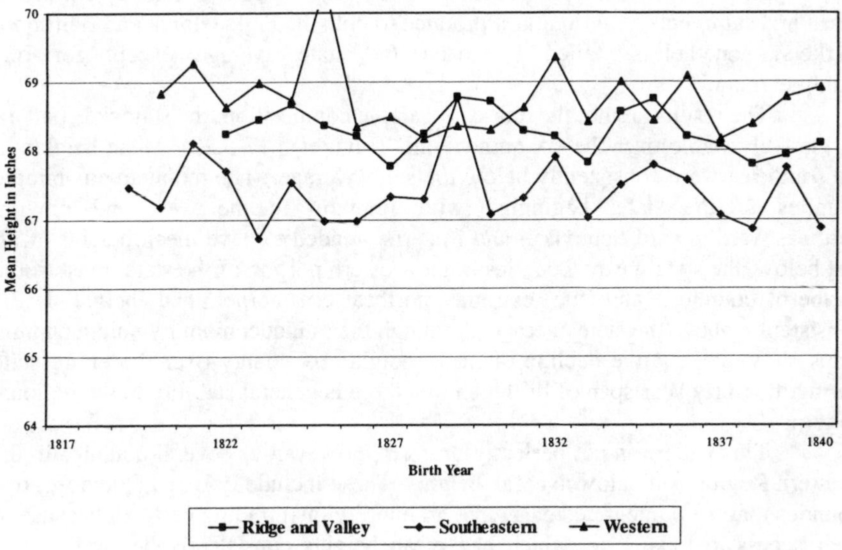

Figure 5.14 Height by Birth Year by Region: 25-45 Year Olds, All Ranks, Infantry

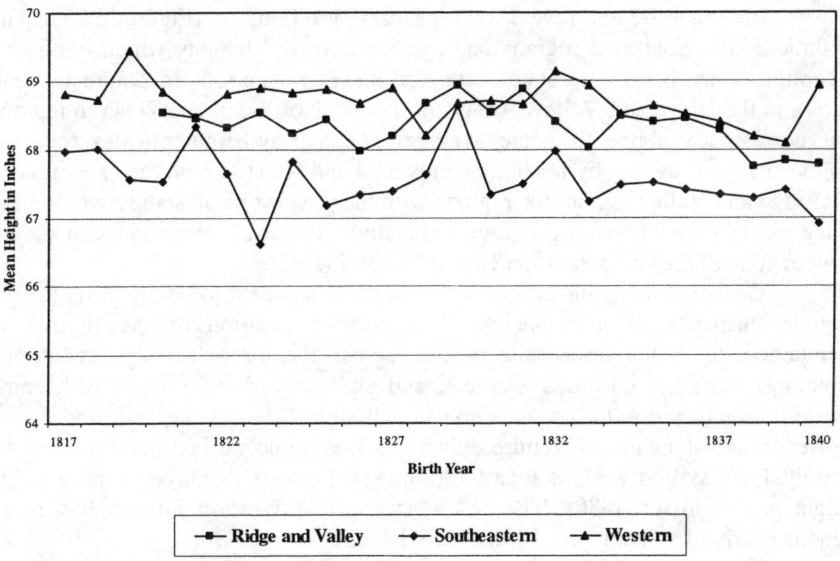

Figure 5.15 Height by Birth Year by Region: 25-49 Year Olds, All Ranks, All Units

It is especially noteworthy that Lancaster County, renowned for its productive farms and shipments of agricultural produce to both the Philadelphia and Baltimore markets, nonetheless, failed to reach the state average except for one quinquennium.

The results are not the quirks of sample composition: the statewide pattern is relatively stable over the six quinquennia (Figures 5.17-5.22). Mean heights in the southeast were consistently below the state average. The mountainous middle counties of the state, beginning with Franklin in the west and moving northeastward toward Schuylkill and Luzerne, tended to have mean heights at, or just below, the state mean. Counties in the western portion of the state, most of the northern counties, and the extreme northeastern corner had height levels consistently above the state average. Although the quinquennium by quinquennium maps show the relative decline of mean heights by county over the entire state during the thirty year span of birth cohorts, there is general stability in the regional pattern.

This pattern is not perfectly uniform, however, as several counties in the Western Region had below average heights. These include Erie and Crawford, two counties that were integrated early into an interregional trading network because of their access to Lake Erie, which had mean heights consistently below the state average. Allegheny County, the most urbanized county in the western region, had height levels below the mean, roughly equivalent to those of Erie and Crawford. The tallest men were found in the most remote counties, Mercer, Lawrence, and Greene.

Regional trends reveal two primary groupings[52] (Figure 5.23). The Anthracite and Southeast regions had age standardized heights which, with one exception, were below the state mean for the entire period. In contrast, mean stature in the Ridge and Valley, Allegheny Forest, Northeast, and Western regions was consistently above the state average. The age-by-height profiles reveal a similar regional ranking by height (Figures 5.24 and 5.25).[53] With the exception of the Ridge and Valley region, the regions with the greatest mean stature were found in the most isolated parts of the state. Yet a slight downward trend in mean stature is evident in all regions across the 1815-1844 period.

Occupational composition variation does not seem to be the basis for the regional disparity in mean height. The relative position of the regions is maintained, as is the basic time profile, across the three largest occupational groupings, farmers, unskilled workers, and skilled workers, though with some greater variability due to the reduction in cell sizes (Figures 5.6, 5.7, and 5.8).[54] However, age standardized stature reductions were concentrated more among the unskilled and skilled workers than with farmers. Farmers displayed a more stable height profile in the 1830s. The 1840-44 cohort of Western farmers had mean heights nearly identical to that of the 1815-19 group.

Regression analysis does not reveal significant change in the statewide pattern described above. Men from the Southeastern and Anthracite Regions were almost a full inch shorter than men from the Western Region. These coefficients,

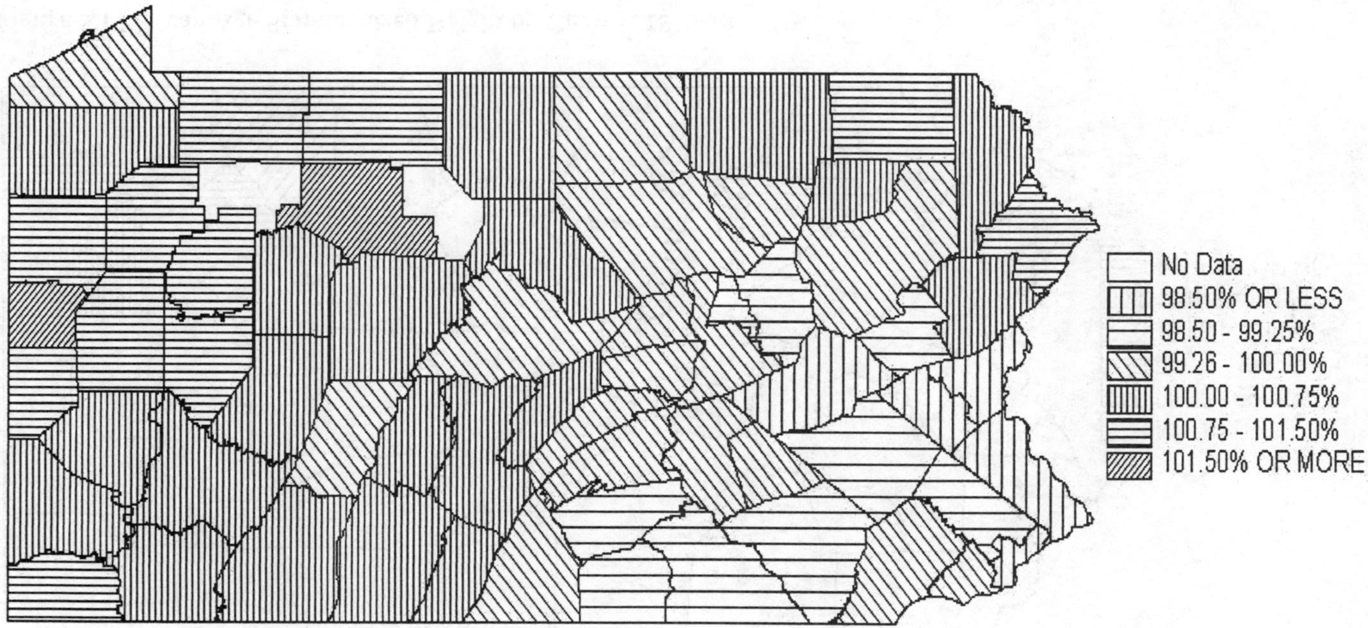

Figure 5.16 Mean Age Standardized Height by County, 1815-44

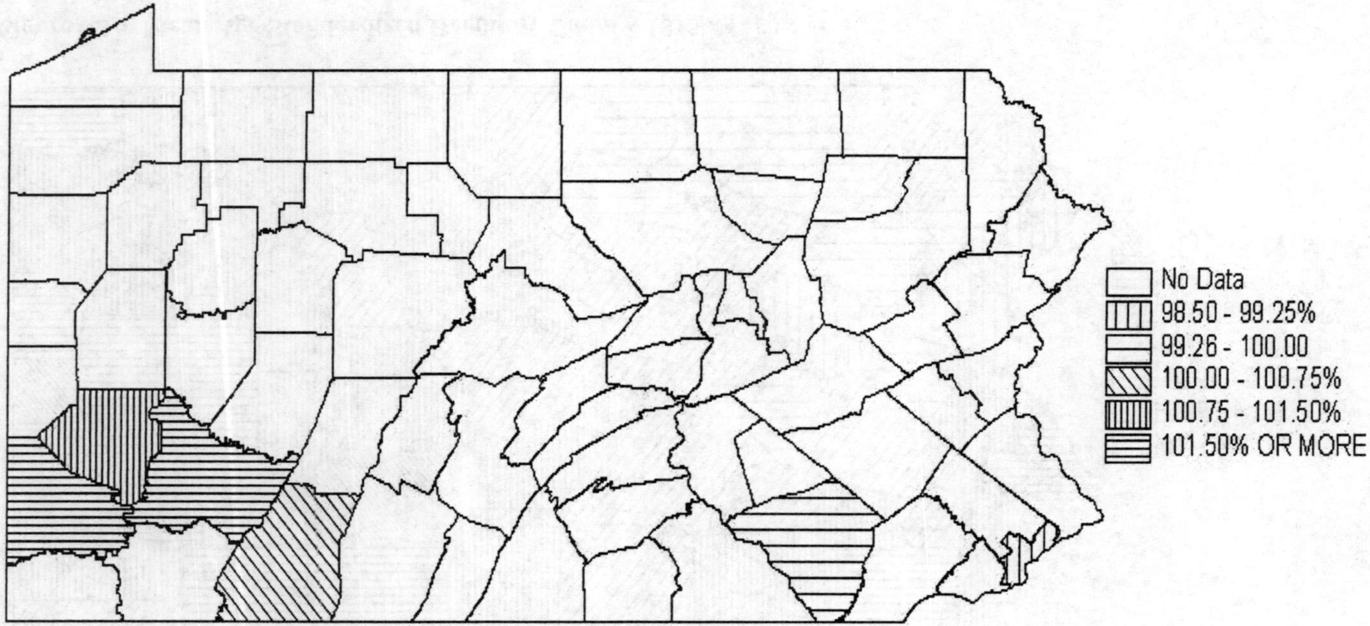

Figure 5.17 Mean Age Standardized Height by County, 1815-19

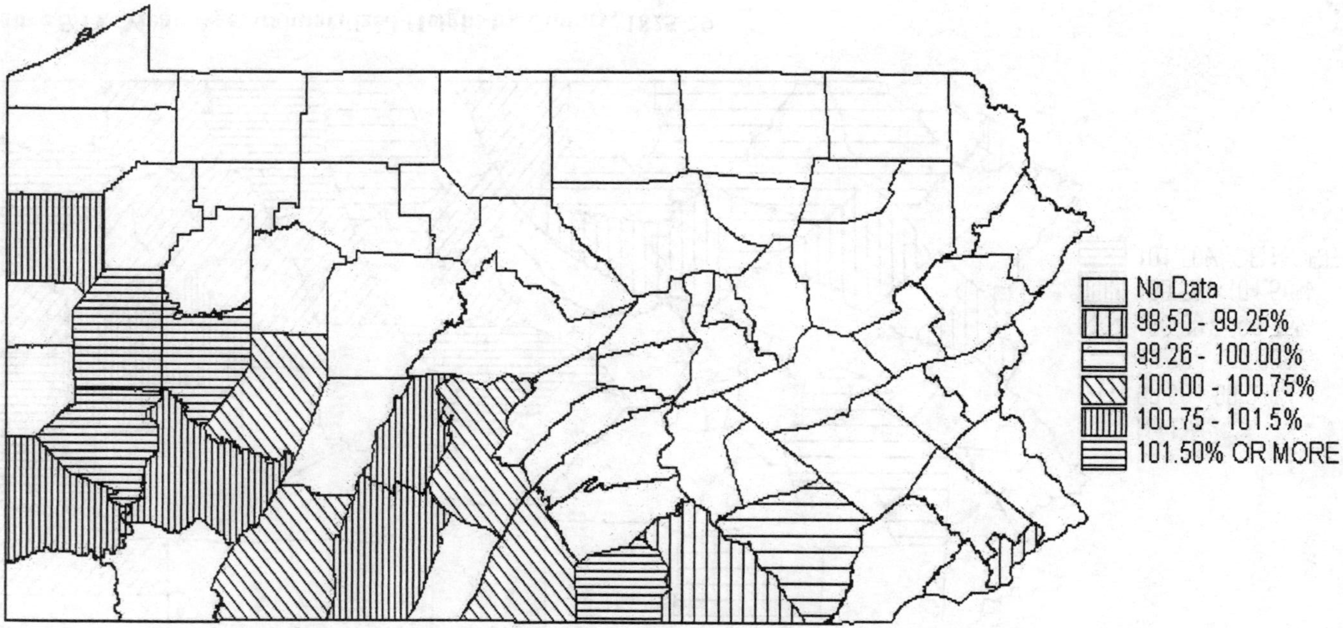

Figure 5.18 Mean Age Standardized Height by County, 1820-24

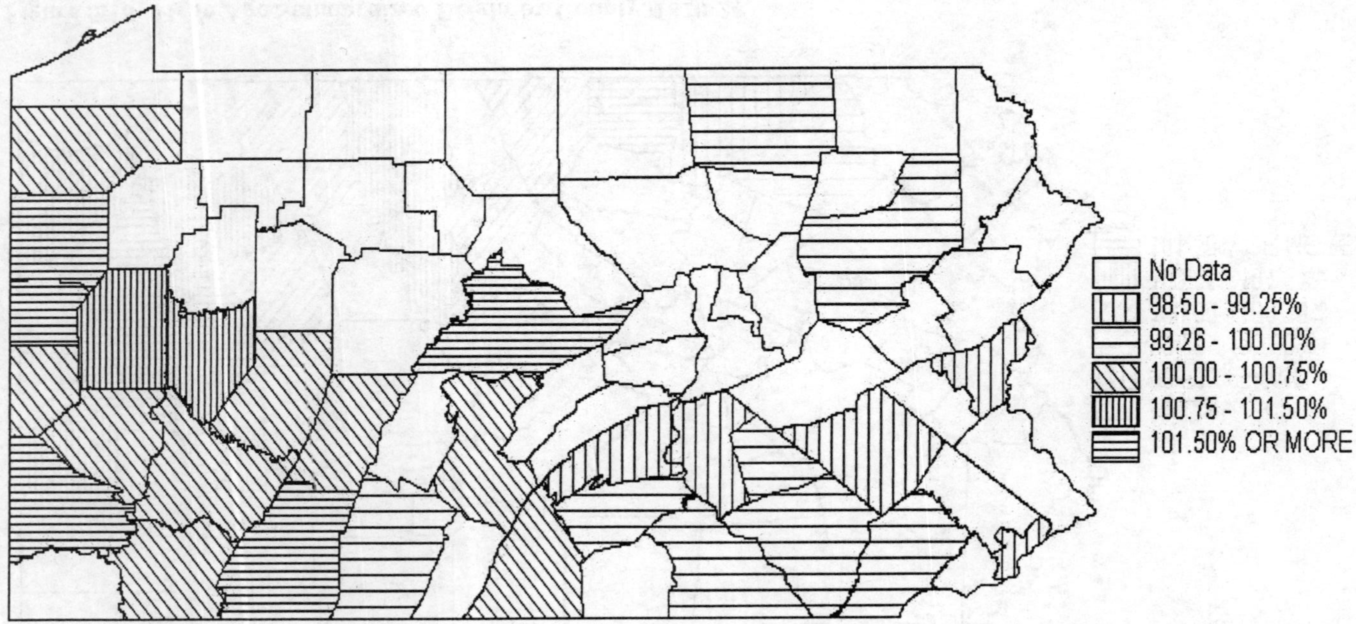

Figure 5.19 Mean Age Standardized Height by County, 1825-29

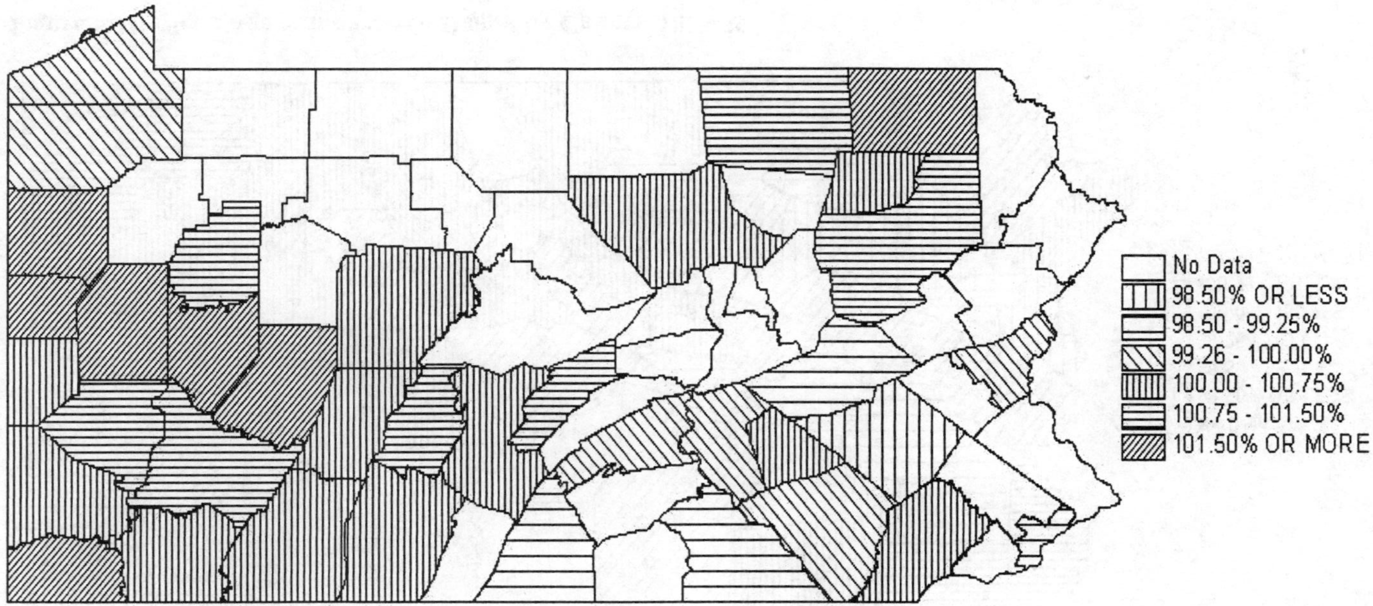

Figure 5.20 Mean Age Standardized Height by County, 1830-34

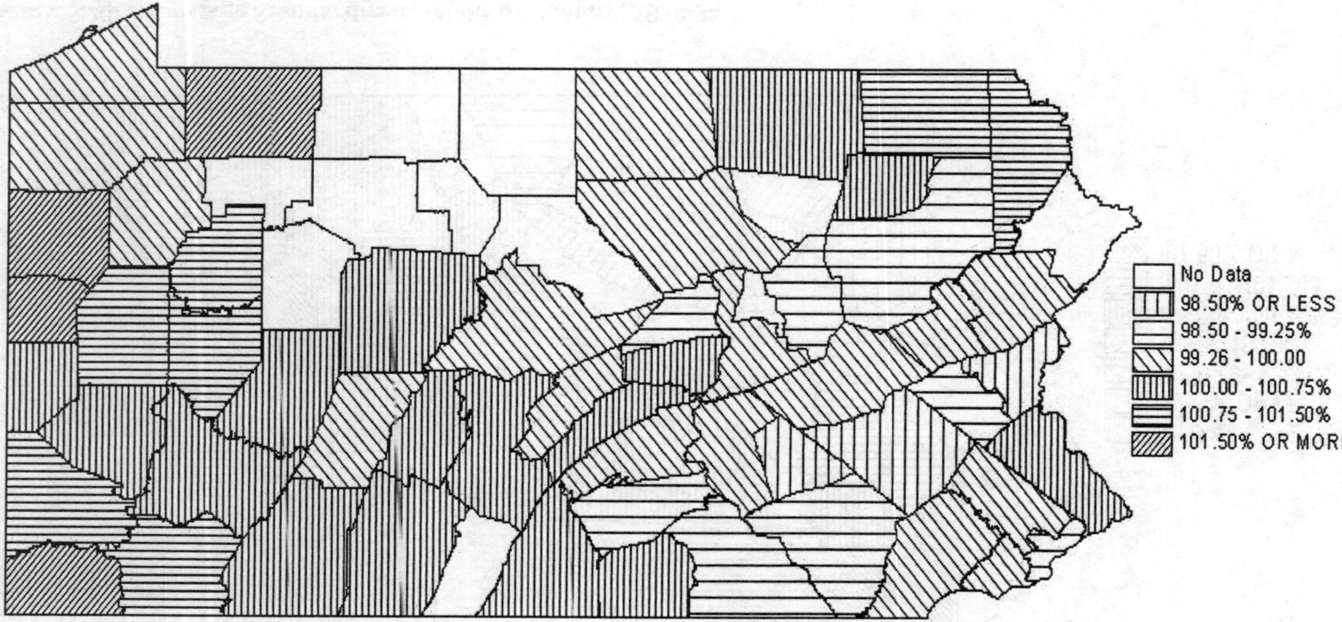

Figure 5.21 Mean Age Standardized Height by County, 1835-39

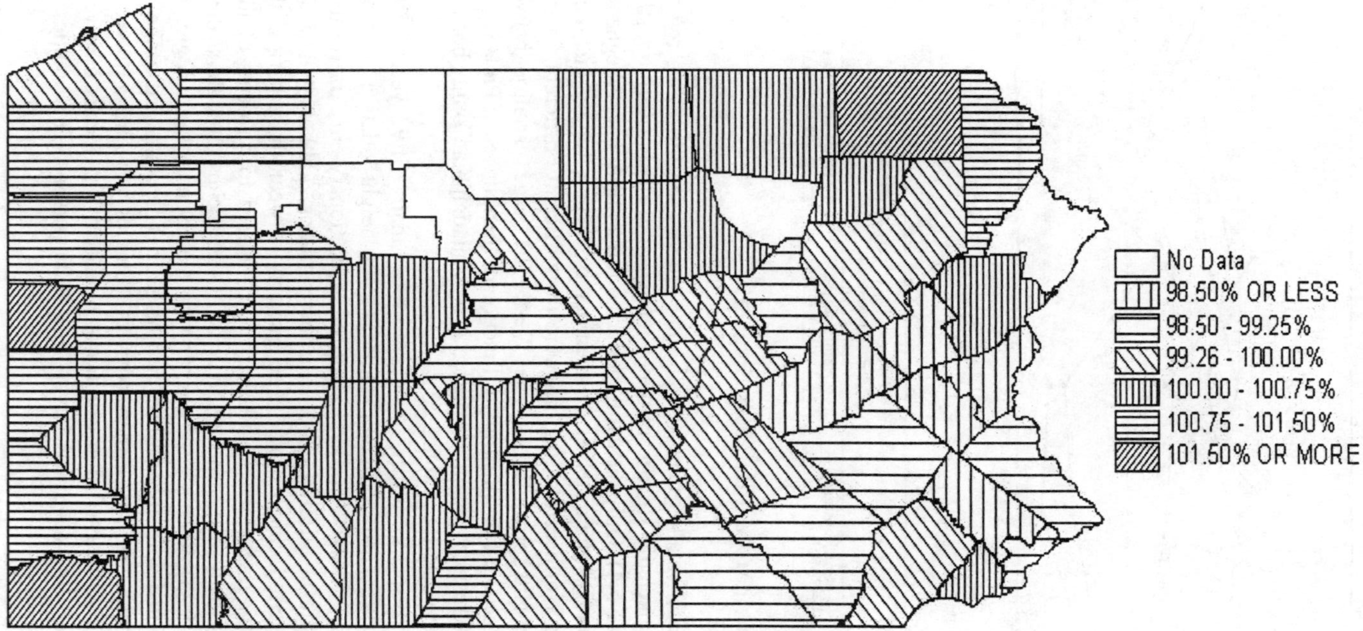

Figure 5.22 Mean Age Standardized Height by County, 1840-44

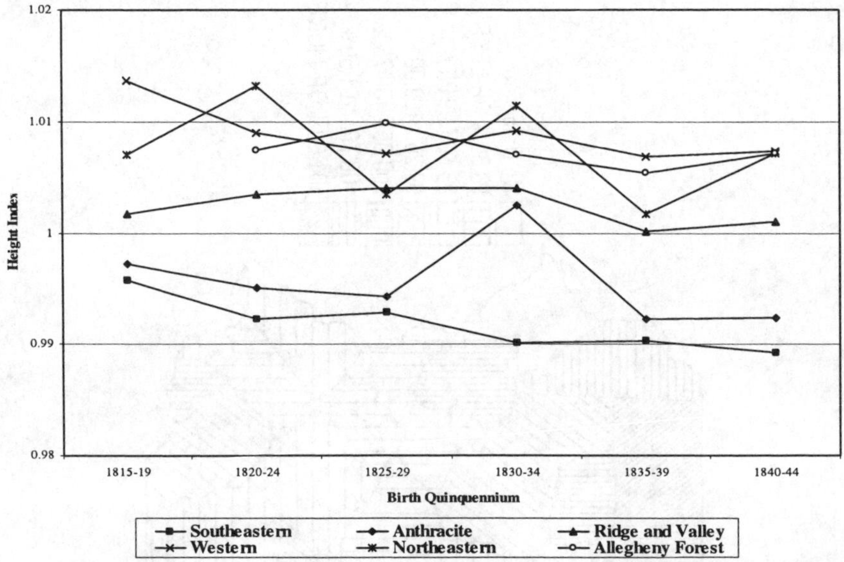

Figure 5.23 Standardized Height by Region

along with much smaller ones (in absolute value) for the other regions, are consistently statistically significant under numerous formulations – mostly at the 0.01 level (Table 5.4). Only the adult men from the undeveloped Allegheny Forest (Columns D and E) were as tall as the men in the Western Region, and those from the Pocono and Northeastern Regions were insignificantly different, in statistical terms, from heights prevailing in the West. The large variation between the Southeast and the West is not simply a function of the number of Philadelphians in the sample. The results remain unaffected if all Philadelphia County born men are removed from the data set (Table 5.13).

Pennsylvania's urban residents less than fifty years after the Revolutionary War had a significant deficit in height relative to their rural neighbors. Sokoloff and Villaflor's study of revolutionary-era American soldiers found no significant difference between these groups,[55] although later work on early national period samples did.[56] The disparity between those born in the most urbanized county in the state, Philadelphia, compared to residents of the 'non-urban' counties of the Western Region, was 1.0-1.5 inches throughout the growth years[57] (Figure 5.25). Even after accounting for their Southeastern Region of birth, which is associated with about a one inch height deficit compared to the Western Region, the mean stature of men born in counties containing towns with a population of 25,000+ carried an additional penalty of 0.5 inches relative to men born in counties with no towns larger than 5000 persons. This implies that the

Table 5.13 Sub-Regions within the Western Region

Allegheny County	*Mountain/Mineral*
Allegheny County	Armstrong
	Cambria
Lake Transport	Indiana
Erie	Somerset
Crawford	
	Northern Hinterland
Southern Hinterland	Beaver
Fayette	Butler
Greene	
Washington	*Isolated Agricultural*
Westmoreland	Lawrence
	Mercer

difference between rural men born in the Western Region and those born in Philadelphia was a substantial 1.5 inches. Between the birth cohorts of the 1770s and the 1820s, conditions changed significantly enough so that Pennsylvanians born in Philadelphia County were more that an inch shorter than residents of the most rural counties.

The large sample of men drawn from the Western Region allows a more disaggregated analysis of this area.[58] The region was divided into six sub-regions. Sub-regions were determined by geography, topography, the nature of economic activity, and the relationship to Pittsburgh, the region's major city. Because of its urban character, Allegheny County is considered separately. The far southwest corner of the state, which had the oldest agricultural settlements and most mature agricultural system in Western Pennsylvania, is considered as the Southern Hinterland, made up of Fayette, Greene, Washington, and Westmoreland Counties. Its name reflects its connection to the Pittsburgh market via the Monongehela and Youghigheny Rivers. The Mountain/Mineral sub-region, made up of Armstrong, Cambria, Indiana, and Somerset Counties, had difficult terrain, only moderately productive agricultural soils, and large deposits of bituminous coal. Butler and Beaver Counties, tied to Pittsburgh by the Ohio River as well as by a series of overland routes, comprised the Northern Hinterland. Throughout most of the antebellum period they were predominantly agricultural, although industrial production began to develop about 1860 especially along the Ohio River. Two productive agricultural counties, Mercer and Lawrence, formed the Isolated Agricultural sub-region. They were not settled until very late in the eighteenth century, and until late in the antebellum period transportation routes did not effectively connect them to the rest of the region. In the far northwest corner of the state, Erie and Crawford Counties made up the Lake Transport sub-region. With

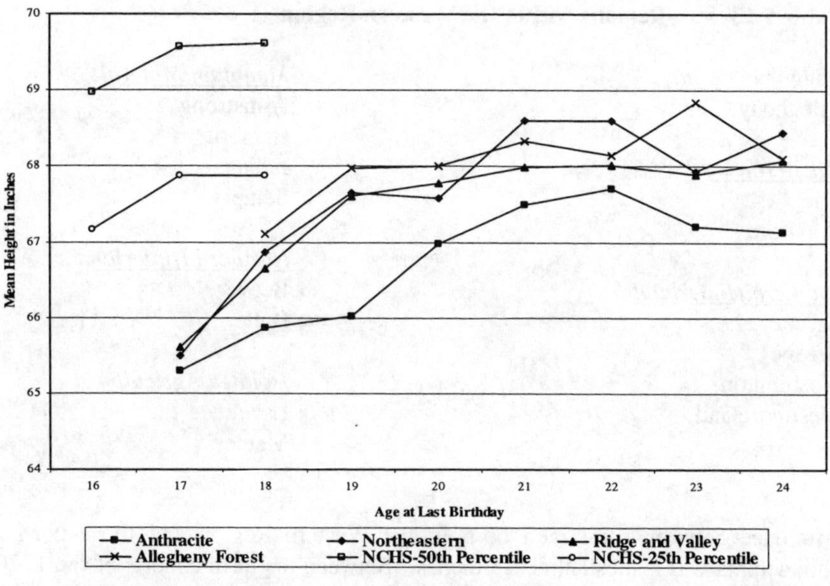

Figure 5.24 Height by Age: Non-Urban Birth Regions

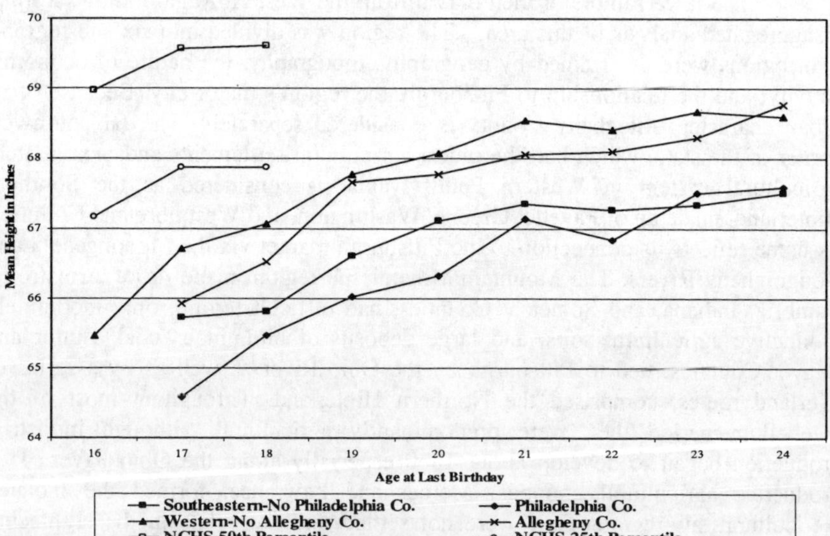

Figure 5.25 Height by Age: Urban Birth Regions

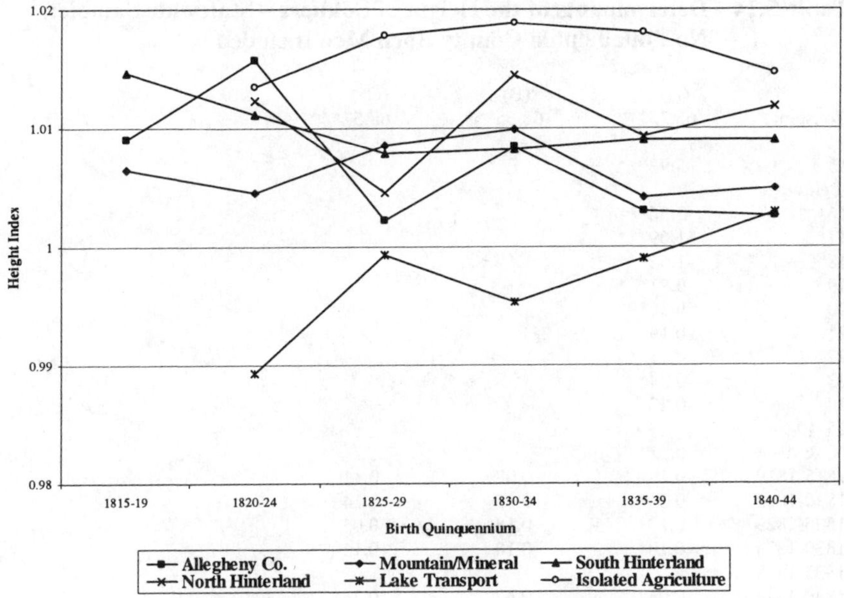

Figure 5.26 Standardized Height: Western Sub-Regions

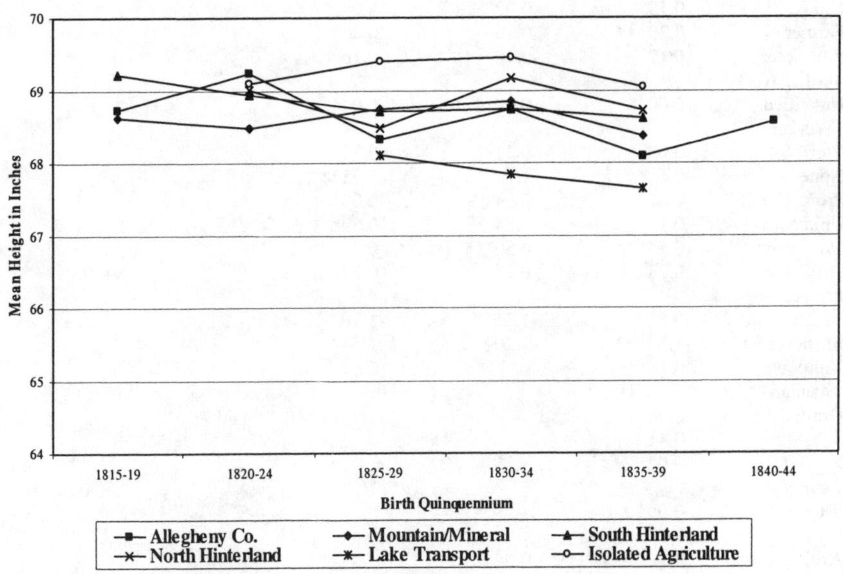

Figure 5.27 Adult Male Height: Western Sub-Regions

Table 5.14 Determinants of the Height of Soldiers – Statewide Sample: No Philadelphia County Born Men Included

	(A)	(B)	(C)
Constant	68.23***	68.55***	68.57***
15 & Below	-5.93***		
16	-3.56***		
17	-1.69***		
18	-1.52***		
19	-0.91***		
20	-0.56***		
21	-0.19		
22	-0.31**		
23	-0.24*		
24	-0.23		
25-49			
50 & Above	0.52		
1815-1819	-0.18	0.08	0.11
1820-1824	0.24*	0.15	0.14
1825-1829	0.20*	0.18	0.05
1830-1834	0.18*	0.18	0.15
1835-1839			
1840-1844	0.03	-0.67	-0.86*
1845-1849	-0.10		
1861	0.60***	0.46***	0.52***
1862	0.18**	0.04	-0.05
1863	-0.22	0.25	0.25
1864			
1865	0.13	0.02	0.09
Farmer	0.29***	0.13	0.26*
Proprietor	-0.12	-0.10	-0.16
Skilled Worker			
Unskilled Worker	0.00	0.09	0.04
Work Site	0.03	0.21	0.34
None	0.61**	1.71	1.72***
Professional	0.42	0.23	-0.03
Unknown	0.14	0.34	0.59*
Non-comm	0.55***	0.50***	0.48***
Officer	0.28	0.25	0.27
Private			
Artisan	-0.81*	-1.35**	-1.10
Musician	-1.53***	-1.20*	-1.54*
Unknown	0.18***		
'Standard'			
Drafted	0.08		
Substitute	0.41		
Recruit	-0.02		
Bounty Rcpnt	-0.09*		
Infantry			
Artillery	0.12	0.04	
Reserve Inf.	-0.33*	-0.78*	
Cavalry	0.28***	0.23	

Table 5.14 (continued)

	(A)	(B)	(C)
Stayer			
Migrant	-0.08	-0.21*	-0.17
Southeast	-0.99***	-0.96***	-1.02***
Anthracite	-1.06***	-0.86***	-0.90***
Pocono	-0.18	-0.87	-1.41**
Northeast	-0.24**	-0.34***	-0.41*
Ridge & Valley	-0.29***	-0.44***	-0.50***
Allegheny Forest	-0.28**	-0.12	0.11
West			
Largest City Size in Enlistment County			
Under 5K			
5K to 10K		-0.39***	-0.42**
10K to 25K		-0.01	-0.01
25K+		-0.05	-0.18
Largest City Size in Birth County			
Under 5K			
5K to 10K		-0.36**	-0.30
10K to 25K		-0.50***	-0.20***
N	9047[a]	2367[b]	1963[c]
Adjusted R^2	0.13	0.06	0.06
F	30.0***	5.04***	5.08***

*** significant at the 0.01 level

** significant at the 0.05 level

* significant at the 0.10 level

---

[a] Intercept represents a 25-49 year old private, a standard enlistee in 1864, who enlisted in the infantry in the same county in which he was born, who was a skilled worker born between 1835 and 1840 in the Western Region.

[b] Intercept represents a private, age 25-49, a standard enlistee in 1864, who enlisted in the infantry in the same county in which he was born, a county which had no town larger than 5000 persons either at his birth or at the time of enlistment, and who was a skilled worker born between 1835 and 1840 in the Western Region. This regression contains only standard enlistees aged 25-49.

[c] Intercept represents a private, age 25-49, a standard enlistee in 1864, who enlisted in the infantry in the same county in which he was born, a county which had no town larger than 5000 persons either at his birth or at the time of enlistment, and who was a skilled worker born between 1835 and 1840 in the Western Region. This regression contains only standard enlistees aged 25-49 from infantry units.

Table 5.15 Determinants of the Height of Soldiers – Western Sample

	(A)	(B)	(C)
Constant	68.17***	68.12***	68.12***
15 & Below	-4.18***		
16	-3.30***		
17	-1.74***		
18	-1.45***		
19	-0.74***		
20	-0.49***		
21	-0.14		
22	-0.22		
23	-0.04		
24	-0.10		
25-49			
50 & Above	-1.12		
1815-1819	0.40*	0.44*	0.64**
1820-1824	0.20	0.27	0.44**
1825-1829	0.23*	0.29*	0.20
1830-1834	0.29**	0.37***	0.33**
1835-1839			
1840-1844	0.01	0.24	-0.07
1845-1849	-0.11		
1861	0.71***	0.77***	0.86***
1862	0.47***	0.45***	0.33*
1863		0.42	0.32
1864			
1865	0.21*	0.37*	0.42*
Farmer	0.50***	0.44***	0.43***
Proprietor	-0.18	-0.16	0.17
Skilled Worker			
Unskilled Worker	0.00	0.19	0.22
Work Site	0.78**	0.39	0.54
None	0.66***	0.09	1.26
Professional	0.33	0.69	0.81
Unknown	0.20	0.42	0.64
Non-comm	0.67***	0.47***	0.53***
Officer	0.49	0.17	0.15
Private			
Artisan	-0.20	-0.41**	0.15
Musician	-2.04***	-0.05*	-0.44*
Unknown	0.02		
'Standard'			
Drafted	0.16		
Substitute	-0.47		
Recruit	0.21		
Bounty Rcpnt	0.07*		

Table 5.15(continued)

	(A)	(B)	(C)
Infantry			
Artillery	0.41***	0.50***	
Reserve Inf.	0.18	0.52	
Cavalry	0.32***	0.41***	
Stayer			
Migrant	0.01	0.14	0.06
Mountain/ Mineral	-0.37***	-0.47**	-0.45*
Allegheny	-0.55***	0.83	0.59
Southern Hinterland	-0.33***	-0.47**	-0.56**
Northern Hinterland	-0.18	-0.14	0.18
Lake	-0.90***	-1.39***	-1.32***
Transport			
Isolated Agricultural			
Largest City Size in Enlistment County			
Under 5K			
5K to 10K	-0.14*	-0.12	-0.09
10K to 25K	-0.37	-0.21	-0.24
25K+	0.02	-0.09	-0.19
Largest City Size in Birth County			
Under 5K			
5K to 10K	0.39	-1.01	-1.17
10K to 25K	-0.08	-1.48	-1.24
N	8034[a]	2263[b]	1541[c]
Adjusted R^2	0.12	0.04	0.05
F	22.5***	3.8***	3.4***

*** significant at the 0.01 level
** significant at the 0.05 level
* significant at the 0.10 level

[a] Intercept represents a 25-49 year old private, a standard enlistee in 1864, who enlisted in the infantry in the same county in which he was born, who was a skilled worker born between 1835 and 1840 in the Western Region. Unknown rank signifies a man from Fogel's sample.

[b] Intercept represents a private, age 25-49, a standard enlistee in 1864, who enlisted in the infantry in the same county in which he was born, a county which had no town larger than 5000 persons either at his birth or at the time of enlistment, and who was a skilled worker born between 1835 and 1840 in the Western Region. This regression contains only standard enlistees aged 25-49. Unknown rank signifies a man from Fogel's sample.

[c] Intercept represents a private, age 25-49, a standard enlistee in 1864, who enlisted in the infantry in the same county in which he was born, a county which had no town larger than 5000 persons either at his birth or at the time of enlistment, and who was a skilled worker born between 1835 and 1840 in the Western Region. This regression contains only standard enlistees aged 25-49 from infantry units. Unknown rank signifies a man from Fogel's sample.

Table 5.16 Determinants of the Height of Soldiers – Statewide Sample: Single Economic/Demographic Variables with Regional Dummy

	(A)	(B)	(C)	(D)	(E)
Constant	67.72***	67.50***	67.33***	67.22***	67.46***
1820-1824	0.41**	0.40**	0.40**	0.38**	0.41**
1825-1829	0.19	0.16	0.16	0.15	0.18
1830-1834	0.30**	0.28**	0.28**	0.28**	0.30**
1835-1839					
1840-1844	-0.07	-0.07	-0.07	-0.06	-0.07
1861	0.59***	0.59***	0.59***	0.61***	0.58***
1862	0.33*	0.31*	0.30*	0.31**	0.33**
1863/64					
1865	0.32**	0.29*	0.29*	0.30*	0.31*
Farmer	0.38***	0.29**	0.30**	0.25*	0.36**
Proprietor	0.25	0.24	0.24	0.26	0.23
Skilled Worker					
Unskilled Worker	-0.00	-0.07	-0.06	-0.07	-0.02
High Status	0.06	0.01	0.01	0.01	0.04
Unknown	0.47	0.40	0.42	0.36	0.48
Stayer					
Migrant	0.18	0.11	0.12	0.06	0.18

Table 5.16 (continued)

	(A)	(B)	(C)	(D)	(E)
Southeast	-0.81***	-0.81***	-0.80***	-0.70***	-0.91***
Anthracite	-0.80**	-0.64**	-0.66**	-0.54*	-0.77**
PNF	-0.02	-0.08	0.01	-0.16	-0.03
West					
Protein		0.24***			
Calorie			0.09***		
Swine				0.61***	
Wealth					0.001**
N	1907	1907	1907	1907	1907
Adjusted R^2	0.05	0.05	0.05	0.06	0.05
F	6.7***	7.4***	7.2***	7.7***	6.6***

*** significant at the 0.01 level
** significant at the 0.05 level
* significant at the 0.10 level

Note: Intercept represents a man aged 25-45, a standard infantry enlistee, who enlisted during 1863 or 1864 in the same county in which he was born, and who was a skilled worker born between 1835 and 1839 in the Western Region of Pennsylvania.

Table 5.17 Determinants of the Height of Soldiers – Statewide Sample: Single Economic/Demographic Variables with Regional Dummy

	(A)	(B)	(C)	(D)	(E)
Constant	68.47***	67.42***	67.59***	67.83***	67.74***
1820-1824	0.38**	0.40**	0.41**	0.41**	0.42**
1825-1829	0.19	0.18	0.18	0.17	0.19
1830-1834	0.29**	0.29**	0.31**	0.30**	0.31**
1835-1839					
1840-1844	-0.09	-0.05	-0.06	-0.04	-0.05
1861	0.59***	0.60***	0.60***	0.64***	0.60***
1862	0.27*	0.25	0.31*	0.33**	0.36**
1863/64					
1865	0.30*	0.31*	0.31*	0.35**	0.30*
Farmer	0.32**	0.30**	0.36**	0.31**	0.35**
Proprietor	0.27	0.26	0.25	0.25	0.24
Skilled Worker					
Unskilled Worker	-0.06	-0.04	-0.00	-0.03	-0.02
High Status	0.14	0.11	0.05	0.05	0.02
Unknown	0.24	-0.30	0.41	0.45	0.49
Stayer					
Migrant	0.10	0.12	0.13	0.14	0.15

Table 5.17 (continued)

	(A)	(B)	(C)	(D)	(E)
Southeast	-0.74***	-0.52***	-0.89***	-0.81***	-0.67***
Anthracite	-0.60*	-0.54	-0.70**	-0.84***	-0.80**
PNF	-0.03	-0.10	-0.15	-0.10	-0.02*
West					
Water Tran.	-0.83***				
Home Mfctr.		0.18***			
Dairy			0.09***		
Mrkt Grdn.				-0.45**	
Land Value					-0.0003**
N	1907	1907	1907	1907	1907
Adjusted R^2	0.06	0.05	0.05	0.05	0.05
F	8.1***	7.1***	6.9***	6.6***	6.7***

*** significant at the 0.01 level
** significant at the 0.05 level
* significant at the 0.10 level

Note: Intercept represents a man aged 25-45, who enlisted in the infantry as a standard enlistee in the same county in which he was born, who enlisted during 1863 or 1864, and who was a skilled worker born between 1835 and 1839 in the Western Region of Pennsylvania.

Table 5.18 Determinants of the Height of Soldiers – Statewide Sample: Single Economic/Demographic Variables with Regional Dummy

	(A)	(B)	(C)	(D)	(E)
Constant	67.75***	67.26***	67.85***	67.79***	67.73***
1820-1824	0.41**	0.41**	0.40**	0.41**	0.42**
1825-1829	0.19	0.18	0.17	0.18	0.19
1830-1834	0.31**	0.30**	0.30**	0.30**	0.31**
1835-1839					
1840-1844	-0.05	-0.04	-0.04	-0.04	-0.05
1861	0.60***	0.62***	0.61***	0.62***	0.60***
1862	0.36**	0.34**	0.33**	0.35**	0.36**
1863/64					
1865	0.30*	0.34*	0.32*	0.33*	0.30*
Farmer	0.35**	0.32**	0.34**	0.32**	0.35**
Proprietor	0.25	0.26	0.25	0.25	0.24
Skilled Worker					
Unskilled Worker	-0.03	-0.03	-0.01	-0.03	-0.02
High Status	0.02	0.05	0.03	0.03	0.02
Unknown	0.49	0.47	0.44	0.47	0.50
Stayer					
Migrant	0.15	0.14	0.13	0.14	0.15

Table 5.18 (continued)

	(A)	(B)	(C)	(D)	(E)
Southeast	-0.67***	-0.68***	-0.72***	-0.74***	-0.68***
Anthracite	-0.80**	-0.80**	-0.78**	-0.85***	-0.80**
PNF	-0.03	-0.11	-0.11	-0.06	-0.02
West					
Pop. Density	-0.0003**				
Agric. Emp. %		0.007**			
% Pop. 2.5K+			-0.004*		
% Pop. 10K+				-0.006**	
% Pop. 25K+					-0.007**
N	1907	1907	1907	1907	1907
Adjusted R^2	0.05	0.05	0.05	0.05	0.05
F	6.7***	6.6***	6.5***	6.7***	6.7***

*** significant at the 0.01 level
** significant at the 0.05 level
* significant at the 0.10 level

Note: Intercept represents a man aged 25-45, who enlisted in the infantry during 1863 or 1864 as a standard enlistee in the same county in which he was born, and who was a skilled worker born between 1835 and 1839 in the Western Region of Pennsylvania.

Table 5.19 Determinants of the Height of Soldiers – Statewide Sample: Single Economic/Demographic Variables with Regional Dummy

	(A)	(B)
Constant	68.00***	67.78***
1820-1824	0.40**	0.39**
1825-1829	0.19	0.18
1830-1834	0.31**	0.30**
1835-1839		
1840-1844	-0.06	-0.04
1861	0.50***	0.61***
1862	0.22	0.35**
1863/64		
1865	0.35*	0.33
Farmer	0.35**	0.33**
Proprietor	0.25	0.29
Skilled Worker		
Unskilled Worker	-0.03	-0.03
High Status	0.06	0.02
Unknown	0.41	0.42
Stayer		
Migrant	0.14*	0.15

Table 5.19 (continued)

	(A)	(B)
Southeast	-0.79***	-0.75***
Anthracite	-0.83**	-0.84***
PNF	-0.16	-0.05
West		
Largest City Size in Enlistment County		
Under 5K		
5K to 10K	-0.46***	
10K to 25K	-0.11	
25K+	-0.34**	
Largest City Size in Birth County		
Under 5K		
5K to 10K		0.07*
10K to 25K		-0.20
25K+		-0.48**
N	1907	1907
Adjusted R^2	0.05	0.05
F	6.2***	6.0***

*** significant at the 0.01 level
** significant at the 0.05 level
* significant at the 0.10 level

Note: Intercept represents a man aged 25-45, who enlisted during 1863 or 1864 in the infantry as a standard enlistee in the same county in which he was born (a county which at the time of enlistment had no town of over 5000 population), and who was a skilled worker born between 1835 and 1839 in the Western Region of Pennsylvania in a county with no town larger than 5000 persons.

only moderate per capita crop production levels, this sub-region was the nexus of transshipment of goods from western Pennsylvania to Buffalo and other lake ports (Table 5.13 and Figure 4.2).

Mean heights varied widely across the region. In the most isolated agricultural lands of Mercer and Lawrence Counties, adult mean heights were a full inch over the average for Erie and Crawford Counties, with smaller differences between the other sub-regions (Figures 5.26 and 5.27). These differences are consistent in size and significance (.01 level) using several different multivariate models (Table 5.15). The differences in height between the Isolated Agricultural area and the Mountain/Mineral Region and the Southern Hinterland were about half as large. After adjusting for other variables, Allegheny County had mean heights slightly less than one-half inch below those of the Isolated Agricultural region. The differences in height between the Northern Hinterland and the Isolated Agricultural Region were insignificant.

The temporal patterns of height in the Western sub-regions were somewhat different from those in the rest of the state. Except for the Lake Transport Region which had heights between one and one and one-half per cent below those of the rest of the West, heights across the Western Region varied in a narrow band between 1.5-1.75 per cent higher than the state mean (Figure 5.26). Region-wide temporal decline is evident only in the last quinquennium. Prior to that, stature declines were concentrated in Allegheny County. The pronounced decline in heights statewide during this period is not as clear in the West.[59]

An important pattern *within* the Western Region is similar to that across the rest of the state. Men born in the most recently settled sub-region, the counties least connected by transportation routes, the Isolated Agricultural Region, were the tallest. Those areas with the greatest concentration of population and most connected with the other regions, Allegheny County, the Lake Transport, and Mountain/Mineral Regions, had noticeably lower mean heights.

Variation by County Economic Characteristics

The trends described above are not artifacts of sample composition and cannot be explained by age or occupational variation within the sample. Earlier chapters discussed the hypothesis which explains antebellum stature variation by the propinquity to food resources and by remoteness from urban centers with their burdensome disease environments and their markets for food. Regional, occupational, and age-standardized analysis of variation in height indicates that the regional patterns expected on the basis of this hypothesis are obtained in this sample of Pennsylvanians as well. Areas least densely populated, least tightly connected by transportation routes, and most agriculturally based had mean stature levels significantly above regions at the other end of the developmental continuum. Even these small regions, however, were characterized by disparate economic and social circumstances. These patterns should, therefore, also be evaluated at a level of aggregation below the regional one in order to account for more localized variation. Controlling for this variation, however, requires techniques beyond those already used in presenting stature trends. After establishing proxy variables, which represented propinquity to nutrients, disease exposure, and participation in markets, multivariate regression analysis was used to evaluate the correlates of height.

In order to eliminate the influence of small categories of observations which might be unrepresentative and to stabilize the regression results, the sample was pared rather extensively. Only infantrymen, who enlisted as 'standard' enlistees, between 25 and 45 years of age, and who were born in counties a) without border changes between 1820 and 1845 and b) for which all relevant economic data were available, were included in this reduced sample. A total of 1907 men from 29 counties fit these characteristics and are included in the statewide county level regression analysis. A similar sub-set was created for men born in the Western Region of the state. A total of 1004 men from ten counties were available for analysis within this region.[60]

A series of proxies was developed to characterize the economies of the counties in the antebellum period.[61] Most data used in this analysis were drawn directly from the U.S. Census.[62] However, several variables were obtained from data gathered by Craig and Weiss, and by Craig, Palmquist and Weiss on agricultural surpluses in 1840 and access to water transportation routes in 1850.[63] The level of economic development is represented by the proportion of the population involved in agriculture. Propinquity to nutrients is proxied by the number of swine per capita, the per capita dollar value of dairy production, and the number of per capita surplus calories per day (in thousands) and grams of surplus protein (in hundreds) generated in the birth county.[64] Several potential proxies for the intensity of the disease environment were tested. These include population density, the percentage of the county population living in places with populations over 2500, over 10,000, and over 25,000, as well as the size of the largest city (in the census year nearest to the year of birth). The extent of market participation was proxied by the per capita value of market garden production and by the per capita value of home manufactures. Access to economic markets was proxied by 1845 average land values as well as by the presence of a navigable water transport route in 1850.[65] Anticipating that wealth would provide access to nutritional resources, the per capita value of agricultural and manufacturing assets in the county of birth in 1850 was also included in the equation.[66] Dummy variables to control for occupation, the year of enlistment, 'migrant' status, and the quinquennium of birth were also included, as was a dummy for the region of birth. The latter served as a proxy variable for some of the unexplained, but regionally associated, variation.

Investigation of the statewide and western data revealed that most of the county level independent variables were highly correlated with one another.[67] As a result the economic and demographic variables were entered into the regression one at a time. Results tended not to be robust when several of the newly created proxy variables were included in the regression. If removal from markets for agricultural and other goods gave a stature advantage to nineteenth-century Pennsylvanians, it would be anticipated that a positive sign (increasing stature levels) would be associated with the coefficient for per capita home manufactures, as high levels of this variable would signal low levels of market involvement. A negative sign (declining stature levels) would be anticipated for increasing levels of population density (disease exposure), town size in the county of birth, increasing land values, and the value of market gardening. Economic and market development indicated by lower levels of employment in agriculture would also be reflected in lower height levels, i.e., negative regression coefficients.

Table 5.20 Statewide Means and Standard Deviations for County Level Regression Variables (29 Counties)

	Including Philadelphia Co.		Excluding Philadelphia Co.	
	Mean	Standard. Deviation	Mean	Standard Deviation
Population Density (persons/sq. mile)	112.9	347.1	48.8	29.4
Protein Surplus (Per Capita, Per Day)	128.2	85	135	77
Calorie Surplus (Per Capita, Per Day)	5206	1969	5380	1764
Wealth Per Capita, 1850 (Agric. and Mnfctr)	$357	$143	$365	$139
Value of Dairy Production Per capita	$3.12	$2.79	$3.20	$2.81
Value of Home Manufactures Per Capita	$1.39	$1.30	$1.44	$1.29
Number of Swine Per Capita	0.91	0.40	0.94	0.38
Value of Land Per Acre 1845	$85	$339	$22	$21
Value of Market Garden Production Per Capita	$0.10	$0.23	$0.08	$0.20
Percentage of County Workforce in Agricultural Sector	65.1	20.8	67.2	17.9
Percentage of County Population in Towns of 2500-10,000	19.2	24.1	16.4	19.3
Percentage of County Population in Towns of 10,000-25,000	4.3	17.2	1.4	7.3
Percentage of County Population in Towns of 25,000+	2.5	13.2	0	0

Note: Unless indicated all figures refer to 1840

It is unclear what the sign on the coefficient for per capita swine levels, protein and calorie surpluses, dollar value of dairy production, and water transport availability should be. The ready accessibility of nutrients represented by the presence of large numbers of hogs, dairy products, surplus protein and calories, and market access via water routes would be factors which theoretically would

Table 5.21 Western Means and Standard Deviations for County Level Regression Variables

	Including Allegheny. Co.		Excluding Allegheny. Co.	
	Mean	Standard Deviation	Mean	Standard Deviation
Population Density (persons/sq. mile)	40.0	27.2	32.1	11.2
Protein Surplus (Per Capita, Per Day)	133	79	145	74
Calorie Surplus (Per Capita, Per Day)	5246	1961	5510	1881
Wealth Per Capita, 1850 (Agric. and Mnfctr)	$286	$99	$286	$104
Value of Dairy Production Per Capita	$2.16	$1.27	$2.27	$1.30
Value of Home Manufactures Per Capita	$2.19	$1.51	$2.41	$1.42
Swine Per Capita	1.04	0.38	1.11	0.33
Value of Land Per Acre 1845	$11	$11	$7	$4
Value of Market Garden Production Per Capita	$0.16	$0.33	$0.10	$0.29
Percentage of County Workforce in Agricultural Sector	71.7	12.6	75.4	5.22
Percentage of County Population in Towns of 2500-10,000	17.4	19.3	12.8	13.5
Percentage of County Population in Towns of 10,000-25,000	3.8	12.1	0	0
Percentage of County Population in Towns of 25,000+	0	0	0	0

Note: Unless indicated all figures refer to 1840

provide greater access to nutrition. If, however, these simply indicated the presence of animals destined for slaughter and/or calories destined for sale elsewhere, and water route access simply a means of bringing people to a locale, then these conditions would mean increased disease exposure without the benefit of increased protein or calorie consumption.[68] The wealth variable, indicating access to nutrients both near and far, is anticipated to have a positive sign.

Regressions were run including these variables on the restricted statewide sample as described above. The exercise was then repeated excluding the men born in the city and county of Philadelphia in order to ascertain the extent to which the results were influenced by this rather atypical region. For both the statewide and western samples, regression coefficients for the non-economic/non-demographic variables remain the same as reported above. The inclusion of these new proxy variables does not have an effect on those results. The basic time profile of stature between 1820 and 1839 remains as previously described. Statistical significance is lacking for the birth cohorts in the Western Region, however. The time pattern is somewhat flatter in the West as the 1820-24 to 1825-29 decline was smaller. The two samples differ with regard to the stature of the 1840-44 cohort. Statewide, this cohort had a mean stature slightly below that of the 1835-39 group. The coefficient for the 1840-44 birth cohort in the Western Region is positive, quite large, but insignificant.

Even after accounting for the economic variables, farmers had a significant stature advantage of four-tenths of an inch or larger, depending upon the model. Other occupational variables did not reach the level of statistical significance, although the near equivalence of the stature of skilled and unskilled workers remained. Migrants in both samples were taller than stayers, but not at a statistically significant level.

Statewide analysis The new proxy variables were entered individually in order to avoid multicollinearity as discussed above. Several variables consistently appear the most closely linked to stature variation across the 29 counties in the statewide sample[69] (Figures 5.28-5.39 and Tables 5.16-5.19). Regardless of the model, the per capita number of swine and the presence of water transportation routes within the county of birth are two variables with the largest consistent relationship to stature variation. Their coefficients have opposite signs, as expected. The presence of a large number of hogs per capita in the county of birth is associated with greater stature, while the presence of a navigable water route is associated with lesser stature. When observations for Philadelphia County and dummy regional variables are included in the model, a one standard deviation change in the level of swine per capita[70] yields a two-third inch change in anticipated stature levels, while the coefficient on the dummy for the presence of water transportation in the county of birth is -0.83. Other strongly influential variables in statewide-sample regressions include protein and calorie surpluses per capita, the dollar value of dairy production, and the dollar value of home manufacturing. Each is associated with approximately a two-tenth of an inch increase in stature for each one standard deviation positive change in the independent variables. A series of variables with negative coefficients including the dollar value of market gardening, the mean land value, and population density (each generally significant at the 0.05 level or below) are not as statistically significant, nor do they have such a large absolute influence on stature (each about 0.1 inch per standard deviation change in the independent variables). The percentage of the work force employed in agriculture also had a significant effect on stature levels (+0.15 inch/standard deviation, 0.05 level of significance). Dummy variables for the presence of a town in the county of birth or enlistment generally carried negative coefficients ranging from a -0.48 for birth in a county containing a town of 25,000 or more persons to -0.34 for enlistment in such a county. The coefficient on birth in a county containing a town of 5-10,000 population was negligible (0.07). In sum, the signs of the variables were quite consistent with the proposed hypothesis. The proxies for propinquity to nutrients (protein and calorie surpluses, swine stocks, and dairy production levels) were all positively correlated with stature, as in some other samples.[71] The positive impact of ready access to nutrients apparently outweighed the negative influence of disease exposure which might also have been associated with these indicators. Distance from markets and urban centers proxied by low dollar values of market gardening, low population concentration levels, and high home manufacturing levels were all correlated with greater stature and thus higher net nutritional status. Connections to markets proxied by the availability of water transportation, high dollar value of market gardening, and high population concentration levels were associated with lower stature.

These statewide results did not arise from the statistical dominance and uniqueness of the Philadelphia-born in the sample. When the same set of regressions is rerun without men born in Philadelphia County, the results are essentially the same (Tables 5.22-5.25). Signs, in most instances, remained as expected and were consistent with the first set of regressions. Some significance levels fell, though, partly due to the smaller number of observations, partly as an indication that Philadelphia did have a substantial impact on the results. However, protein and calorie surpluses, swine stock size per capita, the dollar value of home manufactures, and dairy production all remain significant at the 0.01 level, and the size of their impact on stature remains approximately equivalent to their earlier effect, except for swine levels. The effect of a one standard deviation change in swine stocks has only half as much impact on stature levels when the Philadelphia born are eliminated from the sample.[72] The size and signs of the coefficients for the presence of water transport and city size in the county of enlistment remain. Therefore, the link between market participation and stature levels is not simply a function of the effects of the huge Philadelphia urban center on its residents. Rather, the net nutritional effect of a large city spreads well beyond the urban area's boundaries.

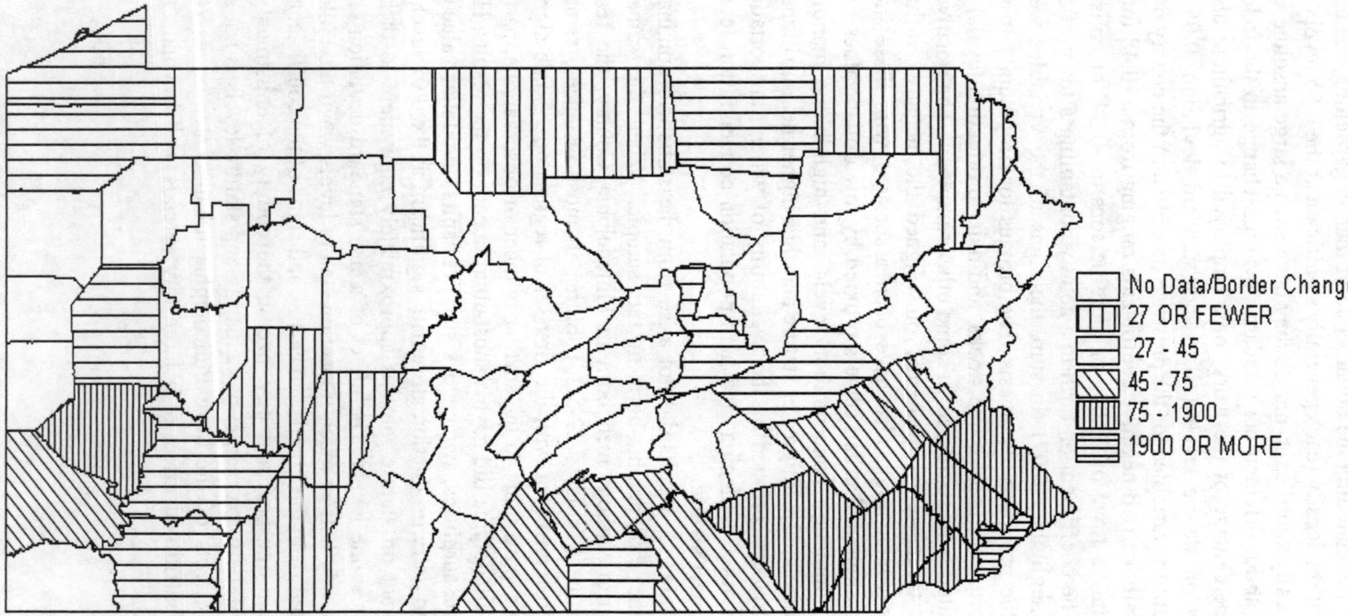

Figure 5.28 Population Density (PSM) – 1840

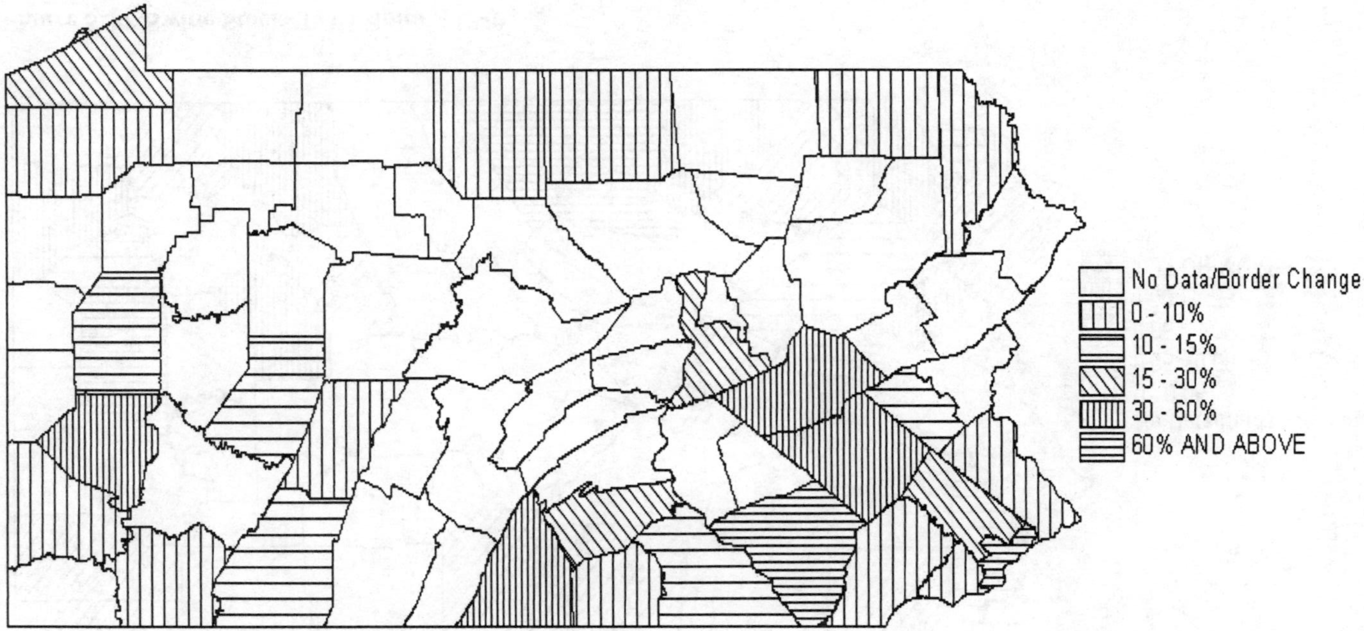

Figure 5.29 Percentage of County Population in Towns of 2500+ –1840

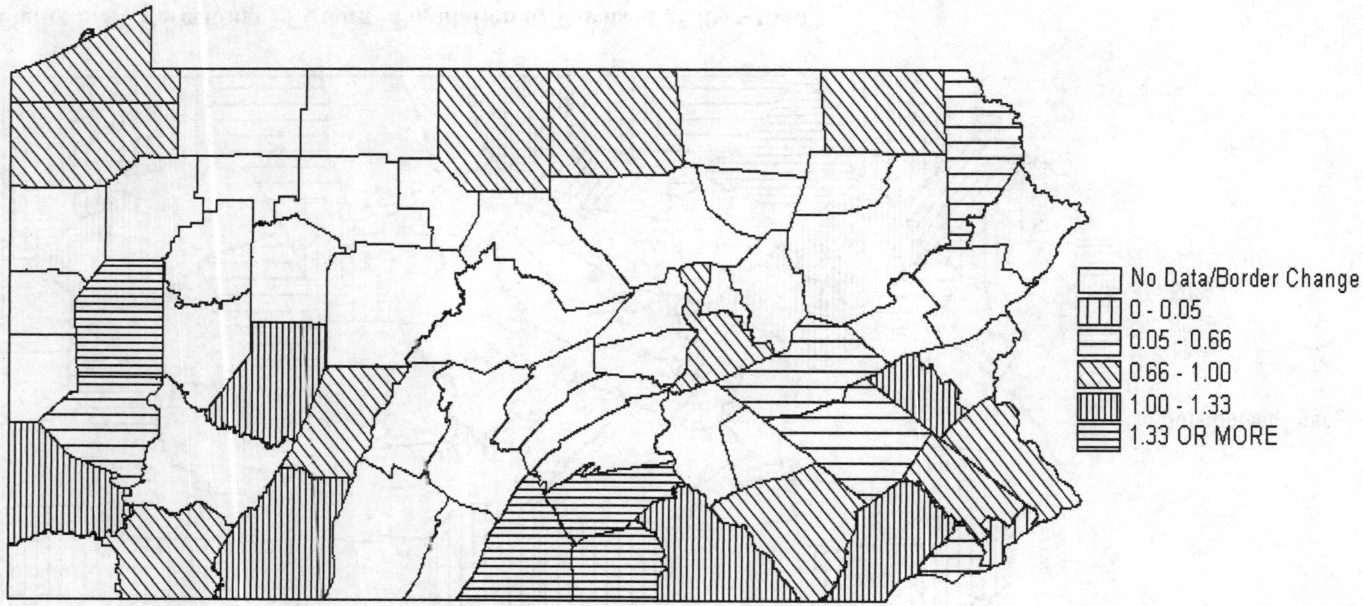

Figure 5.30 Swine Stocks Per Capita – 1840

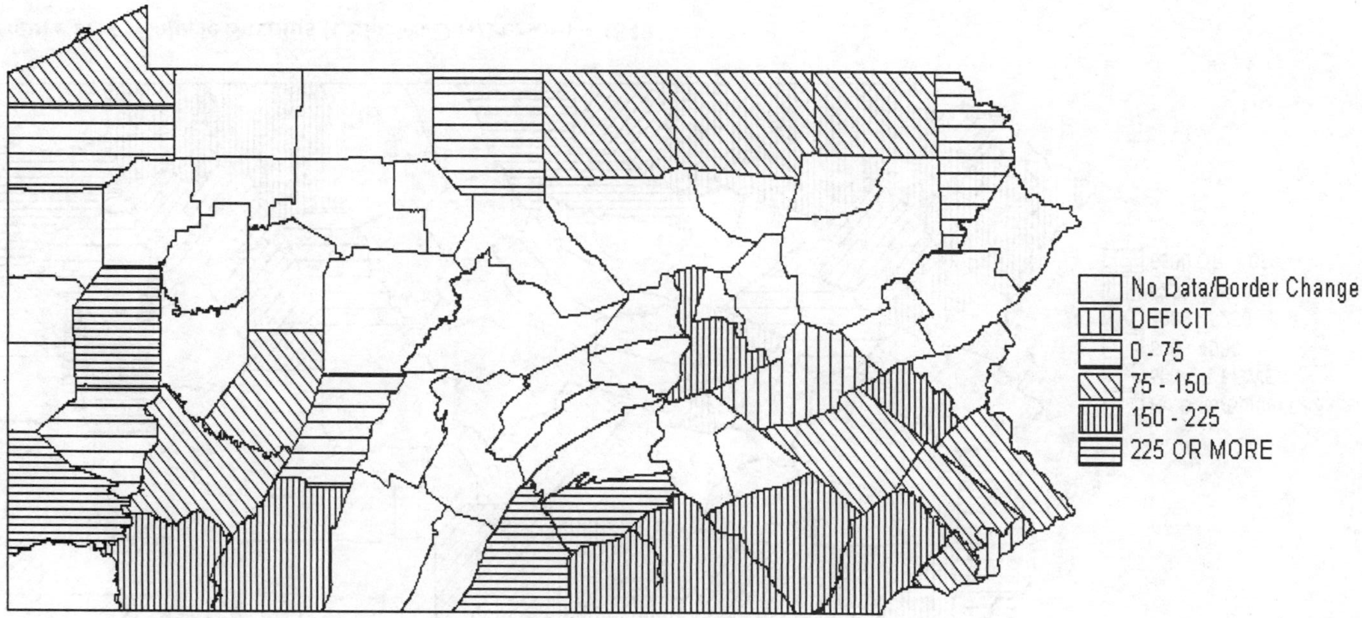

Figure 5.31 Protein Surplus (Grams/Day/Person) – 1840

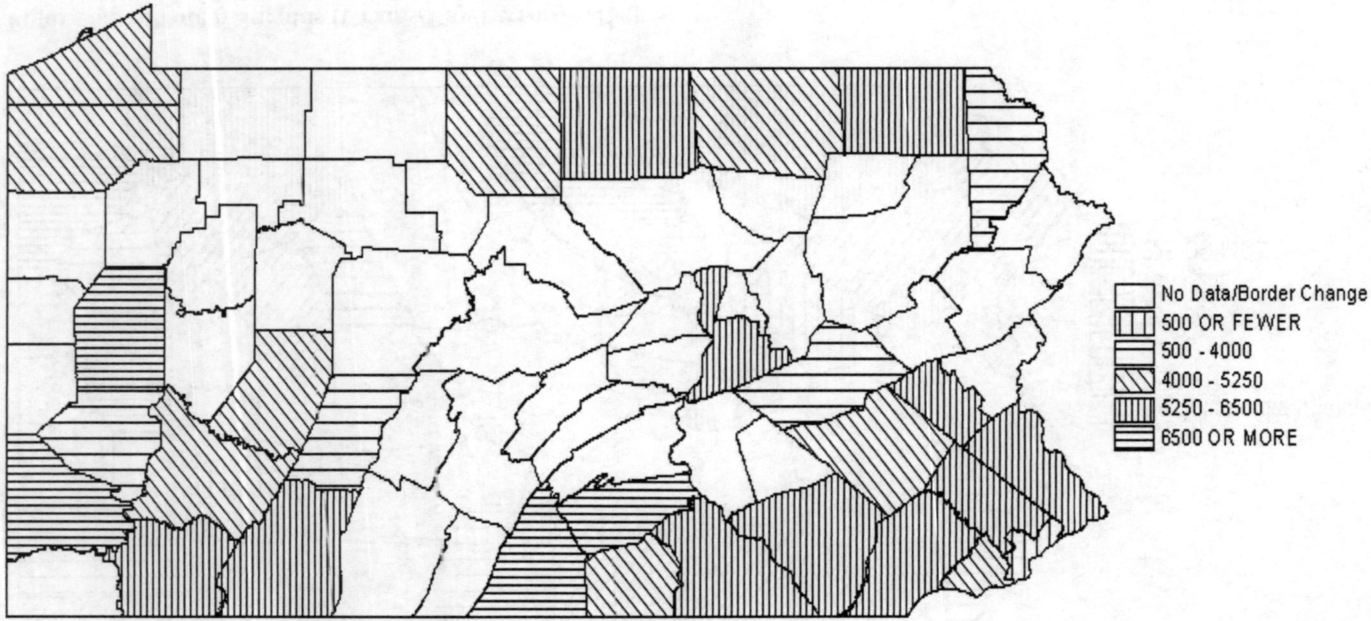

Figure 5.32 Calorie Surplus (Calories/Day/Person) – 1840

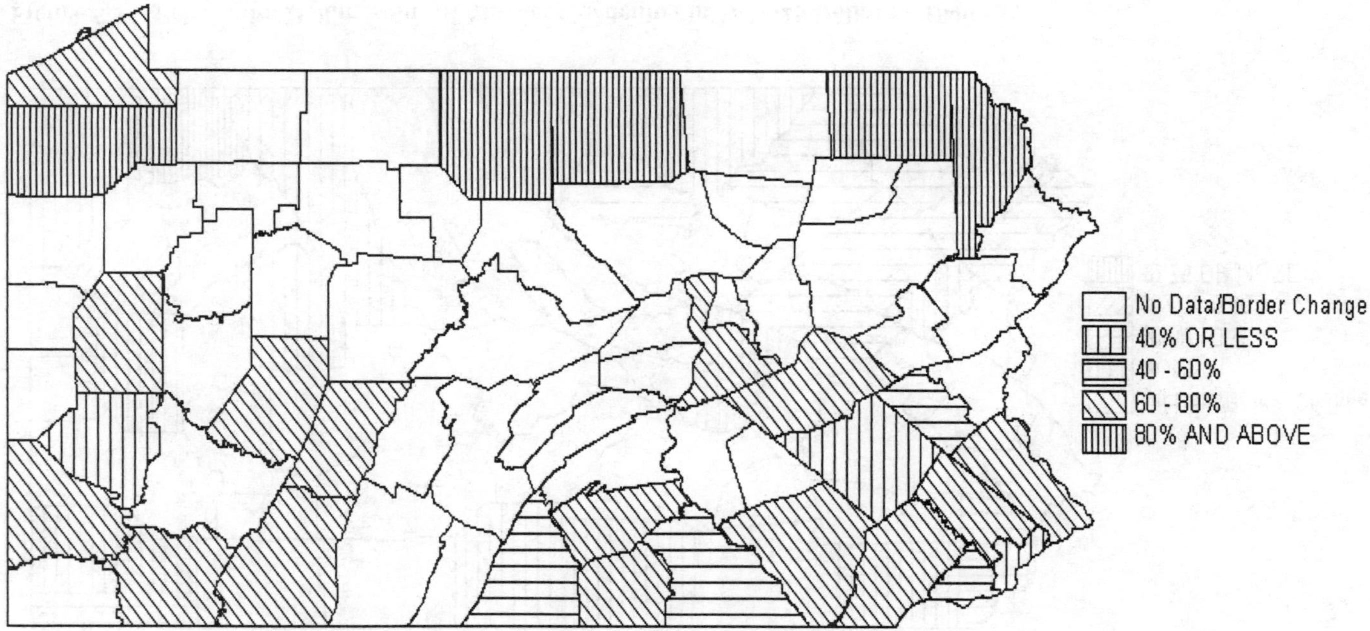

Figure 5.33 Percentage of County Work Force in Agriculture – 1840

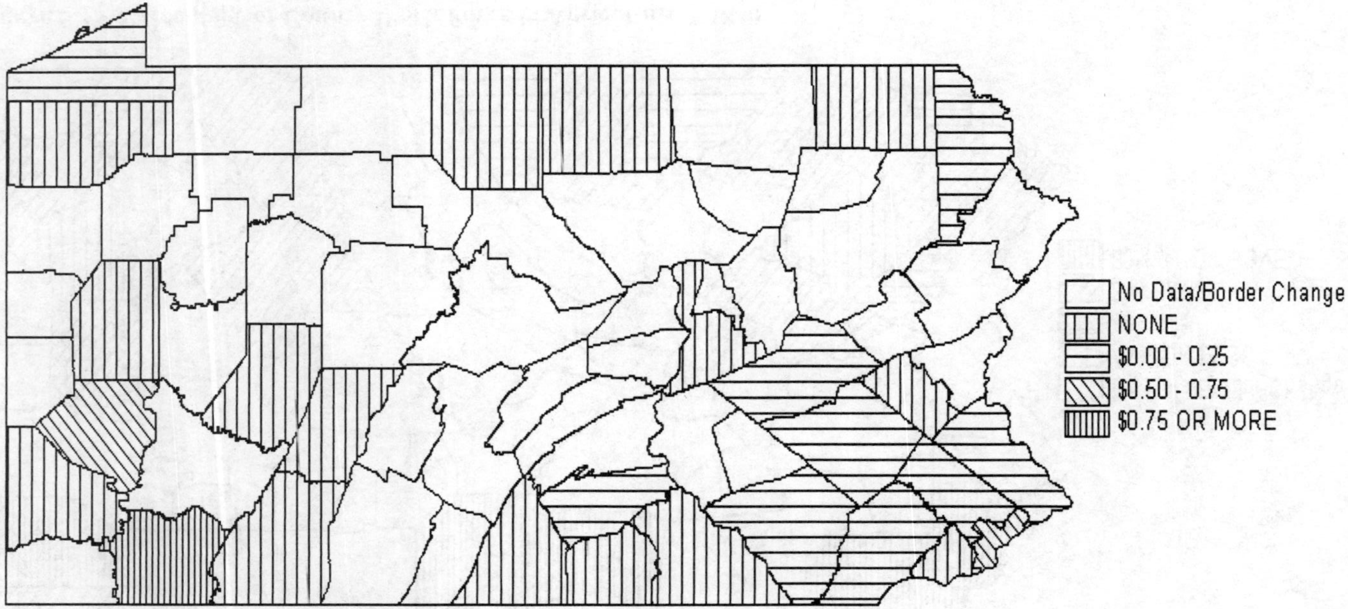

Figure 5.34 Per Capita Dollar Value of Market Gardening in 1821-25 Dollars – 1840

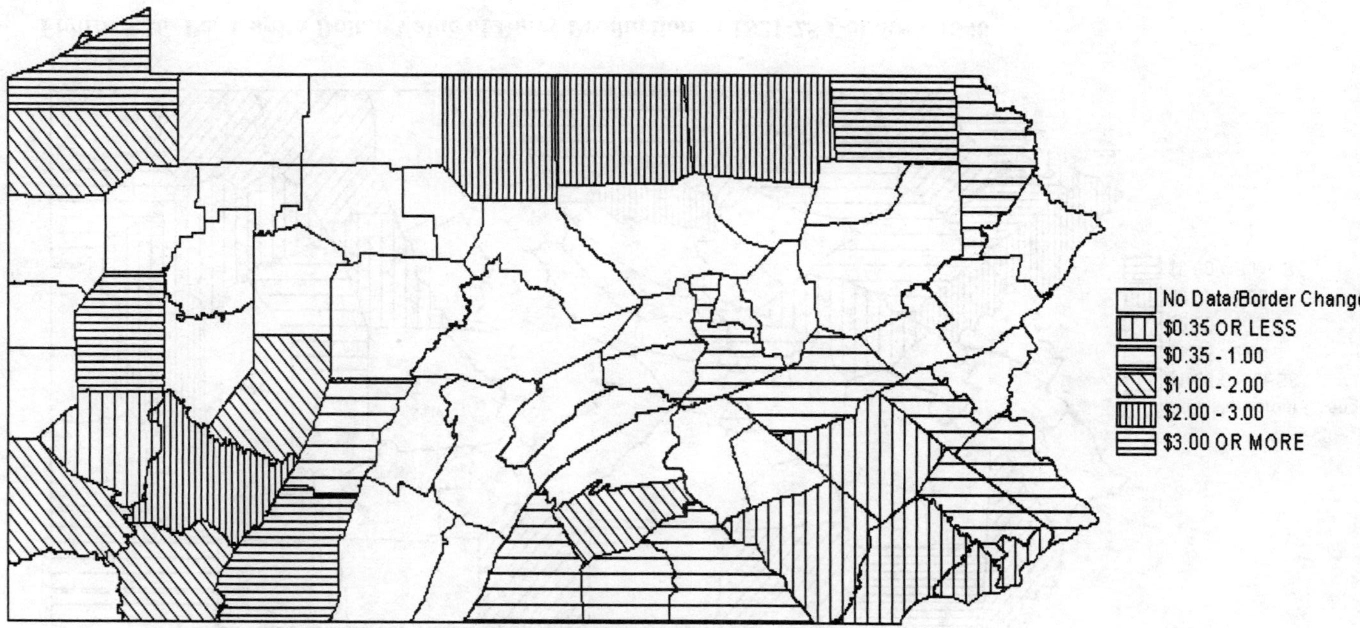

Figure 5.35 Per Capita Dollar Value of Home Manufactures in 1821-25 Dollars – 1840

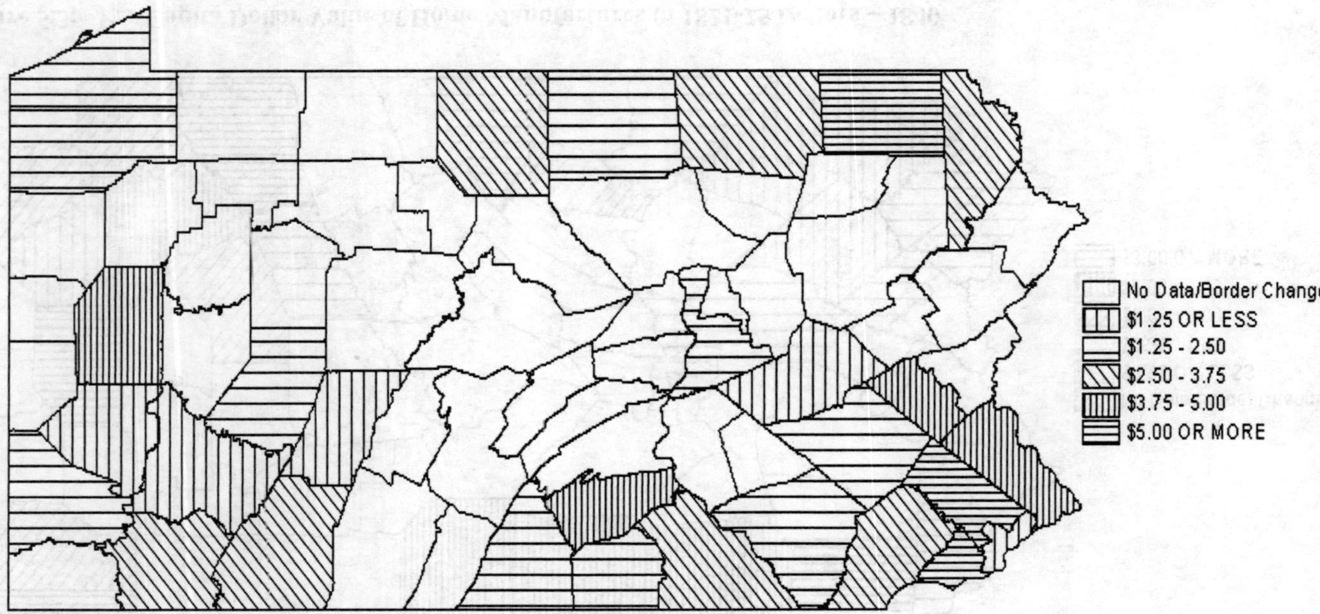

Figure 5.36 Per Capita Dollar Value of Dairy Production in 1821-25 Dollars – 1840

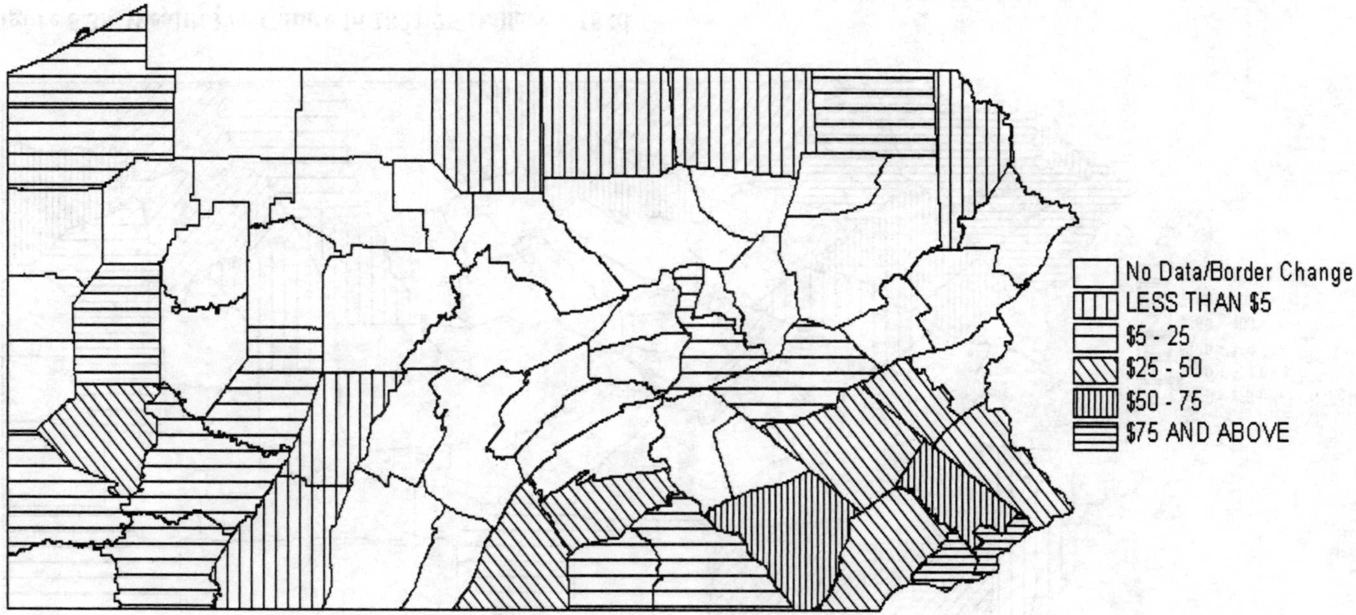

Figure 5.37 Mean Per Acre Land Values in 1821-25 Dollars – 1840

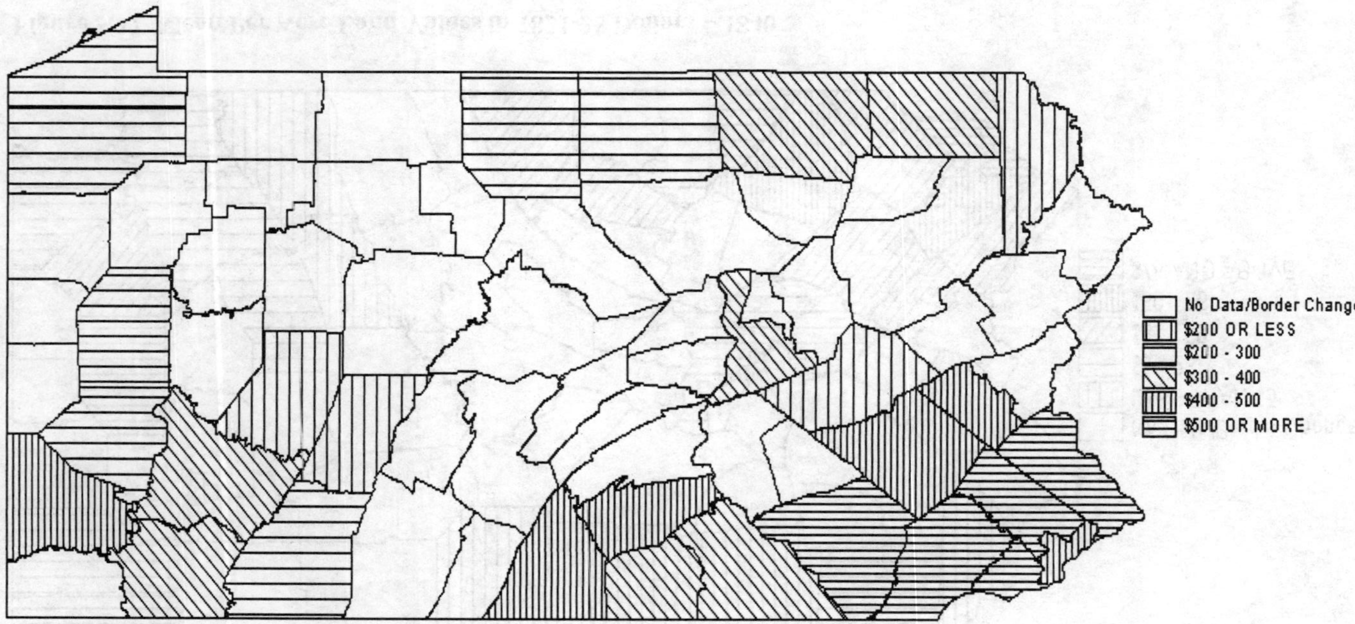

Figure 5.38 Wealth Per Capita in 1821-25 Dollars – 1840

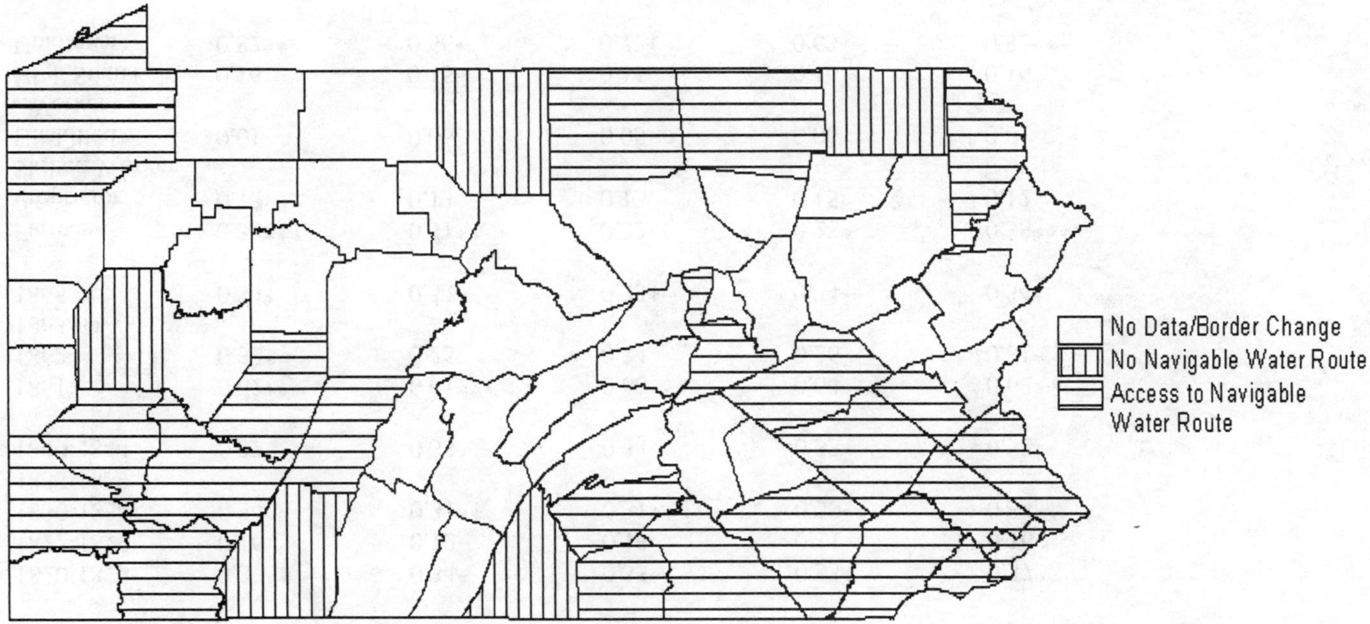

Figure 5.39 Navigable Water Routes – 1850

Table 5.22 Determinants of the Height of Soldiers – Statewide Sample: Single Economic/Demographic Variables with Regional Dummy, No Philadelphia County-Born Men

	(A)	(B)	(C)	(D)	(E)
Constant	67.72***	67.44***	67.28***	67.16***	67.66***
1820-1824	0.37**	0.34*	0.35*	0.33*	0.37**
1825-1829	0.16	0.12	0.13	0.11	0.16
1830-1834	0.34**	0.31**	0.31**	0.30**	0.34**
1835-1839					
1840-1844	-0.32	-0.35	-0.34	-0.33	-0.32
1861	0.62***	0.61***	0.60***	0.64***	0.62***
1862	0.32*	0.25	0.24	0.26	0.31*
1863/64					
1865	0.34*	0.34*	0.33*	0.34*	0.34*
Farmer	0.38***	0.31**	0.33**	0.28*	0.38***
Proprietor	0.12	0.13	0.13	0.15	0.12
Skilled Worker					
Unskilled Worker	-0.01	-0.06	-0.05	-0.06	-0.01
High Status	0.16	0.15	0.16	0.16	0.16
Unknown	0.82**	0.66*	0.72*	0.63	0.82**
Stayer					
Migrant	0.15	0.11	0.12	0.05	0.16

Table 5.22 (continued)

	(A)	(B)	(C)	(D)	(E)
Southeast	-0.67***	-0.87***	-0.82***	-0.72***	-0.71***
Anthracite	-0.84***	-0.64**	-0.68**	-0.55*	-0.83***
PNF	-0.05	0.07	-0.01	-0.15	-0.05
West					
Protein		0.30***			
Calorie			0.10***		
Swine				0.69***	
Wealth					-0.0002
N	1720	1720	1720	1720	1720
Adjusted R^2	0.04	0.04	0.04	0.05	0.04
F	5.3***	5.7***	5.5***	5.9***	5.00***

*** significant at the 0.01 level
** significant at the 0.05 level
* significant at the 0.10 level

Note: Intercept represents a man aged 25-45, a standard infantry enlistee, who enlisted during 1863 or 1864 in the same county in which he was born, and who was a skilled worker born between 1835 and 1839 in the Western Region of Pennsylvania. No men born in Philadelphia County are included in this regression.

Table 5.23 Determinants of the Height of Soldiers – Statewide Sample: Single Economic/Demographic Variables with Regional Dummy, No Philadelphia County-Born Men

	(A)	(B)	(C)	(D)	(E)
Constant	68.44***	67.45***	67.60***	67.77***	67.76***
1820-1824	0.35*	0.36**	0.37**	0.37**	0.37**
1825-1829	0.16	0.16	0.15	0.15	0.16
1830-1834	0.33**	0.33**	0.34**	0.33**	0.33**
1835-1839					
1840-1844	-0.34	-0.31	-0.31	-0.31	-0.31
1861	0.62***	0.64***	0.62***	0.64***	0.63***
1862	0.25	0.23	0.29*	0.31*	0.32*
1863/64					
1865	0.33*	0.33*	0.34*	0.36**	0.34*
Farmer	0.33**	0.31**	0.37**	0.36**	0.37**
Proprietor	0.15	0.14	0.13	0.13	0.13
Skilled Worker					
Unskilled Worker	-0.06	-0.05	0.00	-0.01	-0.01
High Status	0.25	0.22	0.17	0.17	0.16
Unknown	0.55	0.63	0.75*	0.80**	0.81**
Stayer					
Migrant	0.07	0.09	0.11	0.14	0.14

Table 5.23 (continued)

	(A)	(B)	(C)	(D)	(E)
Southeast	-0.64***	-0.42***	-0.78***	-0.71***	-0.62***
Anthracite	-0.64**	-0.59*	-0.75**	-0.86***	-0.83***
PNF	-0.05	-0.12	-0.16	-0.08	-0.07
West					
Water Tran.	-0.79***				
Home Mfctr.		0.17***			
Dairy			0.07***		
Mrkt Grdn.				-0.23	
Land Value					-0.002
N	1720	1720	1720	1720	1720
Adjusted R^2	0.05	0.04	0.04	0.04	0.04
F	6.6***	5.6***	5.4***	5.0***	5.0***

*** significant at the 0.01 level
** significant at the 0.05 level
* significant at the 0.10 level

Note: Intercept represents a man aged 25-45, who enlisted in the infantry as a standard enlistee in the same county in which he was born, who enlisted during 1863 or 1864, and who was a skilled worker born between 1835 and 1839 in the Western Region of Pennsylvania. No men born in Philadelphia County are included in this regression.

Table 5.24 Determinants of the Height of Soldiers – Statewide Sample: Single Economic/Demographic Variables with Regional Dummy, No Philadelphia County-Born Men

	(A)	(B)	(C)	(D)	(E)
Constant	67.86***	67.49***	67.74***	67.75***	
1820-1824	0.36**	0.37**	0.37**	0.37**	
1825-1829	0.15	0.16	0.16	0.16	
1830-1834	0.33**	0.33**	0.34**	0.33**	
1835-1839					
1840-1844	-0.31	-0.31	-0.31	-0.31	
1861	0.65***	0.63***	0.62***	0.63***	
1862	0.32*	0.31*	0.32*	0.31*	
1863/64					
1865	0.37**	0.36*	0.34*	0.36*	
Farmer	0.35**	0.37**	0.38**	0.37**	
Proprietor	0.14	0.13	0.13	0.13	
Skilled Worker					
Unskilled Worker	-0.02	-0.01	-0.01	-0.02	
High Status	0.16	0.17	0.16	0.16	
Unknown	0.78*	0.81**	0.81**	0.81**	
Stayer					
Migrant	0.13	0.14	0.15	0.14	

Table 5.24 (continued)

	(A)	(B)	(C)	(D)	(E)
Southeast	-0.62***	-0.66***	-0.67***	-0.70***	
Anthracite	-0.86***	-0.84***	-0.84***	-0.87***	
PNF	-0.10	-0.09	-0.06	-0.07	
West					
Pop. Dnsty	-0.002				
Ag. Emp. %		0.003			
% Pop. 2.5K+			-0.0006		
% Pop. 10K+				-0.003	
% Pop. 25K+					none
N	1720	1720	1720	1720	0
Adjusted R^2	0.04	0.04	0.04	0.04	
F	5.0***	5.0***	5.0***	5.0***	

*** significant at the 0.01 level
** significant at the 0.05 level
* significant at the 0.10 level

Note: Intercept represents a man aged 25-45, who enlisted in the infantry during 1863 or 1864 as a standard enlistee in the same county in which he was born, and who was a skilled worker born between 1835 and 1839 in the Western Region of Pennsylvania. No men born in Philadelphia County are included in this regression.

Table 5.25 Determinants of the Height of Soldiers – Statewide Sample: Single Economic/Demographic Variables with Regional Dummy, No Philadelphia County-Born Men

	(A)	(B)
Constant	68.00***	67.77***
1820-1824	0.36*	0.34*
1825-1829	0.16	0.15
1830-1834	0.35**	0.33**
1835-1839		
1840-1844	-0.32	-0.31
1861	0.50***	0.64***
1862	0.19	0.31*
1863/64		
1865	0.33*	0.37**
Farmer	0.37**	0.36**
Proprietor	0.12	0.14
Skilled Worker		
Unskilled Worker	-0.02	-0.02
High Status	0.16	0.16
Unknown	0.74*	0.81**
Stayer		
Migrant	0.11*	0.14

Table 5.25 (continued)

	(A)	(B)
Southeast	-0.65***	-0.75***
Anthracite	-0.83**	-0.88***
PNF	-0.16	-0.08
West		
Largest City Size:	in Enlistment County	in Birth County
Under 5K		
5K to 10K	-0.47***	-0.08
10K to 25K	-0.14	-0.20
25K+	-0.23	----
N	1720	1720
Adjusted R^2	0.04	0.04
F	4.9***	4.7***

*** significant at the 0.01 level
** significant at the 0.05 level
* significant at the 0.10 level

Note: Intercept represents a man aged 25-45, who enlisted during 1863 or 1864 in the infantry as a standard enlistee in the same county in which he was born (a county which at the time of enlistment had no town of over 5000 population), and who was a skilled worker born between 1835 and 1839 in the Western Region of Pennsylvania in a county with no town larger than 5000 persons. No men born in Philadelphia County are included in this regression.

Table 5.26 Determinants of the Height Of Soldiers – Statewide Sample: Single Economic/Demographic Variables without Regional Dummy

	(A)	(B)	(C)	(D)	(E)
Constant	67.24***	67.03***	66.84***	66.73***	67.29***
1820-1824	0.35**	0.35**	0.35**	0.34*	0.35**
1825-1829	0.18	0.16	0.16	0.14	0.18
1830-1834	0.32**	0.31**	0.31**	0.29**	0.32**
1835-1839					
1840-1844	-0.08	-0.07	-0.07	-0.05	-0.08
1861	0.68***	0.69***	0.68***	0.70***	0.68***
1862	0.51***	0.48***	0.46***	0.45***	0.50***
1863/64					
1865	0.31*	0.29*	0.29	0.28	0.31*
Farmer	0.65***	0.57***	0.56***	0.48***	0.64***
Proprietor	0.35	0.34	0.34	0.34	0.35
Skilled Worker					
Unskilled Worker	0.01	-0.06	-0.05	-0.07	0.01
High Status	0.22	0.20	0.18	0.21	0.22
Unknown	0.44	0.40	0.41	0.35	0.43
Stayer					
Migrant	0.16	0.09	0.09	0.01	0.16

Table 5.26 (continued)

	(A)	(B)	(C)	(D)	(E)
Protein		0.24***			
Calorie			0.10***		
Swine				0.75***	
Wealth					-0.0002
N	1907	1907	1907	1907	1907
Adjusted R^2	0.02	0.03	0.03	0.04	0.02
F	4.7***	5.6***	5.5***	6.8***	4.3***

*** significant at the 0.01 level
** significant at the 0.05 level
* significant at the 0.10 level

Note: Intercept represents a man aged 25-45, who enlisted during 1863 or 1864 as a standard enlistee in the same county in which he was born, and who was a skilled worker born between 1835 and 1839.

Table 5.27 Determinants of the Height of Soldiers – Statewide Sample: Single Economic/Demographic Variables without Regional Dummy

	(A)	(B)	(C)	(D)	(E)
Constant	68.13***	67.05***	67.12***	67.35***	67.42***
1820-1824	0.34*	0.37**	0.36**	0.36**	0.39**
1825-1829	0.18	0.17	0.18	0.17	0.18
1830-1834	0.31**	0.30**	0.32**	0.32**	0.32**
1835-1839					
1840-1844	-0.09	-0.06	-0.06	-0.06	-0.06
1861	0.68***	0.65***	0.69***	0.73***	0.67***
1862	0.42***	0.29	0.50***	0.51***	0.50***
1863/64					
1865	0.30*	0.31*	0.31*	0.34*	0.27
Farmer	0.55***	0.36**	0.64***	0.58**	0.51***
Proprietor	0.36	0.32	0.35	0.36	0.32
Skilled Worker					
Unskilled Worker	-0.06	-0.06	0.01	-0.02	-0.04
High Status	0.29	0.17	0.20	0.19	0.11
Unknown	0.22	0.19	0.42	0.41	0.45
Stayer					
Migrant	0.07	0.08	0.12	0.12	0.11

Table 5.27 (continued)

	(A)	(B)	(C)	(D)	(E)
Water Tran.	-0.93***				
Home Mfctr.		0.28***			
Dairy			0.05**		
Mrkt Grdn.				-0.43**	
Land Value					-0.0005***
N	1907	1907	1907	1907	1907
Adjusted R^2	0.04	0.05	0.03	0.03	0.04
F	7.1***	7.7***	4.7***	4.7***	6.1***

*** significant at the 0.01 level
** significant at the 0.05 level
* significant at the 0.10 level

Note: Intercept represents a man aged 25-45, who enlisted in the infantry during 1863 or 1864 as a standard enlistee in the same county in which he was born, and who was a skilled worker born between 1835 and 1839.

Table 5.28 Determinants of the Height of Soldiers – Statewide Sample: Single Economic/Demographic Variables without Regional Dummy

	(A)	(B)	(C)	(D)	(E)
Constant	67.44***	66.55***	67.63***	67.40***	67.40***
1820-1824	0.39**	0.38**	0.36**	0.37**	0.39**
1825-1829	0.18	0.16	0.15	0.17	0.18
1830-1834	0.32**	0.31**	0.30**	0.32**	0.32**
1835-1839					
1840-1844	-0.06	-0.05	-0.04	-0.06	-0.06
1861	0.68***	0.71***	0.69***	0.72***	0.67***
1862	0.50***	0.47***	0.46***	0.51***	0.50***
1863/64					
1865	0.28	0.35*	0.32*	0.33*	0.27*
Farmer	0.51***	0.45***	0.48***	0.53***	0.52***
Proprietor	0.32	0.34	0.34	0.35	0.32
Skilled Worker					
Unskilled Worker	-0.04	-0.05	-0.02	-0.04	-0.04
High Status	0.11	0.11	0.07	0.15	0.11
Unknown	0.45	0.41	0.36	0.42	0.45
Stayer					
Migrant	0.11	0.09	0.05	0.10	0.11

Table 5.28 (continued)

	(A)	(B)	(C)	(D)	(E)
Pop. Density	-0.0005***				
Agric. Emp. %		0.01***			
% Pop. 2.5K+			-0.008***		
% Pop. 10K+				-0.008***	
% Pop. 25K+					-0.01***
N	1907	1907	1907	1907	1907
Adjusted R^2	0.04	0.04	0.03	0.03	0.04
F	6.1***	6.0***	5.6***	5.4***	6.0***

*** significant at the 0.01 level
** significant at the 0.05 level
* significant at the 0.10 level

Note: Intercept represents a man aged 25-45, who enlisted during 1863 or 1864 in the infantry as a standard enlistee in the same county in which he was born, who was a skilled worker born between 1835 and 1839.

Table 5.29 Determinants of the Height of Soldiers – Statewide Sample: Single Economic/Demographic Variables without Regional Dummy

	(A)	(B)
Constant	67.75***	67.47***
1820-1824	0.36**	0.42**
1825-1829	0.18	0.18
1830-1834	0.31**	0.32**
1835-1839		
1840-1844	-0.08	-0.07
1861	0.53***	0.66***
1862	0.30*	0.48***
1863/64		
1865	0.37*	0.26*
Farmer	0.52***	0.48***
Proprietor	0.32	0.30
Skilled Worker		
Unskilled Worker	-0.03	-0.03
High Status	0.16	0.09
Unknown	0.29	0.42
Stayer		
Migrant	0.11	0.09

Table 5.29 (continued)

	(A)	(B)
Largest City Size in Enlistment County		
Under 5K		
5K to 10K	-0.62***	
10K to 25K	-0.61***	
25K+	-0.48***	
Largest City Size in Birth County		
Under 5K		
5K to 10K		-0.33
10K to 25K		-0.07
25K+		-0.96***
N	1907	1907
Adjusted R^2	0.03	0.04
F	5.1***	5.5***

*** significant at the 0.01 level
** significant at the 0.05 level
* significant at the 0.10 level

Note: Intercept represents a man aged 25-45, who enlisted during 1863 or 1864 in the infantry as a standard enlistee in the same county in which he was born (a county which at the time of enlistment had no town of over 5000 population), and who was a skilled worker born between 1835 and 1839 in a county with no town larger than 5000 persons.

Table 5.30 Determinants of the Height of Soldiers – Western Region: Single Economic/Demographic Variables without Sub-Region Dummy

	(A)	(B)	(C)	(D)	(E)
Constant	67.35***	67.10***	66.94***	66.75***	67.44***
1820-1824	0.49*	0.46*	0.47**	0.46*	0.49**
1825-1829	0.38*	0.32	0.34	0.32	0.38*
1830-1834	0.45**	0.40**	0.41**	0.40**	0.45**
1835-1839					
1840-1844	0.67	0.73	0.73	0.74	0.67
1861	0.86***	0.83***	0.82***	0.87***	0.86***
1862	0.38*	0.26	0.26	0.29	0.40*
1863/64					
1865	0.42	0.39	0.37	0.44*	0.43
Farmer	0.53***	0.44**	0.46**	0.39**	0.53***
Proprietor	0.22	0.24	0.24	0.26	0.22
Skilled Worker					
Unskilled Worker	0.29	0.22	0.24	0.22	0.29
High Status	0.46	0.48	0.46	0.55	0.47
Unknown	0.69	0.56	0.63	0.49	0.68
Stayer					
Migrant	0.27	0.17	0.19	0.09	0.26

Table 5.30 (continued)

	(A)	(B)	(C)	(D)	(E)
Protein		0.32***			
Calorie			0.11***		
Swine				0.79***	
Wealth					-0.0004
N	1004	1004	1004	1004	1004
Adjusted R^2	0.02	0.03	0.03	0.03	0.02
F	2.5***	3.1***	2.8***	3.5***	2.3***

*** significant at the 0.01 level
** significant at the 0.05 level
* significant at the 0.10 level

Note: Intercept represents a man aged 25-45, who enlisted during 1863 or 1864 as a standard enlistee in the same county in which he was born, and who was a skilled worker born between 1835 and 1839. These regressions only included men born in the Western Region.

Table 5.31 Determinants of the Height of Soldiers – Western Region: Single Economic/Demographic Variables without Sub-Region Dummy

	(A)	(B)	(C)	(D)	(E)
Constant	68.25***	67.09***	67.11***	67.42***	67.47***
1820-1824	0.48*	0.49**	0.50**	0.49*	0.49*
1825-1829	0.39*	0.38*	0.39*	0.37	0.37
1830-1834	0.45**	0.44**	0.46**	0.44**	0.44**
1835-1839					
1840-1844	0.68	0.72	0.74	0.69	0.70
1861	0.75***	0.87***	0.74***	0.91***	0.91***
1862	0.22	0.27	0.19	0.38*	0.39*
1863/64					
1865	0.28*	0.44*	0.29	0.47*	0.50*
Farmer	0.46**	0.42**	0.46**	0.49***	0.49**
Proprietor	0.26	0.24	0.30	0.22	0.23
Skilled Worker					
Unskilled Worker	0.22	0.22	0.26	0.28	0.27
High Status	0.62	0.61	0.52	0.49	0.49
Unknown	0.25	0.39	0.45	0.66	0.63
Stayer					
Migrant	0.13	0.16	0.16	0.23	0.22

Table 5.31 (continued)

	(A)	(B)	(C)	(D)	(E)
Water Tran.	-0.88***				
Home Mfctr.		0.19***			
Dairy			0.21***		
Mrkt Grdn.				-0.27	
Land Value					-0.007
N	1004	1004	1004	1004	1004
Adjusted R^2	0.04	0.03	0.03	0.02	0.02
F	3.8***	3.2***	3.3***	2.4***	2.4***

*** significant at the 0.01 level
** significant at the 0.05 level
* significant at the 0.10 level

Note: Intercept represents a man aged 25-45, who enlisted during 1863 or 1864 in the infantry as a standard enlistee in the same county in which he was born, and who was a skilled worker born between 1835 and 1839. These regressions only included men born in the Western Region.

Table 5.32 Determinants of the Height of Soldiers – Western Region: Single Economic/Demographic Variables without Sub-Region Dummy

	(A)	(B)	(C)	(D)
Constant	67.54***	66.90***	67.43***	67.40***
1820-1824	0.49*	0.49*	0.49*	0.49*
1825-1829	0.36	0.36	0.37*	0.37
1830-1834	0.44**	0.44**	0.45**	0.44**
1835-1839				
1840-1844	0.70	0.71	0.69	0.69
1861	0.91***	0.92***	0.87***	0.89***
1862	0.39*	0.38*	0.37*	0.38*
1863/64				
1865	0.51*	0.50*	0.45*	0.47*
Farmer	0.48**	0.47**	0.51***	0.50***
Proprietor	0.24	0.23	0.23	0.22
Skilled Worker				
Unskilled Worker	0.26	0.27	0.28	0.27
High Status	0.50	0.49	0.46	0.48
Unknown	0.61	0.64	0.67	0.66
Stayer				
Migrant	0.21	0.22	0.24	0.24

Table 5.32 (continued)

	(A)	(B)	(C)	(D)
Pop. Density	-0.003			
Agric. Emp. %		0.01		
% Pop. 2.5K+			-0.002	
% Pop. 10K+				-0.004***
% Pop. 25K+				
N	1004	1004	1004	1004
Adjusted R^2	0.02	0.02	0.02	0.02
F	2.4***	2.4***	2.3***	2.4***

*** significant at the 0.01 level
** significant at the 0.05 level
* significant at the 0.10 level

Note: Intercept represents a man aged 25-45, who enlisted during 1863 or 1864 in the infantry as a standard enlistee in the same county in which he was born, and who was a skilled worker born between 1835 and 1839. These regressions only included men born in the Western Region.

Table 5.33 Determinants of the Height of Soldiers – Western Region: Single Economic/Demographic Variables without Sub-Region Dummy

	(A)	(B)
Constant	67.52***	67.42***
1820-1824	0.49*	0.39
1825-1829	0.38*	0.36
1830-1834	0.45**	0.44**
1835-1839		
1840-1844	0.66	0.71
1861	0.77***	0.89***
1862	0.30	0.37*
1863/64		
1865	0.38*	0.48*
Farmer	0.51***	0.50***
Proprietor	0.21	0.24
Skilled Worker		
Unskilled Worker	0.27	0.27
High Status	0.46	0.45
Unknown	0.64	0.67
Stayer		
Migrant	0.24	0.23

Table 5.33 (continued)

	(A)	(B)
Largest City Size in Enlistment County		
Under 5K		
5K to 10K	-0.26	
10K to 25K	-0.12	
25K+	-0.10	
Largest City Size in Birth County		
Under 5K		
5K to 10K		0.41
10K to 25K		-0.24
25K+		
N	1004	1004
Adjusted R^2	0.02	0.02
F	2.1***	2.3***

*** significant at the 0.01 level
** significant at the 0.05 level
* significant at the 0.10 level

Note: Intercept represents a man aged 25-45, who enlisted during 1863 or 1864 in the infantry as a standard enlistee in the same county in which he was born (a county which at the time of enlistment had no town of over 5000 population), and who was a skilled worker born between 1835 and 1839 in a county containing no town larger than 5000 persons at the time of his birth. These regressions only included men born in the Western Region.

Statewide regression models described so far have included a variable for the region of birth. It was anticipated that this would serve as a repository for some of the unexplained variation resulting either from variables not known to influence stature or from variables known to be influential but for which no data was collected (e.g. level of income inequality and extent of new immigrants in the population). Irrespective of which economic-demographic variable is included in the regression equation, the regions' coefficients are stable and retain their standing relative to the omitted Western Region (Tables 5.26-5.29). The Southeastern Region's coefficient, between –0.5 and –0.8 inches, is always significant at the 0.01 level, with or without the inclusion of cases from Philadelphia County, while the Anthracite is similar in size but at the 0.05 significance level. The Pocono/Northeast/Allegheny Forest Regions, which were conflated because of the small number of cases from these regions, had negligible differences in stature from the Western Region.[73] Those three regions, the most isolated and distant from markets, had stature levels considerably greater than their more economically integrated neighbors.

Excluding region of birth from the model (Philadelphia County observations included) slightly lowers both the level of significance and amount of variation explained, but with a few notable exceptions, does not affect the general pattern of results. While per capita protein and calorie surpluses and per capita swine stock size remained significant at the 0.01 level and had about the same size effect, the coefficient for home manufacturing per capita increased by 50 per cent and the significance of its equation as a whole was higher than when the region variables were included. The coefficients of the population density and land value variables increased similarly. Meanwhile, the coefficients of both per capita dairy production value and wealth were sharply reduced. Wealth became insignificant, and dairy production, previously significant at the 0.01 level, fell slightly to the 0.05 level. Both these variables seem to gain in explanatory power if a regional dummy variable is included in the regression in order to account for economic and demographic characteristics of the region. This was the case possibly because dairy production levels were high both in areas of the Philadelphia hinterland and in some more isolated locales. Some of the other variables, more unambiguously associated with market participation (such as home manufacturing, market gardening, land values), were less sensitive to the inclusion of the regional dummy variables than was dairy production and wealth per capita.[74]

Western analysis As was the case with the sub-regional height data, a clear pattern of variation emerged from the regression results[75] (Tables 5.30-5.33). These indicate that soldiers born in the Lake Transport Region were by 0.6 to 1.74 inches shorter than those born in the other parts of the Western Region. The sub-region with the tallest men was the Northern Hinterland, which borders the Isolated Agricultural Region and was most like it in terms of economic and demographic characteristics. Even Allegheny County had a large positive coefficient relative to the Lake Transport sub-region.

The situation in Erie and Crawford County may well relate to developments in the 1820s in the neighboring Empire State. With the completion of the Erie Canal, Pennsylvania's one Great Lakes port, Erie, became a trans-shipment point for goods and travelers. Connections to the rest of the state from Erie traversed Crawford County along two routes. These avenues of commerce may well have also become avenues of infection, which would have contributed to the lower net nutrition status of the area. With the opening of the Erie Canal it is possible that there were increased sales of high protein foods by local farmers to obtain cash with which to purchase now readily available manufactured goods. In addition, income inequality may well have increased as a consequence of the growth of a commercial economy that employed large amounts of unskilled labor in warehousing and hauling, in Erie County and, to a lesser degree, in Crawford. Disease factors associated with large-scale urbanization can probably be eliminated as a cause.[76]

No significant correlation resulted in the western sample when a regression model including one economic/demographic variable along with a dummy variable for region and the other standard dummies (birth quinquennium, enlistment year, occupation, and migrant status) was used to evaluate the relationship with stature. Signs of the coefficients were as expected for the economic variables, with per capita market gardening and the dummy for water transport route presence carrying a negative sign. Variables indicating a lack of market involvement were correlated positively with height. However, only one of the population density or city size variables, enlistment in a county with a city of 25,000 plus residents, carried a negative sign. None of these was statistically significant.

In the statewide regressions described earlier, omitting the regional dummies increased the significance of some of the individual economic/demographic variables. None of those variables achieved statistical significance in the western sample until the regional dummies were removed. Once region was dropped from the regression, the same variables that were the strongest correlates of height in the statewide sample were the strongest in the west. Per capita protein and calorie surpluses, per capita swine stock levels, and the per capita dollar value of home manufacturing and dairy production were all positively correlated with height and significant at the 0.01 level. The only variable with such a high level of significance and a negative coefficient was the presence of a water route in the birth county (-0.88). Coefficients for the value of market gardening and land values also had negative signs as expected, but these did not rise to the 0.10 level of significance. The size of the impact which each of the individual variables had on stature was comparable with the effects apparent in the statewide sample. The variable with the largest effect on stature was the per capita size of the swine stock, with a 0.3 inch increase in stature associated with each one-third of a hog per capita (one s.d.) increase in the stocks. Similar stature effects (+0.27 inches) were correlated with a one standard deviation change in the value of home manufacturing and dairy production values, with smaller effects (+0.24 and +0.22 inches, respectively) resulting from a similar shift in protein and calorie surpluses.

As was the case in the statewide sample, the economic and demographic variables in the Western Region were highly correlated with one another. Regression models utilizing multiple independent economic/demographic variables yielded few consistent results except for the strength of the water transport and per capita swine stock variables. As was the case in the state sample, signs on the coefficients for the percentage of the work force in agriculture, percentage of the population in towns of 2500+ persons, per capita value of home manufacturing and market gardening all reversed from what they presented as single variables. Greater reliance can be placed on the single variable equations, as they had equal or greater explanatory power and levels of significance equivalent to the multiple variable models.

Conclusion

The analysis presented above confirms and expands upon earlier findings within the literature. Pennsylvanians who fought in the American Civil War had a mean height that ranged between the 20–35th percentile of modern height standards. However, they were probably among the tallest populations in their world, with considerably greater stature than their European contemporaries.[77] Men born in western Pennsylvania were taller than average and had height levels between those of their Midwestern neighbors and their 'cousins' in Philadelphia. Statewide stature levels reflect the relatively easy access to nutrients, the extremely productive soil, the favorable climate, as well as the low level of large-scale urbanization in early nineteenth-century Pennsylvania. Similar stature levels would not be achieved by the majority of even West Europeans until the turn of the twentieth century.[78]

The decline in mean stature described by most studies of the antebellum United States is uniformly evident in these samples as well. It is more clearly apparent in the statewide sample and concentrated more among skilled and unskilled workers than in other occupational categories. Farmers' heights in the Western Region show very little decline in this period. They also tended, as did farmers across Pennsylvania, to have mean heights greater than most other occupation groups.

One can infer on the basis of physical stature that men of meaner and meaner estate were pulled into the Civil War as it dragged on. Proprietors and other upper-middle-class persons comprised an increasingly smaller proportion of the enlistees between 1863 and 1865. The latter's mean height reflected their social and political advantages. A height gradient by military rank, somewhat related to the occupational gradient but not fully explained by it, was identified. This seems to be more a functional outgrowth of height variation than a cause of height differences.

The hypothesis which animated this study is supported by its findings. Analysis of both samples indicates that men from counties which were the least involved in market activity and least developed economically were significantly taller than men in more market integrated locales. Stature was positively and strongly correlated with the production of home manufactures and negatively related to the level of market gardening. Men from counties with the largest proportions of their work force in agriculture tended to be taller, as were men from counties without water transport routes – the latter were not linked to distant markets. In antebellum Pennsylvania, being self-sufficient obviously conferred nutritional advantages. Those who were economically 'behind' literally looked down on those who were 'ahead.'

Distance from markets was not the sole factor related to greater stature. Propinquity to nutrients, the per capita levels of swine stocks, dairy production, and protein and calorie surpluses were all positively correlated with height. While having a somewhat weaker effect, county population characteristics also influenced stature trends. Population density and the presence of large cities in the counties of birth and/or enlistment were negatively related to stature. The case of relatively short men in agriculturally productive Lancaster County highlights the interplay of factors. While large quantities of foodstuffs were harvested in this county, and a considerable nutritional surplus produced, this was not sufficient to generate a high nutritional status for the children growing up there. Either the disease effects associated with being close to an urban center or familial choice to market high value protein foods outweighed the effect of being close to large amounts of proteins and calories. As the cases above indicate, the presence of a navigable water route in Erie County and one in Clearfield County are not equivalent because of who and what was at the other end of that water route and how long it took to reach its terminus. Protein and calorie surpluses in Lancaster County, destined for sale in Philadelphia or Baltimore, clearly mean something different from surpluses of similar size in isolated Tioga County. While statistical analysis using various proxies has outlined the relationship between economic and demographic variables and stature, understanding the full pattern also requires understanding the nature of the places and of the connection (or lack thereof) between them.

A combination of economic processes and harsher epidemiological micro-environments associated with the onset of modern economic growth likely were both responsible for the decline in stature during the antebellum decades. Antebellum economic development, the growth of intra-regional markets, the tying together of the countryside by various means of transport played a role in determining net nutritional status, and thus stature of the state's residents. Yet, local context was also important. Further analysis is warranted and potential extensions of this work are discussed in the concluding chapter.

Notes

1 Robert W. Fogel, 'Nutrition and the Decline in Mortality since 1700: Some Preliminary Findings,' in *Long-Term Factors in American Economic Growth,* ed. S. Engerman and R. Gallman (Chicago: National Bureau of Economic Research, 1987), 439-527.

2 The term 'native-born' Pennsylvanian has a more restrictive definition than 'native-born' may carry in some other contexts. For purposes of this study, a native-born Pennsylvanian is not a Pennsylvania resident born in the United States but rather a Pennsylvanian born within the boundaries of the Keystone State.

3 The independent variables will include most of those used to characterize Pennsylvania in Chapter Four and a few others not presented earlier because they are only available for only about one-half of the state's counties.

4 Housed in the U.S. National Archives, these books were compilations of various rolls kept by company clerks. Data were drawn from the descriptive rolls, a roll of men who enlisted when the unit was formed as well as those who enlisted later to take the place of the fallen. It was one of four record books kept at the company level. United States War Department, *United States Army Regulations of 1861 with an Appendix Containing the Changes and Laws Affecting Army Regulations and Articles of War to June 25, 1863* (Washington, D.C.: G.P.O., 1863), 20 and 24. Data for each soldier included name, date of enlistment, age, birth place, place of enlistment, occupation, rank, and remarks about the man's military career. Data collected for each company and applied to each man's data record included company name and unit type (e.g. infantry, artillery). Adjutant General's Office, *Descriptive Books of Volunteer Organizations: Civil War, 1861-65*, Record Group 94, Item 114 (National Archives. Washington, D.C.).

5 The extent to which the sample is representative of the Pennsylvania male population is discussed in the Appendix.

6 For the primary place of origin of the units, see R.A. Sauers, *Advance the Colors: Pennsylvania Civil War Battle Flags* (Harrisburg: Capitol Preservation Committee, 1987); Samuel P. Bates, *Bates's History of Pennsylvania Volunteers, 1861-1865* (Harrisburg: B. Singerly, 1869). See the Appendix for a description of the process of selecting units for inclusion.

7 Robert W. Fogel, Stanley Engerman, et.al., *Union Army Recruits in White Regiments in the United States, 1861-65*, computer file, Study # 9425 (Chicago: University of Chicago, Center for Population Economics\producer\,1990). Ann Arbor, MI: Inter-University Consortium for Political and Social Research\distributor\,1990.

8 To assess the physical well-being of 'migrants,' stature variation will also be explored between men who enlisted in their county of birth and those who did not. While an important subject, the study of migration with the use of Civil War enlistment records is problematic. Although men who enlisted in counties other than their birth counties clearly had to travel to do so, information does not exist on just when in the life of the soldier the migration took place. During the course of the war enlistments increasingly took place at larger regional recruiting stations, rather than locally. Soldiers who re-enlisted may even have done so out of state. Therefore, the place of enlistment is not a very good indicator of migration status.

9 There were many units with secondary recruitment counties. Sauers, *Advance the Colors*, 248-303.

10 Data in Table 5.1 also reflect both the nature of rural–urban migration in antebellum Pennsylvania and the fact that non-native born Pennsylvanians are absent from the sample.

11 United States War Department, *Regulations of the Army of the United States and General Orders in Force on the 17th of February 1881* (Washington, D.C.: GPO, 1881), 354.

12 Charles S. Tripler, *Manual of the Medical Officer of the Army of the United States. Part I. Recruiting and Inspection of Recruits* (Cincinnati: Wrightson and Co., 1858), 11.

13 J.H. Baxter, *Statistics, Medical and Anthropological of the Provost-Marshall-General's Bureau* (Washington: G.P.O., 1875), lix. These limits did not apply to musicians.

14 Baxter also did not note differences in minimum height standards for different types of military units during this period. After the war a maximum was established for stature and weight among men seeking to enter the cavalry. Baxter, *Statistics, Medical*, xlix.

15 This is a function probably of some size preference on the part of those recruiting for these units and the fact that such units were not recruited equally throughout Pennsylvania. In the combined sample the distribution of birth places in the cavalry and the artillery units are disproportionately from a few counties. For example, although men born in Philadelphia, Allegheny and Westmoreland counties comprised only 18.2 per cent of the total sample, 35.1 per cent of all artillery enlistees were born in these three counties. Similarly, although Philadelphia county birth cohorts comprise 6.0 per cent of the merged samples, they account for only 3.1 per cent of cavalry enlistees.

16 On the effect of the minimum height requirement see John Komlos and Joo Han Kim, 'Estimating Trends in Historical Heights,' *Historical Methods* 23 (1990): 116-120.

17 Komlos and A'hearn have extensively tested Fogel's Union Army sample using the Reduced Sample Maximum Likelihood Estimator and found no impact on data trends resulting from left tail truncation. Brian A'hearn, 'The Antebellum Puzzle Revisited: A New Look at the Stature of Union Army Recruits during the Civil War'; and John Komlos, 'On the Biological Standard of Living of African-Americans: the Case of the Civil War Soldiers,' both in *The Biological Standard of Living in Comparative Perspective*, ed. John Komlos and Joerg Baten (Stuttgart: Steiner Verlag, 1998), pp. 250-267, 236-249.

18 Baxter, *Statistics, Medical*, 29.

19 Robert Margo and Richard Steckel, 'Heights of Native Born Whites During the Antebellum Period,' *Journal of Economic History* 43 (1983): 167-174; Baxter, *Statistics, Medical*, 29.

20 'Occupation' was not always recorded in such a way to reflect the person's role in the business or firm. Men noting only a business site are believed to have been owners of these places of business. Theodore Herschberg and Robert Dockhorn, 'Occupational Classification,' *Historical Methods Newsletter* 9 (1976): 68.

21 The slight rebound apparent in 1865 enlistment cohorts in the Western sample may result from 1861 and 1862 enlistees re-enlisting in 1865 and 'bringing' their greater stature into the 1865 cohort. It was possible in some, but not all, cases to identify and appropriately date the original enlistments of this group.

22 See the Appendix for details of the meaning of these categories. 'Recruit' seems to have been used, at least in the records of the company and regimental roll books, to indicate a veteran who had re-enlisted. Sometimes the books noted 'veteran recruit.' This may be a partial explanation for their greater mean height. As re-enlistees, they had originally enlisted in 1861 or 1862 for a three year stint. Men during those two years were taller than the men who enlisted later in the war. See the Appendix for another potential meaning of 'recruit.'

23 Such notations would have been made in the 'Remarks' column.

24 Sylvester K. Stevens, *Pennsylvania: The Keystone State*, Vol. I, *Historical* (New York: The American Historical Co., Inc., 1956), 361.

25 Fogel's 39,000 observation national sample of Civil War enlistees does not include a rank variable. This avenue of interpretation is thus not available when using observations from that data set. However, even though rank was not noted, non-commissioned officers were seemingly included in his sample. Company C of the 76th Pennsylvania Infantry was collected by both Fogel and me. A comparison reveals that Fogel's sample does contain some soldiers who had a rank of sergeant or corporal, however without a rank indication.

26 While most units identified their officers by name and rank, only a few recorded physical descriptions of them. Since the purpose of these physical descriptions was to prove identity on pay day and in the event of desertion it may have been that commanders in the units did not feel it necessary to have descriptions of their officers recorded because of their belief that officers, as gentlemen, would never claim undeserved pay or desert. I thank Michael Meier, National Archives, Military Reference Branch for this insight.

27 In both samples, non-commissioned officers, sergeants, and corporals were about an inch taller and a year older than the men serving under them. After accounting for age, occupation, and other influencing factors, the regression equation reduces the height advantage of non-commissioned officers to between one-half and two-thirds of an inch. The latter finding is quite robust and stable across several regression formulations.

28 The Reserve Corps is discussed further in the Appendix.

29 See Chapter One and James M. Tanner, *A History of the Study of Human Growth* (Cambridge: Cambridge University Press, 1981), 118.

30 Richard Steckel, 'Percentiles of Modern Height: Standards for Use in Historical Research,' *Historical Methods* 29 (1996): 163.

31 Age variation is obviously a critical issue in evaluating inter-group height differentials. As a result, most of the analysis will take account of it. In some cases data will be presented for the entire sample along with data for only the 25-49 year olds (in order to exclude any influence of variation due to the continuation of the growth process). In addition, height standardization by age will be performed in some cases, in order to allow for comparisons with larger sample sizes by including cases on youth.

32 The use of reported occupation of the soldier has some inherent problems. It would be preferable to have information on father's occupation, as that had a more direct influence on the soldier's nutritional and health circumstances during most of his growing years. However, young men in the early nineteenth century entered the labor market before completion of the biological growth process, so their own occupation would also have had an effect on their final height.

33 It is appropriate to say 'most other men' because most had occupations in the skilled and unskilled categories, categories which have lower mean stature than farmers.

34 Except for men without an occupation, the stature advantage of high status occupations over farmers in the unadjusted statewide mean disappeared in the regressions. The advantage apparently was a function of an average age two and a half to six years higher for the proprietor and work site groups. High status occupations have been defined as students, professionals, men listing only a work site, and men with no occupation.

35 Regressions run separately for men born in each of the seven regions all show farmers with a stature advantage over the omitted category (skilled workers) but it is only

significant in the Southeastern Region (without Philadelphia County), Allegheny County, and the Western Region (without Allegheny County). These regional regressions also show that in the Southeastern Region and in Philadelphia County unskilled workers were one-quarter to one-fifth of an inch shorter than their skilled brethren and that this difference is weakly statistically significant (0.10 level).

36 Kenneth L. Sokoloff and Georgia C. Villaflor, 'The Early Achievement of Modern Stature in America,' *Social Science History* 6 (1982): 462-465.

37 R.W. Fogel, S. Engerman, et al., 'Changes in American and British Stature Since the Mid-Eighteenth Century: A Preliminary Report on the Usefulness of Data on Height for the Analysis of Secular Trends in Nutrition, Labor Productivity, and Labor Welfare,' Cambridge, MA: NBER Working Paper #890; Robert Margo and Richard Steckel, 'Heights of Native Born Whites During the Antebellum Period,' *Journal of Economic History* 43 (1983): 171.

38 It is also possible that more of the migrants moved after their growth ceased.

39 See Chapters One and Two.

40 Margo and Steckel, 'Native Born Whites,' 168.

41 Kenneth L. Sokoloff, 'The Heights of Americans in Three Centuries: Some Economic and Demographic Implications' in *The Biological Standard of Living on Three Continents: Further Explorations in Anthropometric History*, ed. John Komlos (Boulder, CO: Westview Press, 1995), 136.

42 Sokoloff, 'Three Centuries,' 136.

43 See John Komlos, 'The Height and Weight of West Point Cadets: Dietary Change in Antebellum America,' *Journal of Economic History* 47 (1987): 897-327, for a complete analysis of this data set.

44 This anomaly of 'very large' 16 and 17 year olds may be a function of the need for a 'young' potential cadet to be as physically developed as the standard 18 year old cadet in order to warrant 'early' admittance.

45 Among the Pennsylvania-born cadets who reported the nature of their residence at the time of enlistment, 196 out of 245 indicated that they resided in a town or city, with only 98 indicating that they resided in a rural area.

46 The 1845-49 quinquennium is omitted from this description. Most men born in that five year span had not completed their growth prior to enlistment. Additionally, almost all these men enlisted in 1863 or later – years known to have seen the enlistment of men of smaller stature.

47 John Komlos, 'Anomalies in Economic History: Reflections on the "Antebellum Puzzle",' *Journal of Economic History* 56 (March, 1996): 202-214.

48 Komlos, 'West Point Cadets,' see Tables 2, 3, 4 and 5.

49 See Chapter Four for a list of the counties in each region, circa 1860.

50 In order to standardize heights, the mean height for each age category was calculated. Each individual height was then divided by the mean height for that age of that individual to give the standardized height as a percentage of the mean over the whole of the 1815-1850 period. An eighteen year old soldier with a height of 66.66" would have an age standardized height of 1.01 if the mean height of eighteen year olds were 66 inches (66.66/66 = 1.01). This technique allows for height comparisons across regional or occupational categories regardless of the age composition of that category.

51 These maps show county boundaries at the beginning of the war, not during the quinquennium of birth. Later regression analysis will include only men who were born

in counties which experienced no border changes during the years between 1820 and 1860.

52 Fifteen observations per period minimum. Unless noted, the charts and maps do not account for county border changes which may have occurred during the antebellum period. No adjustment was made for such changes, except the analysis below does exclude data from counties which experienced border changes during the period under consideration.

53 The figures' titles 'urban' and 'non-urban' refer to the presence or absence of a large urban center, i.e., Philadelphia or Pittsburgh.

54 Cell sizes were so small for several regions that unreasonably large fluctuation existed in the mean heights by quinquennium and they were not plotted.

55 There was a difference between urban and rural residents but it was only significant at the 0.10 level. In their view, the situation was one in which the less well off became concentrated in cities as time went on. Sokoloff and Villaflor, 'Early Achievement,' 463.

56 Sokoloff, 'Three Centuries,' 137.

57 Note that Allegheny County is plotted separately and is *not* part of the Western Region in this graph.

58 Due to the interesting patterns across the West, men who were born in Lawrence County (which actually would have been possible only for those 20 years and younger since Lawrence County was not formed until 1845) were reported as such, even though they would have been born in either Mercer or Beaver County. This is true only for the regional analysis, not the analysis involving county level economic data. Men from all three counties were excluded from that analysis.

59 The Lake Transport region's time trends in age standardized height and mean adult height diverge sharply. The standardized height moves upward toward the values of the other sub-regions, while the absolute mean (based only on men who have completed their growth) declines. This would seem to indicate some divergence in the net nutritional status of men who had not completed their growth from men who had in the late 1820s and 1830s.

60 The statewide regression utilized the data for anyone in the statewide or western samples who fit the noted characteristics. The western analysis included all men who met the noted requirements and who also were born in one of the ten 'western' counties.

61 See Tables 4.4 through 4.16 in Chapter Four for sources of the various indicators.

62 Census data by county was collected from both bound volumes of the census and from a machine readable computer file made available by the ICPSR. Inter-university Consortium for Political and Social Research, *Historical, Demographic, Economic, And Social Data: The United States, 1790-1970* [Computer file] (Ann Arbor, MI: Inter-university Consortium for Political and Social Research [producer and distributor] 1992). United States, *Compendium of the Enumeration of the Inhabitants and Statistics of the United States as obtained at the Department of State from the returns of the Sixth Census*, Sixth Decennial Census, 1840 (Washington: Thomas Allen, 1841).

63 These variables and their calculation are fully described in Lee A. Craig and Thomas Weiss, 'Nutritional Status and Agricultural Surpluses in the Antebellum United States,' NBER Working Paper Series on Historical Factors in Long Run Growth, Historical Paper 99, April 1997 and Lee A. Craig, Raymond B. Palmquist, and Thomas Weiss, 'Transportation Improvements and Land Values in the Antebellum United States: A

Hedonic Approach,' Working Paper 95-2-5, North Carolina State University, May 1997. I adjusted several of their specifications according to whether or not a county had usable access to a navigable waterway, slightly expanding the list of those that did. The initial file supplied only included rivers and canals as waterways. Erie County, according to that definition, did not have access to a waterway. It was one of three counties which had their waterway variables changed.

64 The amounts produced in a county minus the amounts consumed are considered agricultural surpluses.

65 Since canal construction had, for the most part, ended by 1840 and river navigability did not change appreciably between 1840 and 1850, using a variable developed for 1850 does not pose a difficulty in this analysis.

66 Craig and Weiss note that these data were not collected during the 1840 Census. Craig and Weiss, 'Nutritional Surpluses,' 11-12.

67 Correlations tended to be significant at the 0.01 or 0.05 level. Wealth per capita in 1850, per capita dairy production ($ value), home manufactures per capita ($ value), and the presence of water transportation in the birth county were the only variables not highly correlated positively or negatively with at least three of the other indicators. Wealth per capita in 1850 and 1840 dollar value of dairy production were positively correlated.

68 The former has been found in Lee Craig and Thomas Weiss, 'Nutritional Status and Agricultural Surpluses in the Antebellum United States,' in John Komlos and Jörg Baten (ed.), *The Biological Standard of Living in Comparative Perspectives: Proceedings of a Conference Held in Munich January 18-23, 1997* (Stuttgart: Franz Steiner Verlag, 1999), 190-207.

69 See the Appendix for a description of why no counties with border changes were entered into this part of the analysis.

70 Means and standard deviations for all the economic/demographic variables in the statewide and western regression models are found in Tables 5.20 and 5.21.

71 Craig and Weiss, 'Nutritional Status and Agricultural Surpluses.'

72 In evaluating the size of the impact of a one-standard deviation change in the independent variables a new set of means and standard deviations were calculated having eliminated Philadelphia County's values from the calculation. These calculations were then based on data from 28 counties. (see Table 5.20)

73 The Ridge and Valley Region is not present in this analysis as all the counties in that region had border changes between 1820 and 1845.

74 A series of regressions were run including multiple economic/demographic variables. Only the presence of water transport routes consistently retained its statistical significance and size of impact in these cases. The coefficients of the other variables varied. Per capita protein and calorie surpluses differed in their level of significance and coefficient size, depending on which other variables were entered into the equation along with water transport routes. The signs on the coefficients for agricultural employment percentage, per capita value of home manufacturing and market gardening all changed from their expected value and from the value they presented in the single economic/demographic variable model. The overall significance of the equations and the percentage of variation explained increased only marginally. Regressions run with multiple economic/demographic variables but, without a dummy variable for region, produced results in which the expected signs returned to most of the coefficients. However, as was the case in equations with the multiple economic/demographic

variables and regional dummy variables, the coefficients were not stable. They fluctuated widely, depending on the set of variables that were entered. These tables are not reproduced here but are available from the author upon request.

75 The Isolated Agricultural Region is not present because of border changes in both its counties, and thus is not included in this regression analysis.

76 In the Western Region, birth in a town of 10,000 persons or more was associated with a small but strongly significant reduction in stature. However, Erie and Mill Creek in 1840 had a combined population of a little over 6000 inhabitants.

77 This is consistent with other work on Union soldiers. Margo and Steckel, 'Native Born Whites,' 168; Sokoloff, 'Heights of Americans in Three Centuries,' 136.

78 See Chapters One and Two for more details and sources.

Chapter 6
Conclusion

In early nineteenth-century Pennsylvania differences in economic orientation closely associated with length of settlement, natural resource endowments, transportation network linkages, urbanization levels, and the extent to which an area was market integrated all influenced net nutritional status and hence the physical stature of the population. Men from counties distant from markets for goods and services, removed from growing urban areas, and most nearly economically self-sufficient had significantly greater stature than Pennsylvanians born in regions which had gone farther down the path of modern economic growth. These results are consistent with studies of the United States, Europe, and Asia which have indicated that men removed from areas experiencing market integration and early industrialization benefited physically by their distance. Rural agricultural populations tended to be better nourished. Yet, if those rural populations were tightly linked to urban centers by land or water transportation then the propinquity to nutrients yielded little advantage. In the big picture, it is not the population's 'shortness' that mattered. Rather, what mattered was that they likely were less healthy adults and probably lived shorter lives as a consequence. The correlation between stature and various economic and demographic measures is strong. However, the balance of mechanisms by which mean stature was negatively affected requires continued investigation.

Summary of Research Results

While stature varied significantly across various sub-populations, it remained within a relatively tight range. The difference in mean height between the counties at the extremes of the stature continuum over the thirty years under study was two and one-half inches.[1] Regional means varied by less than one and one-half inches.[2] These differences are small compared to the gap between the mean heights of nineteenth-century Americans and Europeans. They are also much smaller than many European eighteenth- and nineteenth-century intra-national social-class stature variances. On average, adult male populations in Pennsylvania achieved final heights between the 25th and 35th percentile of modern standards. These stature levels reflect the relatively easy access to nutrients and low level of large scale urbanization in the early nineteenth-century United States. Similar stature levels would not be achieved by the bulk of the population of many European nations until late in the nineteenth or early in the twentieth century.[3]

Time trends in this data are consistent with earlier work on nineteenth-century white populations with a slight and uneven fall in height from the 1820s through the 1840s, concentrated toward the end of this period. In Pennsylvania, the size of the fall was greatest among skilled and unskilled workers with farmers showing a somewhat flatter profile over time, although a slight reduction is still evident. Farmers in the Southeastern, Anthracite, and Ridge and Valley Regions experienced greater declines than those in the less developed regions of the state.

By the antebellum period stature variation had developed where it had not existed previously, across occupational and regional categories. The occupational pattern of height variation was consistent statewide. Within every region farmers had a noticeably higher mean stature level than most other men. The height of the relatively few men with high status occupations (work site owners, professionals, men without occupation) was as high or slightly higher than farmers in some regions. There were not consistent differences, however, between men who were skilled workers and those who were unskilled. This may be an indication that epidemiological forces in growing urban areas were more potent in creating a calorie consuming environment than positive income differences (higher wages) were in providing nutritional bolstering. It might also be that unskilled workers existed, in each region, in greater proportions in low population density locales which were less of a drain on their caloric intake, giving them an 'equalizer' relative to skilled workers with higher incomes. If the former, it would be another instance, in an age prior to residential segregation by socio-economic status, in which increased income could not buy better health.[4] The latter scenario highlights the physical cost of urban living, the 'costs' associated with higher income, and the importance of evaluating all the impacts of economic development, not just material welfare effects.

Urban–rural stature differentials were also evident in these data. Regression analysis indicated that birth in a county containing a city of 25,000 persons or more was associated with a height one-half to one inch lower than that for men from counties without towns of 5000 or more persons. Birth within counties with towns of either 5-10,000 persons or 10-25,000 population was also associated with lesser height, but the deficits were smaller. Enlistment in counties with towns and cities also was negatively correlated with height, but the men enlisting in small and medium sized towns tended to be shorter than men enlisting in the largest cities.

One of the ideas which motivated this research was the work of Tryon and his study of household manufactures in the United States. He charted, and followers later mapped, the effects on home cloth production in New York State before and after the completion of the Erie Canal.[5] The data, when mapped, showed how home cloth production dropped to nearly nothing in the counties through which the canal passed. Early hopes for this study were for the production of a similar geographic representation of stature variation. The situation with stature, however, has proved to be somewhat more complex. Stature variation was closely related to a series of economic and demographic variables. The strongest positive correlates were the per capita level of swine stocks, the per capita dollar value of home manufactures, and per capita protein and calorie surpluses. These variables held sway in both the statewide and western samples. The presence of a navigable waterway and the dollar value of market gardening were the variables most closely associated with reduced stature. When combined with the coefficients on the variables specifying the region of birth, which show that those regions qualitatively described as most connected via transportation links, most densely populated, and most involved in market transactions had the lowest stature levels, the findings strongly support the hypothesis that distance/removal from economic markets in the early nineteenth-century United States yielded greater net nutritional status.[6] The strong intercorrelation between the independent variables prohibited the successful inclusion of multiple economic and population variables within a single regression model. The balance of influences must be inferred via other clues.

The conclusion emerges that the onset of modern economic growth generated 'hidden' negative externalities that had a substantial impact on human growth. Economic modernization meant that children who were born and grew up in this period of momentous structural transformation, as adults, were not as healthy as their parents. A worsening of the epidemiological environment is not likely to have been the sole cause of this decline in nutritional status.[7]

A complete history of the antebellum decades, in addition to describing significant economic achievements, should also document the 'modernization penalty.'[8] A balanced judgment of the period must acknowledge that the rapid growth in population and in urbanization, the greater inequality in the distribution of income, and the increase in the variability of income resulting from business cycles in the new economy all had a profound impact on the children, youth and young adults of the period. The standard of living did not rise to the same degree for everyone.

Implications and Future Directions

Earlier research has reported height declines among population groups in several countries during the onset of industrialization and agricultural market integration. Within antebellum Pennsylvania, counties characterized by intense market involvement showed evidence of lower levels of mean stature than more isolated regions. However, market involvement, increasing population densities, and transportation network expansion are closely linked in the early stages of modern economic growth. It is not clear whether stature reductions were brought about by a more intense disease environment associated with larger unsanitary urban areas and the increased movement of people; from familial decisions to consume less food, market more, and purchase increasing amounts of manufactured goods; or from an increasingly bifurcated income and wealth distribution which resulted in less income available for food purchases on the part of wage earners. The relative contributions of disease influences and the structural and/or behavioral effects of market integration are still to be fully proportioned.

Some indications of the mix come from particular situations around the state. Erie and Crawford Counties, in northwestern Pennsylvania, had medium to medium low per capita agricultural production levels.[9] Population density and urbanization levels were near the commonwealth average. Yet these counties, part of the distant Western Region, the region with the highest mean stature in Pennsylvania, had height averages significantly below that of the rest of the Western Region and even below the state average for most of this period. There were no extremely large towns in this sub-region.[10] These counties had been, however, the site of extensive river and overland transport since the early 1800s. Connected by Lake Erie to Buffalo, Detroit, and Mackinaw, connected via turnpike to the eastern portion of the state, connected by road to Waterford, the most northerly point of navigation on French Creek and a connection via the Allegheny River to Pittsburgh, Erie County, and Crawford just to its south, were traversed by groups of travelers and traders. Disease spread by these transients may have negatively affected stature in Erie and Crawford Counties. The introduction of disease vectors can be classified as an indirect impact of market integration, a by-product of transportation linkage. Stature reduction resulting from the choice to reduce food consumption[11] and trade agricultural products for manufactured goods could also have been an influencing factor, as could increased inequality. Erie County did produce some, although not a great deal of market garden crops.[12] Commercial growth, particularly in warehousing and hauling, would have utilized large amounts of unskilled labor, creating a low wage group in the county. This situation in the northwest corner of the state strengthens the case for the negative impact of market involvement but does not discretely identify the mechanism(s) by which it was brought about.

Lancaster County's situation provides another instructive anomaly. This county had a reputation during the nineteenth century as one of the dominant agricultural regions of the nation. The reputation was well warranted. Calorie and protein surpluses in 1840 were greater than those of all but five other counties.[13] Its wheat production, 13.4 bushels per capita, was more than twice the state average. Residents of Lancaster County were close to large quantities of food, even large quantities of 'surplus' food. Yet their mean age standardized stature was below the state average for each quinquennium, usually well below. Either the choices individuals made about their surplus, in Lancaster's case the decision generally was to sell, or the choices others made which created a market connection with large urban areas, and thus a link to virulent disease pools, negatively affected men born in Lancaster County. Propinquity to nutrients was not sufficient in this case to ensure a high level of nutritional status. In 1840, Lancaster County, while full of small towns and with a relatively high population density, had no city with a population over 10,000 persons. Local large scale urbanization does not seem to have been the mechanism through which calories were lost. In this regard it is similar to Erie County. Connection via markets does seem to have had a substantial negative impact on the net nutritional status of Lancaster County residents. Whether the outflow of nutrients through sale or the in-flow of disease was the proximate cause can not be ascertained at this time.

Lancaster County's situation as a highly developed commercial agricultural area also raises the question of the extent to which rising levels of income inequality negatively influenced stature.[14]

The slight stature advantage of the Western Region over other relatively undeveloped regions such as the Allegheny Forest, Pocono, and Northeastern Regions were occasionally statistically significant, but they were consistent in direction and size. According to the working hypothesis, after accounting for other influencing factors, stature in these regions would be expected at least to equal that in the Western Region. In some cases their 'remoteness' exceeded that of the West, at least in the 1840s. Explanation might be found in a factor which was discussed, but for which no variable was included in any regression model, work intensity. Much of the land in the Allegheny Forest and Pocono Regions, and to a lesser degree in the Northeastern Region, was marginal for agriculture.[15] To wrest a living out of these soils would have required more effort than in the Western Region where much of the land was more fertile and less rocky.[16] Additional effort continually expended to maintain sufficient crop output might account for this seeming contradiction of greater remoteness but slightly lesser stature. Further, as has been noted repeatedly, these three regions were late in being settled. Some of the men born in these areas who served in the Civil War would have been children of the original European settlers. In the first years of farm-making much time and great amounts of physical effort were necessary to clear the land and make it available for planting. Contemporary sources note how many new settlers barely survived their first years in these wild lands.[17] The lower than anticipated stature of the children of these hardy men and women may be evidence of the parents' back-breaking efforts to establish farms in these regions and the relative difficulty they had providing for their offspring.[18]

In attempting to discern why stature declined over this period researchers would do well to remember that causation often has multiple sources. This research effort, as Fogel noted, is 'an accounting exercise of a particularly complicated nature.'[19] Multiple lines of causation are probable, and the strength of the factors will not likely be the same in relation to all persons. A landless wage worker in Philadelphia does not have the choice between selling more nutrients in order to buy manufactured goods or eating more. He has no land and is constrained from raising food. Likewise, while rising or falling prices will impact how much food the urban wage worker will buy and consume, they will not have nearly as much effect on the self-sufficient farmer. Similarly, rising inequality will have a different effect on an urban wage worker than on a rural farmer. It is not just that the 'accounting task' is difficult; there are also many different groups for whom the sums must be worked, the accounts balanced, and each is likely to have a set of credits and debits unique to his economic and social condition. It is likely that when it is finally possible to describe the causes of the fall in mean stature in the antebellum U.S., different influences will be linked to different groups within the society, and no one cause will fit all.[20]

More detailed data about these areas, particularly more height data drawn from particular counties, might provide additional insights. Work should seek to determine who experienced the greatest declines: merchants, the men who ran businesses in which meeting the public was both a source of profit and of infection; farmers who dealt less with the public but had to decide how much of their high protein foodstuffs to deal away; or wage laborers beset by both the need to purchase food and living in less than healthful urban locales. These types of clues would help build a case, or more appropriately, a series of cases for the prime influences on particular sub-groups of the population.

Similarly, extended samples, not in terms of sample size but in time coverage in the Western Region, would also be of great value. They would allow for an investigation of this area later in the century as it moved from one dominated by agriculture to one which, at least in several counties, even some with very high stature in the antebellum years, became intense centers of industrial production. A comparison of the path followed by the western portion of the state with the course of stature in the Southeastern Region would be instructive. The west did not necessarily, in terms of stature, follow the earlier course of the Southeastern Region simply delayed by decades.

Separating the influence of disease from the choice or inability of nineteenth-century Americans to consume food as they had previously is at the heart of the puzzle. Research in a series of related fields would be of great assistance in attempts to better understand impacts on physical welfare. Several possible lines of investigation were not carried out by this study. It was assumed that stature variation was associated with several factors for which data were not extant. Their influence was allowed to be subsumed in a regional dummy variable. This was a necessary but undesirable situation. However, the strength of the regional dummy is a sign that the assumption was correct. In cross-national studies the level of inequality has been shown to be an important variable for explaining stature variation.[21] While it would be a massive project, worthy of publication separately (in all likelihood in a large series of publications), an investigation of income and wealth distribution in antebellum Pennsylvania would be an invaluable addition to the literature. State tax records as well as the 1850 census (property holdings) are potential sources of data which might shed some light on this issue.

Assessing the level of disease exposure is extremely difficult because the trail 'exposure' leaves behind is influenced by pre-existing nutritional status. A county-level examination of the mortality schedules in the 1850 census, even with their inadequacies, would provide scholars with some idea of the 'effectiveness' of disease exposure, from the infectious agent's perspective. School attendance rates (number of family disease vectors) and/or the extent to which Civil War soldiers from particular counties died of childhood diseases during the war (an 'inverse' sign of earlier exposure) would be indicators of the local level of disease exposure and might also be included as future regression variables.[22]

Similarly valuable, but not as daunting in terms of the initial data collection effort, would be inclusion in the model of measures of foreign-born parentage in each county throughout the period. Parents born outside the United States, primarily in Europe, on average had net nutritional experiences through their own growth years much inferior to those of persons born at the same time in the United States.[23] Auxological literature indicates that it may take several generations for the effect of low net nutritional status to be eliminated from a family's stature profile. County-level data on the percentage of persons of foreign birth[24] in each county would help account for this possibility and in all likelihood better explain regional stature variation.

A related issue, the varying concentration of ethnic groups within each of the counties, may well account for some stature differences. Differences in ethnic foodways (e.g. the desire to consume meat rather than to sell it; customs about consuming or discarding certain portions of various animals, etc.), could have a direct impact on protein/calorie consumption and thus height.[25] If such variation is non-randomly distributed across the state, regional stature trends would be affected. Better knowledge of this factor would also enable clearer explanations of stature variation to be developed.[26]

A pattern in the United States relative to stature and settlement is discernable. When European settlers arrived in North America in the seventeenth century, they encountered/established a nutritional environment much different from the one they had known in Europe. The combination of land resources and a mix of indigenous and European agricultural techniques and crops resulted in food production levels which yielded a substantial increase in the net nutritional status of the European migrants. Mean stature in the United States in the late eighteenth and early nineteenth centuries bears this out. With extremely low population densities and very small urban areas, initially, there were no rural/urban height differences. However, with urban growth and increased occupational variation, by the early nineteenth century such a gradient was quite evident. Does this pattern indicate a 'new continent model' of stature variation which might also have existed in European settler colonies in Canada, Australia, and South Africa after those colonists displaced the aboriginal peoples? Studies of the formative generations of these settler colonies would be an interesting parallel to the work which has been presented here.

The other piece of the puzzle which will help to tie down the ultimate meaning of this work does not involve additional patterns or trends in stature across time or regions, but the exploration of the meaning of what a one, two, or three inch difference in average height between various populations means in practical terms. This is not a new call, but an important one.[27] Is mortality affected,[28] work efficiency, fertility? What other aspects of the human life experience are correlated with this measure of net nutrition?[29] Stature provides a useful cumulative measure of net nutrition and one result of economic processes. Hopefully, this volume will inspire others to undertake work which links stature to other indicators of well-being, making net nutrition's impact and stature's meaning clearer. Such efforts might provide a more complete answer to the question posed by contemporary policy makers and the antebellum American farmer who began this study: 'but taking all things into consideration will he be better off?'[30]

Notes

1 This difference was based on quinquennium averages by county, 20 observations per quinquennium minimum. Expanding either the period of time or raising the minimum number of observations would reduce this figure from the current 2.5 inch spread.
2 This estimate is based on age standardized heights for the various regions. See Figure 5.7.
3 See Chapter One for more details and sources.
4 Richard Steckel, 'The Health and Mortality of Women and Children,' *Journal of Economic History* 48 (1988): 333-345; Eric L. Davin, 'The Era of the Common Child: Egalitarian Death in Antebellum America,' *Mid-America* 75 (1993): 135-163.
5 Rolla M. Tryon, *Household Manufactures in the United States, 1640-1860: A Study in Industrial History* (Chicago: University of Chicago Press, 1917), 304-305; Arthur H. Cole, *American Woolen Manufactures*, Vol. 1. (Cambridge: Harvard University Press, 1926), 181 and 280.
6 In the western region single economic/demographic variables were only statistically significant if sub-regional dummy variables were removed from the equations.
7 Komlos argues this is evident in the fact that the physical stature of persons with high-status occupations did not appear to decline. John Komlos, 'Anomalies in Economic History: Reflections on the "Antebellum Puzzle",' *Journal of Economic History* 56 (March, 1996): 202-214.
8 I thank John Komlos for this idea and wording.
9 This comparison was made with the 29 counties across the state included in the regression analysis, counties without border changes between 1820 and 1845 and those for which all data included in the regression equations exist.
10 If the 1840 populations of Erie and her sister city, Mill Creek, are aggregated they total 6094. Crawford County had no towns with a population above 2500 in that year.
11 This also includes a switch from high value foods (e.g. meats) to less costly ones.
12 Crawford did not produce any market garden goods in 1840 and only five out of ten Western Region counties did.
13 This is compared to the 29 for which these data are available.
14 Lemon reports that by 1800 already 30 per cent of Lancaster County's taxpayers were landless and that a growing artisan class paid only 60 per cent of what other taxpayers paid. James T. Lemon, *The Best Poor Man's Country: A Geographical Study of Early Southeastern Pennsylvania*, (New York: W.W. Norton & Co., Inc., 1972), 94-95.
15 John William Florin, *The Advance of Frontier Settlement in Pennsylvania, 1638-1850: A Geographic Interpretation* (University Park, Pa.: Department of Geography, Pennsylvania State University, 1977), 28-29. The Western Region also had some lands of poor soil quality along its southeastern edge.
16 Florin, *Frontier Settlement*, 28.
17 Stevenson Whitcomb Fletcher, *Pennsylvania Agriculture and Country Life, 1640-1840* (Harrisburg: Pennsylvania Historical and Museum Commission, 1950), 78.
18 The children themselves may have, out of necessity, directed more than the 'average' amount of calories into work during their youth.
19 Robert W. Fogel, 'Nutrition and the Decline in Mortality since 1700: Some Preliminary Findings,' in *Long-Term Factors in American Economic Growth*, ed. S. Engerman and R. Gallman (Chicago: University of Chicago Press for National Bureau of Economic Research, 1987), 506.

20 Likely it will be that varying proportions of causation will be attributed to the various factors across the different sub-groups.

21 Richard Steckel, 'Height and Per Capita Income,' *Historical Methods* 16 (1993): 1-7.

22 I thank Richard Steckel and Van Beck Hall for these ideas about data sources for this type of investigation.

23 U.S. Army soldiers from the Newport, Kentucky barracks in the late 1850s evidenced this disparity. Tripler notes the following mean heights by nativity (ages not given):

American-born	68.1"
Irish-born	66.9"
French-born	66.5"
English-born	65.9"
German-born	65.2"

Charles S. Tripler, *Manual of the Medical Officer of the Army of the United States. Part I. Recruiting and Inspection of Recruits* (Cincinnati: Wrightson and Co., 1858), 11-12. Note also the greater stature among the men from the least industrialized of the European nations.

24 The federal census contains a non-continuous and varied series of data on persons of foreign birth through the antebellum years.

25 A graduate student at the University of Pittsburgh, Jennifer Ford, is conducting research on the material culture of late eighteenth- and early nineteenth-century farmers in Washington and Westmoreland Counties. As part of her work, she is attempting to determine, based on probate inventories, if differences existed between Scotch-Irish and German families in terms of their dietary habits. She notes what she terms 'surprisingly few.' Personal correspondence with Jennifer Ford, March 1998.

26 Some of these topics have been addressed in a recent article. See Michael R. Haines, Lee A. Craig, and Thomas Weiss, 'The Short and the Dead: Nutrition, Mortality, and the "Antebellum Puzzle" in the United States,' *Journal of Economic History* 63 (June 2003): 382-413.

27 Richard Steckel, 'Stature and the Standard of Living,' *Journal of Economic Literature* 33 (1995): 1933.

28 Studies to date show that among nineteenth-century populations height at the individual level is not closely linked to mortality, but weight standardized by height, body mass indexes, seem to be. See for instance, John E. Murray, 'Standards of the Present for People of the Past: Height, Weight, and Mortality among Men of Amherst College, 1834-1949,' *The Journal of Economic History* 57 (September 1997): 585-606; Timothy Cuff, 'The Body Mass Index Values of Nineteenth-Century West Point Cadets: A Theoretical Application of Waaler's Curves to A Historical Population,' *Historical Methods* 26 (1993): 171-183.

29 Two efforts in this regard are already under way. See Steckel's proposal for expanded use of biological quality of life indicators and their inclusion in a 'quality adjusted life year,' Steckel, 'Stature and the Standard of Living,' 1934-35, and Fogel et. al.'s efforts to tie the stature of the Civil War volunteers to their later experience via their military pension records. For early results of some of the latter work, see Dora L. Costa, 'Height, Weight, Wartime Stress, and Older Age Mortality: Evidence from the Union Army Records,' *Explorations in Economic History* 30 (1993): 424-449, and Dora L. Costa, 'Height, Wealth, and Disease among the Native-Born in the Rural Antebellum North,' *Social Science History* 17 (1993): 355-383.

30 *Plough, Loom and Anvil* 4 (1852): 686 cited in Gavin W. Wright, *The Political Economy of the Cotton South: Households, Markets, and Wealth in the Nineteenth-Century* (New York: W.W. Norton and Co., 1978), 71.

Appendix

Data Collection and Evaluation

Introduction

The samples of Civil War soldiers which comprise the bulk of the data analyzed in this study were drawn from the regimental and/or company descriptive books[1] of military units raised in Pennsylvania to fight in the War of the Rebellion. This appendix describes how the samples were drawn, how the men in the sample compare to the male population of antebellum Pennsylvania, and potential problems associated with the data drawn from these sources.

Sample Construction

Two samples of Pennsylvanians who served in the Civil War were taken, totaling nearly 20,000 observations. The first sample was a *statewide* cluster sample at the company level stratified on primary county of recruitment[2] and includes approximately 12,500 cases. It was composed of nearly 10,000 observations collected directly for this project along with 2638 men from 29 Pennsylvania companies included in Robert Fogel's earlier sample of Union soldiers available from the Inter-University Consortium for Social and Political Research.[3]

A list of all Pennsylvania companies (infantry, cavalry, and artillery) which served in the Civil War was developed based on Sauers' *Advance the Colors*. This list was then grouped and sub-divided by primary recruitment county. Companies were then randomly selected from each county's list of companies and the enlistment records of the soldiers belonging to these units were collected. The number of units selected from each county was proportionate to the total number of units organized in that county during the war years at an approximate ratio of 1 to 15. Since 'Fogel's units' were already collected and their counties of origin known, the number of units from each county which existed in Fogel's sample was subtracted from the number of units needed from each county to make a proportionate sample; the result was the number of units per county to be collected directly for this project. Not all counties had companies represented in Fogel's sample; some had more than one. In several cases the 'theoretical' number of units to be drawn from some of the least populated counties was smaller than 1. In those cases several counties within close proximity with similar characteristics were grouped together and a random selection was made to determine which county's unit would be sampled to represent this group of counties.

The second sample, which contains just over 7500 observations, is also a company level cluster sample. However, it was drawn exclusively from units organized in Western Pennsylvania (see Table 4.1 for a listing of the counties included in this region). The number of companies from each county included in this sample is proportionate to the number of units recruited from each county in this region, at a ratio of approximately 1:8.

As the ultimate focus of this study is to evaluate the relationship between the economic environment in antebellum Pennsylvania and changes in physical stature, *only Pennsylvania-born soldiers who enlisted in Pennsylvania units are included in the samples*. These are men whose nutritional, work, and disease experience would have been determined almost exclusively in Pennsylvania.

Data Collected

For each soldier the following information was collected: name, rank, age, height, race (only white units were collected for this project), birth place, birth state, occupation, enlistment year, enlistment place, and some items out of the 'remarks' column pertaining to their enlistment. A company identifier and unit type code (infantry, cavalry, etc.) were also noted for each man. Any man who could have his rank identified had this data collected. (In practice this meant that the data for some officers were not collected.)

Coding of the Data

After the data was made machine readable, duplicates were eliminated.

Rank Men identified as captains or lieutenants were coded as officers. Sergeants and corporals were classified as non-commissioned officers. Men who were identified as buglers, drummers, or musicians were classified as musicians. Numerous types of artisans/artificers were noted in the rolls. These included teamsters, wagonners, blacksmiths, saddlers. All were classified as artisans.

Enlistment type Men were classified as either 'standard' enlistees, draftees, substitutes, recruits, or bounty recipients. Their status was determined from notations made in the 'remarks' column of their record on the descriptive roll. Standard enlistees were men who had no special notation in reference to enlistment in the 'remarks' column of their descriptive book entry. Draftees were men called into service by the force of the federal draft which began in 1863 and who had such a notation in their remarks column. Substitutes were men who were paid a fee for taking someone else's place in the army, while bounty recipients were men who received a bonus or 'bounty' for enlisting or re-enlisting and carried remarks to that effect in their record. No definitive explanation of the 'recruit' notation has been found. It may refer to a re-enlisted veteran, analogous to a 'veteran volunteer' or to an individual who volunteered individually and did so without enlisting within a particular unit but rather was simply assigned to a company by the recruiting officer.[4] As described in Chapter Five, after accounting for differences in the age and occupational differences in these categories of men, few statistically significant differences in stature existed.

Matching 'place' of birth/enlistment with county In order to prepare for county level analysis, it was necessary to assign each enlistee to his county of birth and of enlistment. The military's descriptive rolls most often called for birth place to be recorded at the county level. In actuality, for both birth place and enlistment place, town or county names, sometimes both, were entered into these columns by the company clerk. For men for whom a town name was recorded (or for whom a county name was specified but a city with the same name existed) a match between town and county needed to be made. Since there was not a one-to-one correspondence between towns and counties (e.g. in 1860 nine Pennsylvania counties had census places named Allegheny) and since many county names also were town names (e.g. Erie City and Erie County), the process involved a degree of ambiguity. In order to identify the reliability of a birth or enlistment place county match, a series of quality codes were established and entered into each observation along with the county code. Table A.1 lists the various quality codes and their frequencies in the merged sample (an aggregation of the statewide and western samples) for birth places and enlistment places.

It was possible to determine, with varying degrees of assuredness, the county of birth of 18,337 of the 19,490 soldiers in the merged sample. For 12,928 the birth place county match was a unique one (the town/county listed as birth place in the enlistment records was the only town with that name in the state in the 1860 census, or the county name was unique [no towns had the same name as that county]). The remaining 5409 observations for which birth place–birth county matches were successful were done with some degree of ambiguity. Table A.1 describes how these ambiguous town-county matches were determined, the various levels of assuredness about the matches, and its relative occurrence.

Similarly, it was possible to determine the county of enlistment for 19,043 of the 19,490[5] men in the merged sample. Again, this was done with varying degrees of assuredness as to the match between enlistment place and enlistment county for reasons similar to those noted above. Of the total 19,043 matches, 13,625 were unique ones, with 5418 being made with some degree of ambiguity. Table A.1 indicates the levels of certainty and the frequency of each type of match.

In order to test for the possible effects of inappropriate coding, a series of three regressions utilizing the merged sample were run. In the first, all men except

Table A.1 Birth/Enlistment Place/County Coding Quality Codes: Frequency And Description

Quality Code Description	Birth place	Enlist place
0) No match made Bctycode/Ectycode = 5555-unable to determine 6666-town in breakaway section of county (later part of another county) 7777-unmatched city-county pair 8888-missing data 9999-unintelligible, outside PA	1153 5.9%	447 2.3%
1) Unique Town-County Pairing, Perfect Spelling Match	12,530 64.3%	13,393 68.7%
2) Unique Town-County Pairing, Spelling Irregularities	398 2.0%	232 1.2%
3) Non-Unique Town-County Pairing, Match based on existence of birth town in enlistee's unit's primary recruitment county, birth and enlistment places in same county.	3074 15.8%	4332 22.2%
4) Non-Unique Town-County Pairing, Match based on existence of birth town and enlistment place in same county but not necessarily in enlistee's unit's primary recruitment county.	245 1.3%	211 1.1%
5) Birth/enlistment place not extant in census but town name does exist elsewhere (e.g. gazetteer) in primary recruitment county.	0	1
6) Birth/enlistment place not extant in census but town name (misspelled) does exist elsewhere (e.g. gazetteer) in primary recruitment county.	0	0

Table A.1 (continued)

Quality Code Description	Birth place	Enlist place
7) Birth/enlistment town specified in enlistment records with county name but census has no town by that name. Match made if confirming circumstantial evidence supports such town's existence (e.g. No West Springfield in census in specified county, but Springfield is listed).	11 0.1%	19 0.1%
8) Birth/enlistment town as listed does not exist in census. Town has same name as county. County name assumed.	9	0
9) County level name assumed to be birth/enlistment county. Company all had same town name listed as birth/enlistment place. (Often town names given for places within local county, county names listed when birth or enlistment occurred outside of local county.) Strong circumstantial evidence to support match.	1174 6.0%	20 0.1%
10) County level name assumed to be birth/enlistment county. Company all had same town name listed as birth/enlistment place. (Often town names given for places within local county, county names listed when birth or enlistment occurred outside of local county.) Weak circumstantial evidence to support match.	579 3.0%	14 0.1%
11) Contextual clues leads to assumed birth/enlistment county. Similar to #9 but weaker.	300 1.5%	734 3.8%
12) Code for assignment of prominent town name to its county when other much less prominent towns exist with the same name and an absolute separation can not be made.	17 0.1%	87 0.4%

Table A.2 Determinants of the Height of Soldiers – Merged Sample, Test of Birth and Enlistment Place Quality Codes

	(A)	(B)	(C)	(D)
Constant	68.02***	67.97***	67.84***	67.81***
18	-1.47***	-1.39***	-1.31***	-1.29***
19	-0.79***	-0.76***	-0.66***	-0.68***
20	-0.45***	-0.40***	-0.27	-0.29
21	-0.07	-0.03	0.08	0.05
22	-0.18*	-0.15	-0.11	-0.12
23	-0.08	-0.04	0.02	0.01
24	0.03	0.10	0.12	0.10
25-49				
1815-1819	0.12	0.17	0.30	0.32
1820-1824	0.32***	0.36***	0.35**	0.39***
1825-1829	0.23***	0.28***	0.30**	0.26**
1830-1834	0.29***	0.27***	0.26**	0.25**
1835-1839				
1840-1844	-0.03	-0.06	-0.19	-0.17
1845-1849	-0.17	-0.26*	-0.39**	-0.38*
1861	0.55***	0.52***	0.46***	0.47***
1862	0.37***	0.35***	0.38***	0.40**
1863	-0.20*	-0.26*	-0.18	-0.18
1864				
1865	0.03	0.04	0.10	0.11
Farmer	0.37***	0.42***	0.38***	0.37***
Proprietor	0.05	0.11	0.04	-0.06
Skilled Worker				
Unskilled Worker	-0.01	-0.01	-0.01	0.02
Work Site	0.53**	0.47*	0.56*	0.58*
None	0.68***	0.67***	0.80***	0.77***
Professional	0.27	0.30	0.20	0.21
Unknown	-0.04	-0.03	-0.13	-0.14
'Standard'				
Drafted (1)	-0.05	-0.01	-0.13	-0.07
Substitute (2)	-0.13	0.28	-0.34	-0.42
Recruit (3)	0.12	0.00	-0.18	-0.09
Bounty Rcpnt (4)	-0.21*	-0.25*	-0.35**	-0.37**

Table A.2 (continued)

	(A)	(B)	(C)	(D)
Infantry				
Artillery	0.19**	0.21**	0.28***	0.28***
Reserve Inf.	0.03	0.06	0.07	-0.17
Cavalry	0.28***	0.28***	0.37***	0.37***
Stayer				
Migrant	0.07*	0.10**	0.25*	0.26***
Southeast	-1.01***	-0.96***	-0.92***	-0.93***
Anthracite	-0.90***	-0.86***	-0.85***	-0.86***
Pocono	-0.14	-0.13	0.01	0.06
Northeast	-0.20**	-0.09	-0.06	-0.02
Ridge & Valley	-0.19***	-0.20***	-0.22**	-0.23**
Allegheny Forest	-0.07	-0.02	-0.03	0.05
West				
N[a]	16060[b]	13409[c]	8469[d]	8038[e]
Adjusted R^2	0.12	0.12	0.12	0.12
F	58.5***	49.4***	31.9***	30.1***

*** significant at the 0.01 level
** significant at the 0.05 level
* significant at the 0.10 level

[a] For all regressions the intercept represents a standard infantry enlistee, in 1864, a private who was a skilled worker, born in the Western Region between 1835 and 1839, who was born and enlisted in the same county.
[b] Includes men with all birth and enlistment quality codes.
[c] Includes men with birth and enlistment county quality codes 1, 2, and 3.
[d] Includes men with birth and enlistment county quality codes 1 and 2.
[e] Includes men with birth and enlistment county quality code 1.

those with the three surest birth and enlistment place quality codes (codes 1, 2, and 3) were eliminated from the sample. In the next all men except those with the two surest birth and enlistment place quality codes (codes 1, 2) were eliminated from the sample. The final regression only included men with the quality code signifying a match without ambiguity. In none of the three regressions did coefficients for any of the variables change appreciably. This was even true for the regional dummy variables which maintained their signs and sizes for the most part. The only exceptions were the three regions with the smallest numbers of observations: the Pocono, Northeast, and Allegheny Forest Regions. The dummy coefficients for these regions showed minor fluctuations particularly after men with birth and enlistment quality codes of '3' were removed. The robustnesss of these results indicates that confidence in the study's coding procedures is not misplaced.

Comparison with Other Populations

Sample Composition vs Pennsylvania Civil War Military

Table A.3 provides a detailed description of the samples available by unit type, i.e. infantry, artillery, cavalry, reserved infantry.[6] The sample is composed primarily of infantry men. The proportions of each unit type vary between the state and western samples. Artillery units are over-represented in both, while cavalry units are over-represented in the western and under-represented in the state, as compared to the actual proportions of these units. Reserve Corps infantry units are also somewhat under-represented in both samples. Although no separate height minima or maxima were found for enlistees in cavalry or artillery units during the Civil War, such regulations did exist before and after the war. For this reason in some regression analysis non-infantry units were eliminated from the study.

Privates make up the vast majority of individuals in the sample, although a few officers and many non-comms are also included, along with a variety of artisans (blacksmiths, teamsters, etc.).[7] Since most companies had a small contingent of musicians, these individuals were also recorded in the data set.[8] The observations obtained from Fogel's sample contained no rank variable although examination of the one unit which both research teams collected shows that non-commissioned officers are present in Fogel's sample.

The majority of men in the samples enlisted during 1861, 1862 and 1864 (see Table A.4). These were also the years of heaviest enlistment in Pennsylvania units, although there is considerable year-to-year variation in the sample. In particular there was under-representation of 1861 and 1863 enlistees and over-representation of those who enlisted in 1864 and 1865. Some of this variation probably results from the fact that many of the 1861 enlistees were short term, i.e. 90-day enlistees, of whom fewer records seem to have survived. Some of the 1864 and 1865 enlistees may have been re-enlistees who originally joined the war effort

Table A.3 Pennsylvania Civil War Companies by Type of Unit

	Total Companies from Pennsylvania[a]		Sample Enlistment Totals Statewide		Western	
	Number	Percent	Number	Percent	Number	Percent
Infantry	1590	77.3%	9800	82.0%	5131	68.1%
Reserve Corps (Infantry)	130	6.3	255	2.1	248	3.3
Cavalry	280	13.6	1187	9.9	1617	21.5
Artillery	57	2.8	711	5.9	541	7.2
Total	2057		11953		7537	

[a] Figures from Sauers, *Advance the Colors*, pp. 249-295.

Table A.4 Pennsylvania Civil War Soldiers by Year of Enlistment

	Total Enlistees[a] Pennsylvania Units		Samples[b] Statewide		Western	
	Number	Percent	Number	Percent	Number	Percent
1861	130,594	37.9%	2936	24.6%	2217	29.4%
1862	71,100	20.6	2166	18.1	1932	25.6
1863	43,046	12.5	640	5.4	298	4.0
1864	73,828	21.4	4661	39.0	2173	28.8
1865	25,840	7.5	1550	13.0	917	12.2
Total	344,408		11953		7537	

[a] Figures from Sauers, *Advance the Colors*, p. 247.

[b] Only includes men born in Pennsylvania who enlisted in units organized by Pennsylvania.

in 1861 or 1862. Within the descriptive rolls there was frequently circumstantial evidence of this being the case. Hence, some men classified by this study as enlisting in the latter years may have been classified by Sauers as 1861 or 1862 enlistees.[9]

Over 97 per cent of soldiers in both samples had recorded ages between 18 and 49, although the complete range of ages is from 13 through 64. Eighteen was the official minimum age for entry into the Union army – although Gould's sample of over one million men indicates that about one per cent were officially listed as under 18 years of age.[10] (Prior to 1862 someone below 21 years of age could enter the service only with parental permission. This age was decreased to 18 in 1863.)[11] The actual percentage is likely to have been greater due to the number of men who fabricated their age in order to enlist.[12] After September 1862, 45 was the maximum age for entry into the Union Army, prior to that older individuals were accepted.[13] Age distributions of this sample by year of enlistment reflect the decline of these older men in the sample.

Sample vs Pennsylvania's Male Population in 1860

Writers who have characterized the Union army have described it as full of a wide array of men of divergent backgrounds and experiences, drawn widely if not proportionately from all social classes.[14] The 334,000 white men who enlisted in Pennsylvania units represent between 50 and 62 per cent of white Pennsylvania males in the 18-45 age category in 1860.[15] Fogel estimates that 95 per cent of American males, age 18-25, were examined for service in Civil War units, with approximately three-quarters being accepted.[16] Looking specifically at the sample of Union soldiers currently under examination, several characteristics can be noted.

Table A.5 Age Distribution

Age Range	Pennsylvania White Male Population, 1860	Civil War Enlistees (Native-Born) Sample Statewide	Western
15-19	10.3%	27.6%	28.1%
20-29	16.9	51.6	53.7
30-39	12.9	15.6	13.2
40+	17.8	5.1	5.1

Source: United States, *Population of the United States in 1860; Compiled from the Original Returns of the Eighth Census*, Eighth Decennial Census, 1860 (Washington: G.P.O., 1864), 406-409.

Men in the age categories of 15-19 and 20-29 are vastly over-represented in the sample as compared with their proportion in the population generally (Table A.5). Men 30-39 and 40+ are greatly under-represented.

The soldiers' occupations were primarily craftsmen, farmers, or unskilled laborers, consistent with the population generally. As would be expected, farmers made up a larger proportion of the soldiers in the western sample than in the statewide one, again consistent with agricultural employment proportions in the Western Region. Wiley notes that his sample of 14,000 plus observations yielded an occupational distribution in which just under half of the soldiers were farmers and another ten per cent laborers.[17] The lower percentage of farmers and higher percentage of laborers in this Pennsylvania sample is consistent with the higher degree of urbanization found in Pennsylvania than in the nation as a whole in the 1860s.[18] Some authors have argued that the Union Army, particularly in the later years of the war, included a much higher proportion of men of mean estate than characterized the population generally.[19] Occupational distribution by year of enlistment indicates no consistent shift in pattern between the occupational categories of skilled laborer, farmer, or unskilled laborer.[20] After 1862, however, the proportion of proprietors and low white collar workers does fall off in both the statewide and western samples. This shift coincides with the rise of the draft and the use of substitutes and commutation fees beginning in 1863.[21] Table A.6 indicates the distribution of occupations by category for the state, as per the 1860 census, and for the statewide and western samples.[22] Tables A.7 and A.8 provide a similar breakdown by year of enlistment and shows the declining proportion of enlistees in the upper socio-economic ranks.[23]

Researchers using this type of data will be safe if they limit their generalizations to that portion of the antebellum Pennsylvania population which was native-born and classified as either skilled or unskilled workers or farmers. Professionals and proprietors are somewhat under-represented in this sample. Additionally, it cannot be determined whether or not the professionals and proprietors who did enlist were men at the edge of their professions or the leaders in their fields. While the latter may have been the case early in the war, it probably was not the case later on.

Regional Distribution of Enlistees

Table A.9 indicates the regional breakdown of population in 1860 by residence for Pennsylvania and then region of birth and region of enlistment for the men in the statewide sample. Focus is best placed on a comparison of 1860 state population proportions by region and the distribution of enlistees by region as date of birth and date of enlistment might well have been separated by a minimum of almost two decades. The lack of any foreign-born individuals in the sample is also a factor to consider in evaluating the distribution of enlistees relative to current residence. Areas with a large foreign-born population would be under-represented in the

Table A.6 Occupational Distribution by Category, Merged Sample[a]

	Pennsylvania Male Population[b]	Native-Born Enlistees Statewide Sample	Western Sample
Professional	1.4%	0.6%	0.6%
Proprietor/ Low White Collar[c]	9.9	5.2	6.0
Skilled Worker	28.0	32.5	29.9
Unskilled Worker	30.5	28.9	22.2
Farmer	28.7[d]	29.6	38.7
Student/ No occupation	0.5	0.8	1.3
Unknown	0.9	2.4	1.3

[a] These distributions were calculated by applying Herschberg and Dockhorn's classification scheme both to the 1860 statewide distribution of occupations listed in the census and to the lists of occupations recorded in the enlistment records. Herschberg and Dockhorn, 'Occupational Classification,' 59-98.

[b] United States, *Population of the United States in 1860; Compiled from the Original Returns of the Eighth Census*, Eighth Decennial Census, 1860 (Washington: G.P.O., 1864), 440-441.

[c] This category also includes Herschberg and Dockhorn's 'work site only' category (men who only listed their work site, e.g. cloth factory, not profession). They believe such men to have been the owners of such operations.

[d] This figure includes men classified who identified themselves as farmers or farm laborers to the census takers. It does not include unskilled laborers. In all likelihood a percentage of these men would have also been involved in farm labor.

Table A.7 Occupational Distribution by Category, Statewide Sample[a]

	Pennsylvania Male Population 1860[b]	Pennsylvania Statewide Sample Civil War Enlistees (Native-Born) 1861	1862	1863/64	1865
Professional/ Proprietor	1.4%	0.5%	0.6%	0.6%	0.5%
Low White Collar[c]	9.9	5.8	7.0	4.3	4.5
Skilled Worker	28.0	36.7	29.9	30.1	36.1
Unskilled Worker	30.5	24.4	18.9	34.7	31.9
Farmer	28.7[d]	28.5	36.9	28.7	25.1
Student/ No occupation	0.5	0.5	1.5	0.7	0.8
Unknown	0.9	3.6	5.2	0.9	1.1

[a] These distributions were calculated by applying Herschberg and Dockhorn's classification scheme both to the 1860 statewide distribution of occupations listed in the census and to the lists of occupations recorded in the enlistment records. Herschberg and Dockhorn, 'Occupational Classification,' 59-98.

[b] United States, *Population of the United States in 1860; Compiled from the Original Returns of the Eighth Census*, Eighth Decennial Census, 1860 (Washington: G.P.O., 1864), 440-441.

[c] This category also includes Herschberg and Dockhorn's 'work site only' category (men who only listed their work site, e.g. cloth factory, not profession). They believe such men to have been the owners of such operations.

[d] This figure includes men classified who identified themselves as farmers or farm laborers to the census takers. It does not include unskilled laborers. In all likelihood a percentage of these men would have also been involved in farm labor.

Table A.8 Occupational Distribution by Category, Western Sample[a]

	Pennsylvania Male Population 1860[b]	Pennsylvania Western Sample Civil War Enlistees (Native-Born) 1861	1862	1863/64	1865
Professional/ Proprietor	1.4%	0.6%	0.6%	0.4%	0.7%
Low White Collar[c]	9.9	7.5	7.8	3.6	5.0
Skilled Worker	28.0	34.3	24.2	27.5	37.6
Unskilled Worker	30.5	25.8	14.6	24.5	23.4
Farmer	28.7[d]	28.8	49.2	42.0	31.6
Student/ No occupation	0.5	0.9	2.5	1.1	0.7
Unknown	0.9	2.1	1.0	0.9	1.0

a These distributions were calculated by applying Herschberg and Dockhorn's classification scheme both to the 1860 statewide distribution of occupations listed in the census and to the lists of occupations recorded in the enlistment records. Herschberg and Dockhorn, 'Occupational Classification,' 59-98.

b United States, *Population of the United States in 1860; Compiled from the Original Returns of the Eighth Census*, Eighth Decennial Census, 1860 (Washington: G.P.O., 1864), 440-441.

c This category also includes Herschberg and Dockhorn's 'work site only' category (men who only listed their work site, e.g. cloth factory, not profession). They believe such men to have been the owners of such operations.

d This figure includes men classified who identified themselves as farmers or farm laborers to the census takers. It does not include unskilled laborers. In all likelihood a percentage of these men would have also been involved in farm labor.

Table A.9 State Regional Population Proportions in 1860 and Sample Regional Population Proportions

	Proportion of State's 1860 Population By Residence	Proportion of Statewide Sample by Birth Place	Proportion of Statewide Sample by Enlistment Place
Southeastern Region			
with Philadelphia Co.	44.3%	34.0%	32.6%
without Philadelphia Co.	24.8	24.6	20.5
Philadelphia Co.	19.5	9.3	12.1
Anthracite Region	11.9	13.0	22.5
Pocono Region	1.9	0.7	0.2
Northeastern Region	4.4	5.6	5.7
Ridge and Valley Region	7.0	15.8	9.5
Allegheny Forest Region	6.7	5.0	4.9
Western			
with Allegheny County	23.9	25.9	24.5
without Allegheny County	17.7	21.3	17.0
Allegheny County alone	6.2	4.7	7.5

Source: United States, *Population of the United States in 1860; Compiled from the Original Returns of the Eighth Census*, Eighth Decennial Census, 1860 (Washington: G.P.O., 1864), 440-441.

sample, but that is because the 1860 population distribution includes persons of American nativity born outside of Pennsylvania and persons of foreign birth. Thus, the low number of enlistees compared to the 1860 population for the Southeast Region and Philadelphia County in particular is quite reasonable. The lower proportion of persons who were born in the Southeast, and again Philadelphia County, than were present there in 1860 also is reflective of the high levels of rural-to-urban migration which would have been taking place during this period and might also explain some of the opposite pattern in the Ridge and Valley.[24]

Potential Problems with the Data

Effect of Foreign-Born Parents on Heights of 'Native-Born Pennsylvanians'

Under ideal conditions not only would anthropometric researchers know the enlistee's place of birth but also his parents' (as well as his father's occupation). Chapter Two noted the generational effect which exists in physical stature. The sons of immigrants, of which there are no doubt many in this sample, but who unfortunately cannot be identified, would, under the same environmental conditions (calorie intake, work, disease), not grow to be as tall as multi-generational 'native-born' men. In the eighteenth century, it took several generations for Europeans to reach the U.S. 'standard' after arriving in this country. In this study, no variable was entered into the multivariate model to account for the percentage of the population in the birth county which was of foreign parentage. Further exploration of this issue and an attempt to account for percentage of foreign-born within the birth county would provide some indication of the extent to which this was an important influence on height variation within Pennsylvania.

Sample Selectivity because of Left-Tail Truncation

The use of military samples always brings with it problems of selectivity. Some military forces establish height minima which serve as a screening device to keep out 'under-sized' men. Obviously, this raises concerns when stature is the dependent variable in a study which utilizes military data. (See Chapter Five for a description of the height minima which existed over the course of the Civil War.) Fortunately, the extensive work which has been done on the heights of Civil War recruits has allayed many fears in this regard. Work by Margo and Steckel as well as by Komlos, and A'hearn finds no evidence that truncation affected trend results among the Civil War sample.[25] Additionally, the Civil War Army's status as one of mass participation rather than professional or small groups of volunteers makes this type of selectivity problem less important than it might be otherwise.[26]

Visual inspection of this sample at the company level reveals no consistent pattern of left-tail truncation. The height minima which existed for standard enlistees throughout the war (there were no minima for drafted men[27]) were so low relative to the mean height that few men would have been screened out, absent the very young who were still growing. The only visual evidence of left-tail truncation occurs within the Reserve Corps infantry which seems to have enforced some, although not absolute, scrutiny over the heights of its men. Kolmogorov-Smirnov tests run on the height distributions did not reject the hypothesis of normality for any of the unit types except the Reserve Corps infantry. Similar tests run by enlistment year also did not reject the normality hypothesis.

Figures A.1 – A.4 indicate that the time trend in height for populations which had completed their growth are not affected by the elimination of the left-tails of the distribution even as it neared the mean. Regression analysis on the statewide sample shows that progressive elimination of observations on the left side of the distribution, while raising the value of the constant, did not affect the pattern of relationships between the explanatory variables and the dependent one[28] (Table A.10). Analysis of the sample proceeded without reference to left-tail truncation, although cavalry, artillery, and Reserve Infantry units were eliminated from the sample due to potential size preferences with these particular units.[29]

Problems with Heaping and Rounding

In samples drawn from institutional records, height distributions often show evidence of 'heaping' of observations on whole or half inches. This may occur because of laziness on the part of the recorder, or as a result of poor measurement technique. The observations in the sample do show some heaping as described. Fogel et. al's work with the Union Army sample and other military samples indicates that neither heaping nor rounding, due to their self-canceling nature, have important effects on trends evident in the data.[30]

Removal of Men from Counties Experiencing Border Changes

During the presentation of the analysis of stature and its relationship to the economic characteristics of the soldiers' birth counties, men born in counties which had experienced border changes between 1820 and 1845 were excluded from this analysis. The rationale for this was that it was impossible to link firmly a man who had provided his birth county as his nativity with the economic data for his county if the borders had changed. It was not possible to tell if a man had given the county of his birth at the time of his birth or the time of enlistment. For example, in 1845 Lawrence County was created out of portions of Mercer and Beaver Counties, the latter two literally giving up land to form the new county. If a man born in 1840 provided his birth place as Mercer County, it was not possible to decipher whether he had been born in Mercer County as it existed in 1861 (after the creation of Lawrence County) or in 1840 (the date of his birth and before the creation of Lawrence County). Similarly, if a man gave his birth county as

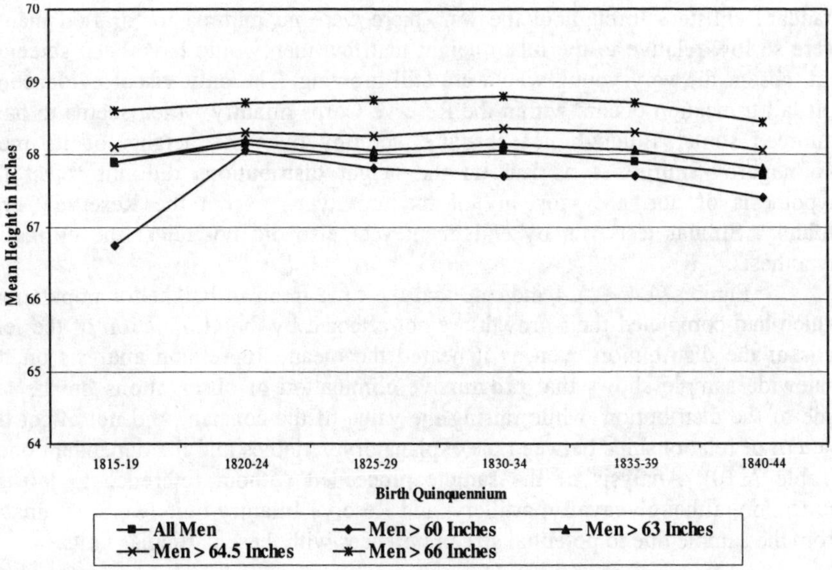

Figure A.1 Truncation Evaluation: Infantry, Aged 21-49

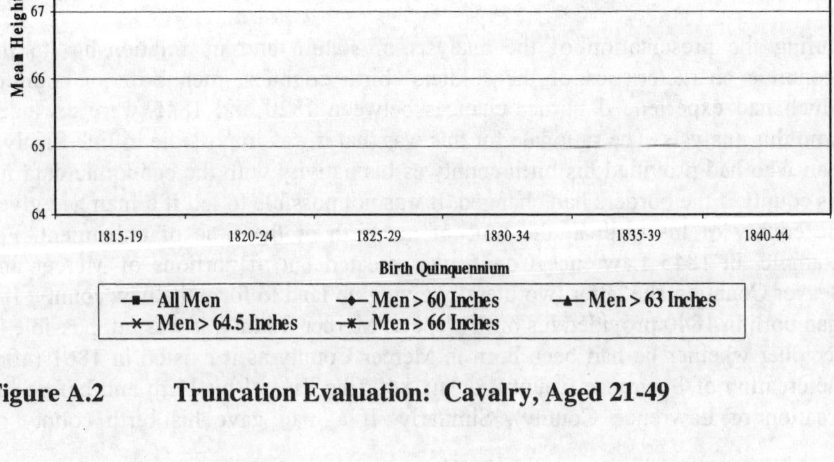

Figure A.2 Truncation Evaluation: Cavalry, Aged 21-49

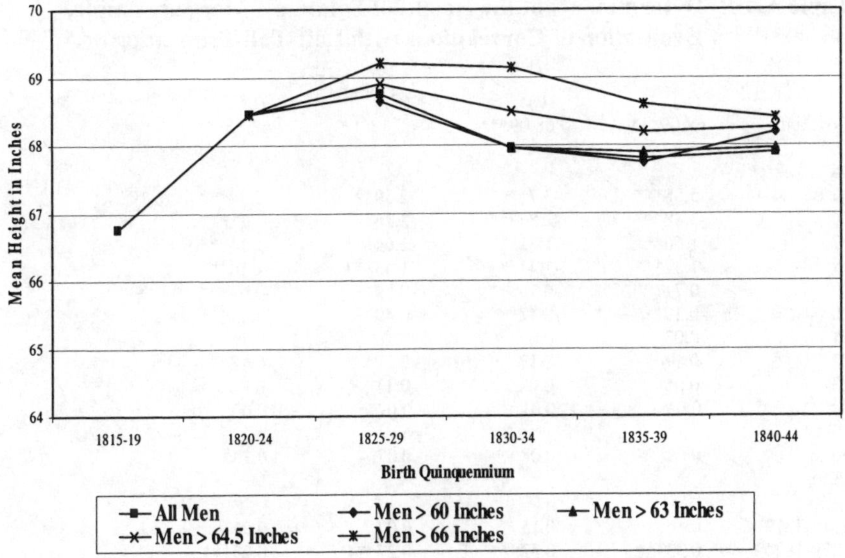

Figure A.3 Truncation Evaluation: Artillery, Aged 21-49

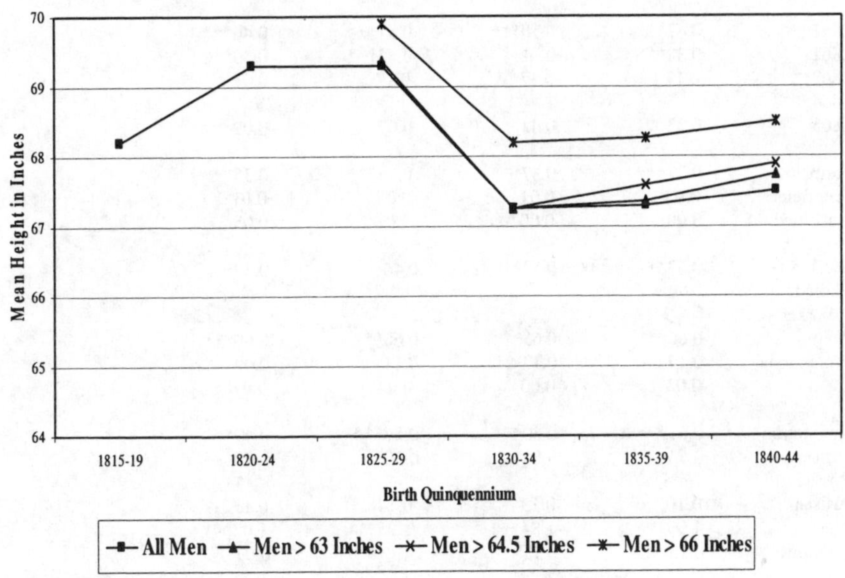

Figure A.4 Truncation Evaluation: Reserve Infantry, Aged 21-49

Table A.10 Determinants of the Height of Soldiers – Merged Sample, Evaluation of Correlations with Left-Tail Truncation

	(A)	(B)	(C)	(D)
Constant	68.09***	68.09***	68.12***	68.55***
15 & Below	-5.08***	-3.71***	-2.59** *	-2.54***
16	-3.38***	-2.84***	-2.26***	-1.71***
17	-1.66***	-1.71***	-1.64***	-1.14***
18	-1.37***	-1.41***	-1.43***	-1.16***
19	-0.71***	-0.75***	-0.79***	-0.63***
20	-0.39***	-0.42***	-0.49***	-0.44***
21	-0.03	-0.07	-0.16	-0.16
22	-0.17	-0.17	-0.19*	-0.18*
23	-0.06	-0.08	-0.11	-0.06
24	0.03	0.01	0.02	0.00
25-49				
50 & Above	0.08	0.08	0.07	0.13
1815-1819	0.16	0.15	0.07	0.05
1820-1824	0.33***	0.32***	0.27***	0.23**
1825-1829	0.25***	0.24***	0.21**	0.20**
1830-1834	0.30***	0.30***	0.27***	0.26***
1835-1839				
1840-1844	-0.05	-0.03	0.03	0.03
1845-1849	-0.27*	-0.23	-0.14	-0.12
1861	0.47***	0.50***	0.51***	0.46***
1862	0.30***	0.31**	0.33***	0.30***
1863	-0.17	-0.17	-0.17	0.01
1864				
1865	0.03	0.02	0.07	0.02
Farmer	0.37***	0.37***	0.36***	0.35***
Proprietor	-0.03	-0.01	-0.05	-0.01
Unskilled Worker	0.00	-0.00	-0.02	0.05
Work Site	0.53**	0.53**	0.46	0.39*
Skilled Worker				
None	0.66***	0.65***	0.66***	0.60***
Professional	0.17	0.17	0.11	0.09
Unknown	-0.03	-0.00	-0.04	-0.07
Non-comm	0.61***	0.60***	0.57***	0.49***
Officer	0.56*	0.54*	0.50*	0.38
Private				
Artisan	-0.10	-0.13	-0.14	-0.17
Musician	-1.99***	-1.84***	-1.25***	-1.02***
Unknown	0.13**	0.15**	0.13**	0.07

Table A.10 (continued)

	(A)	(B)	(C)	(D)
'Standard'				
Drafted (1)	0.12	0.12	0.09	-0.03
Substitute (2)	0.13	0.12	0.10	0.32
Recruit (3)	0.09	0.08	0.02	0.17
Bounty Rcpnt (4)	-0.16	-0.15	-0.12	-0.04
Infantry				
Artillery	0.22***	0.21***	0.18**	0.18**
Reserve Inf.	0.04	0.02	-0.04	-0.21*
Cavalry	0.33***	0.32***	0.31***	0.24***
Stayer				
Migrant	0.04	0.04	0.02	-0.02
Southeast	-0.97***	-0.98***	-0.89***	-0.75***
Anthracite	-0.90***	-0.91***	-0.82***	-0.61***
Pocono	-0.18	-0.19	-0.23	-0.19
Northeast	-0.29***	-0.31***	-0.30***	-0.28***
Ridge & Valley	-0.29***	-0.30***	-0.30***	-0.23***
Allegheny Forest	-0.11	-0.12	-0.11	-0.07
West				
Largest City Size in Enlistment County				
Under 5K				
5K to 10K	-0.30***	-0.29***	-0.25**	-0.22**
10K to 25K	-0.02	0.00	-0.01	-0.05
25K+	-0.07	-0.06	0.00	-0.03
Largest City Size in Birth County				
Under 5K				
5K to 10K	-0.02	-0.03	-0.04*	-0.07
10K to 25K	-0.26***	-0.26***	-0.30***	-0.28***
25K+	-0.36***	-0.35***	-0.36***	-0.37***
N[1]	16525[2]	16511[3]	16194[4]	15084[5]
Adjusted R^2	0.15	0.14	0.13	0.10
F	54.8***	52.9***	46.2***	33.4***

*** significant at the 0.01 level
** significant at the 0.05 level
* significant at the 0.10 level

---

[1] Intercept represents a 25-49 year old private, a standard enlistee in 1864, who enlisted in the infantry in the same county in which he was born (a county which at the time of birth and enlistment did not have a town containing more than 5000 persons), who was a skilled worker born between 1835 and 1839 in the Western Region.

[2] Contains observations regardless of height.

[3] Contains only observations with heights greater than or equal to 60 inches.

[4] Contains only observations with heights greater than or equal to 63 inches.

[5] Contains only observations with heights greater than 64.5 inches.

Lawrence County and he was born before 1845, clearly he was incorrect. Lawrence County did not exist before 1845. However, it was impossible to tell if he should be associated with Mercer or Beaver, either. There was no way to associate him with any particular county around the years of his birth. County creation and border changes made firmly linking men from such counties to the county of their youth, and thus to the economic data which characterized it, impossible. While this reduced the strength of the regression results because of reduced sample sizes, there was no other alternative that would ensure the use of appropriately coded data.

Notes

1 These books, housed in the U.S. National Archives, were compilations of various rolls kept by company clerks. Data was drawn from the descriptive rolls, a roll of men who enlisted when the unit was formed as well as those who enlisted later to take the place of the fallen. A duplicate copy of this roll was forwarded to the regiment which kept its own regimental descriptive book. United States, War Department, *United States Army Regulations of 1861 with an Appendix Containing the Changes and Laws Affecting Army Regulations and Articles of War to June 25, 1863* (Washington, D.C.: G.P.O., 1863), Article XII, 20 and 24.

2 Sauers' *Advance the Colors* was the source for primary county of recruitment for each company. Primary recruitment county was the county in which the unit was raised from which the bulk of its men came. There are several historical studies of Pennsylvania units in the Civil War, and some controversy over the determination of which counties supplied troops to which units. (Sauers' work seems to be an improvement on Samuel Bates' *Bates' History of the Pennsylvania Volunteers, 1861-1865* (Harrisburg: B. Singerly, 1869); R. A. Sauers, *Advance the Colors: Pennsylvania Civil War Battle Flags* (Harrisburg: Capitol Preservation Committee, 1987). Figures here are before 'cleaning' of the data.

3 Robert W. Fogel, Stanley Engerman, et. al., *Union Army Recruits in White Regiments in the United States, 1861-1865*, computer file, Study # 9425 (Chicago, University of Chicago, Center for Population Economics \producer\, 1990), Ann Arbor, MI: Inter-university Consortium for Political and Social Research \distributor\, 1990.

4 Sauers, *Advance the Colors*, 247.

5 This is the total men in the two samples *after* eliminating cases with uninterpretable data of some sort.

6 Reserved Infantry units were part of the Reserve Volunteer Corps formed by Pennsylvania when Lincoln's first call for volunteers was vastly oversubscribed. Many members of these units, initially held in 'reserve,' answered desperate calls for more volunteers shortly thereafter. These units' height distributions show more evidence than any other of left-tail truncation. It may be that, particularly in light of the great initial response to Lincoln's call, the officers forming these units were very selective. J.R. Sypher, *History of the Pennsylvania Reserve Corps* (Lancaster, PA: Elias Barr and Co., 1865), 18-20.

7 While most units identified who their officers were, few recorded physical descriptions of them. Since these physical descriptions were used to prove identity on pay day and in the event of desertion it may have been that commanders in the units did not feel it

necessary to have descriptions of their officers recorded because of their belief that officers, as gentlemen, would never claim undeserved pay or desert. I thank Michael Meier, National Archives, Military Reference Branch, for this insight.

8 'Rank,' for the purpose of the data set, also indicates status as an artisan or a musician. Because interest in socio-economic status was behind our interest in any relationship between rank and height, it was decided to collect rank at entry. This would seem to be more indicative of socio-economic status as opposed to final rank which might be influenced by events during the conflict which might lead to promotion.

9 Sauers, *Advance the Colors*, 247.

10 Benjamin A. Gould, *Investigations in the Military and Anthropological Statistics of American Soldiers* (New York: Hurd and Houghton [for the U.S. Sanitary Commission], 1869), 38. Wiley's sample indicated just over one per cent of the enlistees to be under age 18. Bell I. Wiley, *The Life of Billy Yank: The Common Soldier of the Union* (Indianapolis: Bobbs-Merrill Co., Inc., 1952), 299.

11 United States, War Department, Adjutant General's Office, *Regulations for the Recruiting Service of the Army of the United States Both Regular and Volunteer* (Washington, D.C.: GPO, 1862), 8; United States, War Department, *United States Army Regulations of 1861 with an Appendix Containing the Changes and Laws Affecting Army Regulations and Articles of War to June 25, 1863* (Washington, D.C.: G.P.O., 1863), 519.

12 Wiley, *Life of Billy Yank*, 299. This might also help account for some of the unusual fluctuations in the height by age patterns around ages 17 and 18 and 21 and 22.

13 United States, War Department, Adjutant General's Office, *Regulations for the Recruiting Service*, 8.

14 Wiley, *The Life of Billy Yank*; James W. Geary, *We Need Men: The Union Draft in the Civil War* (DeKalb, IL: University of Northern Illinois Press, 1991).

15 The manner in which population by age data is presented in the census precludes a more precise calculation of this figure.

16 Robert Fogel, Stanley L. Engerman, and James Trussell, 'Exploring the Uses of Data on Height: The Analysis of Long Term Trends in Nutrition, Labor Welfare, and Labor Productivity.' *Social Science History* 6 (1982): 401-421.

17 Wiley, *Life of Billy Yank*, 303-304.

18 It should be noted that there is some ambiguity in the farmer/laborer dichotomy in that it can be assumed that many of the men who specified themselves as laborers would have been so in farm settings. Thus some of this difference may also result from the classification of some laborers as farm workers.

19 Geary, *We Need Men*, 95.

20 Some trends in the data may be masked by re-enlistees who were included in the 1864 and 1865 enlistment year categories.

21 The size of this shift may be understated in this sample because it does not include foreign-born individuals.

22 These distributions were developed by applying to the occupation summary in the 1860 U.S. Census and the reported occupations collected from the Civil War enlistment records which were the data source for this study, the occupational categorizations scheme used in the Philadelphia Social History Project. See Theodore Herschberg and Robert Dockhorn, 'Occupational Classification,' *Historical Methods Newsletter* 9 (1976): 59-98.

23 Note that the higher proportion of farmers in the western sample than in the statewide one is consistent with their greater presence in the western counties generally.

24 As has been noted in an earlier chapter, the fact that a man enlisted in a particular county does not mean that he resided there. So while enlistment distributions can be evaluated against current residence distributions this caveat must be kept in mind.

25 Margo and Steckel, 'Native Born Whites,' 168; Brian A'hearn, 'The Antebellum Puzzle Revisited: A New Look at the Stature of Union Army Recruits during the Civil War,' in *The Biological Standard of Living in Comparative Perspective*, Vol. I, *The Americans, Asia, and Australia*, ed. John Komlos and Joerg Baten (Stuttgart: Steiner Verlag, 1998).

26 Fogel, et. al., 'Secular Changes,' 454.

27 J.H. Baxter, *Statistics, Medical and Anthropological of the Provost-Marshall-General's Bureau* (Washington: G.P.O., 1875), lix.

28 This is known as the Komlos-Kim Method. John Komlos and Joo Han Kim, 'Estimating Trends in Historical Heights,' *Historical Methods* 23 (1990): 116-120.

29 In 1825 a man needed to stand 5'6" tall to enter the infantry, but 5'8" to enter the artillery. United States War Department, *General Regulations for the Army, or Military Institutes* (Washington, D.C.: Davis and Force, 1825), 354.

30 Fogel, 'Secular Changes,' 455.

Bibliography

PRIMARY SOURCES

Manuscript Sources (Paper)

Adjutant General's Office. *Descriptive Books of Volunteer Organizations: Civil War, 1861-65*. Record Group 94, Item 114. National Archives. Washington, D.C.

Manuscript Sources (Computer File Compilations)

Fogel, Robert W. and Stanley Engerman et. al. *Union Army Recruits in White Regiments in the United States, 1861-1865*, computer file, ICPSR Study #9425. Chicago: University of Chicago, Center for Population Economics \producer\, 1990. Ann Arbor, MI: Inter-university Consortium for Political and Social Research \distributor\, 1990.

Inter-University Consortium for Political and Social Research. *Historical Demographic, Economic and Social Data: The United States, 1790-1970* \computer file\, ICPSR Data Set 0003. Ann Arbor: ICPSR \producer and distributor\, 1992.

Komlos, John. *Height and Weight of West Point Cadets, 1843-1894*, computer file, ICPSR Study #9468. Pittsburgh: University of Pittsburgh \producer\, 1985. Ann Arbor, MI: Inter-university Consortium for Political and Social Research \distributor\, 1991.

Government Documents and Publications

Bartholow, Roberts. *A Manual of Instructions for Enlisting and Discharging Soldiers: With Special Reference to the Medical Examination of Recruits, and the Detection of Disqualifying and Feigned Diseases*. Philadelphia: J.B. Lippincott, 1863; reprint San Francisco: Norman Publishers, 1991.

Baxter, J.H. *Statistics, Medical and Anthropological of the Provost-Marshall-General's Bureau*. Washington: G.P.O., 1875.

Coolidge, Richard H. *Hints on the medical examination of recruits for the Army, and discharge of soldiers from service on surgeon's certificate*. Philadelphia: J.B. Lippincott and Co., 1856.

Coxe, Tench. *A Statement of the Arts and Manufactures of the United States of America for the Year of 1810*. Philadelphia: A. Cornman, 1814; reprint New York: Luther M. Cornwall, Co., 1914.

Henderson, Thomas. *Hints on the medical examination of recruits for the Army, and discharge of soldiers from service on surgeon's certificate*. Philadelphia: Haswell, Barrington, and Haswell, 1840.

Pennsylvania Department of Agriculture. 'Agriculture in Pennsylvania: A Study of Trends, County and State Since 1840,' by George Fiske Johnson. *General Bulletin* No. 484. Harrisburg: Department of Agriculture, 1929.

Pennsylvania Senate. 'Report of the Board of Revenue Commissioners, transmitted to the Governor, in pursuance of an act of the 29th of April 1844.' *Journal of the Senate*, 1845, Vol. II, Document 53, 303-320. Harrisburg: J. M. G. Lescure, 1845.

Pennsylvania Senate. 'Communication from the State Treasurer, Enclosing Tables of the Valuation fixed on the Several Counties of the Commonwealth,' by the Board of Revenue Commissioners. *Journal of the Senate*, 1845, Vol. II, Document 54, 321-326. Harrisburg: J. M. G. Lescure, 1845.

Tripler, Charles S. *Manual of the Medical Officer of the Army of the United States. Part I. Recruiting and Inspection of Recruits*. Cincinnati: Wrightson and Co., 1858.

United States. *Returns of The Whole Number of Persons within the Several Districts of the United States According to 'An Act Providing for the Second Census...'*. Second Decennial Census, 1800. Washington: Duane, 1801.

________. *Compendium of the Enumeration of the Inhabitants and Statistics of the United States as obtained at the Department of State from the returns of the Sixth Census*. Sixth Decennial Census, 1840. Washington: Thomas Allen, 1841.

________. *The Seventh Census of the United States: 1850*. Seventh Decennial Census, 1850. Washington: Robert Armstrong, 1853.

________. *Population of the United States in 1860; Compiled from the Original Returns of the Eighth Census*. Eighth Decennial Census, 1860. Washington: G.P.O., 1864.

________. *Agriculture of the United States in 1860; Compiled from the Original Returns of the Eighth Census*. Eighth Decennial Census, 1860. Washington: G.P.O., 1864.

United States. Army. *Statistical Report on the Sickness and Mortality in the Army of the United States . . . from January, 1819, to January 1839*, by Samuel Forry. Washington: Gideon, 1840.

________. *Statistical Report on the Sickness and Mortality in the Army of the United States . . . from January, 1855, to January 1860*, by Richard Coolidge. Washington: Gideon, 1860.

United States. Bureau of the Census. *Sixteenth Census of the United States: 1940, Agriculture*, Vol.1. Washington, D.C.: G.P.O., 1942.

________. *The History and Growth of the United States Census*, by Carroll D. Wright. Washington: Government Printing Office, 1900; reprint: New York: Johnson Reprint Corp., 1966.

________. *Historical Statistics of the United States, Colonial Times to 1970, Part 1*. Washington, D.C.: G.P.O., 1975.

United States. Census Office. *Census for 1820*. Fourth Decennial Census, 1820. Washington: Gales and Seaton, 1821.

________. *Fifth Census; or, Enumeration of the Inhabitants of the United States, 1830*. Fifth Decennial Census, 1830. Washington: Duff Green, 1832.

United States. Treasury Department. *Aggregate Amount of each description of persons within the United States of America and the Territories thereof, agreeably to actual enumeration made according to law in the Year 1810*. Third Decennial Census, 1810. Washington, 1811.

United States. War Department. *General Regulations for the Army, or Military Institutes*. Washington, D.C.: Davis and Force, 1825.

________. *United States Army Regulations of 1861 with an Appendix Containing the Changes and Laws Affecting Army Regulations and Articles of War to June 25, 1863*. Washington, D.C.: G.P.O., 1863.

________. *General Orders of the War Department Embracing the Years 1861, 1862, and 1863. Adapted Specially for the Use of the Army and Navy of the United States* by Thomas O'Brien and Oliver Diefendorf. New York: Derby and Miller, 1864.

________. *Compendium of General Orders, 1861-[1863]*. Washington, D.C.: G.P.O., 1866.

________. *Regulations of the Army of the United States and General Orders in Force on the 17th of February 1881*. Washington, D.C.: GPO, 1881.

United States. War Department. Adjutant General's Office. *Regulations for the Recruiting Service of the Army of the United States Both Regular and Volunteer*. Washington, D.C.: GPO, 1862.

SECONDARY SOURCES

Ackerknecht, Erwin H. *A Short History of Medicine*. Baltimore: Johns Hopkins University Press, 1982.

Adams, Donald R. Jr. 'Wage Rates in Philadelphia, 1790-1830.' *Journal of Economic History* (1968): 404-417.

Agnew, Daniel. *A History of the Region of Pennsylvania North of the Ohio and West of the Allegheny River*. Philadelphia: Kay and Brother, 1887.

Agriculture, Its Early History and Development in Pennsylvania, and its Present Status. Harrisburg: Bureau of Industrial Statistics, 1875.

A'Hearn, Brian. 'The Antebellum Puzzle Revisited: A New Look at the Stature of Union Army Recruits during the Civil War.' In *The Biological Standard of Living in Comparative Perspective*, Vol. I, *The Americans, Asia, and Australia*, ed. John Komlos and Joerg Baten. Stuttgart: Steiner Verlag, 1999.

Allen, William R. *International Trade Theory: Hume to Ohlin*. New York: Random House, 1965.

American Public Works Association. *History of Public Works in the United States, 1776-1976*. Chicago: American Public Works Association, 1976.

'An Abstract of the Returns made by the Commissioners of the City of Philadelphia and the Several Counties of the Commonwealth of Pennsylvania.' *Hazard's Register* (July 1828): 12-13.

Anderson, Niles. *Roads to the Forks*. Pittsburgh: Historical Society of Western Pennsylvania, 1976.

Andriot, Donna. *Population Abstract of the United States*. McLean, VA: Documents Index Inc., 1993.

Aron, Jean-Paul, Paul Dumont, and Emmanuel Le Roy Ladurie, *Anthropologie du Conscrit Francais*. Paris: Mouton, 1972.

Baer, Christopher T. *Canals and Railroads of the Mid-Atlantic States, 1800-1860*. Wilmington, DE: Regional Economic History Research Center, Eleutherian Mills-Hagley Foundation, 1981.

Bairagi, Radheshyam. 'A Comparison of Five Anthropometric Indices for Identifying Factors of Malnutrition.' *American Journal of Epidemiology* 126 (1987): 258-267.

Baker, Reginald Paul. 'Economic Development and Rural Social Structure: Pennsylvania in 1860.' Ph.D. dissertation, University of Pittsburgh, 1977.

Baldwin, Leland D. 'The Rivers in the Early Development of Western Pennsylvania.' *Western Pennsylvania Historical Magazine* 16 (1933): 79-98.

________. *The Keelboat Age on Western Waters*. Pittsburgh: University of Pittsburgh, 1941.

Barron, Hal S. 'Listening to the Silent Majority: Change and Continuity in the Nineteenth-Century Rural North.' In *Agriculture and National Development: Views on the Nineteenth-Century*, ed. Lou Ferleger, 3-23. Ames, IA: Iowa State University Press, 1990.

Bartlett, Virginia K. *Keeping House: Women's Lives in Western Pennsylvania, 1790-1850*. Pittsburgh: Historical Society of Western Pennsylvania and the University of Pittsburgh, 1994.

Bateman, Fred and Jeremy Atack. *To Their Own Soil: Agriculture in the Antebellum North*. Ames: University of Iowa Press, 1987.

Bates, Samuel P. *Bates's History of Pennsylvania Volunteers, 1861-1865*. Harrisburg: B. Singerly, 1869.

Baumann, Roland M. *Dissertations on Pennsylvania History, 1886-1976: A Bibliography*. Harrisburg: Pennsylvania Historical and Museum Commission, 1978.

Behrmann, Jere R. and Anil B. Deolaliker. 'Health and Nutrition.' In *Handbook of Development Economics*, ed., H. Chenery and T.N. Srinivasan, 633-711. Amsterdam: Elsevier Science Publishers, 1988.

Berry, Brian J. *America's Utopian Experiments: Communal Havens from Long-Wave Crises*. Hanover, N.H.: University Press of New England, 1992.

Berry, Thomas S. 'Wholesale Commodity Prices in the Ohio Valley, 1816-1860.' Ph.D. dissertation, Harvard University, 1938.

Bezanson, Anne, Robert D. Gray, and Miriam Hussey. *Wholesale Prices in Philadelphia, 1784-1861*. Philadelphia: University of Pennsylvania Press, 1936.

Bidwell, Percy W. and John I. Falconer. *History of Agriculture in the Northern United States, 1620-1860*. Washington, D.C.: Carnegie Institution of Washington by The Lord Baltimore Press, 1925.

Bielecki, T. and J. Charzewski. 'Body Height and Upward Social Mobility.' *Annals of Human Biology* 10 (1983): 403-408.

Bielecki, T. 'Physical Growth as a Measure of the Economic Well-being of Populations; the Twentieth-Century.' In *Human Growth*, 2nd ed.; Vol. 3, ed. F. Falkner and J.M. Tanner, 283-305. New York: Plenum, 1986.

Binder, Frederick Moore. *Coal Age Empire: Pennsylvania Coal and its Utilization to 1860*. Harrisburg: Pennsylvania Historical and Museum Commission, 1974.

Bongaarts, John. 'Does Malnutrition Affect Fecundity? A Summary of the Evidence.' *Science* 208 (1980): 564-569.

Boserup, Ester. *The Conditions of Agricultural Growth: The Economics of Agrarian Change under Population Pressure*. Chicago: Aldine Publishing Co., 1965.

Bowles, G. T. *New Types of Old Americans at Harvard and at Eastern Women's Colleges*. Cambridge, MA: Harvard University Press, 1952.

Brinkman, Henk Jan, J.W. Drukker, and Brigitte Slot. 'Height and Income: A New Method for the Estimation of Historical National Income Series.' *Explorations in Economic History* 25 (1988): 227-264.

Brittan, Samuel. *Participation Without Politics: An Analysis of the Nature and Role of Markets*. London: Institute of Economic Affairs, 1975.

Bruchey, Stuart. 'The Business Economy of Marketing Change, 1790-1840: A Study of the Sources of Efficiency.' In *Farming in the New Nation: Interpreting America's Agriculture, 1790-1840*, ed. Darwin P. Kelsey, 211-226. Washington, D.C.: The Agricultural History Society, 1972.

Brudevoll, J.E., K. Liestol, and L. Walloe. 'Menarcheal Age in Oslo during the Last 140 Years.' *Annals of Human Biology* 6 (1979): 407-416.

Bryzski, Anthony J. 'The Lehigh Canal and Its Effect on the Economic Development of the Region through which it Passes, 1818-1873.' Unpublished dissertation, New York University, 1957.

Buck, Solon J. and Elizabeth H. Buck. *The Planting of Civilization in Western Pennsylvania*. Pittsburgh: University of Pittsburgh Press, 1939.

Buckler, J.M.H. *A Reference Manual of Growth and Development*. Oxford: Blackwell Scientific Publications, 1979.

Burrowes, Thomas. *State-book of Pennsylvania*. Philadelphia: Uriah Hunt and Son, 1846.

Cameron, Noel. 'The Methods of Auxological Anthropometry.' In *Human Growth: A Comprehensive Treatise*, 2nd ed., Vol. 3, ed. F. Falkner and J.M. Tanner, 263-281. New York: Plenum, 1986.

________. 'Measurement Issues Related to Anthropometric Assessment of Nutritional Status.' In *Anthropometric Assessment of Nutritional Status*, ed. John H. Himes, 347-364. New York: Wiley-Liss, Inc., 1991.

Cantor, Robin A. *Making Markets: An Interdisciplinary Perspective on Economic Exchange*. Westport, CN: Greenwood Press, 1992.

Carmichael, Ann G. 'Infection, Hidden Hunger and History.' *Journal of Interdisciplinary History* 14 (1983): 249-64.

Cassedy, James H. *Medicine and American Growth, 1800-1860*. Madison: University of Wisconsin Press, 1986.

Cather, Willa. 'Neighbor Rosicky.' In *Obscure Destinies*. New York: Alfred A. Knopf, 1941.

Caves, Richard E. *Trade and Economic Structure: Models and Methods*. Cambridge, MA: Harvard University Press, 1963.

Caves, Richard E., Jeffrey A. Frankel, and Ronald W. Jones. *World Trade and Payments: An Introduction*, 5th ed. Glenview, IL: Scott Foresman/Little Brown Higher Education, 1990.

Chen, Kuan-I. 'Agricultural Production in Pennsylvania, 1840-1950.' Ph.D. dissertation, Pennsylvania State University, 1954.

Chen, Lincoln C., A.K.M. Alauddin Chowdhury, and Sandra L. Huffman. 'Anthropometric Assessment of Energy-Protein Malnutrition and Subsequent Risk of Mortality among Preschool Aged Children.' *American Journal of Clinical Nutrition* 33 (1980): 1836-1845.

Chenery, Hollis and Moises Syrquin. *Patterns of Development, 1950-1970*. New York: Oxford University Press, 1975.

Chudacoff, Howard P. *The Evolution of American Urban Society*. Englewood Cliffs, N.J.: Prentice-Hall, 1975.

Clark, Gregory, Michael Huberman, and Peter H. Lindert. 'A British Food Puzzle, 1770-1850.' *Economic History Review* 48 (1995): 215-237.

Cohen, Majorie Griffen. *Women's Work, Markets, and Economic Development in Nineteenth-Century Ontario*. Toronto: University of Toronto Press, 1988.

Cole, A.H. *American Woolen Manufactures*, Vol. 1. Cambridge: Harvard University Press, 1926.

________. *Wholesale Commodity Prices in the United States, 1700-1861*. Cambridge: Harvard University Press, 1938; reprint, New York: Johnson Reprint Co., 1969.

Cole, T.J. 'A Critique of the NCHS Weight for Height Standards.' *Human Biology* 57 (1985): 183-196.

Collard, David A. *Prices, Markets, and Welfare*. New York: Crane, Russak, 1972.

Conk, Margo Anderson. *U.S. Census and Labor Force Change: A History of Occupation Statistics*. Ann Arbor: UMI Research Press, 1980.

Costa, Dora L. 'Height, Weight, Wartime Stress, and Older Age Mortality: Evidence from the Union Army Records.' *Explorations in Economic History* 30 (1993): 424-449.

________. 'Height, Wealth, and Disease among the Native-Born in the Rural Antebellum North.' *Social Science History* 17 (1993): 355-383.

________. 'Health, Income, and Retirement Behavior: Evidence from Nineteenth-Century America.' National Bureau of Economic Research Working Paper 4537. Cambridge, MA: National Bureau of Economic Research, 1993.

Cox, Thomas R. 'Transition in the Woods: Log Drivers, Raftsmen, and the Emergence of Modern Lumbering in Pennsylvania.' *Pennsylvania Magazine of History and Biography* 104 (January 1980): 345-364.

Craig, Lee A., Raymond B. Palmquist, and Thomas Weiss. 'Transportation Improvements and Land Values in the Antebellum United States: A Hedonic Approach.' Manuscript #95-2-5, North Carolina State University, 1997.

Craig, Lee A. and Thomas Weiss. 'Nutritional Status and Agricultural Surpluses in the Antebellum United States,' NBER Working Paper Series on Historical Factors in Long Run Growth, Historical Paper 99, April 1997.

Cuff, David J., William J. Young, Edward K. Muller, Wilbur Zelinsky, and Ronald F. Abler. *The Atlas of Pennsylvania*. Philadelphia: Temple University Press, 1989.

Cuff, Timothy. 'A Weighty Issue Revisited: New Evidence on Commercial Swine Weights and Pork Production Trends in Mid-Nineteenth-Century America.' *Agricultural History* 66 (1992): 55-74.

________. 'The Body Mass Index Values of Mid-Nineteenth-Century West Point Cadets: A Theoretical Application of Waaler's Curves to A Historical Population.' *Historical Methods* 26 (1993): 171-183.

________. 'Historical Anthropometrics-Theory, Method, and State of the Field.' In *The Biological Standard of Living on Three Continents: Further Explorations in Anthropometric History*, ed. John Komlos, 1-18. Boulder, CO: Westview Press, 1995.

Curti, Merle. *The Making of An American Community: A Case Study of Democracy in a Frontier County*. Stanford, CA: Stanford University Press, 1959.

Damon, Albert. 'Secular Trend in Height and Weight within Old American Families at Harvard, 1870-1965.' *American Journal of Physical Anthropology* 29 (1968): 45-50.

________. 'Stature Increase among Italian-Americans: Environmental, Genetic, or Both?' *American Journal of Physical Anthropology* 23 (1965): 401-408.

________. *Human Biology and Ecology*. New York: W.W. Norton and Co., 1977.

Danhof, Clarence. *Change in Agriculture: The Northern United States, 1820-1870*. Cambridge: Harvard University Press, 1969.

Dasgupta, Partha. 'Well-being and the Extent of Its Realization in Poor Countries.' *Economic Journal* 100, supplement 1 (1990): 1-32.

David, Paul. 'The Growth of Real Product in the United States Before 1840: New Evidence, Controlled Conjectures.' *Journal of Economic History* 27 (1967): 151-197.

Davin, Eric L. 'The Era of the Common Child: Egalitarian Death in Antebellum America.' *Mid-America* 75 (1993): 135-163.

Davis, Lance, Richard Easterlin, and William Parker, cd. *American Economic Growth: An Economist's History of the United States*. New York: Harper and Row Publishers, 1972.

Day, Sherman. *Historical Collections of the State of Pennsylvania*. Philadelphia: G.W. Gorton, 1843; reprint, Long Island, N.Y.: Ira J. Friedman, Inc., 1969.

DeGeorge, Jon E. 'The Commercial Development of Erie County, 1810-1825.' *Journal of Erie Studies* 4 (1975): 20-51.

DeGeorge, Theresa G. 'The Economic Development of the Port of Erie and Related Avenues of Trade, 1825-1845.' *Journal of Erie Studies* 4 (1975): 52-71.

Deolaliker, A.B. 'Do Health and Nutrition Influence Labor Productivity in Agriculture? Econometric Estimates for Rural India.' *Review of Economics and Statistics* 70 (1988): 406-413.

DePuy, LeRoy B. 'The Walnut Street Prison: Pennsylvania's First Penitentiary.' *Pennsylvania History* 18 (1951): 130-144.

Drake, Daniel. *A Systematic Treatise, Historical, Etiological, and Practical, on the Principal Diseases of the Interior Valley of North America*. Cincinnati: Smith, 1850.

Dublin, Thomas. *Women at Work: The Transformation of Work and Community in Lowell, Massachusetts, 1826-1860*. New York: Columbia University Press, 1979.

Dunaway, Wayland F. *A History of Pennsylvania*. New York: Prentice-Hall, 1948.

Dupuy, R. Ernest. *The National Guard: A Compact History*. New York: Hawthorn Books, Inc., 1971.

Dyer, Frederick. *A Compendium of the War of the Rebellion*. Des Moines: By the author, 1908; reprint: The Press of Morningside Bookshop, 1978.

Dykstra, Ann. 'Region, Economy and Party: The Roots of Policy Formation in Pennsylvania.' Ph.D. dissertation, University of Pittsburgh, 1988.

Eaton, Rebecca. *A Geography of Pennsylvania*, 2nd ed. Philadelphia: Edward C. Biddle, 1837.

Egle, William H. *An Illustrated History of the Commonwealth of Pennsylvania: Civil, Political, and Military*. . . Harrisburg: DeWitt C. Goodrich & Co., 1876.

Eisenberg, N., K. Roth and K.A. Bryniarski and E. Murray. 'Sex Differences in the Relationship of Height to Children's Actual and Attributed Social and Cognitive Competencies.' *Sex Roles* 11 (1984): 719-734.

Ellis, Elizabeth G. *Bibliography of Pennsylvania History*. Harrisburg: Pennsylvania Historical and Museum Commission, 1957.

________. *List of Basic Pennsylvania State Publications for Depository Libraries*. Harrisburg: Government Publications Section, Pennsylvania State Library, 1967.

________. *Year's Work in Pennsylvania Studies*. Harrisburg: Pennsylvania State Library, 1970.

________. *Bibliography of Pennsylvania History: A Supplement*. Harrisburg: Pennsylvania Historical and Museum Commission, 1976.

Eltis, David. 'Nutritional Trends in Africa and the Americas: Heights of Africans, 1819-1839.' *Journal of Interdisciplinary History* 12 (1982): 453-475.

________. 'Welfare Trends Among the Yoruba in the Early Nineteenth-Century: The Anthropometric Evidence.' *Journal of Economic History* 50 (1990): 521-540.

Engerman, Stanley. 'The Height of U.S. Slaves.' *Local Population Studies* 16 (1976): 45-50.

Ent, Col Uzal. W. *The First Century: A History of the 28th Infantry Division*. Harrisburg: Stackpole Books, 1979.

Erhardt, Carl L. and Joyce E. Berlin. *Mortality and Morbidity in the United States*. Cambridge: Harvard University Press, 1974.

Espenshade, A. Howry. *Pennsylvania Place Names*. State College, PA: The Pennsylvania State College, 1925.

Eveleth, Phyllis B. and James M. Tanner. *Worldwide Variation in Human Growth*. Cambridge: Cambridge University Press, 1976.

Eveleth, Phyllis B. 'Population Differences in Growth: Environmental and Genetic Factors.' In *Human Growth: A Comprehensive Treatise*, 2nd ed., Vol. 3, ed. F. Falkner and J.M. Tanner, 221-239. New York: Plenum, 1986.

Everett, Edward G. *Pennsylvania's Mobilization for War, 1860-61*. Ph.D. dissertation, University of Pittsburgh, 1954.

Fishlow, Albert. 'Internal Transportation.' In *American Economic Growth: An Economist's History of the United States*, ed. Lance Davis, Richard Easterlin, and William N. Parker, 468-472. New York: Harper and Row, 1972.

Fletcher, Stevenson Whitcomb. *Pennsylvania Agriculture and Country Life, 1640-1840*. Harrisburg: Pennsylvania Historical and Museum Commission, 1950.

________. *Pennsylvania Agriculture and Country Life, 1840-1940*. Harrisburg: Pennsylvania Historical and Museum Commission, 1955.

Florin, John William. *The Advance of Frontier Settlement in Pennsylvania, 1638-1850: A Geographic Interpretation*. University Park, PA: Department of Geography, Pennsylvania State University, 1977.

Floud, Roderick. 'The Heights of Europeans since 1750: A New Source for European Economic History.' In *Stature, Living Standards, and Economic Development: Essays in Anthropometric History*, ed. John Komlos, 10-24. Chicago: University of Chicago Press, 1994.

Floud, Roderick and Kenneth Wachter. 'Poverty and Physical Stature, Evidence on the Standard of Living of London Boys 1770-1870.' *Social Science History* 6 (1982): 422-452.

Floud, Roderick, Kenneth Wachter, and Annabel Gregory. 'The Physical State of the British Working Class, 1870-1914: Evidence from Army Recruits.' National Bureau of Economic Research, Working Paper 1661, 1985.

Floud, Roderick, Kenneth Wachter, and Annabel Gregory. *Height, Health, and History: Nutritional Status in the United Kingdom, 1750-1980*. Cambridge, England: Cambridge University Press, 1990.

Floud, Roderick, Kenneth Wachter, and Annabel Gregory. 'Measuring Historical Heights – Short Cuts or the Long Way Round: A Reply to Komlos.' *Economic History Review* 46 (1993): 145-154.

Floud, Roderick, Kenneth Wachter, and Annabel Gregory. 'Further Thoughts on the Nutritional Status of the British Population.' *Economic History Review* 46 (1993): 367-368.

Floud, Roderick and Bernard Harris. 'Health, Height and Welfare: Britain, 1700-1980.' Unpublished manuscript. London Guildhall University and University of Southampton, 1995.

Fogel, Robert W. *Railroads and American Economic Development: Essays in Econometric History*. Baltimore: Johns Hopkins University Press, 1964.

________.'The Aging of Union Army Men: A Longitudinal Study, 1830-1940.' Unpublished grant proposal, University of Chicago, 1986.

________. 'Physical growth as a measure of the economic well-being of populations; the eighteenth- and nineteenth-centuries.' In *Human Growth: A Comprehensive Treatise*, 2nd ed., Vol. 3, ed. F. Falkner and J.M. Tanner, 263-281. New York: Plenum, 1986.

________. 'Nutrition and the Decline in Mortality since 1700: Some Preliminary Findings.' In *Long-Term Factors in American Economic Growth*, ed. Stanley Engerman and Robert Gallman, 439-527. Chicago: National Bureau of Economic Research, 1987.

________. *Without Consent or Contract: The Rise and Fall of American Slavery*. New York: W.W. Norton Co., 1989.

________. 'The Conquest of High Mortality and Hunger in Europe and America: Timing and Mechanisms.' In *Favorites of Fortune: Technology, Growth, and Economic Development Since the Industrial Revolution*, ed. P. Higonnet, D.S. Landes, and H. Rosovsky, 33-71. Cambridge, MA: Harvard University Press, 1991.

________. 'New Sources and New Techniques for the Study of Secular Trends in Nutritional Status, Health, Mortality, and the Process of Aging.' *Historical Methods* 26 (1993): 5-43.

________. 'The Relevance of Malthus for the Study of Mortality Today: Long-Run Influences on Health, Mortality, Labor Force Participation, and Population Growth.'

NBER Working Paper Series on Historical Factors in Long Run Growth, Working Paper #54. Cambridge, MA, 1994.

Fogel, Robert W., Stanley L. Engerman, James Trussell, Roderick Floud, Clayne L. Pope, and Larry T. Wimmer. 'The Economics of Mortality in North America, 1650-1910: A Description of a Research Project.' *Historical Methods* 11 (1978): 75-108.

Fogel, Robert W., Stanley Engerman, et al. 'Changes in American and British Stature Since the Mid-Eighteenth-Century: A Preliminary Report on the Usefulness of Data on Height for the Analysis of Secular Trends in Nutrition, Labor Productivity, and Labor Welfare.' Cambridge, MA: National Bureau of Economic Research. Working Paper #890, 1982.

Fogel, Robert W., Stanley L. Engerman, and James Trussell. 'Exploring the Uses of Data on Height: The Analysis of Long Term Trends in Nutrition, Labor Welfare, and Labor Productivity.' *Social Science History* 6 (1982): 401-421.

Fogel, Robert W., Stanley L. Engerman, Roderick Floud, Gerald Friedman, Robert Margo, Kenneth Sokoloff, Richard Steckel, James Trussell, Georgia Villaflor and Kenneth Wachter. 'Secular Changes in American and British Stature and Nutrition.' *Journal of Interdisciplinary History* 14 (1983): 445-481.

Fogel, Robert W. and Stanley Engerman. 'The Slave Breeding Thesis.' In *Without Consent or Contract: The Rise and Fall of American Slavery. Conditions of Slave Life and the Transition to Freedom: Technical Papers*, Vol. II, 455-472. New York: W.W. Norton and Company, 1992.

Freeman, A. Myrick. *International Trade: An Introduction to Method and Theory*. New York: Harper and Row, 1971.

Freudenberger, Herman and Gaylord Cummins. 'Health, Work, and Leisure Before the Industrial Revolution.' *Explorations in Economic History* 13 (1976): 1-12.

Friedman, Gerald C. 'The Heights of Slaves in Trinidad.' *Social Science History* 6 (1982): 482-515.

Frisancho, Robert A. 'Nutritional Influences on Human Growth and Maturation.' *Yearbook of Physical Anthropology* 21 (1978): 174-191.

Frisch, Rose E. 'Population, Food Intake, and Fertility.' *Science* 199 (1978): 22-30.

Gallman, Robert. 'The Statistical Approach: Fundamental Concepts as Applied to History.' In *Approaches to American Economic History*, ed. G.R. Taylor and L.R. Ellsworth, 87-105. Charlottesville: University of Virginia Press, 1971.

________. 'The Pace and Pattern of American Economic Growth.' In *American Economic Growth: An Economist's History of the United States*, ed. Lance Davis, Richard Easterlin, and William N. Parker, 15-60. New York: Harper and Row, 1972.

Garn, S.M. and D.C. Clark. 'Nutrition, growth, development and maturation: findings from the ten-state nutrition survey of 1968-1970.' *Pediatrics* 56 (1975): 309-316.

Garrison, J. Ritchie. 'Farm Dynamics and Regional Exchange: The Connecticut Valley Beef Trade, 1670-1850.' *Agricultural History* 61 (1987): 1-17.

Geary, James W. *We Need Men: The Union Draft in the Civil War*. DeKalb, IL: University of Northern Illinois Press, 1991.

Geissler, Catherine and Derek J. Oddy. 'Introduction.' In *Food, Diet and Economic Change: Past and Present*, ed. Catherine Geissler and Derek J. Oddy, 1-9. Leicester: Leicester University Press, 1993.

Gibson, A. and T.C. Smout. 'From Meat to Meal: Changes in Diet in Scotland.' In *Food, Diet and Economic Change: Past and Present*, ed. Catherine Geissler and Derek J. Oddy, 10-34. Leicester: Leicester University Press, 1993.

Gordon, Thomas F. *A Gazetteer of the State of Pennsylvania*. Philadelphia: T. Belknap, 1833.

Gould, Benjamin A. *Investigations in the Military and Anthropological Statistics of American Soldiers*. New York: Hurd and Houghton [for the U.S. Sanitary Commission], 1869.

Greene, L.S. and F.E. Johnston, ed. *Social and Biological Predictors of Nutritional Status, Physical Growth and Neurological Development*. New York: Academic Press, 1980.

Greulich, W.W. 'A Comparison of the Physical Growth and Development of American-Born and Native Japanese Children.' *American Journal of Physical Anthropology* 15 (1957): 489-515.

_______. 'Some Secular Changes in the Growth of American-born and Native Japanese Children.' *American Journal of Physical Anthropology* 45 (1976): 553-568.

Habicht, J.P., R. Martorell, C. Yarbrough, R.M. Malina, and R.E. Klein. 'Height and Weight Standards for Pre-School Children: How Relevant are Ethnic Differences in Growth Potential.' *The Lancet* 7858 (April 6, 1974): 611-615.

Haines, Michael R., Lee A. Craig, and Thomas Weiss. 'The Short and the Dead: Nutrition, Mortality, and the "Antebellum Puzzle" in the United States.' *Journal of Economic History* 63 (June 2003): 382-413.

Haites, Erik F., James Mak, Gary M. Walton. *Western River Transportation: The Era of Early Internal Development, 1810-1860*. Baltimore: Johns Hopkins University Press, 1975.

Hamill, P.V., F.E. Johnston, and S. Lemeshow. 'Body Weight, Stature and Sitting Height: White and Negro Youths 12-17 years.' Rockville, MD: U.S. Dept of Health, Education and Welfare, HRA-74-1608, 1973.

Hamill, P.V., T.A. Drizd, C.L. Johnson, R.R. Reed and A.F. Roche. 'NCHS growth charts, 1976.' *Vital Statistics Report*, HRA 76-1120, vol. 25, #3, supplement. Rockville, MD, 1976.

Harper, R. Eugene. *The Transformation of Western Pennsylvania, 1770-1800*. Pittsburgh: University of Pittsburgh Press, 1991.

Harris, Bernard. 'Health, Height, and History: An Overview of Recent Developments in Anthropometric History.' *Social History of Medicine* 7 (1994): 297-320.

Harrison, G.A. 'Human Adaptability with Reference to the IBP Proposals for High Altitude Research.' In *The Biology of Human Adaptability*, ed. P.T. Baker and J.S. Weiner, 509-519. Oxford: Clarendon Press, 1966.

Hartz, Louis. *Economic Policy and Democratic Thought: Pennsylvania, 1776-1860*. Cambridge: Harvard University Press, 1948.

Hayami, Yujiro and Vernon W. Ruttan. *Agricultural Development: An International Perspective*, rev. ed. Baltimore: Johns Hopkins University Press, 1985.

Healy, M.J.R. 'Notes on the Statistics of Growth Standards.' *Annals of Human Biology*, 1 (1974): 41-46.

________. 'Statistics of Growth Standards.' In *Human Growth: A Comprehensive Treatise*, 2nd ed., Vol. 3, ed. F. Falkner and J.M. Tanner, 47-58. New York: Plenum, 1986.

Heckscher, Eli F. *An Economic History of Sweden*. Cambridge, MA: Harvard University Press, 1954.

Henretta, James A. 'Families and Farms: Mentalite in Pre-Industrial America.' *William and Mary Quarterly*, 3rd series, 35 (1978): 3-32.

Herschberg, Theodore and Robert Dockhorn. 'Occupational Classification.' *Historical Methods Newsletter* 9 (1976): 59-98.

Hertzberg, H.T.E. 'Albert Damon's Contributions to Engineering Anthropology.' *American Journal of Physical Anthropology* 42 (1975): 455-460.

Higginbottom, Sanford W., William A. Hunter, and Donald H. Kent. *Pennsylvania and the Civil War: A Handbook*. Harrisburg: Pennsylvania Historical and Museum Commission, 1961.

Higman, Barry W. 'Growth in Afro-Caribbean Slave Populations.' *American Journal of Physical Anthropology* 50 (1979): 373-385.

Hill, Jim Dan. *The Minute Man in Peace and War: A History of the National Guard*. Harrisburg: The Stackpole Company, 1964.

History of Cumberland and Adams Counties, Pennsylvania. Chicago: Warner, Beers & Co., 1886.

Hoffman, Frederick L. *Army Anthropometry and Medical Rejection Statistics*. Newark, N.J.: Prudential Press, 1918.

Horrell, Sara and Jane Humphries. 'Women's Labor Force Participation and the Transition to the Male Breadwinner Family, 1790-1865.' *Economic History Review* 48 (1995): 89-117.

Hunter, Louis C. 'Influence of the Market upon Techniques in the Iron Industry in Western Pennsylvania up to 1860.' *Journal of Economic and Business History* 1 (1929): 241-281.

________. *Factors in the Early Pittsburgh Iron Industry*. Cambridge, MA: Harvard University Press, 1932.

Ismail, S.J. 'Diet and Disease During the First Industrial Revolution: England as a Developing Country (1795-1850).' Ph.D. dissertation, Cornell University, 1977.

James, H. F. *Agricultural Industry of Southeastern Pennsylvania: A Study in Economic Geography*. Ph.D. dissertation, University of Pennsylvania, 1927.

Johannson, S.R. Review of *The Origins of Human Disease*, by Thomas McKeown. *Journal of Interdisciplinary History* 21 (1991): 118-122.

Jones, Chester Lloyd. *The Economic History of the Anthracite-Tidewater Canals*. Philadelphia: University of Pennsylvania Press, 1908.

Jones, Fred Mitchell. 'Middlemen in the Domestic Trade of the United States, 1800-1860.' *Illinois Studies in the Social Sciences* 21 (1937): 1-81.

Jordan, Thomas E. 'Linearity, Gender, and Social Class in Economic Influences on Heights of Victorian Youth.' *Historical Methods* 24 (1991): 116-123.

Karpinos, Bernard D. 'Height and Weight of Selective Service Registrants Processed for Military Service During World War II.' *Human Biology* 40 (1958): 292-321.

________. 'Current Height and Weight of Youths of Military Age.' *Human Biology* 33 (1961): 335-354.

Kelly, Donald S. 'Patterns of Pioneer Migration and Population in Mid-Western Pennsylvania.' Ph.D. dissertation, Ball State University, 1975.

Kent, Donald H. 'The Story of the Allegheny Gateway Region.' *Journal of Erie Studies* 61 (1973): 10-20.

Kent, Donald H. and Harry E. Whipkey, ed. *Descriptive List of the Map Collection in the Pennsylvania State Archives*. Harrisburg: Pennsylvania Historical and Museum Commission, 1976.

Kesten, Seymour R. *Utopian Episodes: Daily Life in Experimental Colonies Dedicated to Changing the World*. Syracuse, N.Y.: Syracuse University Press, 1993.

Kiple, Kenneth and Virginia Himmelsteib King. *Another Dimension to the Black Diaspora: Diet, Disease and Racism*. New York: Cambridge University Press, 1981.

Klee, Linnea B. *Culture and Disease in Nineteenth-Century San Francisco*. Ph.D. dissertation, University of California, San Francisco, 1983.

Klein, Philip S. and Ari Hoogenboom. *A History of Pennsylvania*. 2nd ed. University Park, PA: Pennsylvania State University, 1980.

Klein, Theodore B. *The Canals of Pennsylvania and the System of Internal Improvements*. Harrisburg: William Stanley Ray, State Printer, 1901.

Komlos, John. 'Stature and Nutrition in the Habsburg Monarchy: The Standard of Living and Economic Development in the Eighteenth-Century.' *American Historical Review* 90 (1985): 1149-1161.

________. 'Patterns of Children's Growth in East-central Europe in the Eighteenth-Century.' *Annals of Human Biology* 13 (1986): 33-48.

________. 'The Height and Weight of West Point Cadets: Dietary Change in Antebellum America.' *Journal of Economic History* 47 (1987): 897-927.

________. 'The Age at Menarche in Vienna.' *Historical Methods* 22 (1989): 158-163.

________. 'The Age at Menarche and Age at First Birth in an Undernourished Population.' *Annals of Human Biology* 16 (1989): 463-466.

________. *Nutrition and Economic Development in the Eighteenth-Century Habsburg Monarchy*. Princeton: Princeton University Press, 1989.

________. 'Height and Social Status in Eighteenth-Century Germany.' *Journal of Interdisciplinary History* 20 (1990): 607-621.

________. 'Toward an Anthropometric History of African-Americans: The Case of the Free Blacks in Antebellum Maryland.' In *Strategic Factors in Nineteenth-Century American Economic History: A Volume to Honor Robert W. Fogel*, ed. Claudia Goldin and Hugh Rockoff, 267-329. Chicago: University of Chicago Press, 1992.

________. 'Anthropometric History: What is it?' *Magazine of History* (Spring 1992): 3-5.

________. 'A Malthusian Episode Revisited: The Height of British and Irish Servants in Colonial America.' *Economic History Review* 46 (1993): 768-782.

________. 'The Secular Trend in the Biological Standard of Living in the United Kingdom, 1730-1860.' *Economic History Review* 46 (1993): 115-144.

________. 'Further Thoughts on the Nutritional Status of the British Population.' *Economic History Review* 46 (1993): 363-366.

________. 'The Nutritional Status of French Students.' *Journal of Interdisciplinary History* 24 (1994): 493-508.

________. 'The Height of Runaway Slaves in Colonial America, 1720-1770.' In *Stature, Living Standards, and Economic Development: Essays in Anthropometric History*. ed. John Komlos, 93-116. Chicago: University of Chicago Press, 1994.

________. *Stature, Living Standards, and Economic Development: Essays in Anthropometric History*. Chicago: The University of Chicago Press, 1994.

________. *The Biological Standard of Living in Europe and America 1700-1900. Studies in Anthropometric History*. Aldershot, England: Variorum Press, 1995.

________. *The Biological Standard of Living on Three Continents: Further Essays in Anthropometric History*. Boulder: Westview Press, 1995.

________. 'Anomalies in Economic History: Reflections on the "Antebellum Puzzle".' *Journal of Economic History* 56 (March, 1996): 202-214.

________. 'Shrinking in a Growing Economy? the Mystery of Physical Stature during the Industrial Revolution.' *Journal of Economic History* 58 (1998) 3: 779-802.

________. 'On the Biological Standard of Living of African-Americans: the Case of the Civil War Soldiers.' In *The Biological Standard of Living in Comparative Perspectives: Proceedings of a Conference Held in Munich January 18-23, 1997*, ed. John Komlos and Jörg Baten, 236-249. Stuttgart: Franz Steiner Verlag, 1999.

________. Guest Editor, 'Historische Anthropometrie.' *Jahrbuch für Wirtschaftsgeschichte*, 2000, no. 1.

________. 'The Biological Standard of Living of Eighteenth-Century Americans: Taller, Richer, and Healthier.' Unpublished manuscript, University of Munich, 2000.

Komlos, John and Joo Han Kim. 'Estimating Trends in Historical Heights.' *Historical Methods* 23 (1990): 116-120.

Komlos, John, J. Tanner, P.S.W. Davies and T. Cole. 'Growth of Boys in the Stuttgart Carlschule, 1771-1793.' *Annals of Human Biology* 19 (1992): 139-152.

Komlos, John and Peter Coclanis, 'On the "Puzzling" Antebellum Cycle of the Biological Standard of Living: the Case of Georgia.' *Explorations in Economic History*, 34 (Oct. 1997) 4: 433-59.

Komlos, John and Peter Coclanis, 'Nutrition and Economic Development in Post-Reconstruction South Carolina: an Anthropometric Approach.' *Social Science History* 19 (1995): 91-116.

Komlos, John and Timothy Cuff (ed.). *Classics of Anthropometric History: A Selected Anthology*. St. Katharinen, Germany: Scripta Mercaturae, 1998.

Komlos, John and Jörg Baten, *The Biological Standard of Living in Comparative Perspective: Proceedings of a Conference Held in Munich January 18-23, 1997*. Stuttgart: Franz Steiner Verlag, 1999.

Krugman, Paul. *Geography and Trade*. Leuven, Belgium: Leuven University Press, 1991.

Kuh, Diana and Michael Wadworth. 'Parental Height: Childhood Environment and Subsequent Adult Height in a National Birth Cohort.' *International Journal of Epidemiology* 18 (1989): 663-668.

Kunitz, Stephen J. 'Making a Long Story Short: A Note on Men's Height and Mortality in England from the First through the Nineteenth-Centuries.' *Medical History* 31 (1987): 269-280.

Kuznets, S. *Modern Economic Growth: Rate, Structure and Spread*. New Haven: Yale University Press, 1966.

Laidig, Schutjer. 'Agricultural Variation and Human Fertility in Antebellum Pennsylvania.' *Journal of Family History* 6 (1981): 195-204.

Landauer, Thomas K. 'Infantile Vaccinations and the Secular Trend in Stature.' *Ethos* 1 (1973): 499-503.

Lane, Robert E. *The Market Experience*. New York: Cambridge University Press, 1991.

Lebergott, Stanley. *The Americans: An Economic Record*. New York: W.W. Norton and Co., 1984.

Lee, Susan P. and Peter Passell. *A New Economic View of American History*. New York: W.W. Norton and Company, 1979.

Lemon, James T. *The Best Poor Man's Country: A Geographical Study of Early Southeastern Pennsylvania*. New York: W.W. Norton & Co., Inc., 1972.

Le Roy Ladurie, Emmanuel, N. Bernageau, and Y. Pasquet. 'Le Conscrit et l'ordinateur. Perspectives de recherches sur les Archives Militaries du XIXieme siecle Francais.' *Studi Storici* 10 (1969): 260-308.

Le Roy Ladurie, Emmanuel. 'The Conscripts of 1868: A Study of the Correlation between Geographical Mobility, Delinquency and Physical Stature and other Aspects of the Situation of the Young Frenchmen called to do Military Service that Year.' In *The Territory of the Historian*. Translated by Ben and Sian Reynolds. Chicago: University of Chicago Press, 1979.

Lewis, W.A. 'Economic Development with Unlimited Supplies of Labour.' *Manchester School* 22 (1954): 139-91.

Lindstrom, Diane. *Economic Development in the Philadelphia Region, 1810-1850*. New York: Columbia University Press, 1978.

Livesay, Harold C. 'The Changing Distribution System in American Manufacturing, 1815-1860.' Ph.D. dissertation, Johns Hopkins University, 1970.

Livingood, James W. *The Philadelphia-Baltimore Trade Rivalry, 1780-1860*. Harrisburg: Pennsylvania Historical and Museum Commission, 1947.

Machlup, Fritz. *A History of Thought on Economic Integration*. New York: Columbia University Press, 1977.

Mahon, John K. *History of the Militia and the National Guard*. New York: Macmillan Publishing Company, 1983.

Malcolm, L.A. 'Ecological Factors Relating to Child Growth and Nutritional Status.' In *Nutrition and Malnutrition: Identification and Measurement*, ed. A.E. Roche and F. Falkner, 329-352. New York: Plenum Press, 1974.

Mandemakers, C.A. and J.L. Van Zanden. 'The Height of Conscripts and National Income: Apparent Relations and Misconceptions.' *Explorations in Economic History* 30 (1993): 81-97.

Margo, Robert A. and Richard Steckel. 'The Height of American Slaves: New Evidence on Slave Nutrition and Health.' *Social Science History* 6 (1982): 516-538.

Margo, Robert A. and Richard Steckel. 'Heights of Native Born Whites During the Antebellum Period.' *Journal of Economic History* 43 (1983): 167-174.

Margo, Robert A. and Georgia C. Villaflor. 'The Growth of Real Wages in Antebellum America: New Evidence.' *Journal of Economic History* 47 (1987): 873-895.

Marshall, William A. and James M. Tanner. 'Puberty.' In *Human Growth: A Comprehensive Treatise*, 2nd ed., Vol. 2, ed. F. Falkner and J.M. Tanner, 171-209. New York: Plenum, 1986.

Martel, Leslie F. and Henry B. Biller. *Stature and Stigma: The Biopsychosocial Development of Short Males*. Lexington, MA: D.C. Heath and Co., 1987.

Martorell, Reynaldo and Jean-Pierre Habicht. 'Growth in Early Childhood in Developing Countries.' In *Human Growth: A Comprehensive Treatise*, 2nd ed., Vol. 3, ed. F. Falkner and J.M. Tanner, 241-262. New York: Plenum, 1986.

McClelland, Peter D. *Demographic Dimensions of the New Republic: American Interregional Migration, Vital Statistics and Manumission, 1800-1860*. New York: Cambridge University Press, 1982.

McClintock, Walter J. 'The French Creek Feeder and Conneaut Resevoir: 1827-1872.' *Western Pennsylvania Historical Magazine* 22 (1939): 188-200.

McElwee, Thomas B. *Concise History of the Eastern Penitentiary of Pennsylvania*. Philadelphia: Massey, 1935.

McKeown, Thomas. *The Modern Rise of Population*. New York: Academic Press, 1976.

________. *The Role of Medicine: Dream, Mirage or Nemesis?*, 2nd. ed. Princeton: Princeton University Press, 1979.

McMahon, Sarah. 'Provisions Laid Up for the Family: Toward A History of Diet in New England, 1650-1850.' *Historical Methods* 14 (1981): 4-21.

McNeill, William H. *A History of the Human Community*. Englewood Cliffs, NJ: Prentice-Hall, 1993.

M'Cready, Benjamin W. 'On the Influence of Trades, Professions, and Occupations in the United States, in the Production of Disease.' *Transactions of the Medical Society of the State of New York* 3 (1836/37): 91-150.

Menken, Jane, James Trussell, and Susan Watkins. 'The Nutrition Fertility Link: An Evaluation of the Evidence.' *Journal of Interdisciplinary History* 11 (1981): 425-441.

Meredith, H.V. 'Findings from Asia, Australia, Europe and North America on Secular Change in Mean Height of Children, Youths and Young Adults.' *American Journal of Physical Anthropology* 44 (1976): 315-326.

Merrill, Michael. 'Cash is Good to Eat: Self-Sufficiency and Exchange in the Rural Economy of the United States.' *Radical History Review* 3 (1977): 42-71.

Miller, F.J.W., W.Z. Billewicz, and A. M. Thomson. 'Growth from Birth to Adult Life of 442 Newcastle-upon-Tyne Children.' *British Journal of Preventive and Social Medicine* 26 (1972): 224-230.

Miller, Ruby M. *Pennsylvania Maps and Atlases in the Pennsylvania State University Libraries*. University Park, PA: Penn State University Libraries, 1972.

Mosk, C. and S. R. Johansson. 'Income and Mortality: Evidence from Modern Japan.' *Population and Development Review* 12 (1986): 417-428.

Mueller, William H. 'The Genetics of Size and Shape in Children and Adults.' In *Human Growth: A Comprehensive Treatise*, 2nd ed., Vol. 3., ed. F. Falkner and J.M. Tanner, 145-168. New York: Plenum, 1986.

Murdock, Eugene C. *Patriotism Limited, 1862-1865: The Civil War Draft and Bounty System*. Kent, OH: Kent State University Press, 1967.

Murphy, Raymond E. and Marion Murphy. *Pennsylvania: A Regional Geography*. Harrisburg: The Pennsylvania Book Service, 1937.

Murray, John. 'Stature Among Members of a Nineteenth-Century American Shaker Commune.' *Annals of Human Biology* 20 (1993): 121-129.

________. 'Human Capital in Religious Communes: Literacy and Selection Among the Shakers.' *Explorations in Economic History*, 32 (1995): 217-235.

________. 'A New Anthropometric Look at the Status of Women and Children in Oneida Community, 1848-1881.' In *The Biological Standard of Living on Three Continents: Further Explorations in Anthropometric History*, ed. John Komlos, 105-122. Boulder, CO: Westview Press, 1995.

________. 'Standards of the Present for People of the Past: Height, Weight, and Mortality among Men of Amherst College, 1834-1949.' *The Journal of Economic History* 57 (1997): 585-606.

Mushkin, Selma J. 'Health as an Investment.' *Journal of Political Economy* 70 (1962): 129-157.

Mutch, Robert E. 'Yeoman and Merchant in Pre-industrial America: Eighteenth-Century Massachusetts as a Case Study.' *Societas* 7 (1977): 279-302.

Newman, M.T. 'Nutritional Adaptation in Man.' In *Physiological Anthropology*, ed. Albert Damon, 210-259. New York: Oxford University Press, 1975.

Nicholas, Stephen and Richard Steckel. 'Heights and Living Standards of English Workers During the Early Years of Industrialization, 1770-1815.' *Journal of Economic History* 51 (1991): 937-957.

Nicholas, Stephen and Deborah Oxley. 'The Living Standards of Women during the Industrial Revolution, 1795-1820.' *Economic History Review* 46 (1993): 723-749.

Nilsen, Stein T., Per H. Finne, Per Bergsjo and Ola Stamnes. 'Males with Low Birth Weight Examined at 18 Years of Age.' *Acta Paediatrica Scandinavica* 73 (1984): 168-175.

North, Douglass. *The Economic Growth of the United States, 1790-1860*. New York: W.W. Norton, 1966.

Ohlin, Bertil G. *Interregional and International Trade*. Cambridge: Harvard University Press, 1967.

Oppers, V.M. 'The Secular Trend in Growth and Maturation in the Netherlands.' *Tijdschift voor Sociale Geneeskunde* 44 (1966): 539-48.

O'Rourke, Kevin and Jeffrey Williamson. 'Late Nineteenth-Century Anglo-American Factor-Price Convergence: Were Heckscher and Ohlin Right?' *Journal of Economic History* 54 (1994): 892-916.

Owsley, Frank Lawrence. *Plain Folk of the Old South*. Baton Rouge: Louisiana State University Press, 1949; reprint Baton Rouge: Louisiana State University Press, 1982.

Parker, William N. 'Trends in Food Consumption in the United States, 1840-1910: An Experiment in Econometrical History.' Unpublished manuscript presented to the Econometrical Society, 1957.

Paskoff, Paul F. *Industrial Evolution: Organization, Structure and Growth of the Pennsylvania Iron Industry, 1750-1860.* Baltimore and London: Johns Hopkins University Press, 1983.

Pavick, Thomas Peter. 'An Economic History of Southwestern Pennsylvania, 1850-1860.' Ph.D. dissertation, West Virginia University, 1973.

Pendleton, Othmiel A. 'Poor Relief in Philadelphia, 1790-1840.' *Pennsylvania Historical Magazine and Biography* 70 (1946): 161-172.

Pennsylvania Historical Review. *Gazetteer, Post Office, Express and Telegraph Guide: City of Philadelphia: Leading Merchants and Manufacturers.* New York: Historical Publishing Co., 1886.

Perlman, Mark. 'On Health and Economic Development: Some Problems, Methods and Conclusions Reviewed in a Perusal of the Literature.' *Comparative Studies in Society and History* 8 (1966): 433-448.

Perlman, Richard. *Theory of Markets.* Hinsdale, IL: Dryden Press, 1972.

Phisterer, Frederick. *New York in the War of Rebellion, 1861-1865*, 3rd. ed. Albany: J.B. Lynn Co.: 1912.

Pierce, M.D. *Pennsylvania Economic Studies: A Bibliography.* University Park, PA: The Pennsylvania State University, 1983.

Polanyi, Karl. *The Great Transformation: The Social and Economic Origins of Our Time.* Boston: Beacon Press, 1944.

Pope, Clayne L. 'Adult Mortality in America before 1900: A View from Family Histories.' In *Strategic Factors in Nineteenth-Century American Economic History: A Volume to Honor Robert W. Fogel*, ed. Claudia Goldin and Hugh Rockoff, 267-296. Chicago: University of Chicago Press, 1992.

Prazuck, T., A. Fisch, E. Pichard, and Y. Sidibe. 'Lack of Secular Change in Male Adult Stature in Rural Mali (West Africa).' *American Journal of Physical Anthropology* 75 (1988): 471-475.

Preece, M.A. and M.J. Baines. 'A New Family of Mathematical Models Describing the Human Growth Curve.' *Annals of Human Biology* 5 (1978): 1-24.

Pressley, Thomas J. and William H. Scofield, ed. *Farm Real Estate Values in the United States, 1850-1959.* Seattle: University of Washington Press, 1959.

Preston, Samuel H., ed. *Biological and Social Aspects of Mortality and the Length of Life.* Liege: Ordina, 1982.

Prichett, Jonathan B. and Herman Freudenberger. 'A Peculiar Sample: The Selection of Slaves for the New Orleans Market.' *Journal of Economic History* 52 (1992): 109-127.

Pruitt, Bettye Hobbs. 'Self-Sufficiency and the Agricultural Economy of Eighteenth-Century Massachusetts.' *William and Mary Quarterly*, 3rd. series, 41 (1984): 333-364.

Raloff, Janet. 'Paring Protein: Low Protein Cuisines May Slow Aging.' *Science News* 142 (Nov. 21, 1992): 346-347.

Ram, R. and T.W. Schultz. 'Life Span, Health, Savings, and Productivity.' *Economic Development and Cultural Change* 27 (1979): 399-421.

Ranis, G. and J. Fei. 'A Theory of Economic Development.' *American Economic Review* 51 (1961): 533-565.

Rees, Ray, John Komlos, Ulrich Woitek, and Ngo Van Long. 'Slave Prices, Food Allotments, and Heights.' Unpublished manuscript, University of Munich, 2000.

Reiser, Catherine Elizabeth. *Pittsburgh's Commercial Development, 1800-1850.* Harrisburg: Pennsylvania Historical and Museum Commission, 1951.

Research Publications Inc. *Bibliography and Reel Index. A Guide to the Microfilm Edition of U.S. Decennial Census Publications, 1790-1970.* Woodbridge, CN: Research Publications Inc., 1975.

Rhodes, Henry T.F. *Alphonse Bertillon: Father of Scientific Detection.* New York: Abelard-Schuman, Inc., 1956.

Riggs, Paul. 'The Standard of Living in Scotland, 1800-1850.' In *Stature, Living Standards, and Economic Development: Essays in Anthropometric History*, ed. John Komlos, 60-75. Chicago: University of Chicago Press, 1994.

Riley, James C. *Sickness, Recovery, and Death: A History of Forecast of Ill Health.* Iowa City: University of Iowa Press, 1989.

________. 'Height, Nutrition, and Mortality Risk Reconsidered.' *Journal of Interdisciplinary History* 24 (1994): 465-492.

________. 'Stature's Problems.' Unpublished manuscript, Indiana University, 1994.

Roberts, C. 'The Physical Development and the Proportions of the Human Body.' *St. George's Hospital Reports* 8 (1876): 1-48.

Roberts, D.F., L.M. Rozner, and A.V. Swan. 'Age at Menarche, Physique and Environment in Industrial North East England.' *Acta Paediatrica Scandinavica* 60 (1971): 158-164.

Rosen, George. *A History of Public Health.* New York: MD Publications, 1958.

Rostow, W.W. *The Stages of Economic Growth: A Non-Communist Manifesto*, 2nd ed. Cambridge: Cambridge University Press, 1971.

Rothenberg, Winifred B. 'The Market and Massachusetts Farmers, 1750-1855.' *Journal of Economic History* 41 (1981): 283-314.

________. 'The Emergence of a Capital Market in Rural Massachusetts, 1730-1838.' *Journal of Economic History* 45 (1985): 781-808.

________. 'The Emergence of Farm Labor Markets and the Transformation of the Rural Economy: Massachusetts, 1750-1855.' *Journal of Economic History* 48: (1988): 537-566.

________. *From Market-Places to a Market Economy: The Transformation of Rural Massachusetts, 1750-1850.* Chicago: University of Chicago Press, 1992.

Rothstein, Morton. 'The Antebellum South as a Dual Economy: A Tentative Hypothesis.' *Agricultural History* 41 (1967): 373-382.

Rubin, Julius. 'Canal or Railroad?: Imitation or Innovation in the Response to the Erie Canal in Philadelphia, Baltimore, and Boston.' *Transactions of the American Philosophical Society* 51, part 7 (1961).

Rule, John. *The Labouring Classes in Early Industrial England, 1750-1850.* London: Longman, 1986.

Sandberg, Lars G. and Richard Steckel. 'Soldier, Soldier, What Made you Grow so Tall? A Study of Height, Health and Nutrition in Sweden, 1720-1881.' *Economy and History* 23 (1980): 91-105.

Sandberg, Lars G. and Richard Steckel. 'Heights and Economic History: The Swedish Case.' *Annals of Human Biology* 14 (1987): 101-110.

Sandberg, Lars G. and Richard Steckel. 'Overpopulation and Malnutrition Rediscovered: Hard Times in 19th-Century Sweden.' *Explorations in Economic History* 25 (1988): 1-19.

Sauers, R.A. *Advance the Colors: Pennsylvania Civil War Battle Flags.* Harrisburg: Capitol Preservation Committee, 1987.

Saylor, Roger B. *The Railroads of Pennsylvania.* University Park, PA: Penn State University Press, 1964.

Schultz, Stanley K. *Constructing Urban Culture: American City Planning, 1800-1920.* Philadelphia: Temple University Press, 1989.

Schumacher, Max George. *The Northern Farmer and His Markets During the Late Colonial Period*. New York: Arno Press, 1975.

Scrimshaw, N.S., C.E. Taylor, and J. E. Gordon. *Interactions of Nutrition and Infection*. Geneva: World Health Organization, 1968.

Sen, Amartya. 'Development: Which Way Now?' *The Economic Journal* 93 (1983): 745-762.

_______. 'The Standard of Living: Lecture I, Concepts and Critiques and The Standard of Living.' In *The Standard of Living: The Tanner Lectures*, ed. G. Hawthorn, 1-19. Cambridge: Cambridge University Press, 1987.

_______. 'The Standard of Living: Lecture II: Lives and Capabilities.' In *The Standard of Living: The Tanner Lectures*, ed. G. Hawthorn, 20-38. Cambridge: Cambridge University Press, 1987.

Schaefer, Donald F. 'A Quantitative Description and Analysis of the Growth of the Pennsylvania Anthracite Coal Industry, 1820 to 1865.' Ph.D. dissertation, University of North Carolina, 1967.

Shannon, Fred A. *The Organization and Administration of the Union Army: 1861-1865*. Vol. I. Cleveland: Arthur H. Clark Company, 1928.

Shay, Ted. 'The Level of Living in Japan, 1885-1938: New Evidence.' In *The Biological Standard of Living on Three Continents: Further Explorations in Anthropometric History*, ed. John Komlos, 173-201. Boulder, CO: Westview Press, 1995.

Simpson, H. N. *Invisible Armies: The Impact of Disease on American History*. Indianapolis: Bobbs-Merrill, 1980.

Sokoloff, Kenneth L. 'The Heights of Americans in Three Centuries: Some Economic and Demographic Implications.' In *The Biological Standard of Living on Three Continents: Further Explorations in Anthropometric History*, ed. John Komlos, 133-150. Boulder, CO: Westview Press, 1995.

Sokoloff, Kenneth L. and Georgia C. Villaflor. 'The Early Achievement of Modern Stature in America.' *Social Science History* 6 (1982): 453-481.

Soltow, Lee. *Men and Wealth in the United States, 1850-1870*. New Haven: Yale University Press, 1975.

_______. 'Inequality Amidst Abundance: Land Ownership in Early Nineteenth-Century Ohio.' *Ohio History* 88 (1979): 133-151.

Stanton, William. *The Leopard's Spots: Scientific Attitudes toward Race in America, 1815-1859*. Chicago: University of Chicago Press, 1960.

Steckel, Richard. 'Slave Height Profiles from Coastwise Manifests.' *Explorations in Economic History* 16 (1979): 363-380.

_______. 'Height and Per Capita Income.' *Historical Methods* 16 (1983): 1-7.

_______. 'A Peculiar Population: The Nutrition, Health, and Mortality of American Slaves from Childhood to Maturity.' *Journal of Economic History* 46 (1986): 721-741.

_______. 'Birth Weights and Infant Mortality among American Slaves.' *Explorations in Economic History* 23 (1986): 173-198.

_______. 'Growth Depression and Recovery: The Remarkable Case of American Slaves.' *Annals of Human Biology* 14 (1987): 111-132.

_______. 'The Health and Mortality of Women and Children.' *Journal of Economic History* 48 (1988): 333-345.

_______. 'Height, Living Standards, and History.' *Historical Methods* 24 (1991): 183-187.

_______. 'Stature and Living Standards in the United States.' In *American Economic Growth and Standards of Living before the Civil War*, ed. R.E. Gallman and J.J. Wallis, 265-310. Chicago: National Bureau of Economic Research by University of Chicago Press, 1992.

_______. 'Health and Nutrition in the American Midwest: Evidence from the Height of Ohio National Guardsmen, 1850-1910.' In *Stature, Living Standards, and Economic Development: Essays in Anthropometric History*, ed. John Komlos, 153-170. Chicago: University of Chicago Press, 1994.

_______. 'Heights and Health in the United States, 1710-1950.' In *Stature, Living Standards, and Economic Development: Essays in Anthropometric History*, ed. John Komlos, 153-170. Chicago: University of Chicago Press, 1994.

_______. 'Stature and the Standard of Living.' *Journal of Economic Literature* 33 (1995): 1903-1940.

_______. 'Percentiles of Modern Height: Standards for Use in Historical Research.' *Historical Methods*, 29 (1996): 157-166.

Steegmann, A. Theodore Jr. '18th-Century British Military Stature: Growth Cessation, Selective Recruiting, Secular Trends, Nutrition at Birth, Cold and Occupation.' *Human Biology* 57 (1985): 77-95.

Steegmann, A. Theodore Jr. and Phillip A. Haseley. 'Stature Variation in the British American Colonies: French and Indian War Records, 1755-1763.' *American Journal of Physical Anthropology* 75 (1988): 413-421.

Stein, Zena, Mervyn Susser, Gerhart Saenger, and Francis Marolla. *Famine and Human Development: The Dutch Hunger Winter of 1944-45*. New York: Oxford University Press, 1975.

Steiner, Paul E. *Disease in the Civil War: Natural Biological Warfare in 1861-65*. Springfield, IL: C.C. Thomas, 1968.

_______. *Medical History of a Civil War Regiment: Disease in the 65th U.S. Colored Infantry*. Clayton, MO: Institute of Civil War Studies, 1977.

Stevens, Sylvester K. *Pennsylvania: The Keystone State*, Vol. I, *Historical*. New York: The American Historical Co., Inc., 1956.

_______. *Pennsylvania: Titan of Industry*. New York: Lewis Historical Publishing Co., 1948.

Stiglitz, J.E. 'Economic Organization, Information, and Development.' In *Handbook of Development Economics*, Vol. I, ed., H. Chenery and T. N. Srinivasan, 93-160. Amsterdam: Elsevier Science Publishers, 1988.

Stradley, Leighton P. *Early Financial and Economic History of Pennsylvania*. New York: Commerce Clearing House, Inc., 1942.

Sullivan, William A. *The Industrial Worker in Pennsylvania, 1800-1840*. Harrisburg: Pennsylvania Historical and Museum Commission, 1955.

Sypher, J.R. *History of the Pennsylvania Reserve Corps*. Lancaster, PA: Elias Barr and Co., 1865.

Syrquin, M. 'Patterns of Structural Change.' In *Handbook of Development Economics*, Vol I., ed. H. Chenery and T. N. Srinivasan, 201-273. Amsterdam: Elsevier Science Publishers, 1988.

Swank, James M. *The Amazing Pennsylvania Canals*. York, PA: Historical Society of York County, 1965.

_______. *Progressive Pennsylvania: A Record of the Remarkable Development of the Keystone State*. Philadelphia: J.B. Lippincott Co., 1908.

Tanner, James M. *Growth at Adolescence*, 2nd ed. Oxford: Blackwell Scientific Publications, 1962.

_______. 'The Regulation of Human Growth.' *Child Development*, 34 (1963): 817-847.

_______. 'Growth and Physique in Different Populations of Mankind: A Proposal for the Establishment of an International Bureau of Growth Studies.' In *The Biology of*

Human Adaptability, ed. P.T. Baker and J.S. Weiner, 44-66. Oxford: Clarendon Press, 1966.

________. 'Trend towards Earlier Menarche in London, Oslo, Copenhagen, the Netherlands, and Hungary.' *Nature* 243 (1973): 95-96.

________. 'Use and Abuse of Growth Standards.' In *Human Growth*, 2nd ed., Vol. 3, ed. F. Falkner and J.M. Tanner. New York: Plenum, 1978.

________. *A History of the Study of Human Growth.* Cambridge: Cambridge University Press, 1981.

________. 'The Potential of Auxological Data for Monitoring Economic and Social Well-Being.' *Social Science History* 6 (1982): 571-581.

________. 'Growth as a Mirror of the Condition of Society: Secular Trends and Class Distinctions.' In *Human Growth: A Multi-Disciplinary Review*, ed. A. Demirjian, 3-34. London: Taylor and Francis, 1986.

________. 'Growth as a Target-Seeking Function, Catch-up and Catch-down growth in Man.' In *Human Growth: A Comprehensive Treatise*, 2nd ed., Vol. 1, ed. F. Falkner and J.M. Tanner, 167-180. New York: Plenum, 1986.

________. *Foetus into Man: Physical Growth from Conception to Maturity*, rev. and enl. ed. Cambridge, MA: Harvard University Press, 1990.

Tanner, James M., R.H. Whitehouse, and M. Takaishi. 'Standards from Birth to Maturity for Height, Weight, Height Velocity, and Weight Velocity: British Children 1965.' *Archives of Disease in Childhood* 41 (1966): 454-471 and 613-635.

Tanner, James M. and P.S.W. Davies. 'Clinical Longitudinal Standards for Height and Height Velocity for North American Children.' *Journal of Pediatrics* 107 (1985): 317-329.

Taylor, George R. *The Transportation Revolution, 1815-1860*, Vol. 4, *The Economic History of the United States*. New York: Rinehart and Company, Inc., 1951.

________. 'American Economic Growth Before 1840: An Exploratory Essay.' *Journal of Economic History* 24 (1964): 427-444.

Thorndale, William and William Dollarhide. *Map Guide to the U.S. Federal Censuses, 1790-1920*. Baltimore: Genealogical Printing, 1987.

Townsend, Thomas S. *The Honors of the Empire State in the War of Rebellion*. New York: A. Lovell and Company, 1889.

Trego, Charles B. *A Geography of Pennsylvania.* Philadelphia: Edward C. Biddle, 1843.

Trotter, Mildred and Goldine Gleser. 'Trends in Stature of American Whites and Negroes Born between 1840 and 1924.' *American Journal of Physical Anthropology* 9 (1951): 427-440.

Trussell, James and Richard Steckel. 'The Age of Slaves at Menarche and Their First Birth.' *Journal of Interdisciplinary History* 8 (1978): 477-505.

Trussell, James and Kenneth Wachter. 'Estimating the Covariates of Historical Heights.' Working Paper #1455. Cambridge, MA: National Bureau of Economic Research, 1984.

Trussell, John B.R. *Pennsylvania Historical Bibliography.* Harrisburg: Pennsylvania Historical and Museum Commission, 1957.

________. *Pennsylvania Historical Bibliography*, Vol. 1. Harrisburg: Pennsylvania Historical and Museum Commission, 1970.

________. *Pennsylvania Historical Bibliography.* Supplement to 1970 edition. Harrisburg: Pennsylvania Historical and Museum Commission, 1979.

Tryon, Rolla M. *Household Manufacturing in the United States, 1640-1860: A Study in Industrial History*. Chicago: University of Chicago Press, 1917.

Ulijaszek, Stanley J. 'Changes in Subsistence Practices and Diet in Papua New Guinea.' In *Food, Diet and Economic Change: Past and Present*, ed. Catherine Geissler and Derek J. Oddy, 183-206. Leicester: Leicester University Press, 1993.

van Wieringen, J.C. 'Secular Growth Changes.' In *Human Growth*, 2nd ed., Vol. 3, ed. F. Falkner and J.M. Tanner, 307-331. New York: Plenum, 1978.

von Thünen, Johann H. *Von Thünen's Isolated State: An English Edition of Der Isolierte Staat*, ed. Peter Hall, translated by Carla M. Wartenberg. Oxford: Pergamon Press Ltd., 1966.

Vexler, Robert I. *Chronology and Documentary Handbook of the State of Pennsylvania*. Dobbs Ferry, N.Y.: Oceana Publications, Inc., 1978.

Wachter, Kenneth, and James Trussell. 'Estimating Historical Heights.' *Journal of the American Statistical Association* 77 (1982): 279-303.

Wachter, Kenneth. 'Graphical Estimation of Military Heights.' *Historical Methods* 14 (1981): 31-42.

Waaler, Hans Th. 'Height, Weight, and Mortality: The Norwegian Experience.' *Acta Medica Scandinavica*, supplement 679, 1984.

Walsh, Margaret. *The Rise of the Midwestern Meatpacking Industry*. Lexington, KY: University of Kentucky Press, 1982.

Walter, John, and Roger Schofield. *Famine, Disease, and the Social Order in Early Modern Society*. New York: Cambridge University Press, 1989.

Ward, W. Peter and Patricia C. Ward. 'Infant Birth Weight and Nutrition in Industrializing Montreal.' *American Historical Review* 89 (1984): 324-345.

Ward, W. Peter. *Birth Weight and Economic Growth: Women's Living Standards in the Industrializing West*. Chicago: University of Chicago Press, 1993.

Weiman, David F. 'Farmers and the Market in Antebellum America: A View from the Georgia Upcountry.' *Journal of Economic History* 47 (1987): 627-647.

Weiner, J.S. 'Major Problems in Human Population Biology.' In *The Biology of Human Adaptability*, ed. P.T. Baker and J.S. Weiner, 2-24. Oxford: Clarendon Press, 1966.

Weiss, Thomas. 'Long Term Changes in U.S. Agricultural Output Per Worker, 1800-1900.' Working Paper 23, National Bureau of Economic Research, Series on Historical Factors in Long Run Growth, 1991.

Welcher, Frank Johnson. *The Union Army, 1861-65: Organization and Operations*. Bloomington: Indiana University Press, 1989.

Wells, Jerome. 'On the Agricultural Performance of Developing Nations, 1950-1985.' *Food Research Institute* 21 (1989): 165-191.

Williamson, Jeffrey and Peter Lindert. *American Inequality: A Macroeconomic History*. New York: Academic Press, 1980.

Williamson, Jeffrey. *Coping with City Growth During the Industrial Revolution*. New York: Cambridge University Press, 1990.

Wolanski, Napoleon. 'Biological Reference Systems in the Assessment of Nutritional Status.' In *Nutrition and Malnutrition: Identification and Measurement*, ed. A.E. Roche and F. Falkner, 213-269. New York: Plenum Press, 1974.

________. 'Heterosis and Homosis in Man.' In *Physical Anthropology of European Populations*, ed. Ilse Schwidetzky, B. Chiarelli, and Olga Necrasov, 213-233. The Hague: Mouton Publishers, 1980.

Woods, Robert and John Woodward, ed. *Urban Disease and Mortality in Nineteenth-Century England*. London: Batsford Academic and Educational Press, 1984.

World Health Organization. 'Use and Interpretation of Anthropometric Indicators of Nutritional Status.' *Bulletin of the World Health Organization* 64 (1986): 929-941.

World Health Organization Expert Committee on Maternal and Child Care. 'New Trends in the Delivery of Maternal and Child Care in Health Services.' WHO Technical Report Series, #600. Geneva: World Health Organization, 1976.

Wright, Gavin. *The Political Economy of the Cotton South: Households, Markets, and Wealth in the Nineteenth-Century*. New York: W.W. Norton and Co., 1978.

Wu, Jialu. 'The Anthropometric History of Pittsburgh and Allegheny County, Pennsylvania, 1890-1945.' *Annals of Human Biology* 19 (1992): 79-86.

________. 'How Severe was the Great Depression? Evidence from the Pittsburgh Region.' In *Stature, Living Standards, and Economic Development: Essays in Anthropometric History*, ed. John Komlos, 129-152. Chicago: University of Chicago Press, 1994.

Index